Natsume's BOOK of FRIENDS

Shojo Beat

Natsume's BOOK of FRIENDS

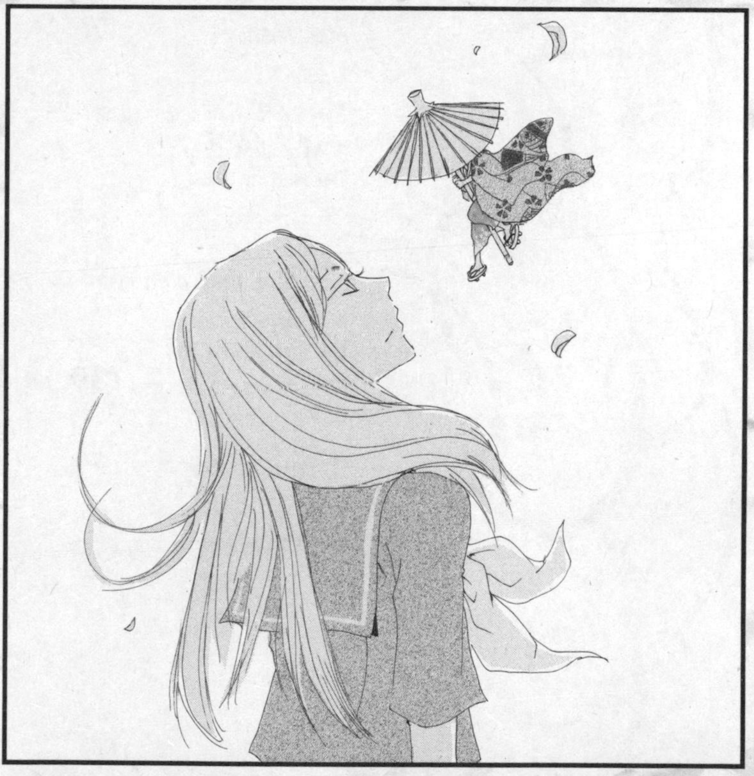

STORY and ART by
Yuki Midorikawa

VOLUME 17

Natsume's BOOK of FRIENDS

VOLUME 17 CONTENTS

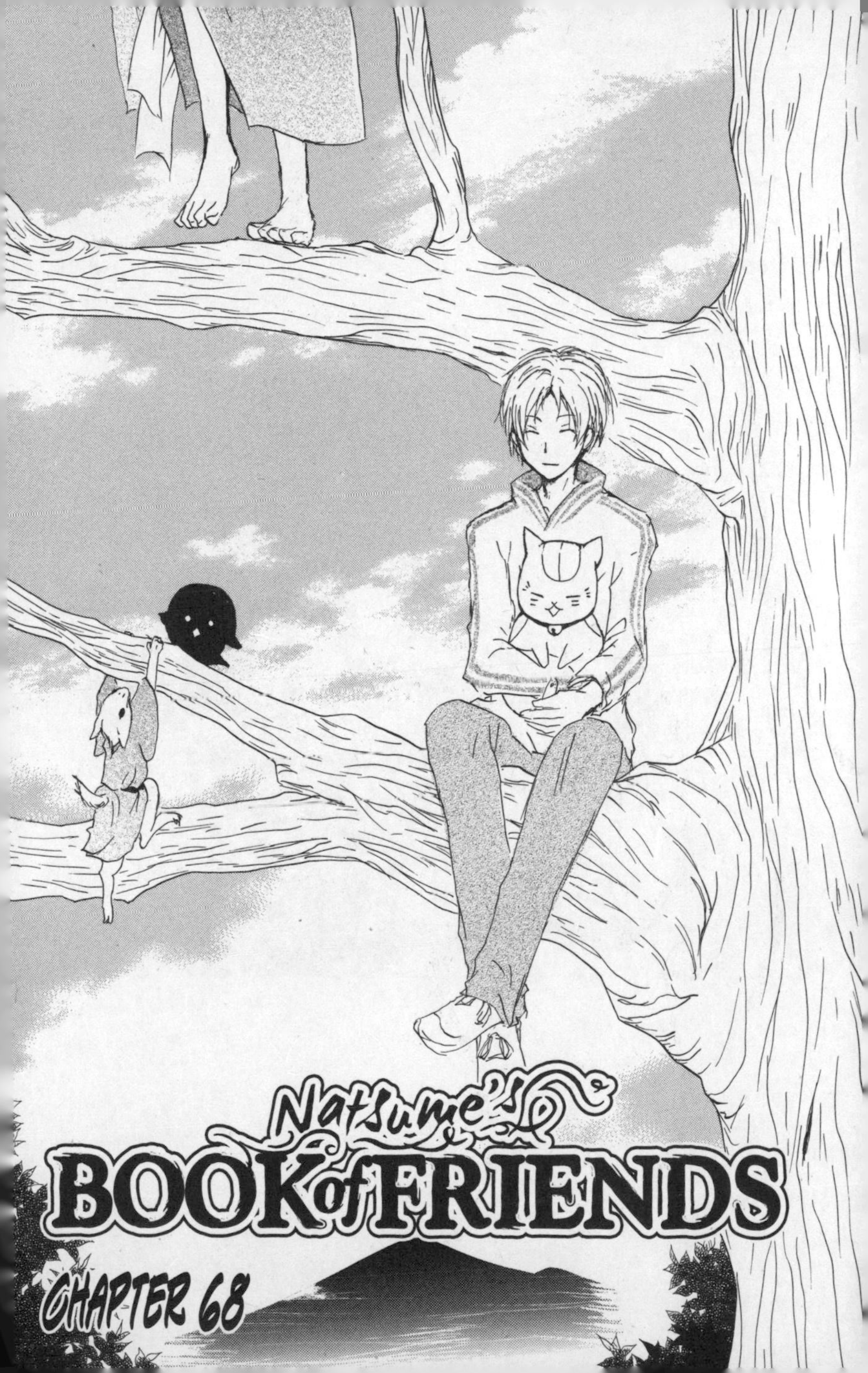
Natsume's
BOOK of FRIENDS
CHAPTER 68

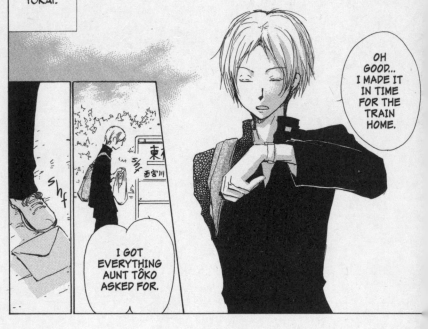

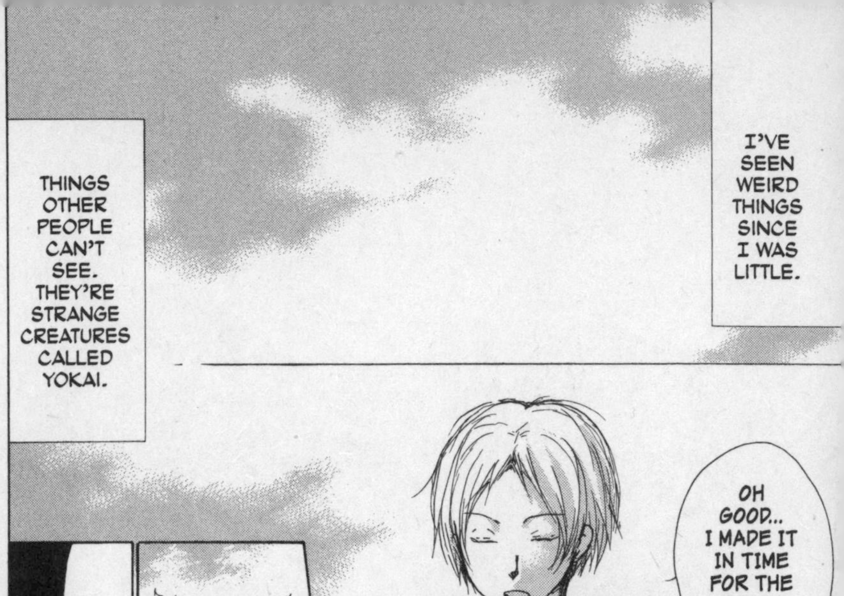
I'VE SEEN WEIRD THINGS SINCE I WAS LITTLE.
THINGS OTHER PEOPLE CAN'T SEE. THEY'RE STRANGE CREATURES CALLED YOKAI.
OH GOOD... I MADE IT IN TIME FOR THE TRAIN HOME.
西宮川
shf
I GOT EVERYTHING AUNT TÔKO ASKED FOR.
shf

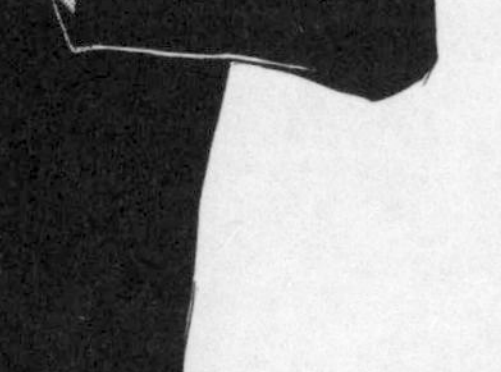

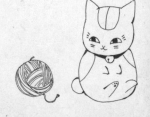

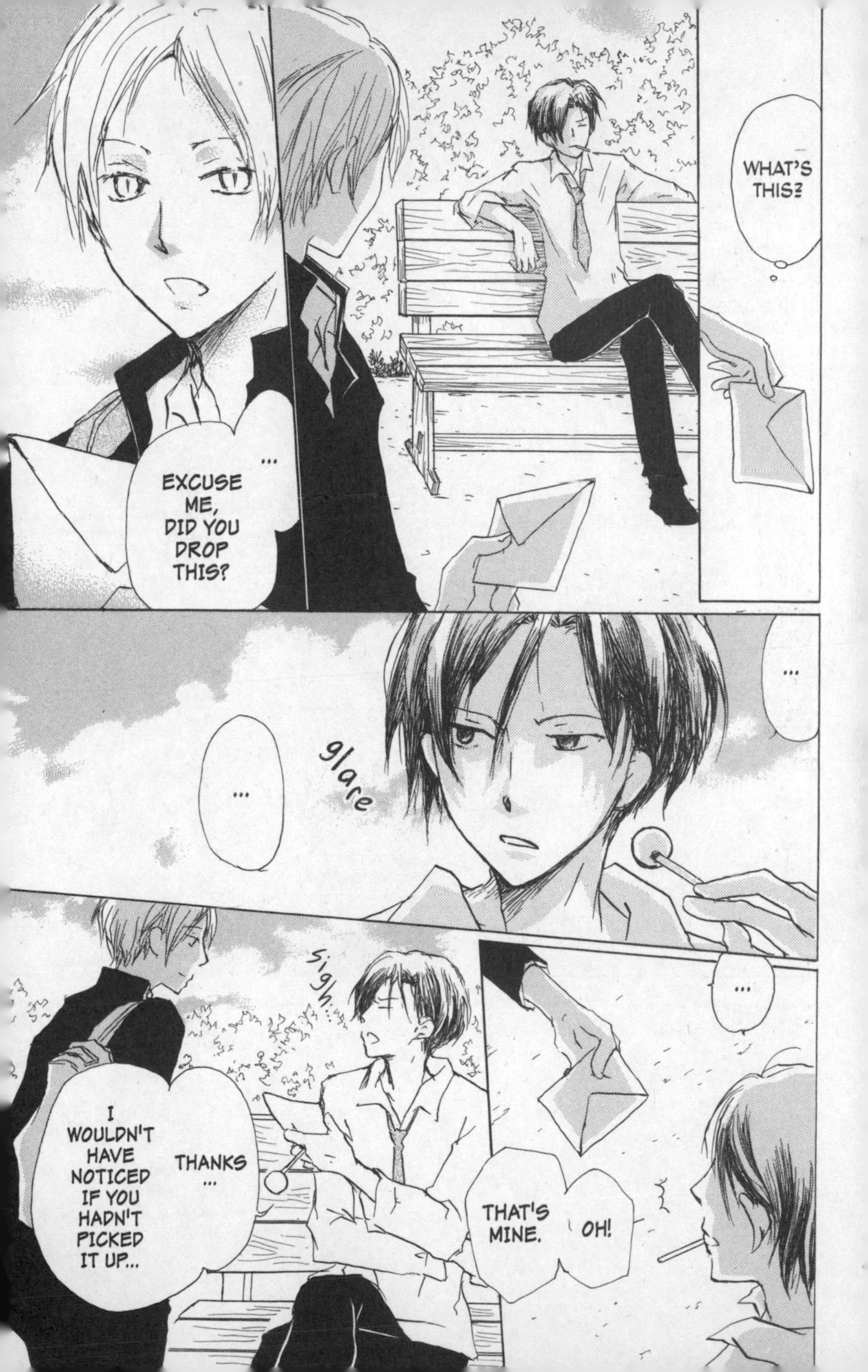
WHAT'S THIS?
... EXCUSE ME, DID YOU DROP THIS?
...
glare
...
...
OH!
THAT'S MINE.
sigh...
THANKS ...
I WOULDN'T HAVE NOTICED IF YOU HADN'T PICKED IT UP...

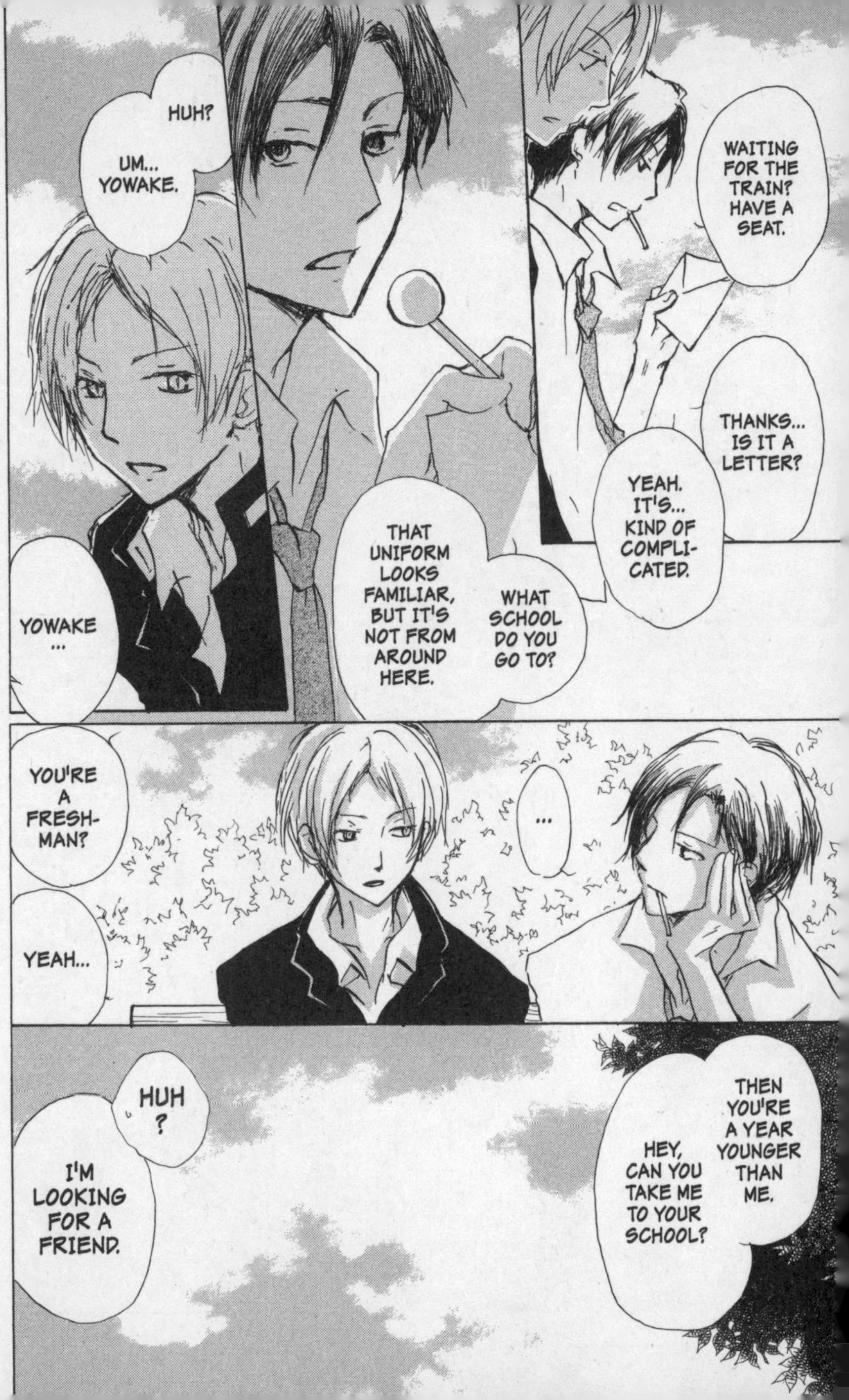
WAITING FOR THE TRAIN? HAVE A SEAT.
THANKS... IS IT A LETTER?
YEAH. IT'S... KIND OF COMPLICATED.
THAT UNIFORM LOOKS FAMILIAR, BUT IT'S NOT FROM AROUND HERE.
WHAT SCHOOL DO YOU GO TO?
HUH?
UM... YOWAKE.
YOWAKE...
...
YOU'RE A FRESHMAN?
YEAH...
THEN YOU'RE A YEAR YOUNGER THAN ME.
HEY, CAN YOU TAKE ME TO YOUR SCHOOL?
HUH?
I'M LOOKING FOR A FRIEND.

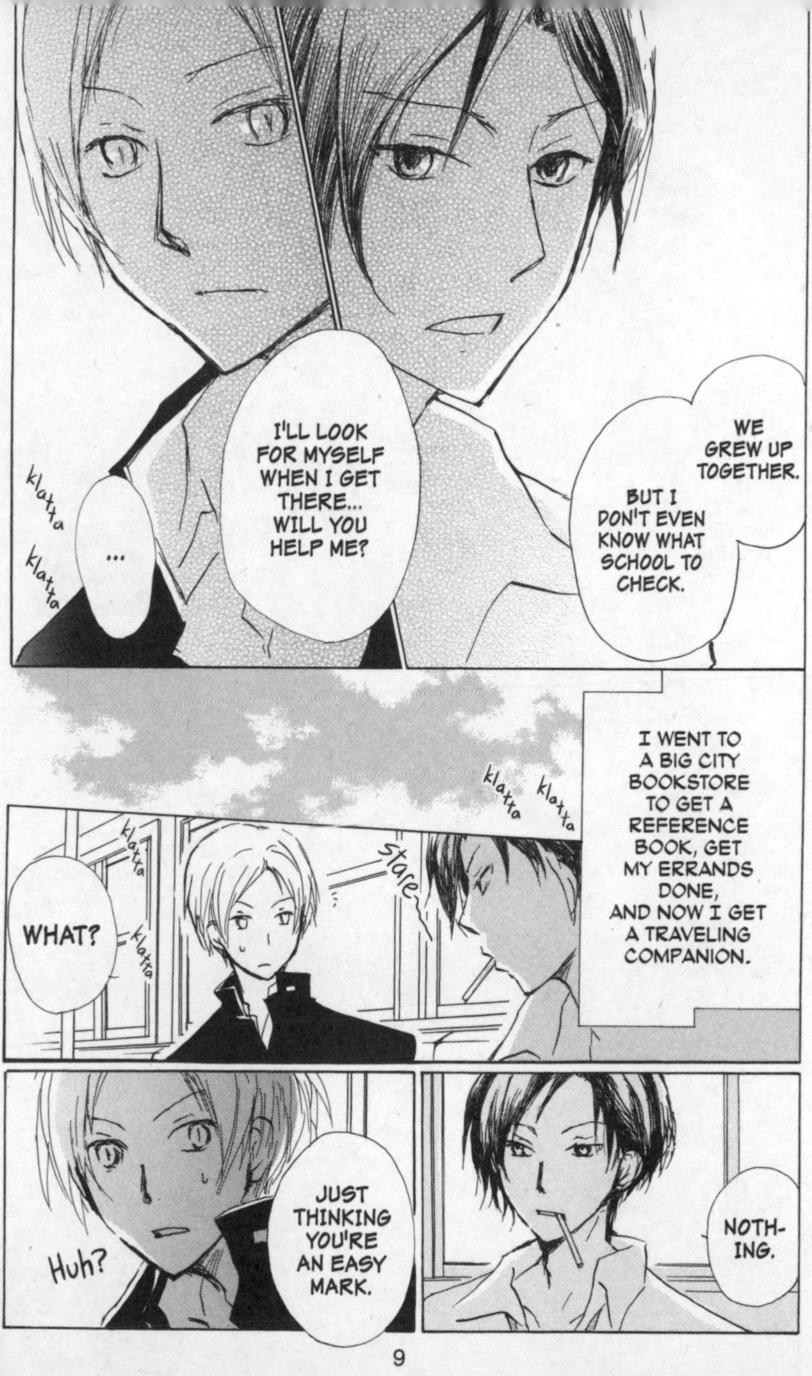
WE GREW UP TOGETHER.
BUT I DON'T EVEN KNOW WHAT SCHOOL TO CHECK.
I'LL LOOK FOR MYSELF WHEN I GET THERE... WILL YOU HELP ME?
...
klatta klatta
I WENT TO A BIG CITY BOOKSTORE TO GET A REFERENCE BOOK, GET MY ERRANDS DONE, AND NOW I GET A TRAVELING COMPANION.
klatta klatta
stare
klatta
WHAT?
klatta
NOTH-ING.
JUST THINKING YOU'RE AN EASY MARK.
Huh?

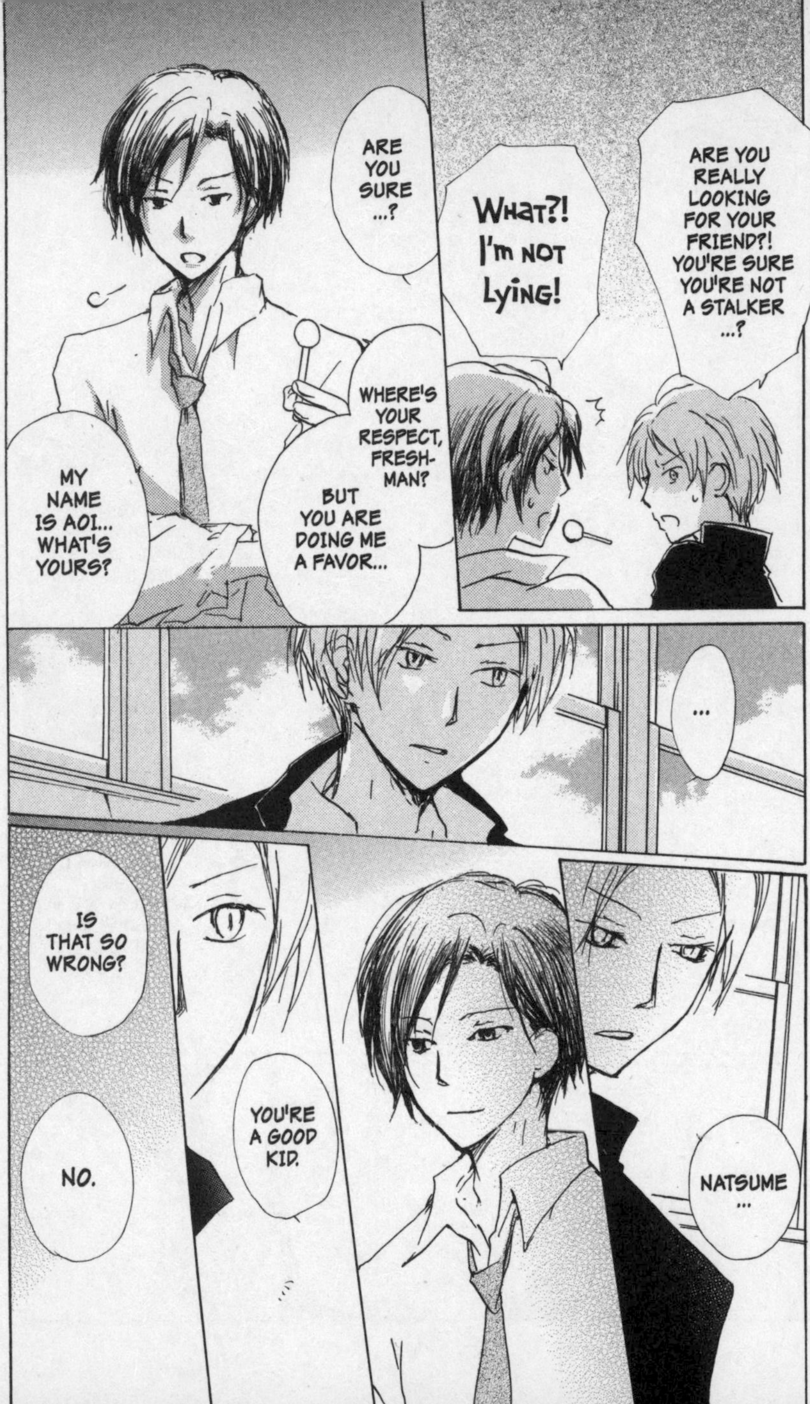
ARE YOU REALLY LOOKING FOR YOUR FRIEND?! YOU'RE SURE YOU'RE NOT A STALKER ...?
WHAT?! I'M NOT LYING!
ARE YOU SURE ...?
WHERE'S YOUR RESPECT, FRESH-MAN?
BUT YOU ARE DOING ME A FAVOR...
MY NAME IS AOI... WHAT'S YOURS?
...
NATSUME ...
YOU'RE A GOOD KID.
IS THAT SO WRONG?
NO.

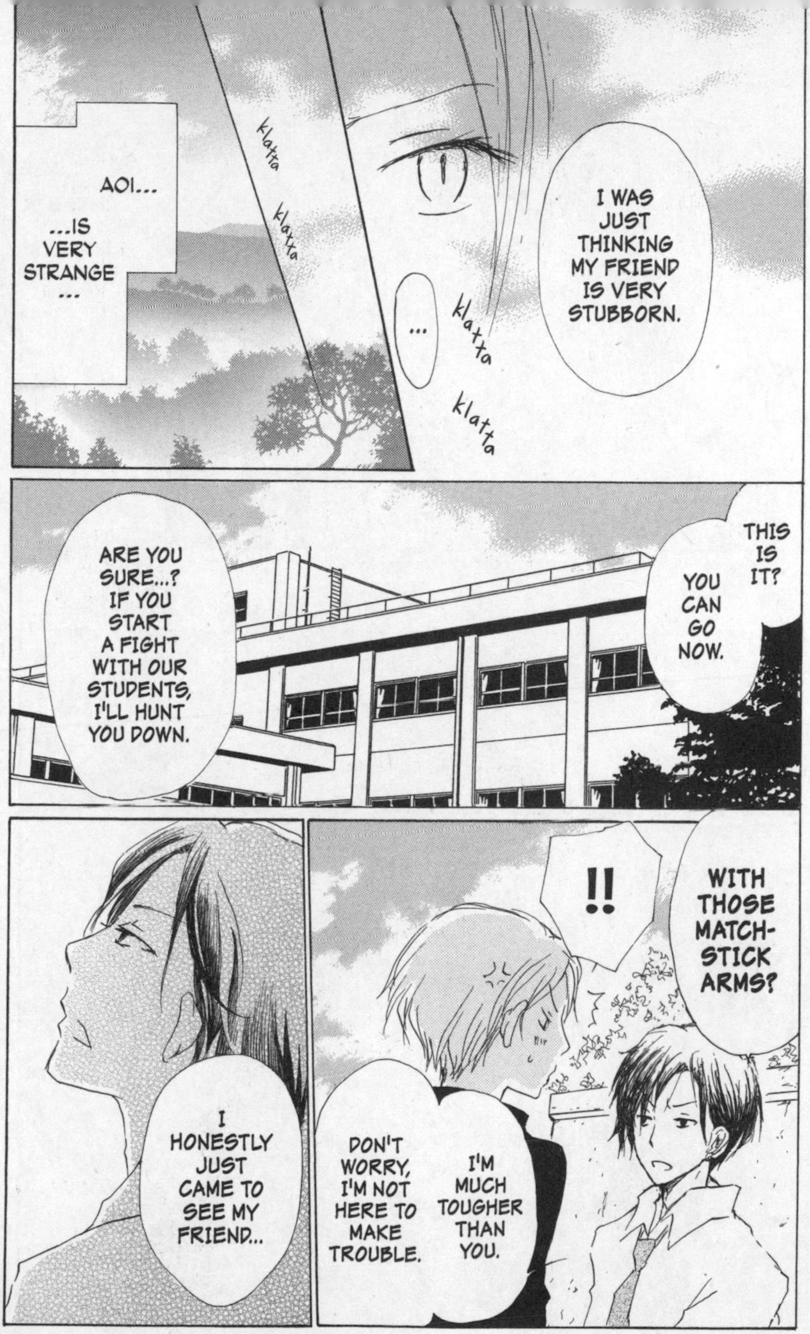
I WAS JUST THINKING MY FRIEND IS VERY STUBBORN.
klatta
klatta
...
klatta
klatta
AOI...
...IS VERY STRANGE ...
THIS IS IT?
YOU CAN GO NOW.
ARE YOU SURE...? IF YOU START A FIGHT WITH OUR STUDENTS, I'LL HUNT YOU DOWN.
WITH THOSE MATCH-STICK ARMS?
!!
DON'T WORRY, I'M NOT HERE TO MAKE TROUBLE.
I'M MUCH TOUGHER THAN YOU.
I HONESTLY JUST CAME TO SEE MY FRIEND...

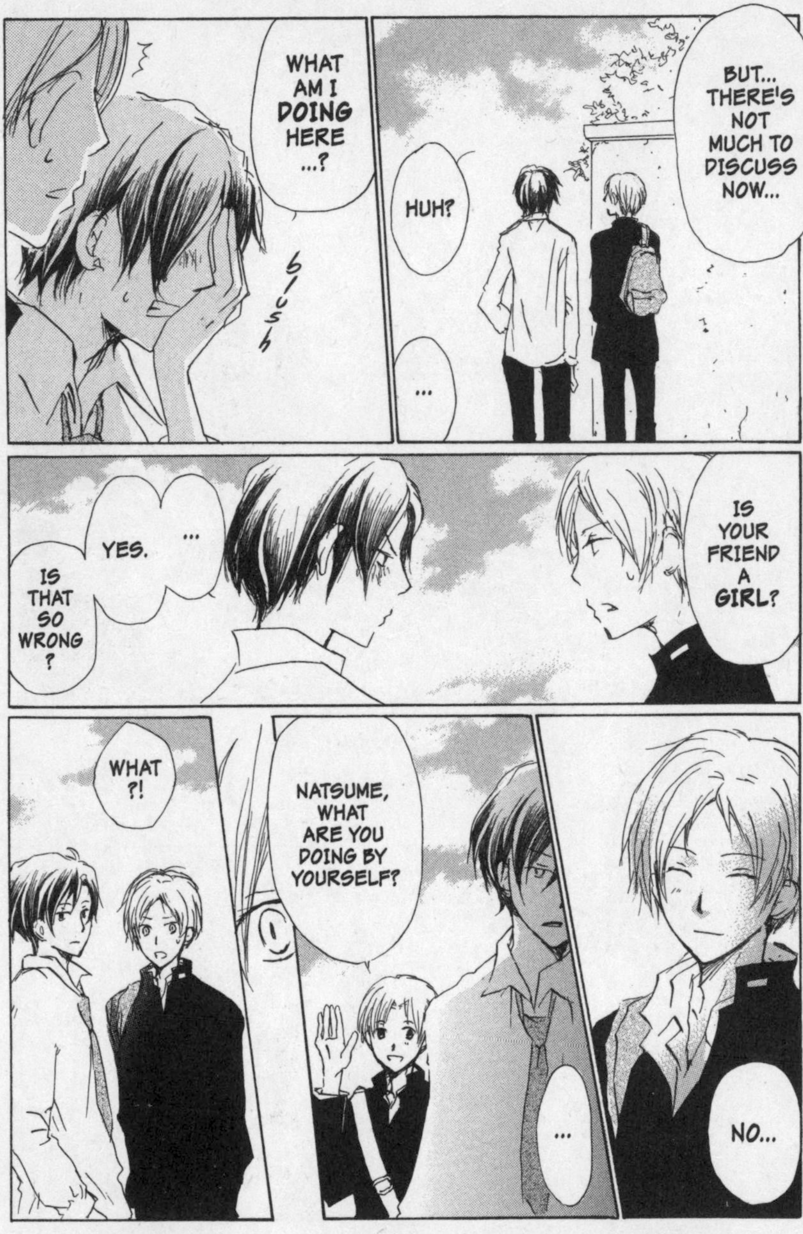
BUT... THERE'S NOT MUCH TO DISCUSS NOW...
HUH?
...
WHAT AM I DOING HERE ...?
blush
IS YOUR FRIEND A GIRL?
...
YES.
IS THAT SO WRONG?
NO...
...
NATSUME, WHAT ARE YOU DOING BY YOURSELF?
WHAT?!

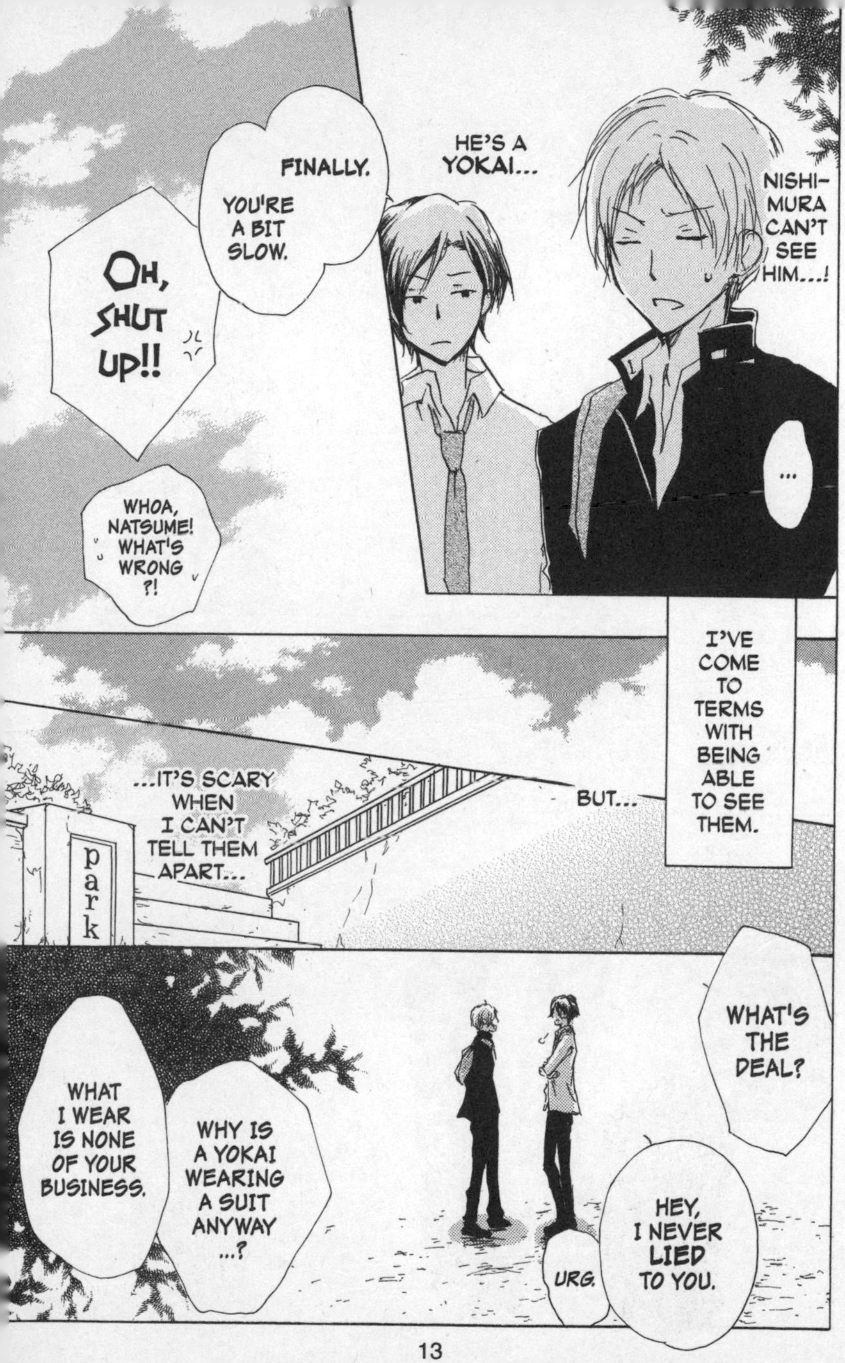
NISHI-MURA CAN'T SEE HIM...!
HE'S A YOKAI...
FINALLY.
YOU'RE A BIT SLOW.
OH, SHUT UP!!
...
WHOA, NATSUME! WHAT'S WRONG?!
I'VE COME TO TERMS WITH BEING ABLE TO SEE THEM.
BUT...
...IT'S SCARY WHEN I CAN'T TELL THEM APART...
park
WHAT'S THE DEAL?
HEY, I NEVER LIED TO YOU.
URG.
WHY IS A YOKAI WEARING A SUIT ANYWAY...?
WHAT I WEAR IS NONE OF YOUR BUSINESS.

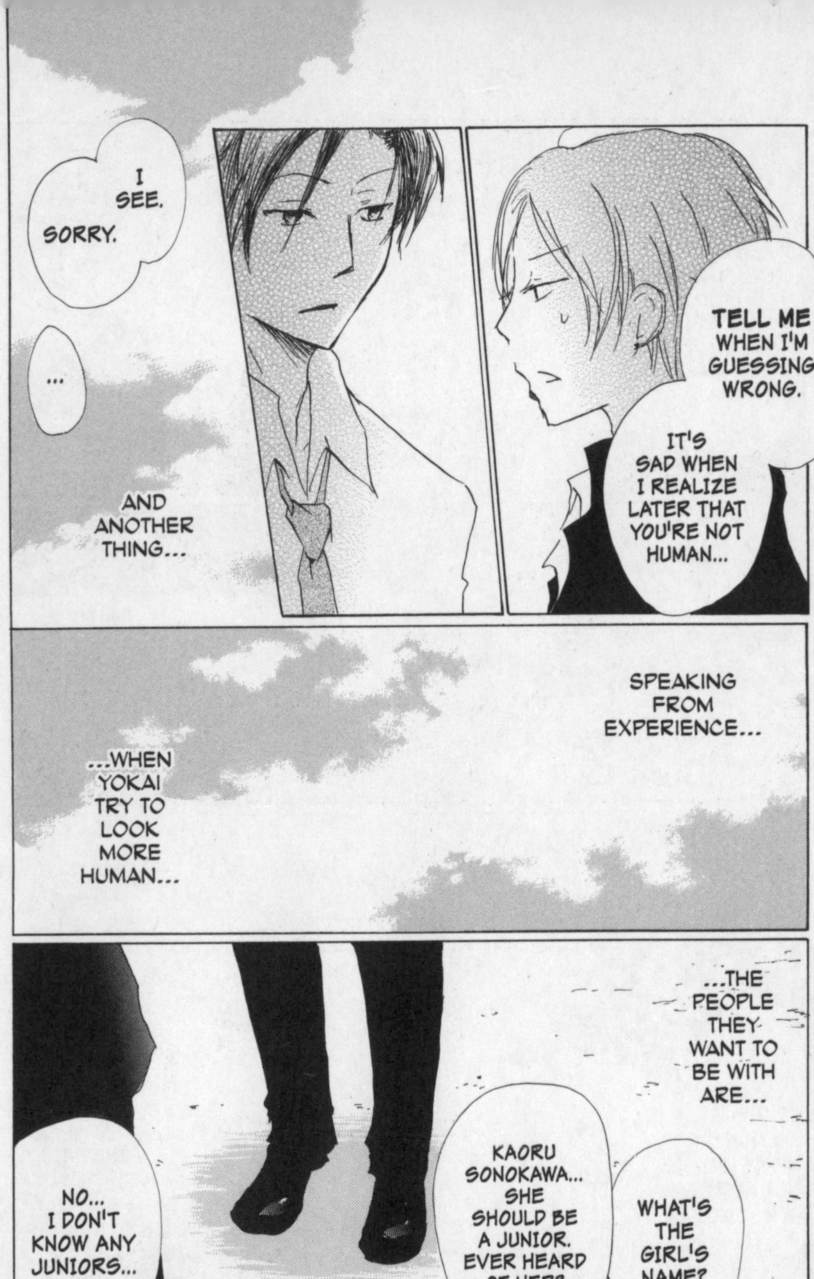
TELL ME WHEN I'M GUESSING WRONG.
IT'S SAD WHEN I REALIZE LATER THAT YOU'RE NOT HUMAN...
I SEE. SORRY.
...
AND ANOTHER THING...
SPEAKING FROM EXPERIENCE...
...WHEN YOKAI TRY TO LOOK MORE HUMAN...
...THE PEOPLE THEY WANT TO BE WITH ARE...
WHAT'S THE GIRL'S NAME?
KAORU SONOKAWA... SHE SHOULD BE A JUNIOR. EVER HEARD OF HER?
NO... I DON'T KNOW ANY JUNIORS...

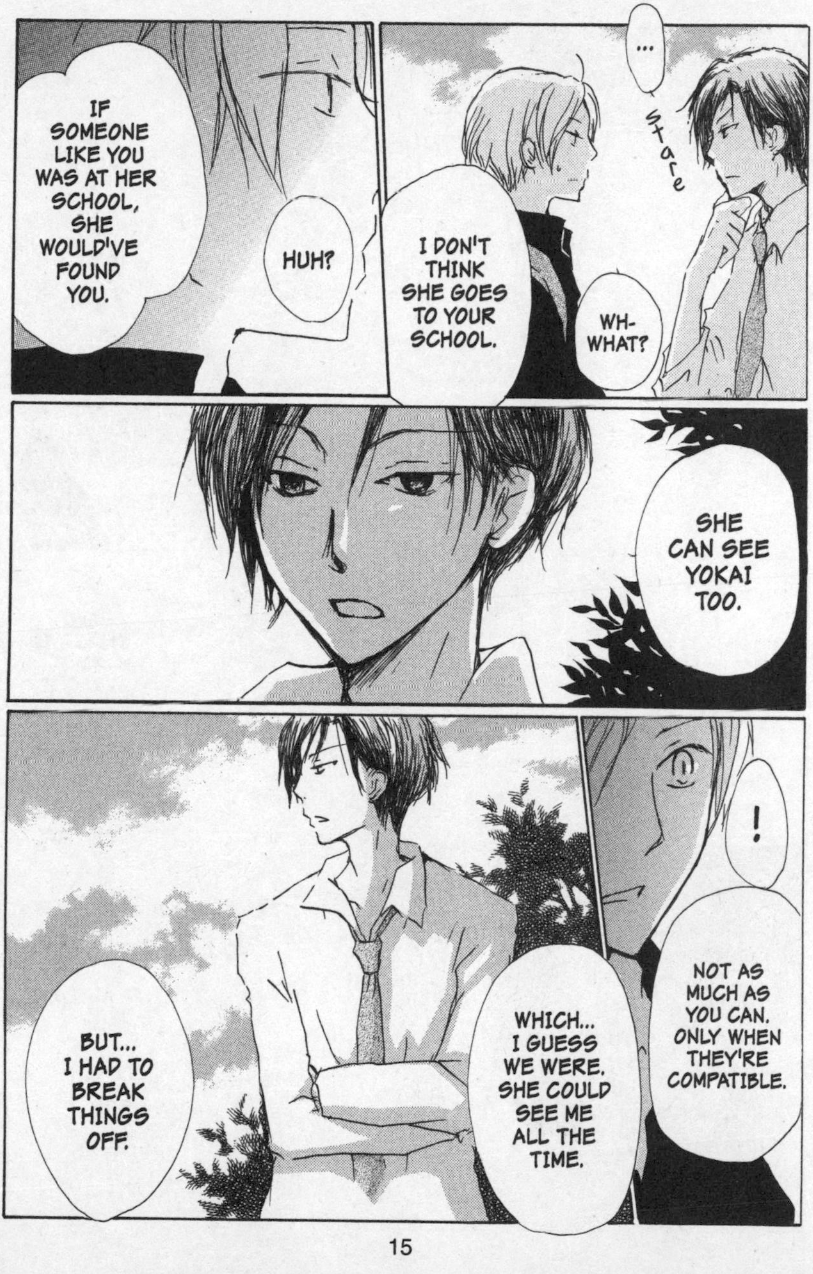
...
Stare
I DON'T THINK SHE GOES TO YOUR SCHOOL.
WH-WHAT?
HUH?
IF SOMEONE LIKE YOU WAS AT HER SCHOOL, SHE WOULD'VE FOUND YOU.
SHE CAN SEE YOKAI TOO.
!
NOT AS MUCH AS YOU CAN. ONLY WHEN THEY'RE COMPATIBLE.
WHICH... I GUESS WE WERE. SHE COULD SEE ME ALL THE TIME.
BUT... I HAD TO BREAK THINGS OFF.

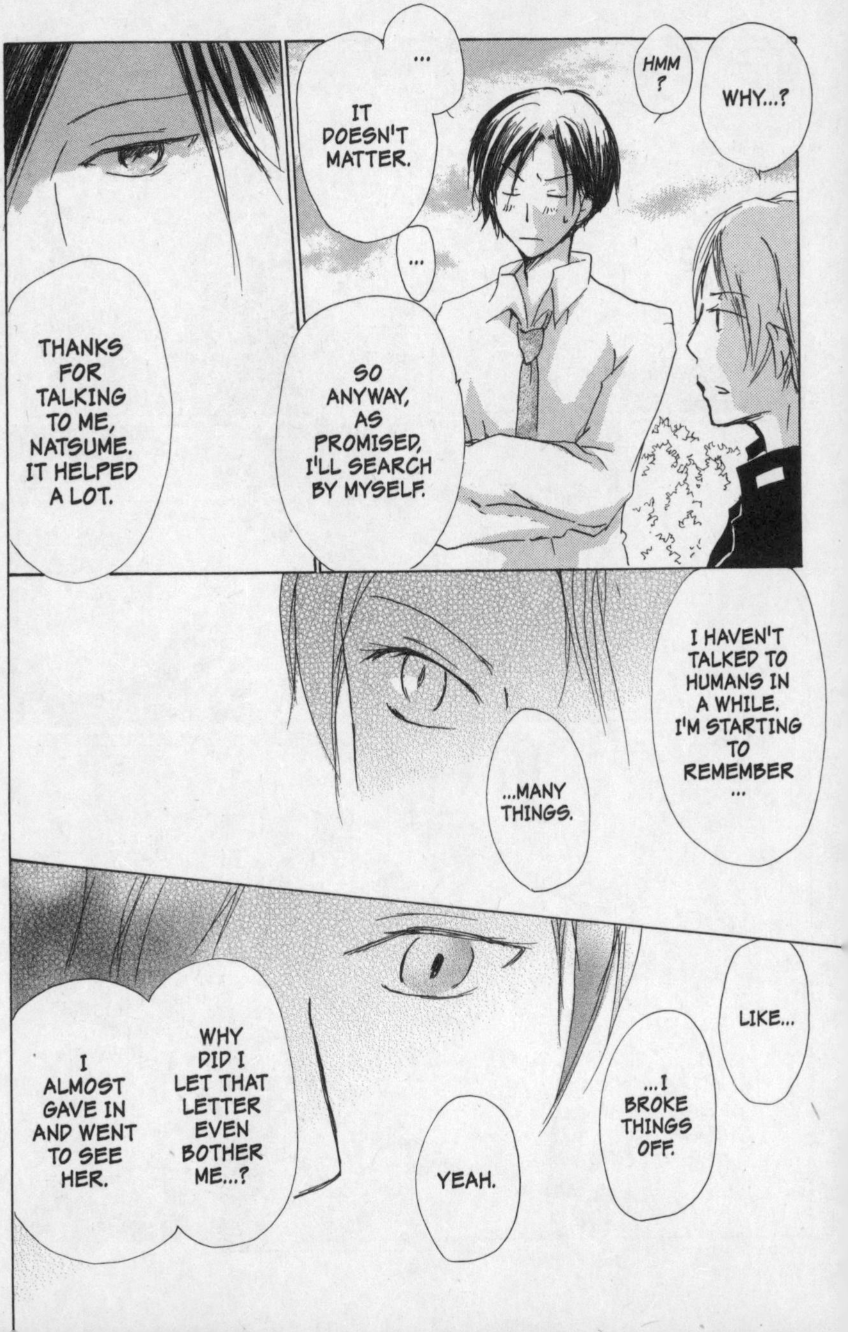
WHY...?
HMM?
...
IT DOESN'T MATTER.
...
SO ANYWAY, AS PROMISED, I'LL SEARCH BY MYSELF.
THANKS FOR TALKING TO ME, NATSUME. IT HELPED A LOT.
I HAVEN'T TALKED TO HUMANS IN A WHILE. I'M STARTING TO REMEMBER...
...MANY THINGS.
LIKE...
...I BROKE THINGS OFF.
YEAH.
WHY DID I LET THAT LETTER EVEN BOTHER ME...?
I ALMOST GAVE IN AND WENT TO SEE HER.

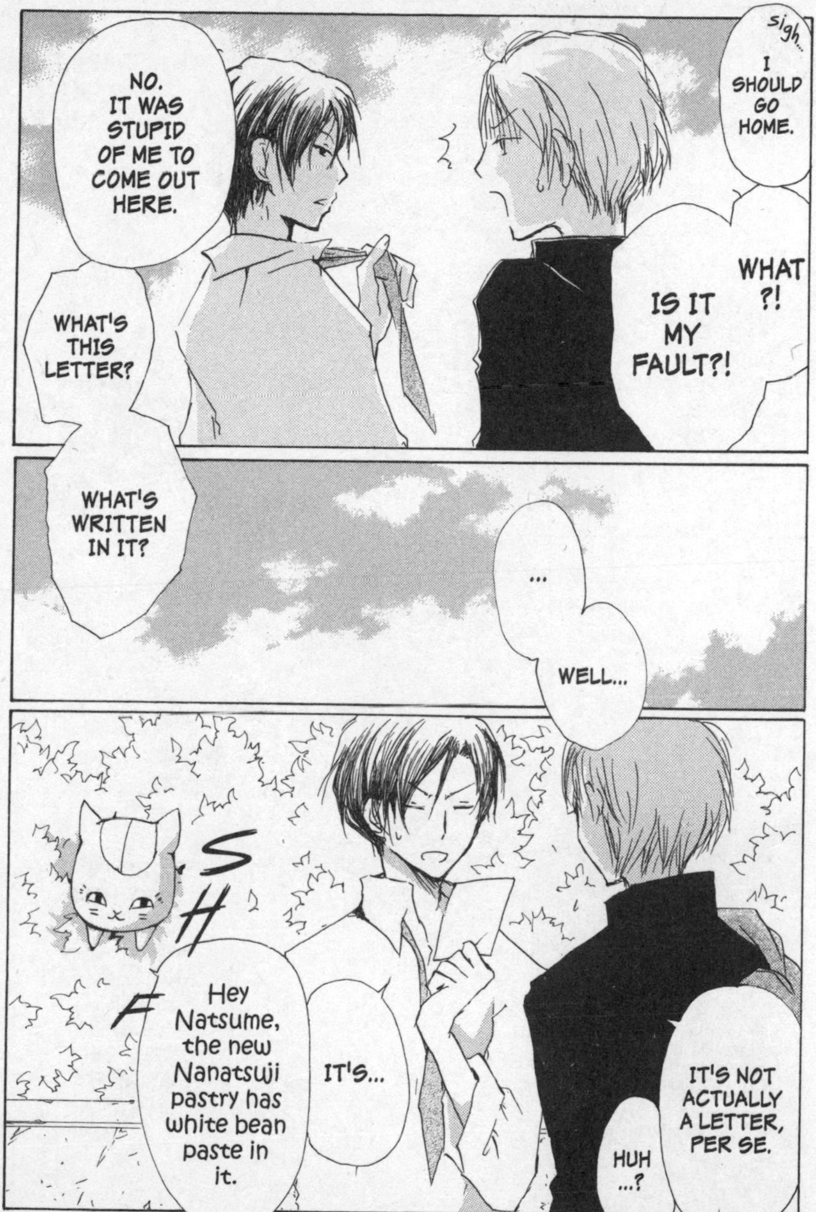
sigh...
I SHOULD GO HOME.
WHAT?!
IS IT MY FAULT?!
NO. IT WAS STUPID OF ME TO COME OUT HERE.
WHAT'S THIS LETTER?
WHAT'S WRITTEN IN IT?
...
WELL...
IT'S NOT ACTUALLY A LETTER, PER SE.
HUH...?
IT'S...
SHF
Hey Natsume, the new Nanatsuji pastry has white bean paste in it.

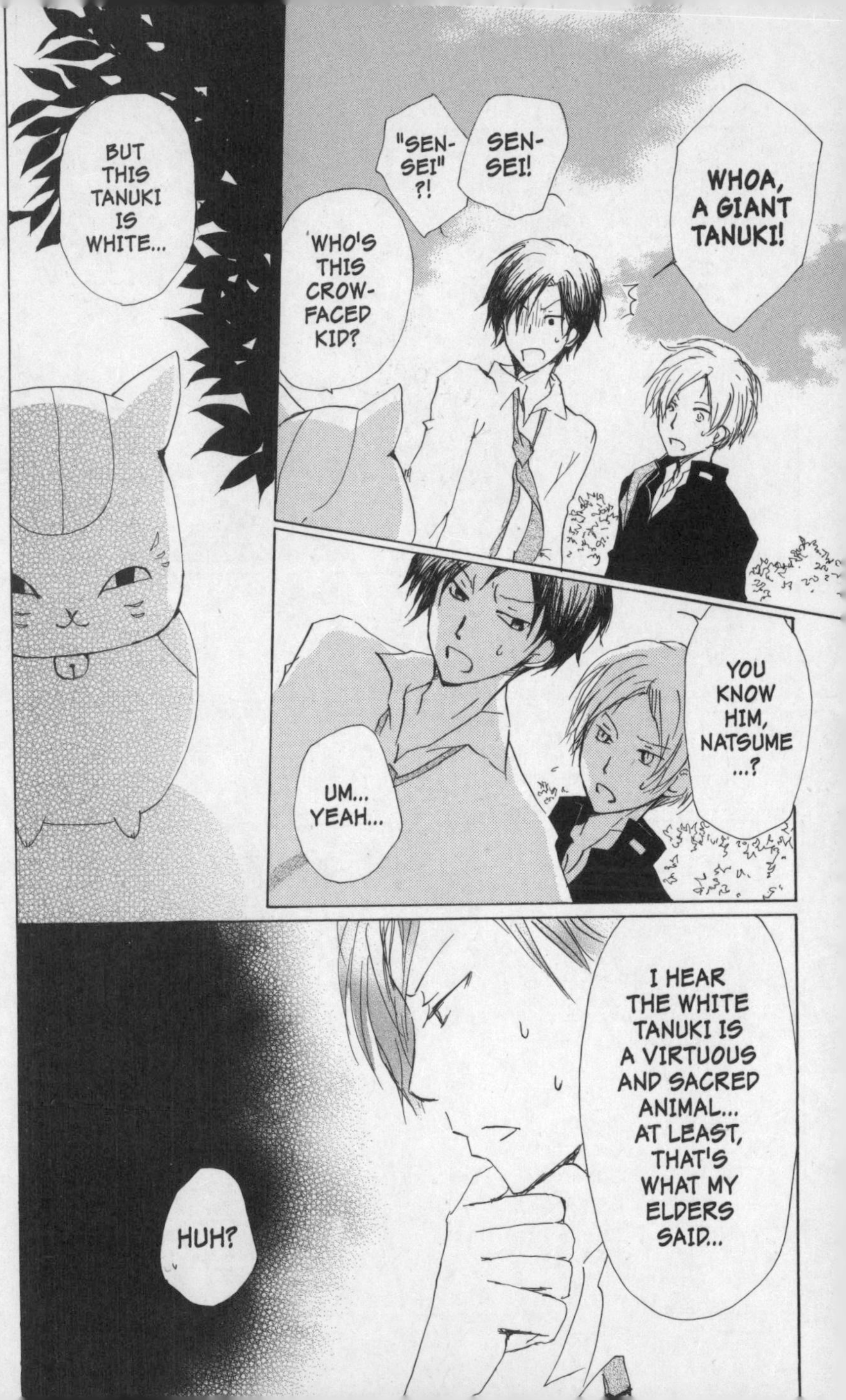
WHOA, A GIANT TANUKI!
SEN-SEI!
"SEN-SEI"?!
WHO'S THIS CROW-FACED KID?
YOU KNOW HIM, NATSUME ...?
UM... YEAH...
BUT THIS TANUKI IS WHITE...
I HEAR THE WHITE TANUKI IS A VIRTUOUS AND SACRED ANIMAL... AT LEAST, THAT'S WHAT MY ELDERS SAID...
HUH?

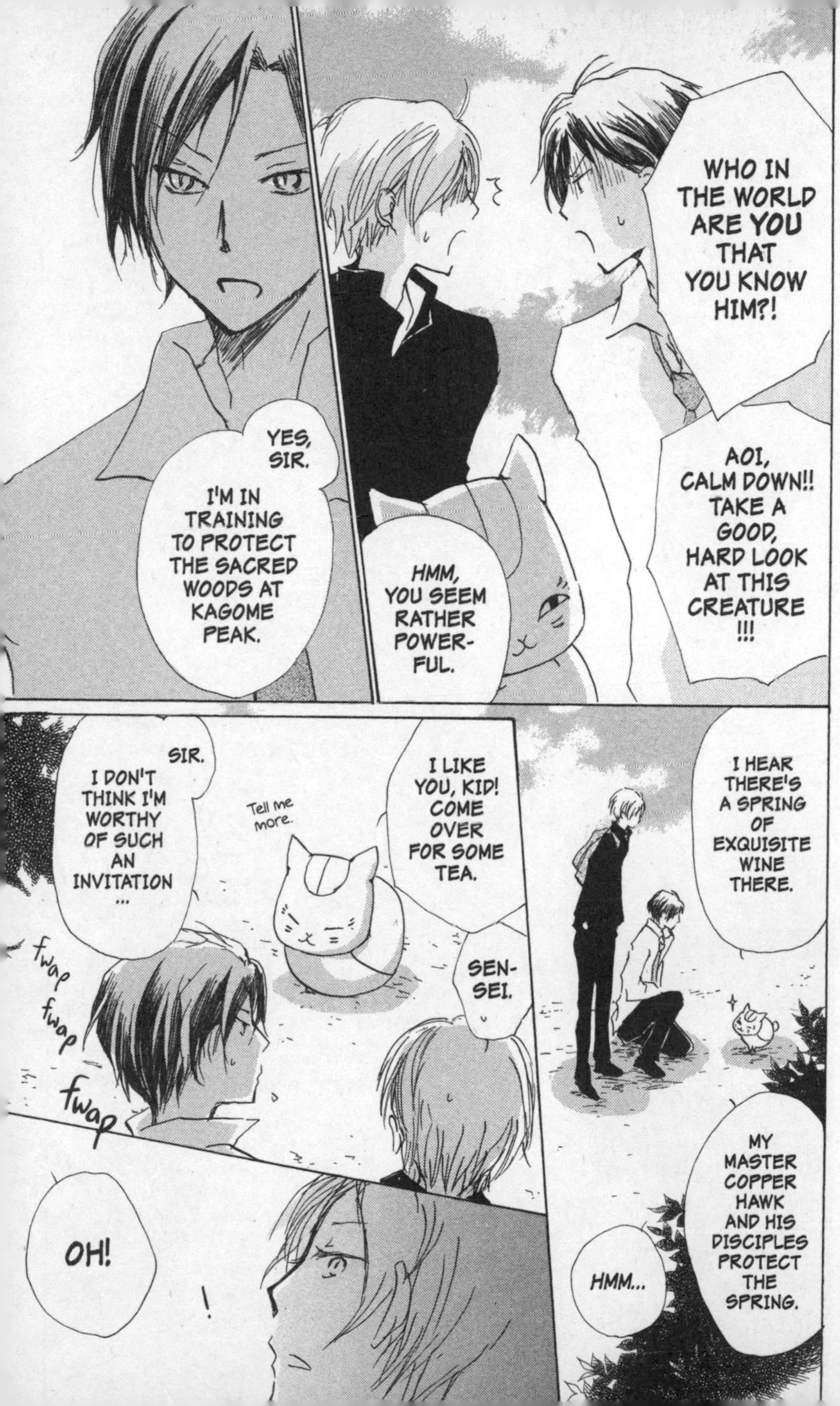
WHO IN THE WORLD ARE YOU THAT YOU KNOW HIM?!
AOI, CALM DOWN!! TAKE A GOOD, HARD LOOK AT THIS CREATURE !!!
HMM, YOU SEEM RATHER POWER-FUL.
YES, SIR.
I'M IN TRAINING TO PROTECT THE SACRED WOODS AT KAGOME PEAK.
I HEAR THERE'S A SPRING OF EXQUISITE WINE THERE.
MY MASTER COPPER HAWK AND HIS DISCIPLES PROTECT THE SPRING.
HMM...
I LIKE YOU, KID! COME OVER FOR SOME TEA.
SIR.
I DON'T THINK I'M WORTHY OF SUCH AN INVITATION ...
Tell me more.
SEN-SEI.
fwap fwap fwap
OH!
!

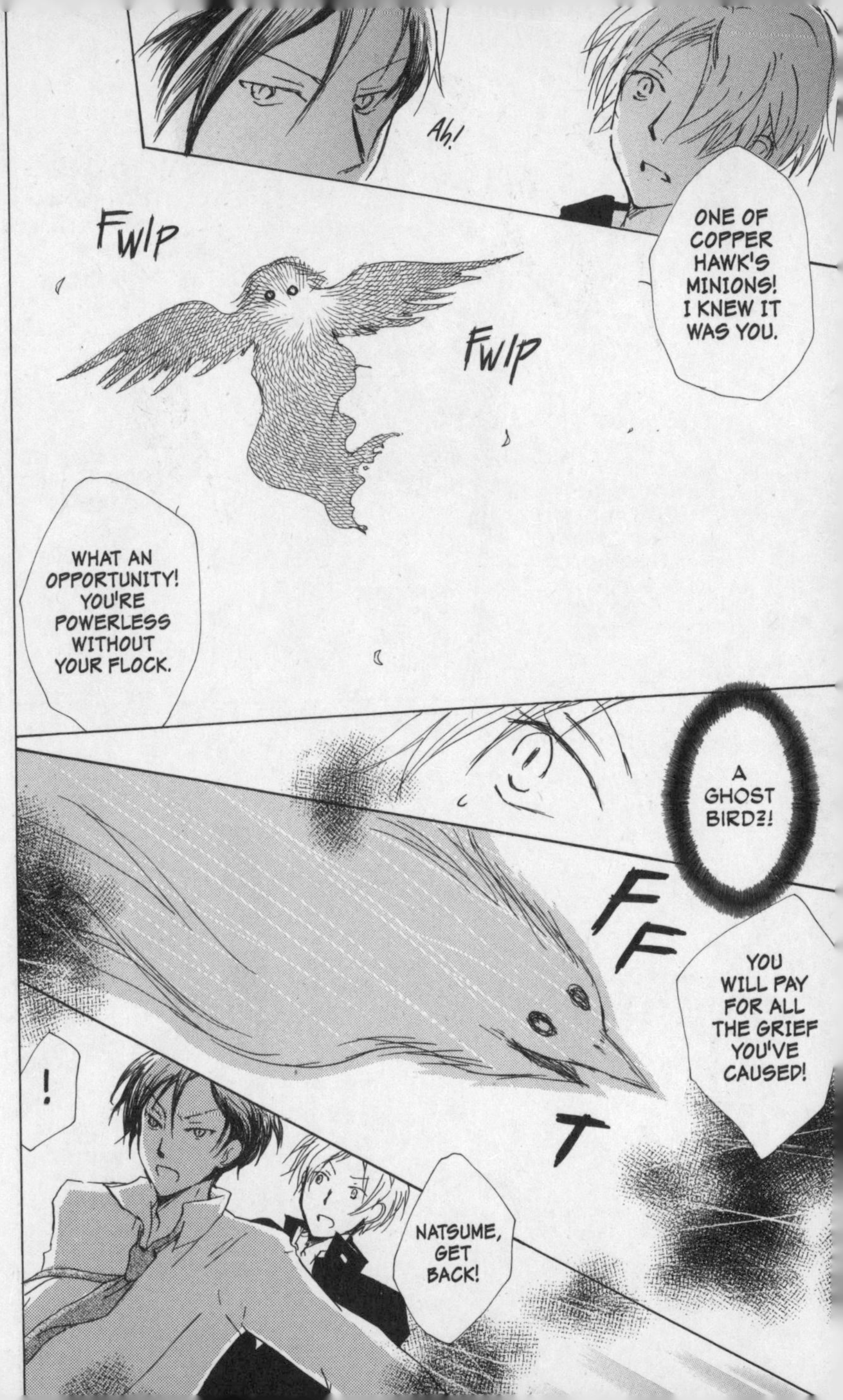

Ah!
ONE OF COPPER HAWK'S MINIONS! I KNEW IT WAS YOU.
FWIP
FWIP
WHAT AN OPPORTUNITY! YOU'RE POWERLESS WITHOUT YOUR FLOCK.
A GHOST BIRD?!
FFT
YOU WILL PAY FOR ALL THE GRIEF YOU'VE CAUSED!
!
NATSUME, GET BACK!

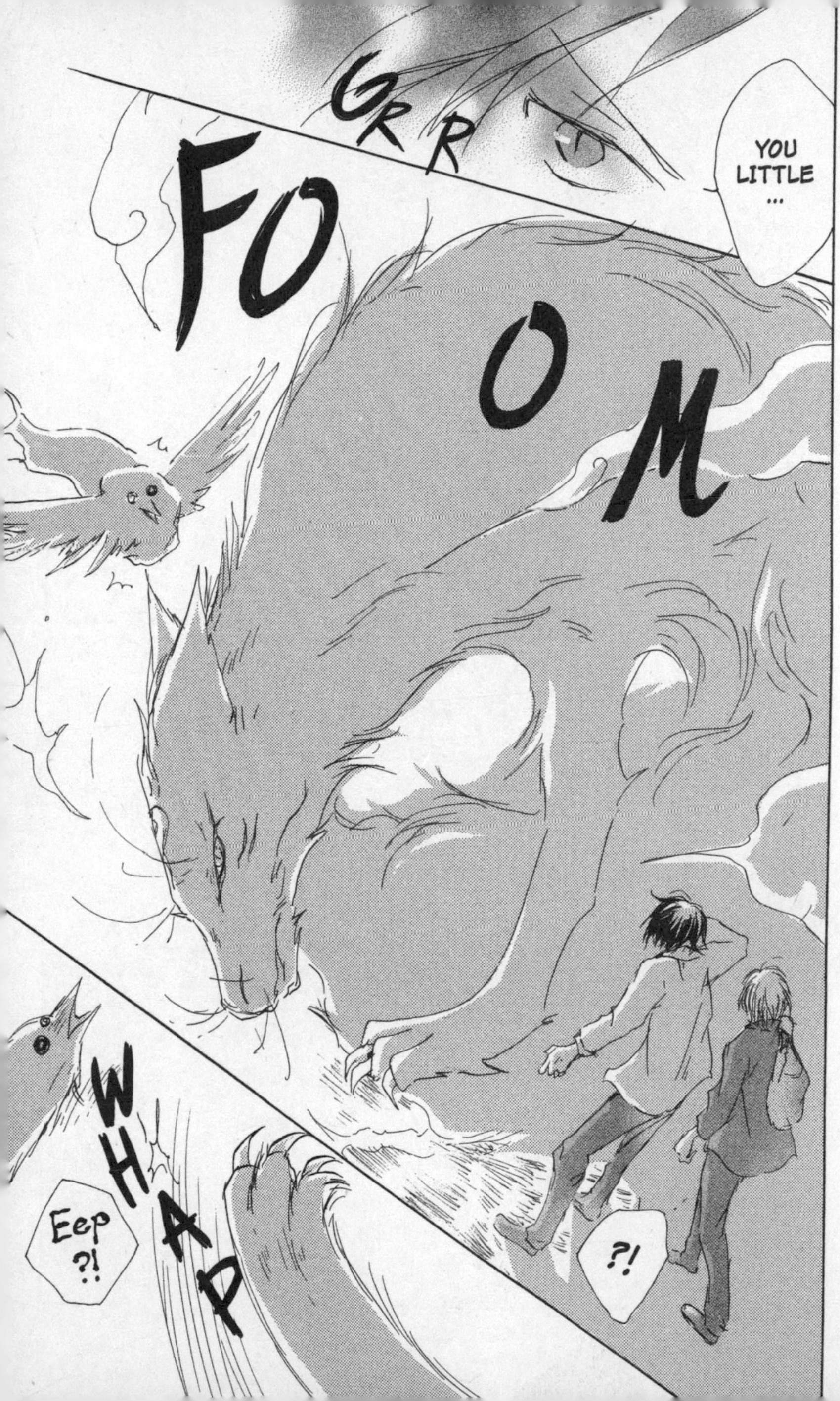
YOU LITTLE ...
GRR
FOOM
?!
WHAP
Eep ?!

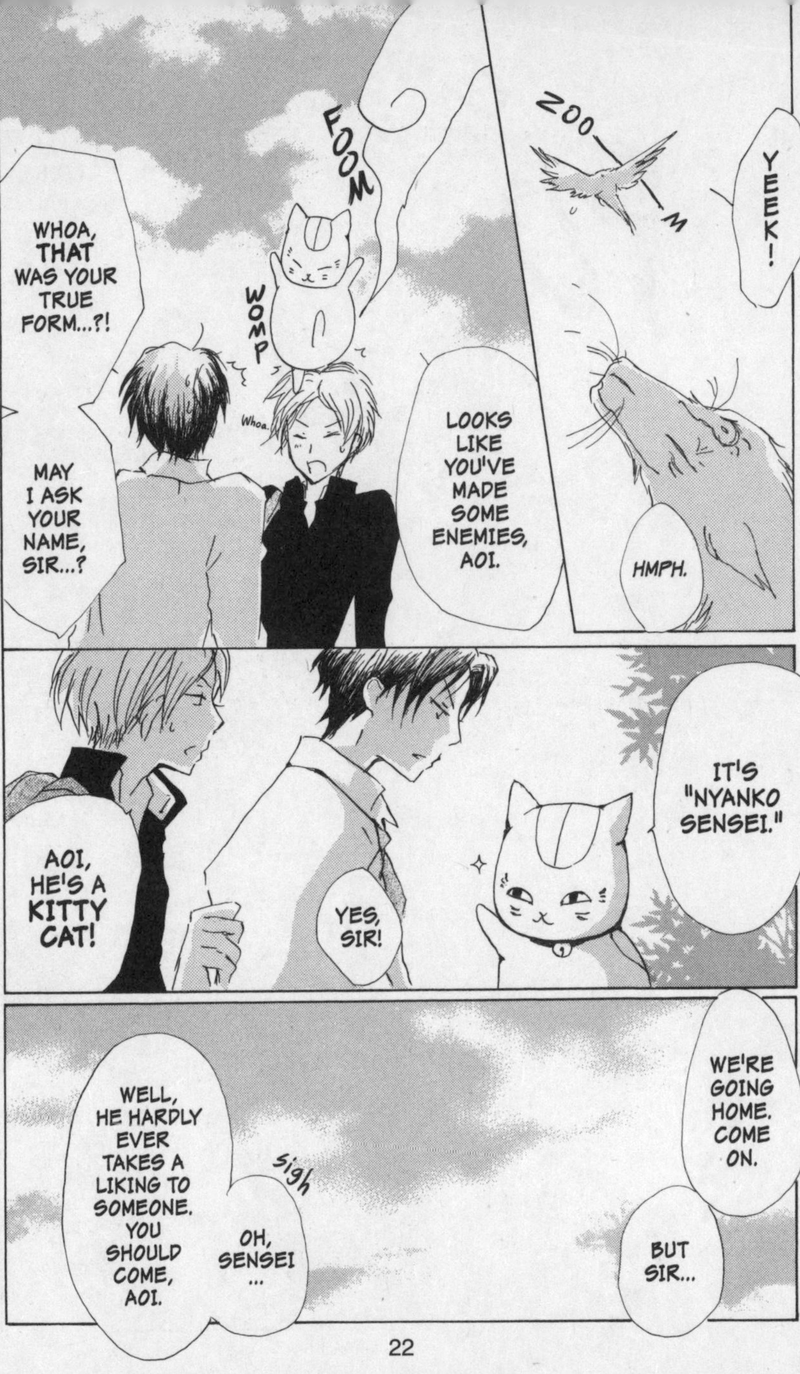
YEEK!
ZOOM
HMPH.
FOOM
LOOKS LIKE YOU'VE MADE SOME ENEMIES, AOI.
WOMP
Whoa.
WHOA, THAT WAS YOUR TRUE FORM...?!
MAY I ASK YOUR NAME, SIR...?
IT'S "NYANKO SENSEI."
YES, SIR!
AOI, HE'S A KITTY CAT!
WE'RE GOING HOME. COME ON.
BUT SIR...
sigh
OH, SENSEI ...
WELL, HE HARDLY EVER TAKES A LIKING TO SOMEONE. YOU SHOULD COME, AOI.

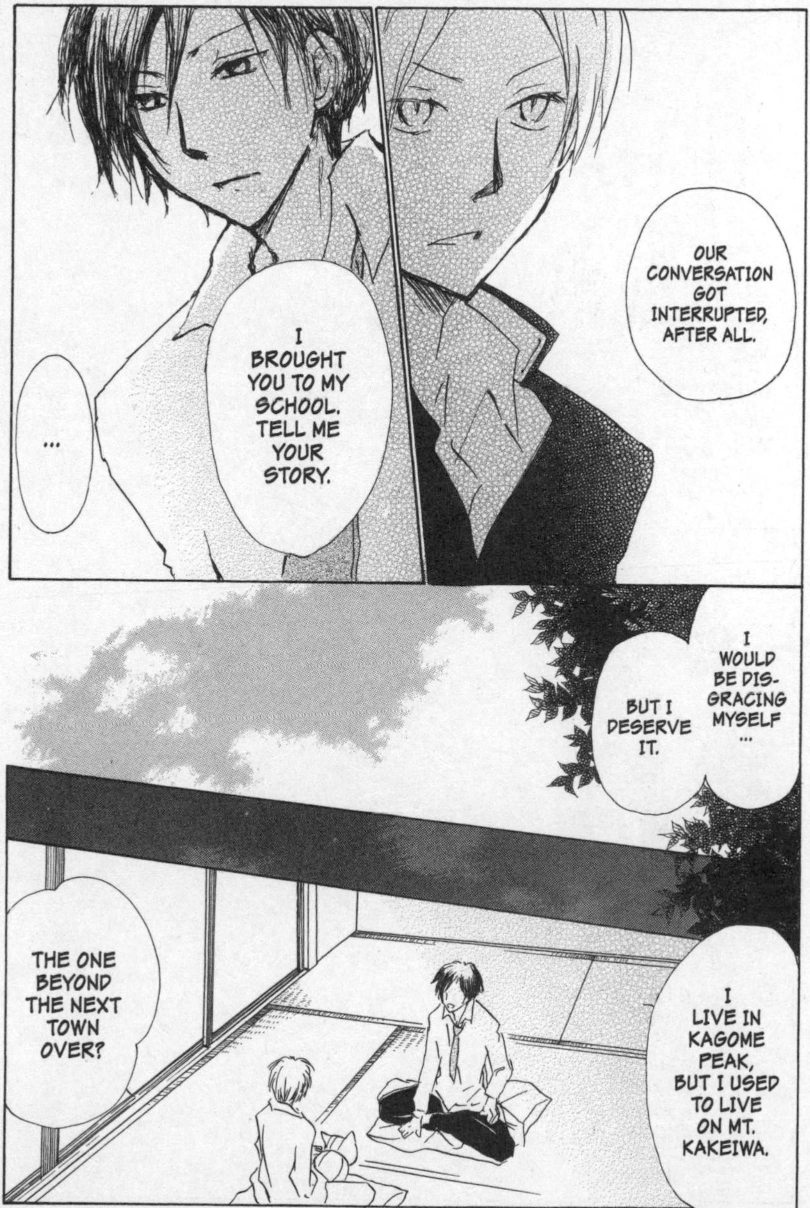
OUR CONVERSATION GOT INTERRUPTED, AFTER ALL.
I BROUGHT YOU TO MY SCHOOL. TELL ME YOUR STORY.
...
I WOULD BE DIS-GRACING MYSELF ...
BUT I DESERVE IT.
I LIVE IN KAGOME PEAK, BUT I USED TO LIVE ON MT. KAKEIWA.
THE ONE BEYOND THE NEXT TOWN OVER?

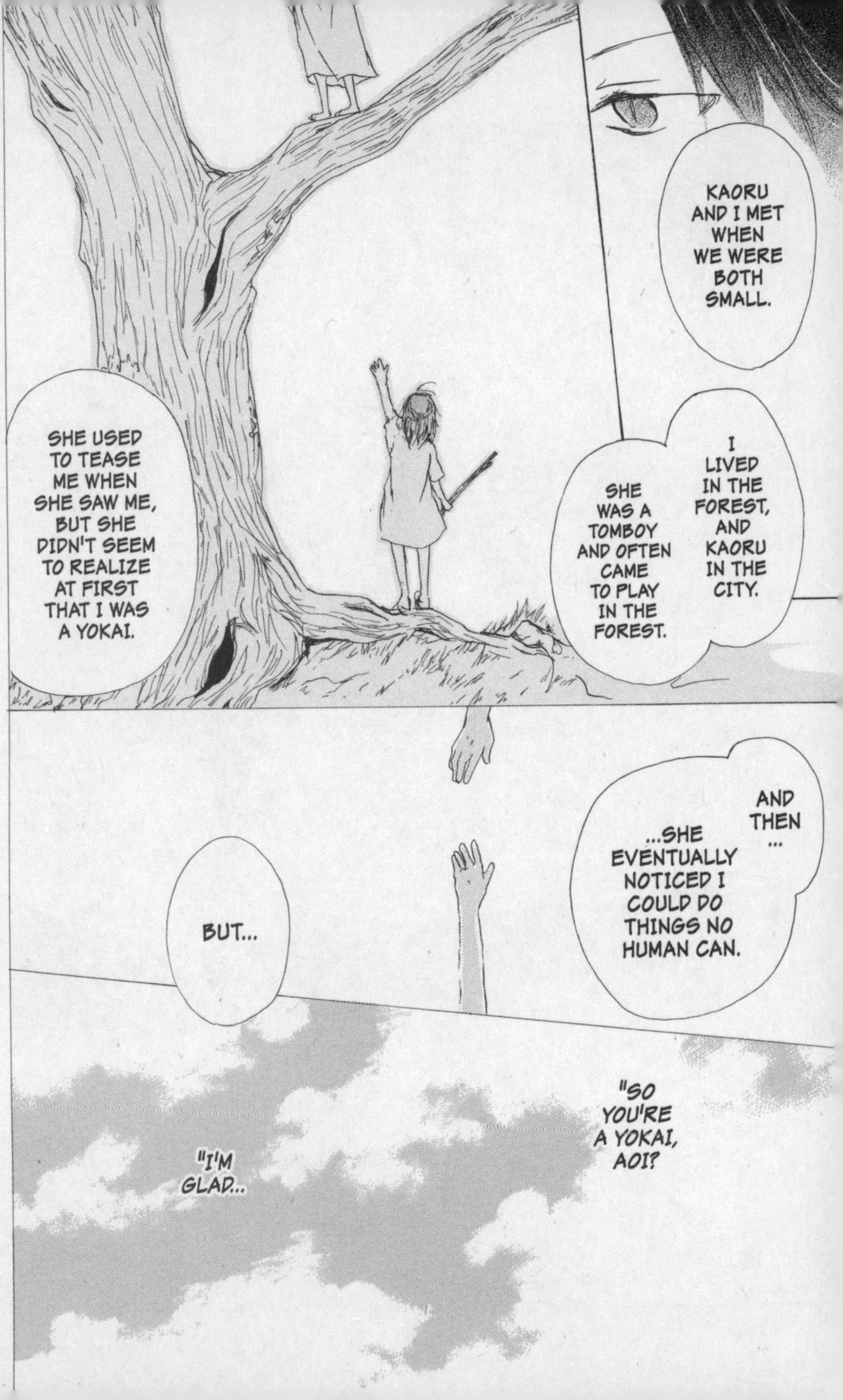
KAORU AND I MET WHEN WE WERE BOTH SMALL.
I LIVED IN THE FOREST, AND KAORU IN THE CITY.
SHE WAS A TOMBOY AND OFTEN CAME TO PLAY IN THE FOREST.
SHE USED TO TEASE ME WHEN SHE SAW ME, BUT SHE DIDN'T SEEM TO REALIZE AT FIRST THAT I WAS A YOKAI.
AND THEN ...
...SHE EVENTUALLY NOTICED I COULD DO THINGS NO HUMAN CAN.
BUT...
"SO YOU'RE A YOKAI, AOI?
"I'M GLAD...

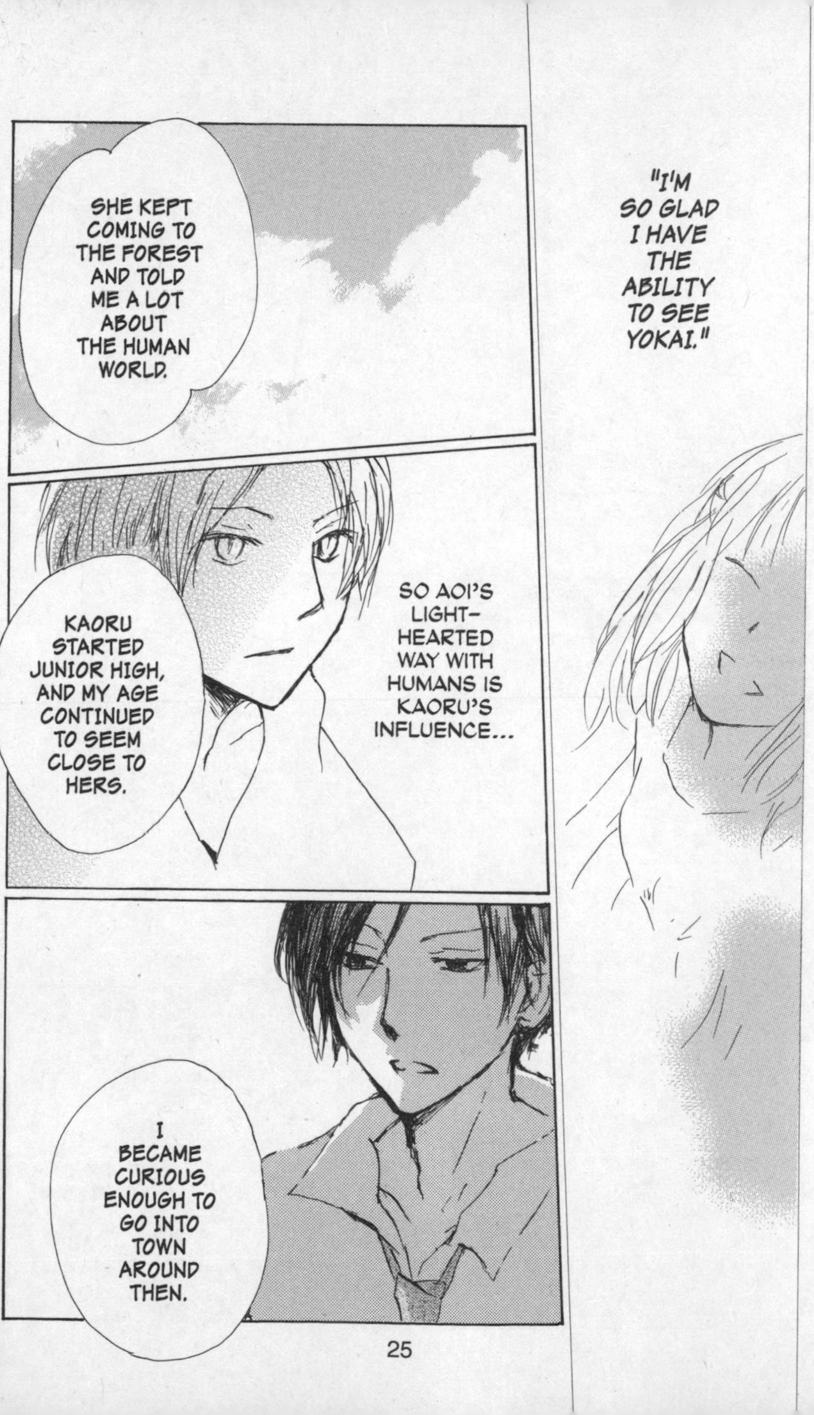
"I'M SO GLAD I HAVE THE ABILITY TO SEE YOKAI."
SHE KEPT COMING TO THE FOREST AND TOLD ME A LOT ABOUT THE HUMAN WORLD.
SO AOI'S LIGHT-HEARTED WAY WITH HUMANS IS KAORU'S INFLUENCE...
KAORU STARTED JUNIOR HIGH, AND MY AGE CONTINUED TO SEEM CLOSE TO HERS.
I BECAME CURIOUS ENOUGH TO GO INTO TOWN AROUND THEN.

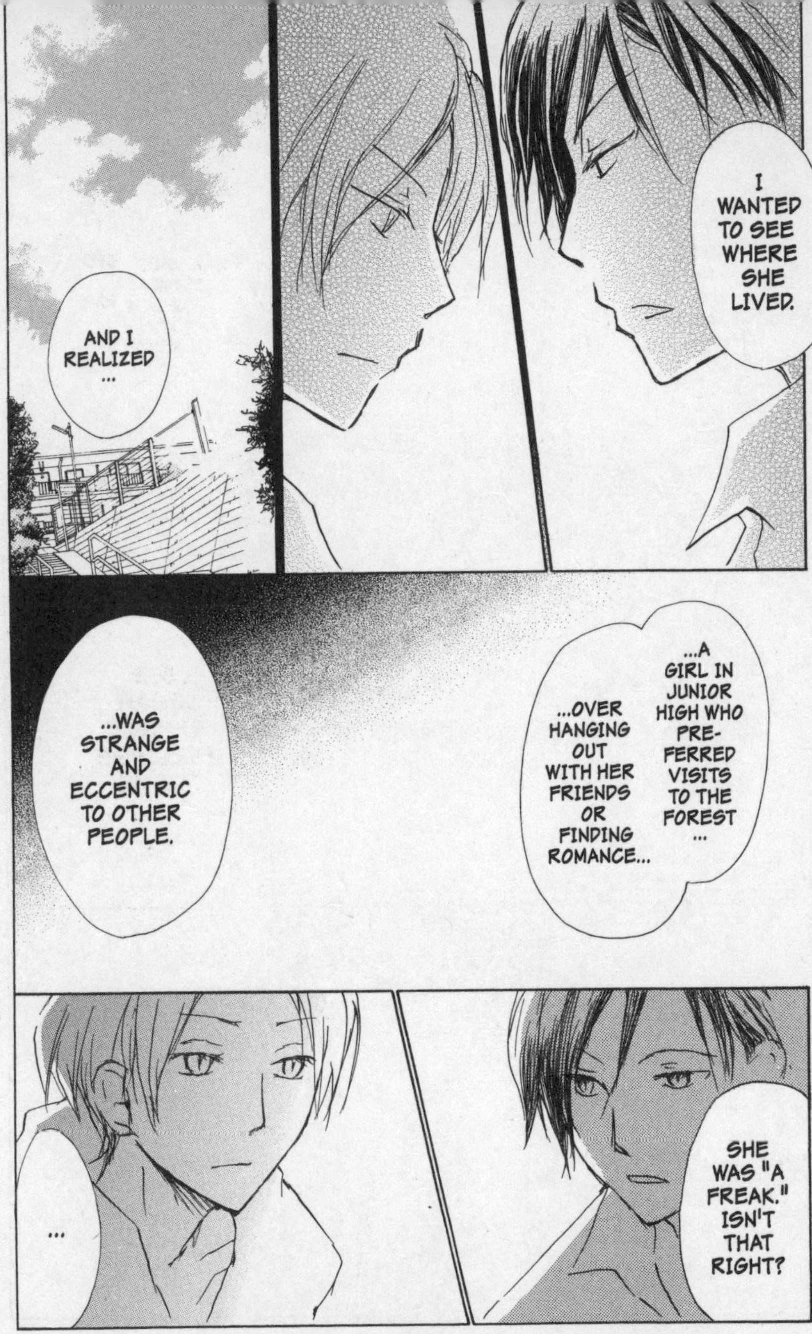
I WANTED TO SEE WHERE SHE LIVED.
AND I REALIZED...
...A GIRL IN JUNIOR HIGH WHO PRE-FERRED VISITS TO THE FOREST...
...OVER HANGING OUT WITH HER FRIENDS OR FINDING ROMANCE...
...WAS STRANGE AND ECCENTRIC TO OTHER PEOPLE.
SHE WAS "A FREAK." ISN'T THAT RIGHT?
...

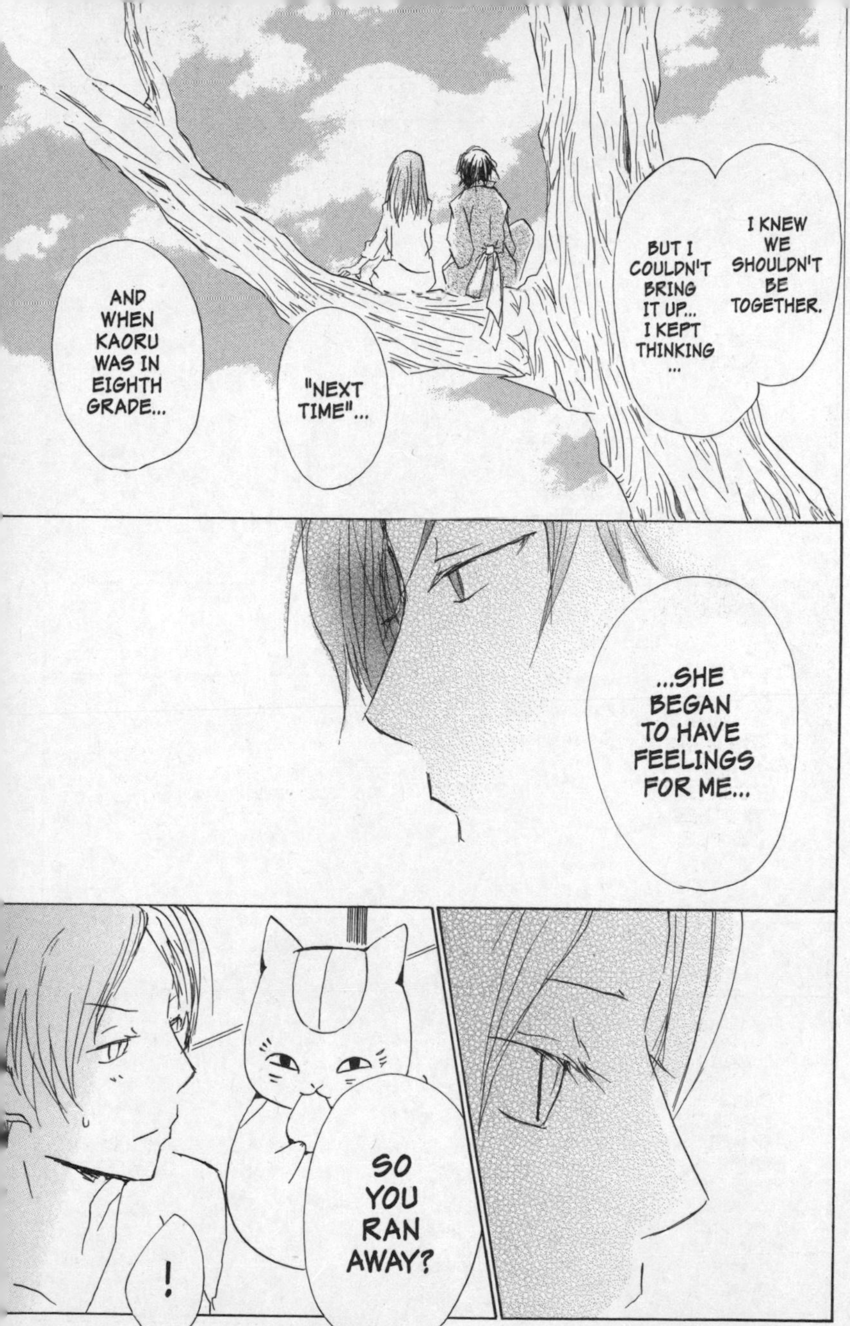
I KNEW WE SHOULDN'T BE TOGETHER.
BUT I COULDN'T BRING IT UP... I KEPT THINKING ...
"NEXT TIME"...
AND WHEN KAORU WAS IN EIGHTH GRADE...
...SHE BEGAN TO HAVE FEELINGS FOR ME...
SO YOU RAN AWAY?
!

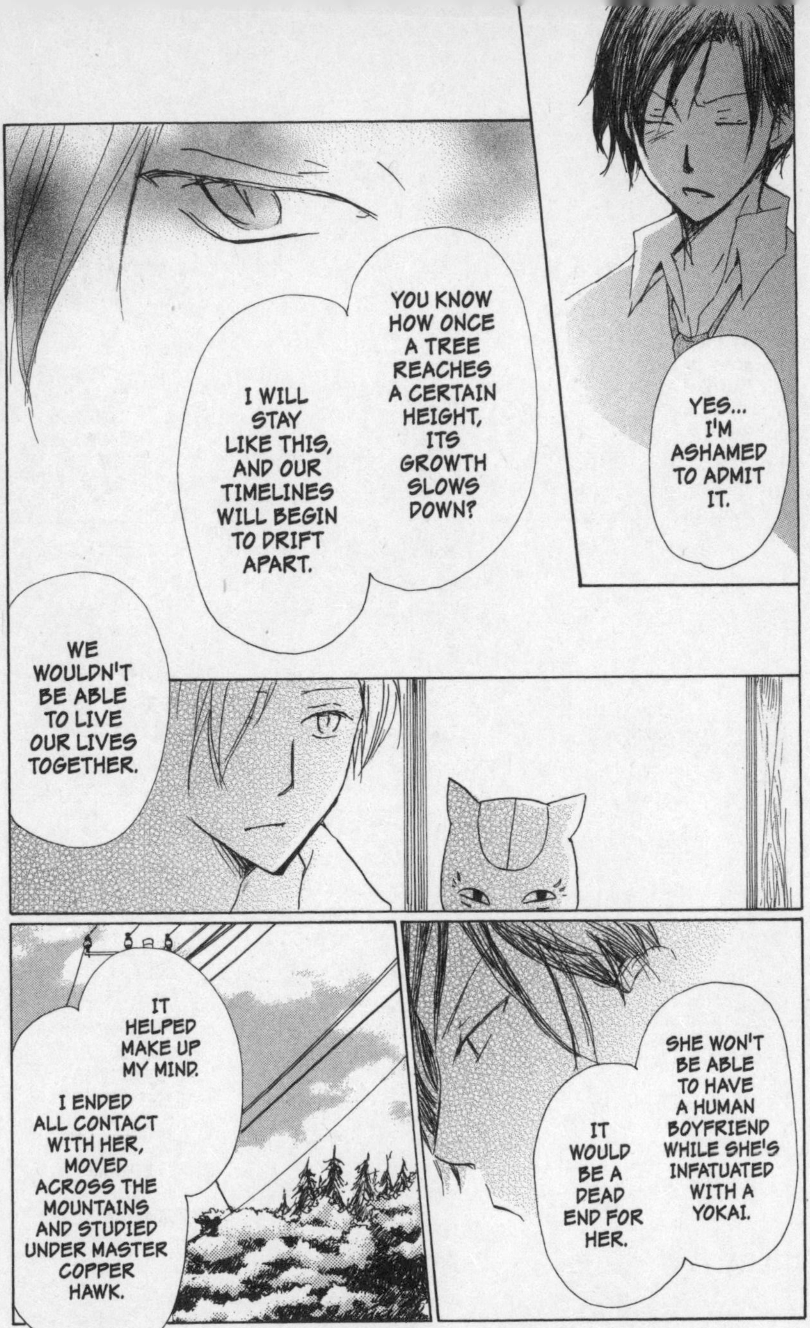
YES... I'M ASHAMED TO ADMIT IT.
YOU KNOW HOW ONCE A TREE REACHES A CERTAIN HEIGHT, ITS GROWTH SLOWS DOWN?
I WILL STAY LIKE THIS, AND OUR TIMELINES WILL BEGIN TO DRIFT APART.
WE WOULDN'T BE ABLE TO LIVE OUR LIVES TOGETHER.
SHE WON'T BE ABLE TO HAVE A HUMAN BOYFRIEND WHILE SHE'S INFATUATED WITH A YOKAI.
IT WOULD BE A DEAD END FOR HER.
IT HELPED MAKE UP MY MIND.
I ENDED ALL CONTACT WITH HER, MOVED ACROSS THE MOUNTAINS AND STUDIED UNDER MASTER COPPER HAWK.

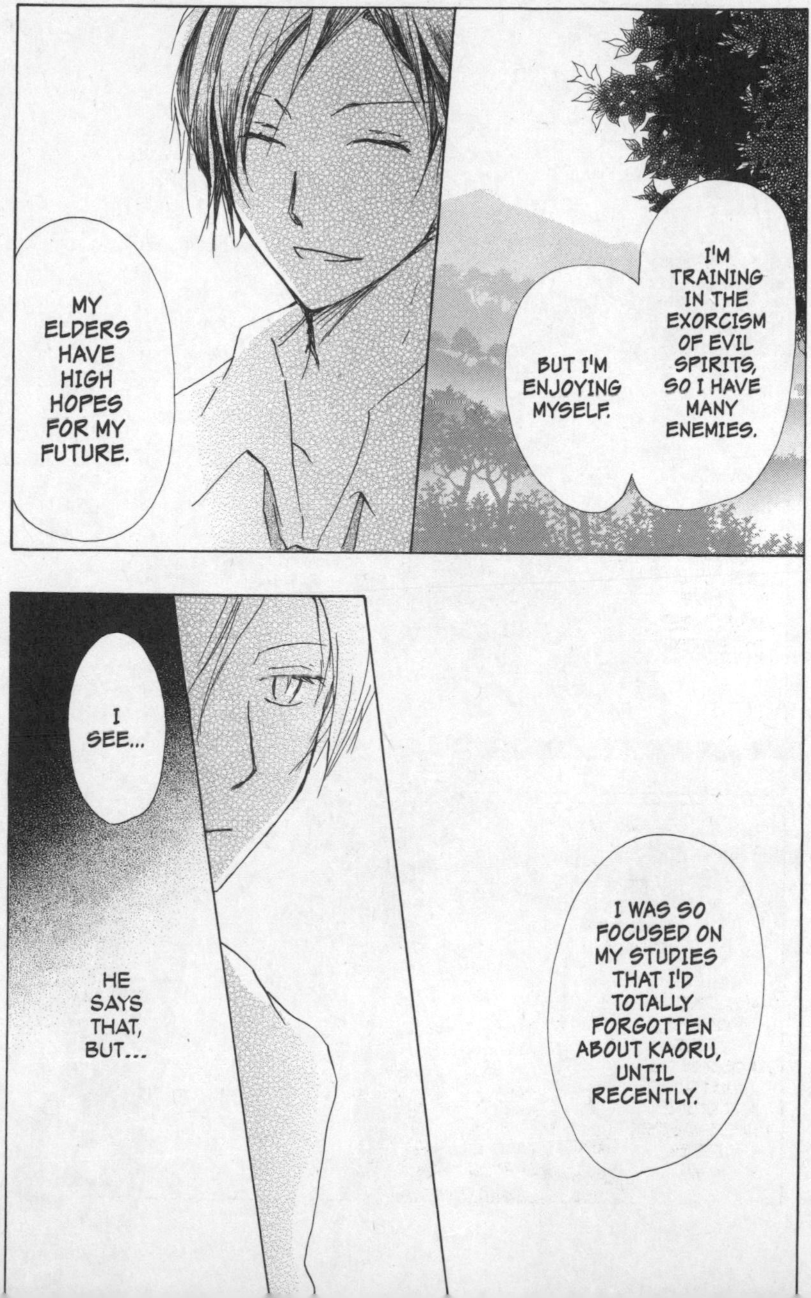
I'M TRAINING IN THE EXORCISM OF EVIL SPIRITS, SO I HAVE MANY ENEMIES.
BUT I'M ENJOYING MYSELF.
MY ELDERS HAVE HIGH HOPES FOR MY FUTURE.
I SEE...
I WAS SO FOCUSED ON MY STUDIES THAT I'D TOTALLY FORGOTTEN ABOUT KAORU, UNTIL RECENTLY.
HE SAYS THAT, BUT...

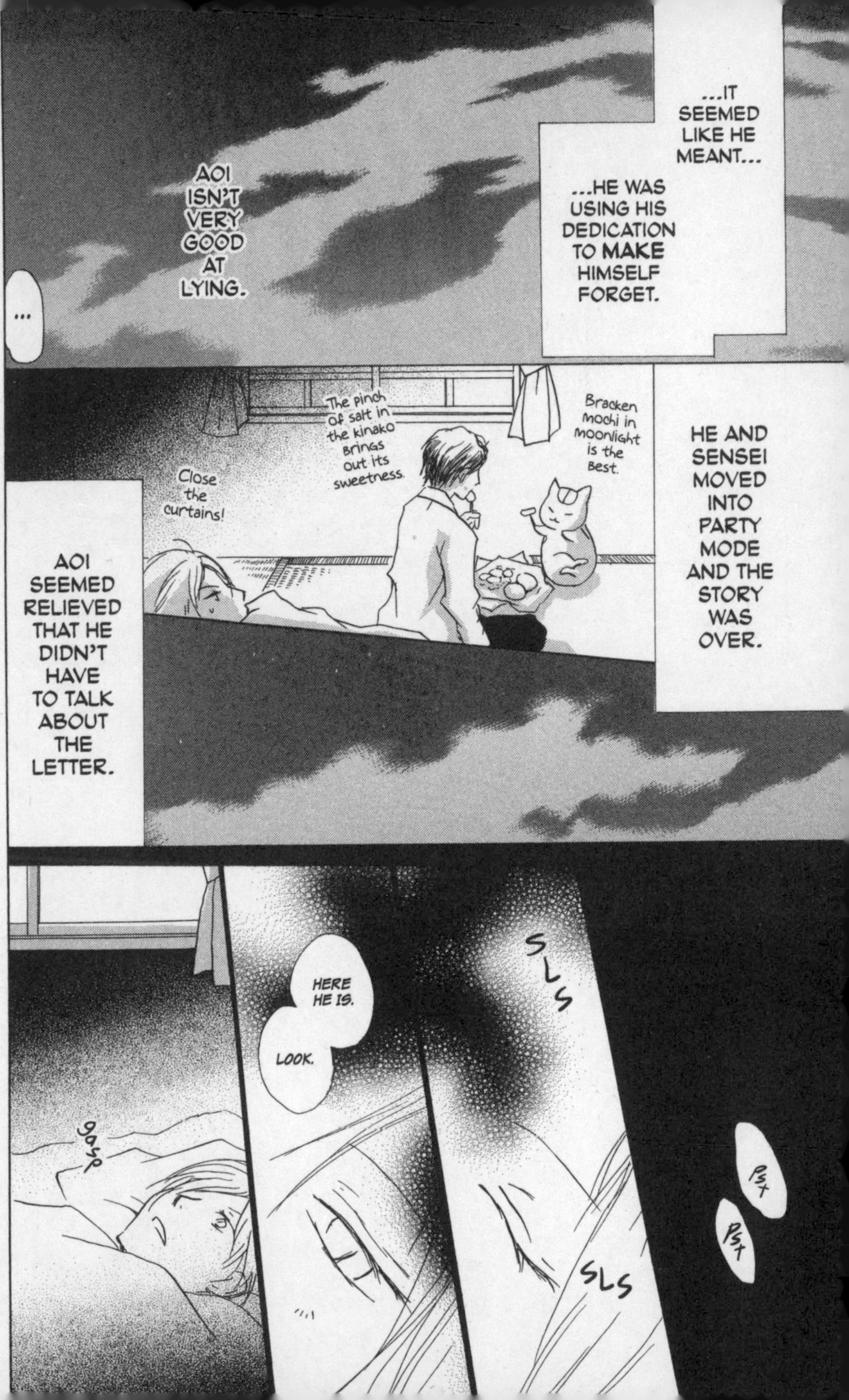
...IT SEEMED LIKE HE MEANT...
...HE WAS USING HIS DEDICATION TO MAKE HIMSELF FORGET.
AOI ISN'T VERY GOOD AT LYING.
...
HE AND SENSEI MOVED INTO PARTY MODE AND THE STORY WAS OVER.
Bracken Mochi in moonlight is the Best.
The pinch of salt in the kinako brings out its sweetness.
Close the curtains!
AOI SEEMED RELIEVED THAT HE DIDN'T HAVE TO TALK ABOUT THE LETTER.
PST
PST
SLS
SLS
HERE HE IS.
LOOK.
gasp

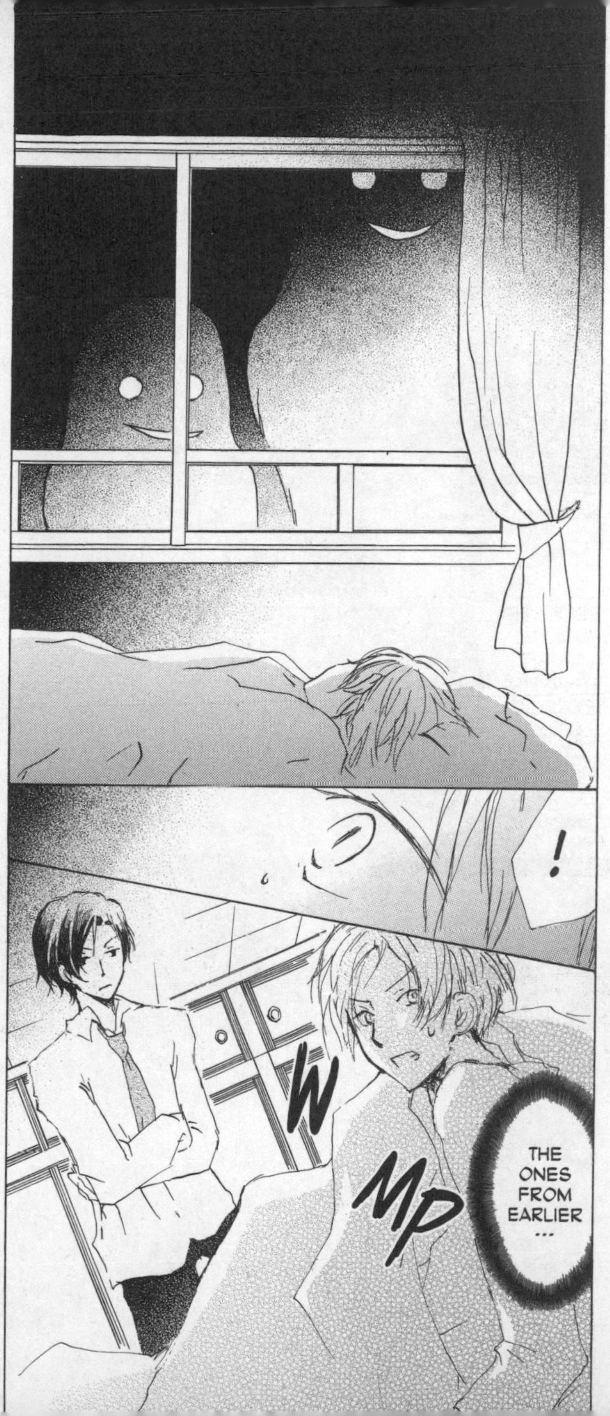
!
WMP
THE ONES FROM EARLIER ...

01

Hello, Midorikawa here. Natsume's Book of Friends is lucky to have reached the 17th volume.

This volume reminds me of fun things, joyful things, as well as things that didn't work out very well. My editor and I spend many a long night debating various topics, working and reworking everything. I always receive such positive energy from the letters my readers send me, and courage from the people who plan all these fun projects and events. I couldn't have come so far without them.

I'd like to keep working hard to draw what I like. Please keep up with your support.

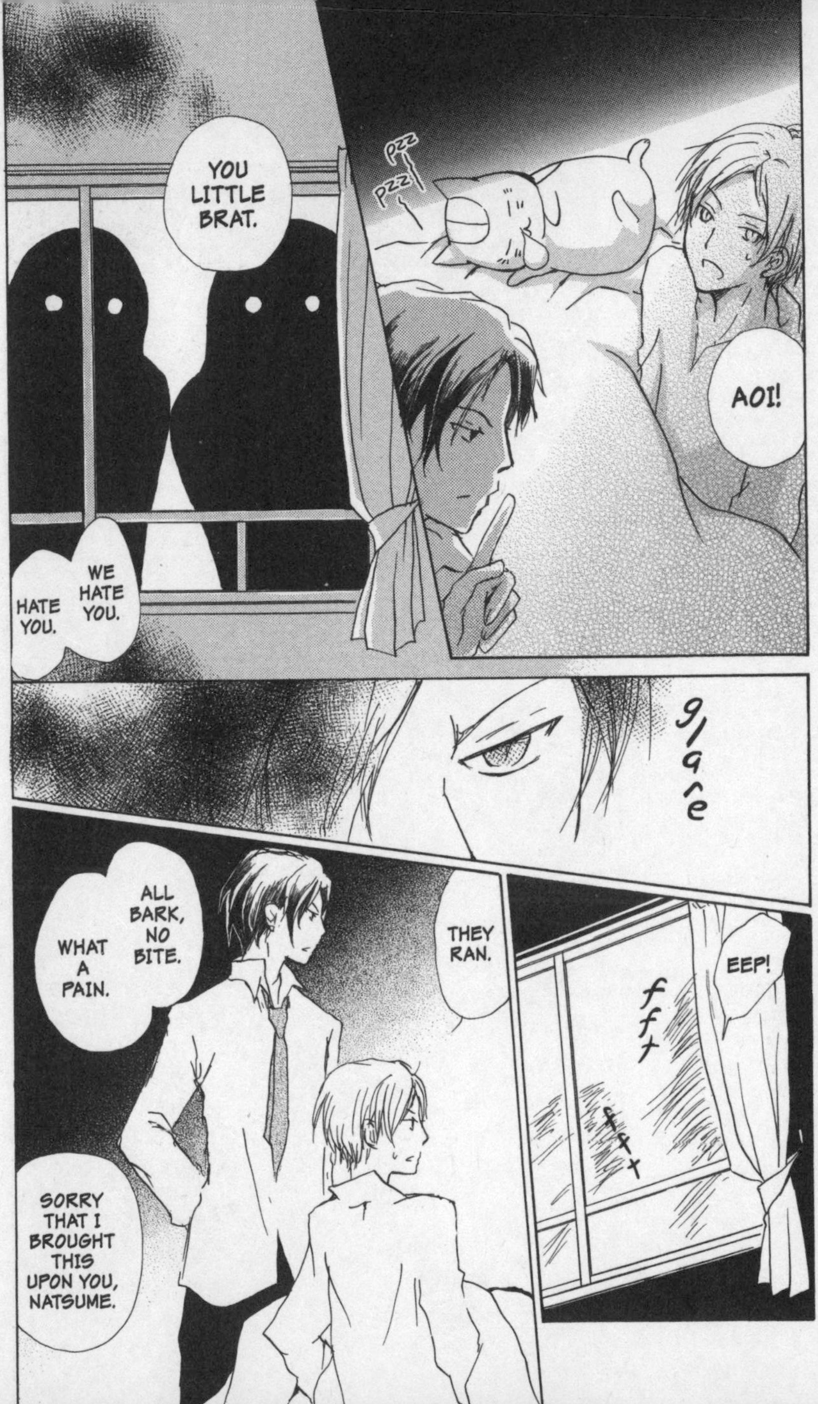
pzz
pzz
AOI!
YOU LITTLE BRAT.
WE HATE YOU.
HATE YOU.
glare
EEP!
fft
fft
THEY RAN.
ALL BARK, NO BITE.
WHAT A PAIN.
SORRY THAT I BROUGHT THIS UPON YOU, NATSUME.

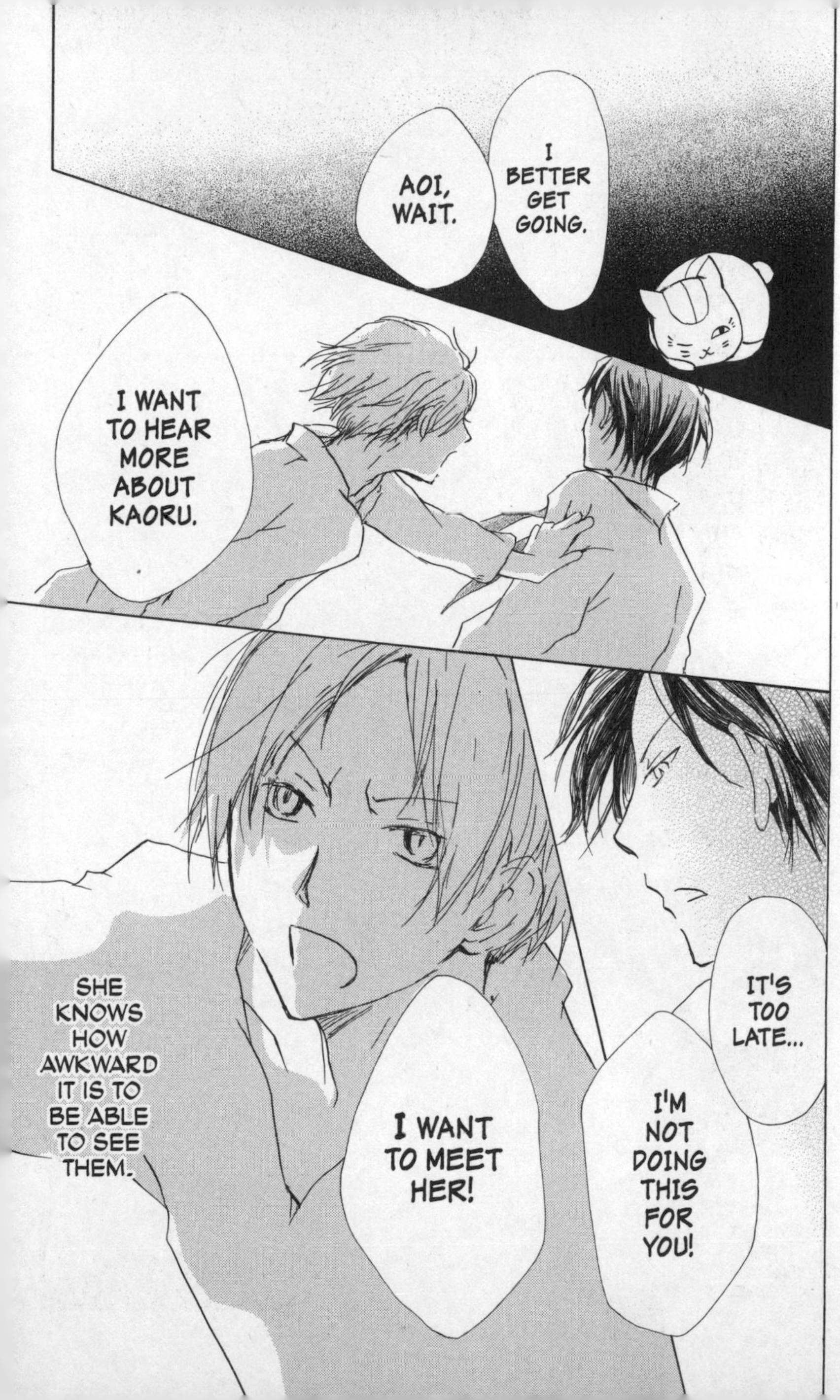
I BETTER GET GOING.
AOI, WAIT.
I WANT TO HEAR MORE ABOUT KAORU.
IT'S TOO LATE...
I'M NOT DOING THIS FOR YOU!
I WANT TO MEET HER!
SHE KNOWS HOW AWKWARD IT IS TO BE ABLE TO SEE THEM.

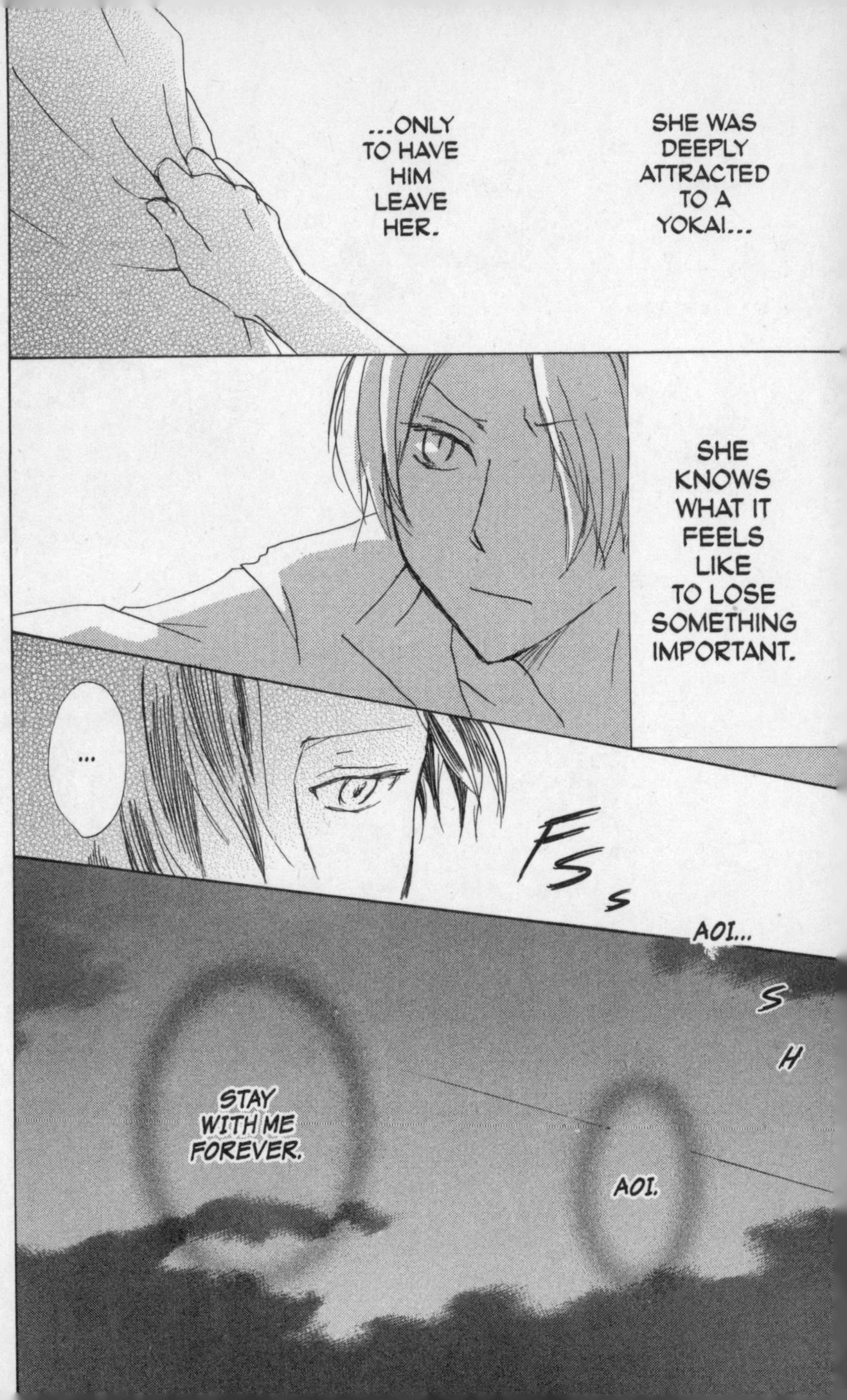
SHE WAS DEEPLY ATTRACTED TO A YOKAI...
...ONLY TO HAVE HIM LEAVE HER.
SHE KNOWS WHAT IT FEELS LIKE TO LOSE SOMETHING IMPORTANT.
...
FSS
AOI...
SH
AOI.
STAY WITH ME FOREVER.

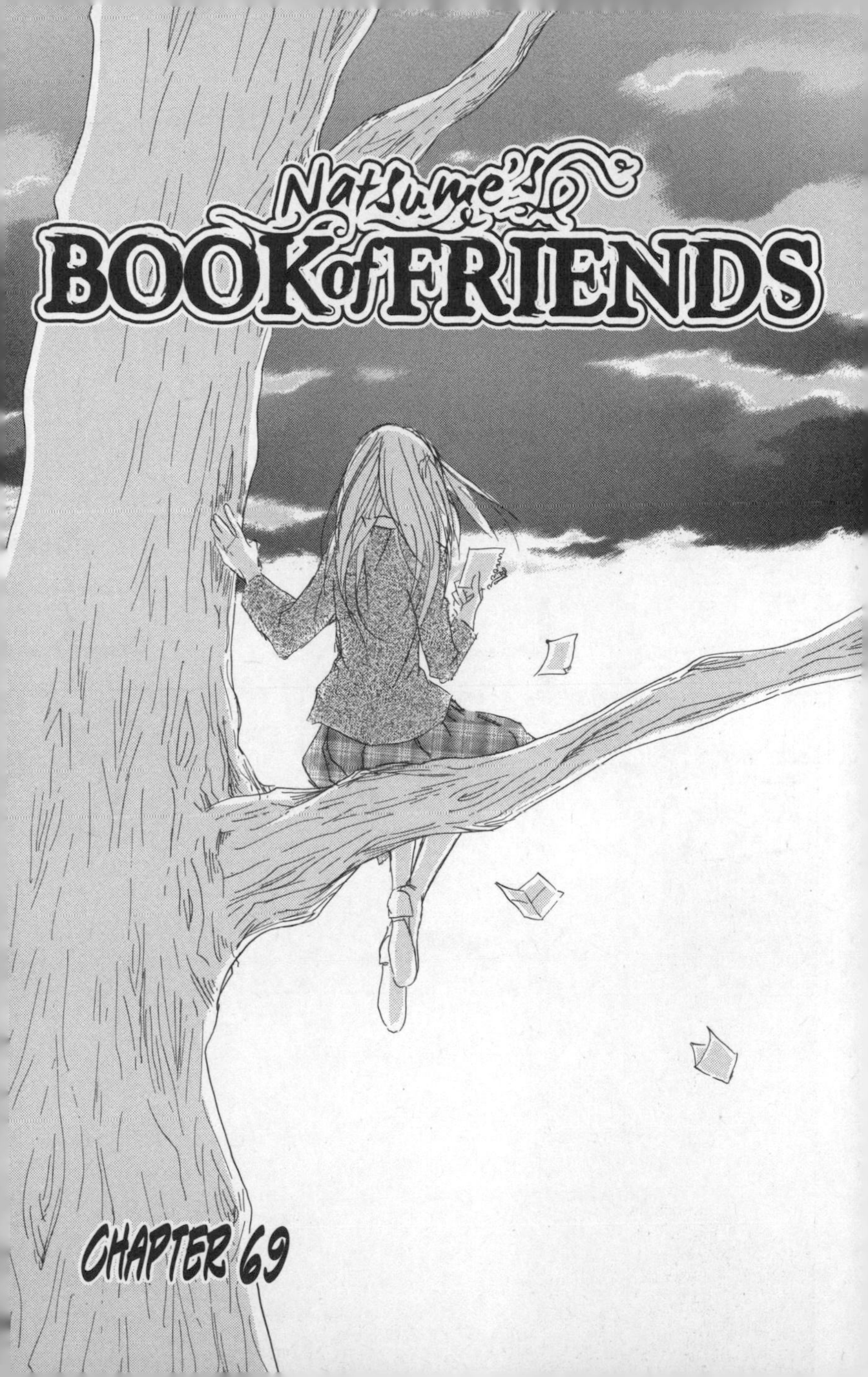
Natsume's
BOOK of FRIENDS
CHAPTER 69

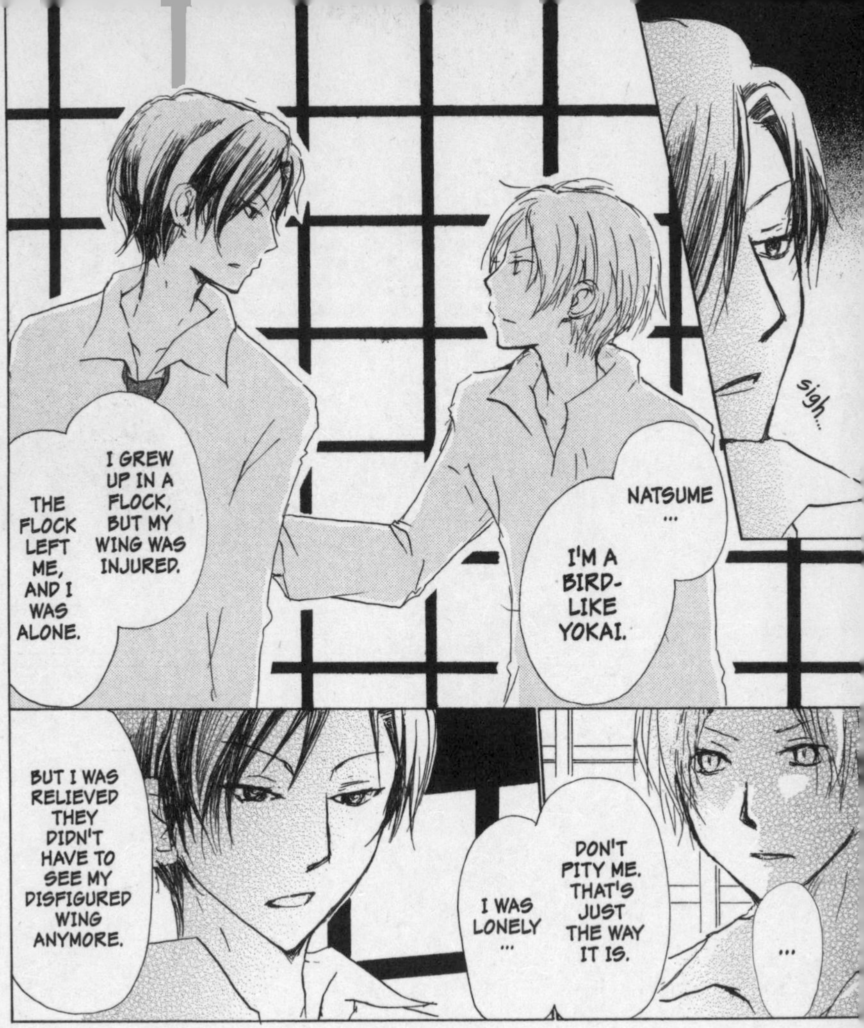
sigh...
NATSUME ... I'M A BIRD-LIKE YOKAI.
I GREW UP IN A FLOCK, BUT MY WING WAS INJURED.
THE FLOCK LEFT ME, AND I WAS ALONE.
...
I WAS LONELY ... DON'T PITY ME. THAT'S JUST THE WAY IT IS.
BUT I WAS RELIEVED THEY DIDN'T HAVE TO SEE MY DISFIGURED WING ANYMORE.

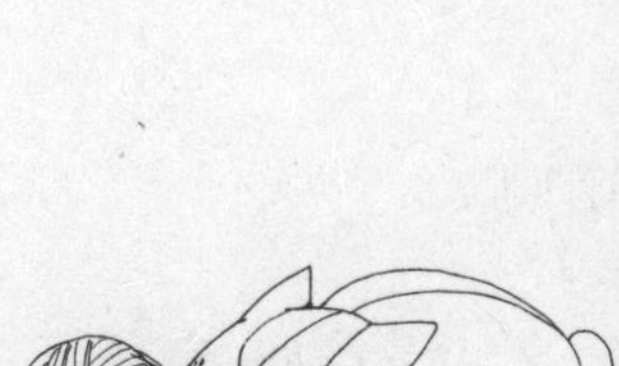

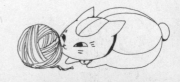

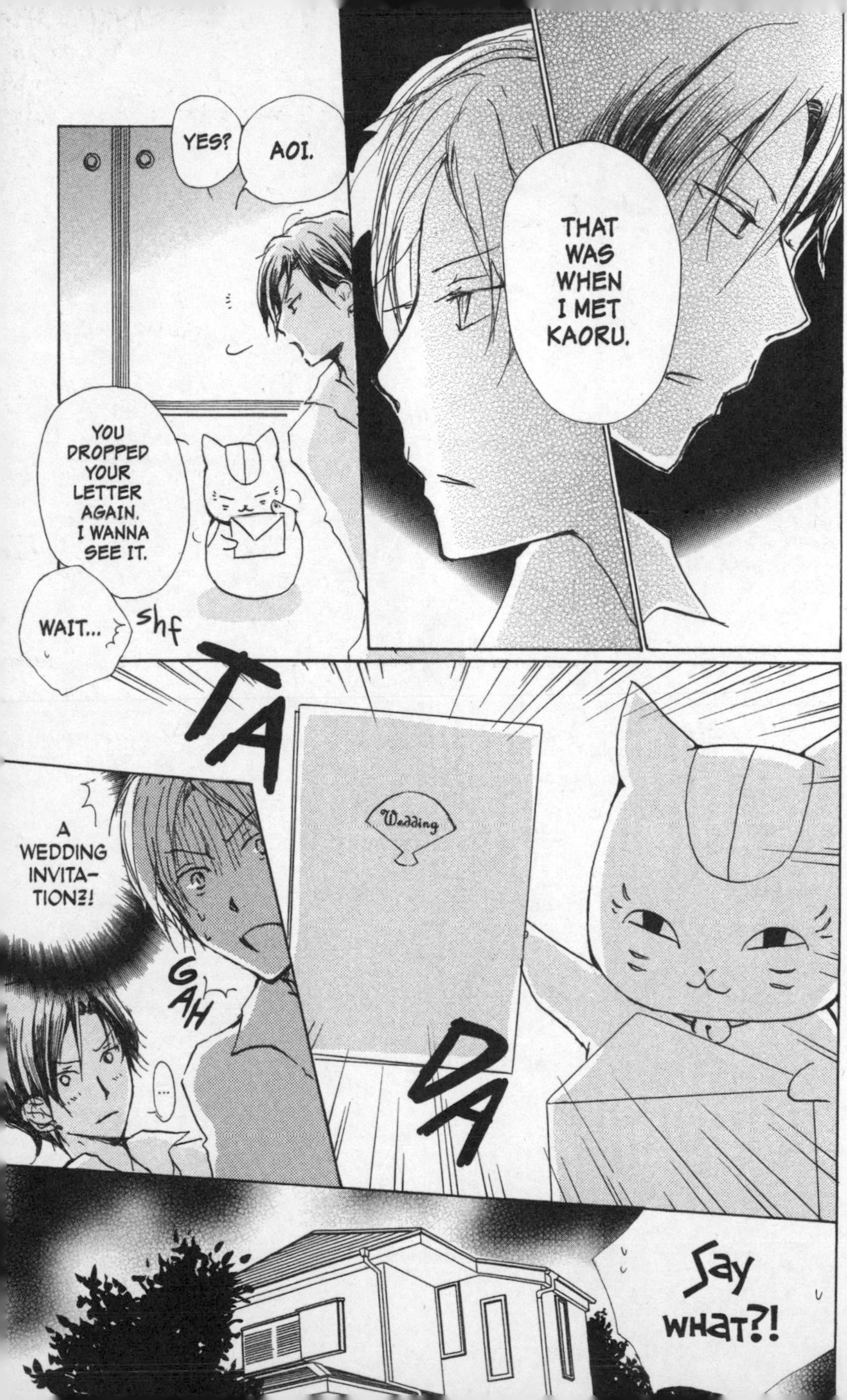
THAT WAS WHEN I MET KAORU.
AOI.
YES?
YOU DROPPED YOUR LETTER AGAIN. I WANNA SEE IT.
WAIT...
shf
TA
Wedding
DA
A WEDDING INVITATION?!
GAH
...
Say WHAT?!

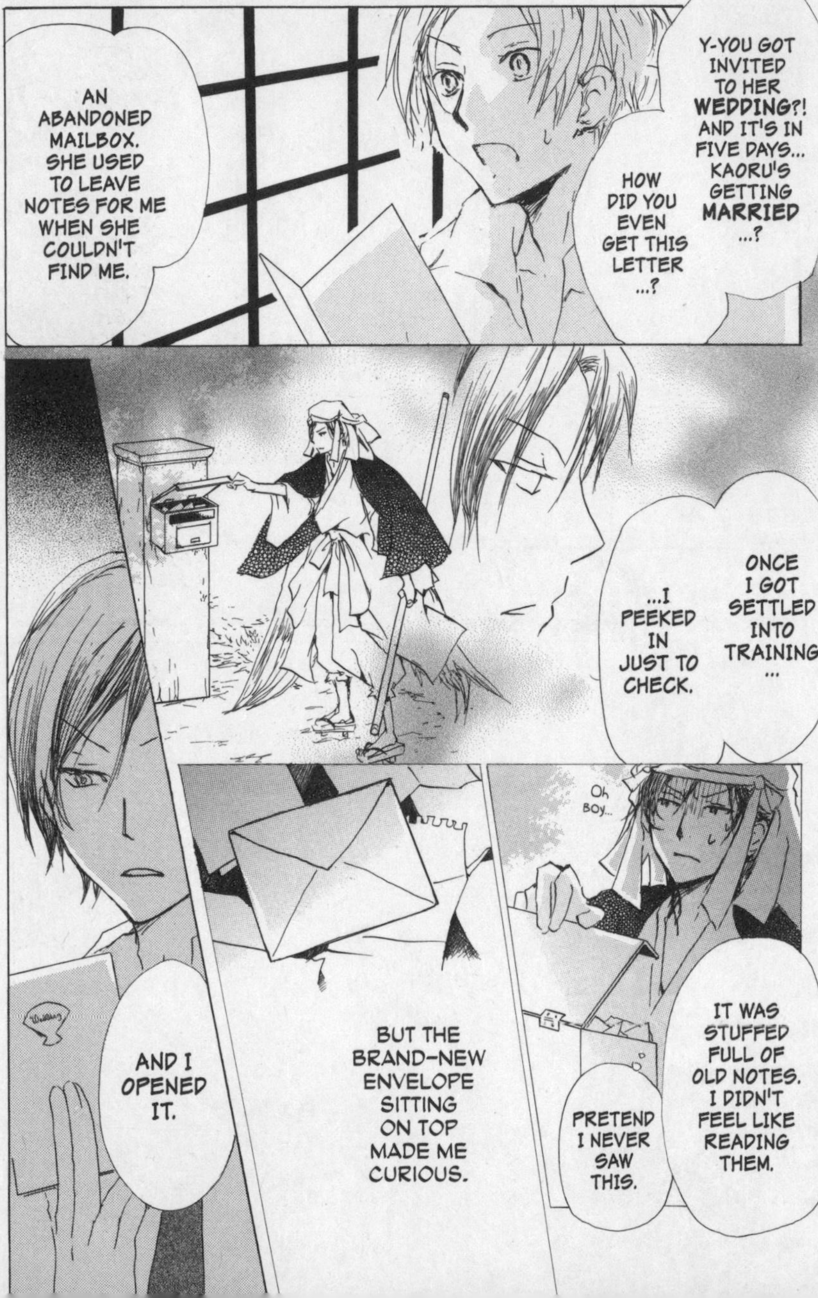
Y-YOU GOT INVITED TO HER WEDDING?! AND IT'S IN FIVE DAYS... KAORU'S GETTING MARRIED ...?
HOW DID YOU EVEN GET THIS LETTER ...?
AN ABANDONED MAILBOX. SHE USED TO LEAVE NOTES FOR ME WHEN SHE COULDN'T FIND ME.
ONCE I GOT SETTLED INTO TRAINING ...
...I PEEKED IN JUST TO CHECK.
Oh boy...
IT WAS STUFFED FULL OF OLD NOTES. I DIDN'T FEEL LIKE READING THEM.
PRETEND I NEVER SAW THIS.
BUT THE BRAND-NEW ENVELOPE SITTING ON TOP MADE ME CURIOUS.
AND I OPENED IT.

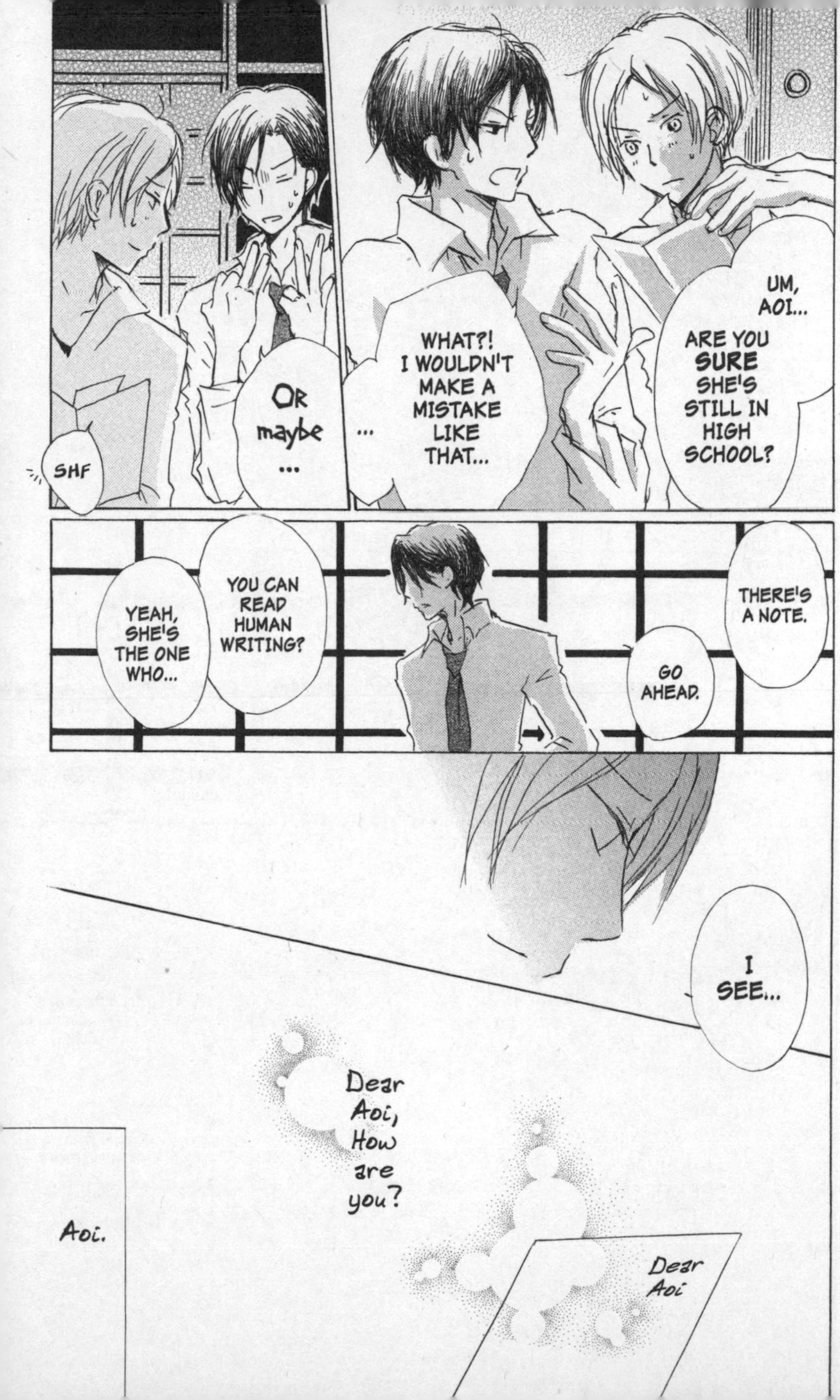
UM, AOI...
ARE YOU SURE SHE'S STILL IN HIGH SCHOOL?
WHAT?! I WOULDN'T MAKE A MISTAKE LIKE THAT...
...
OR maybe ...
SHF
THERE'S A NOTE.
GO AHEAD.
YOU CAN READ HUMAN WRITING?
YEAH, SHE'S THE ONE WHO...
I SEE...
Dear Aoi, How are you?
Dear Aoi
Aoi.

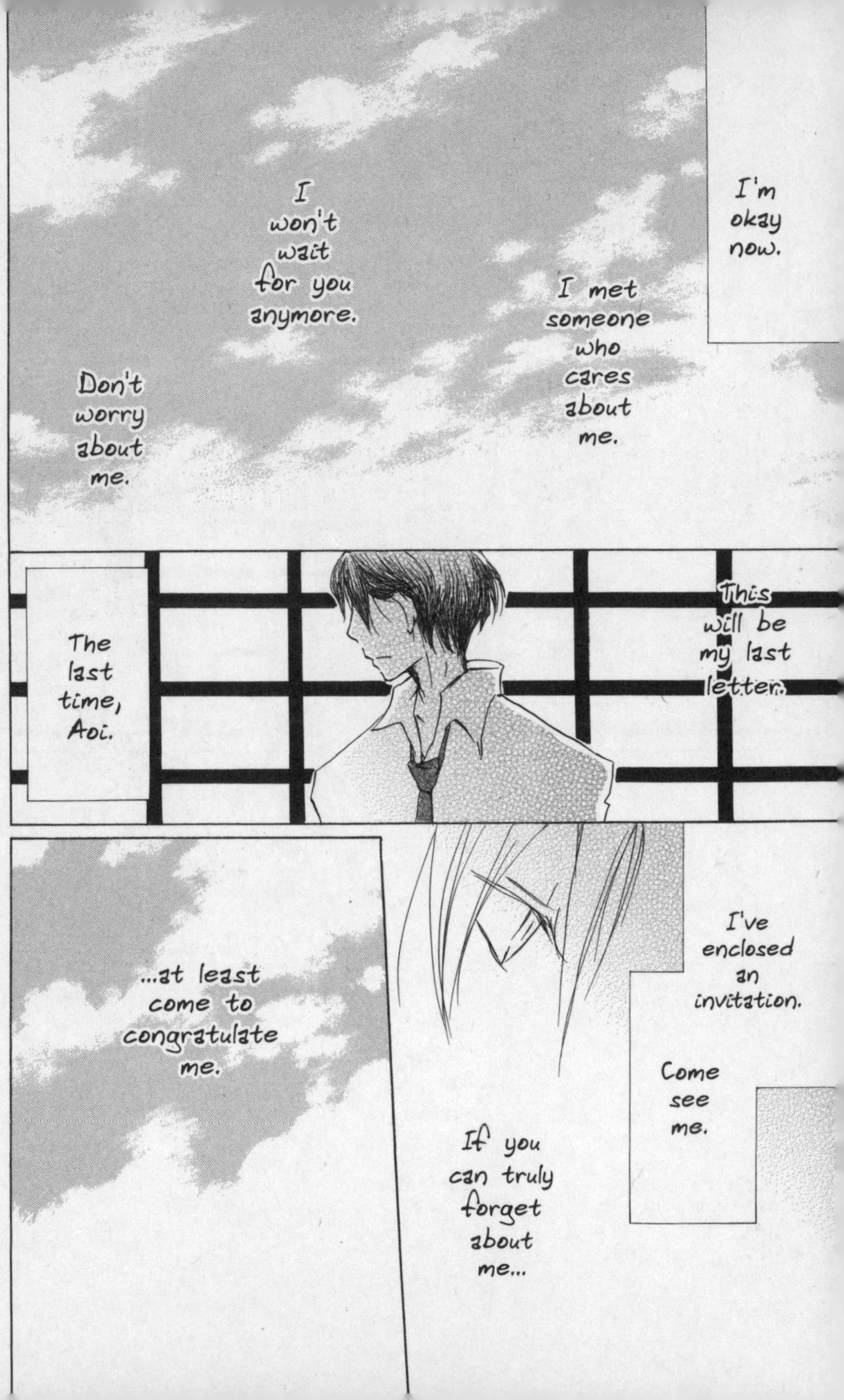
I'm okay now.
I met someone who cares about me.
I won't wait for you anymore.
Don't worry about me.
This will be my last letter.
The last time, Aoi.
I've enclosed an invitation.
Come see me.
If you can truly forget about me...
...at least come to congratulate me.

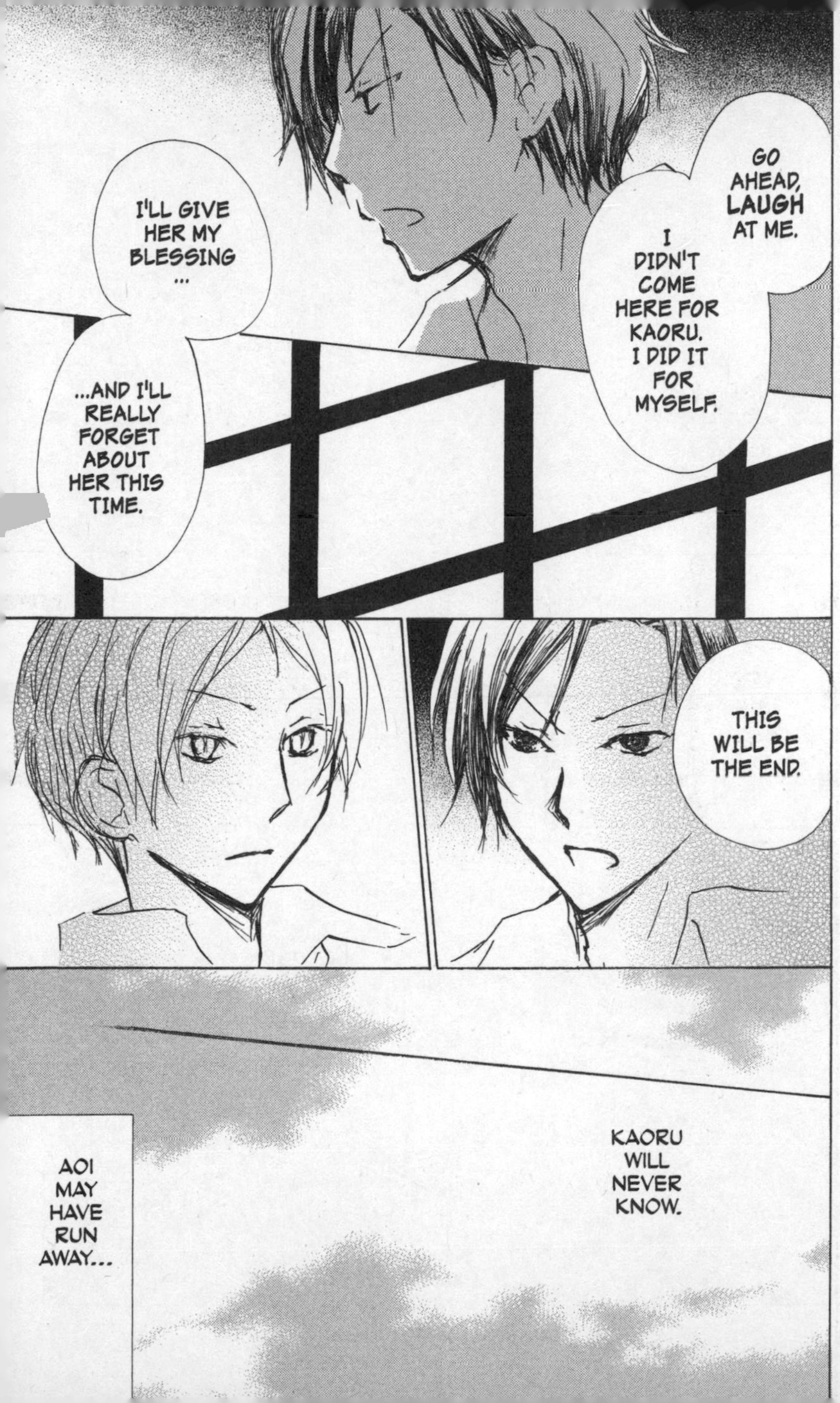
GO AHEAD, LAUGH AT ME.
I DIDN'T COME HERE FOR KAORU. I DID IT FOR MYSELF.
I'LL GIVE HER MY BLESSING ...
...AND I'LL REALLY FORGET ABOUT HER THIS TIME.
THIS WILL BE THE END.
KAORU WILL NEVER KNOW.
AOI MAY HAVE RUN AWAY...

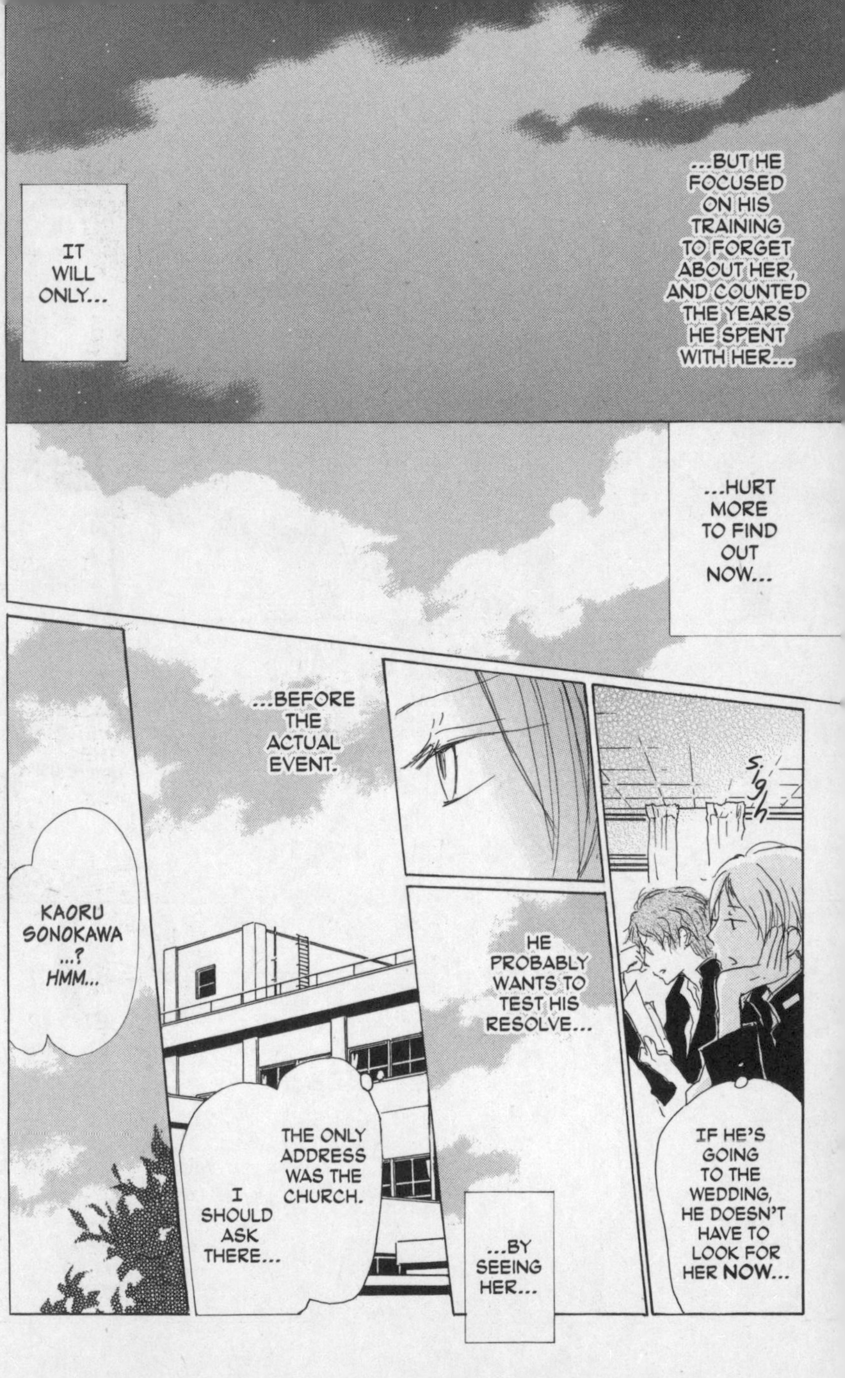
...BUT HE FOCUSED ON HIS TRAINING TO FORGET ABOUT HER, AND COUNTED THE YEARS HE SPENT WITH HER...
IT WILL ONLY...
...HURT MORE TO FIND OUT NOW...
...BEFORE THE ACTUAL EVENT.
sigh
IF HE'S GOING TO THE WEDDING, HE DOESN'T HAVE TO LOOK FOR HER NOW...
HE PROBABLY WANTS TO TEST HIS RESOLVE...
...BY SEEING HER...
KAORU SONOKAWA ...? HMM...
THE ONLY ADDRESS WAS THE CHURCH.
I SHOULD ASK THERE...

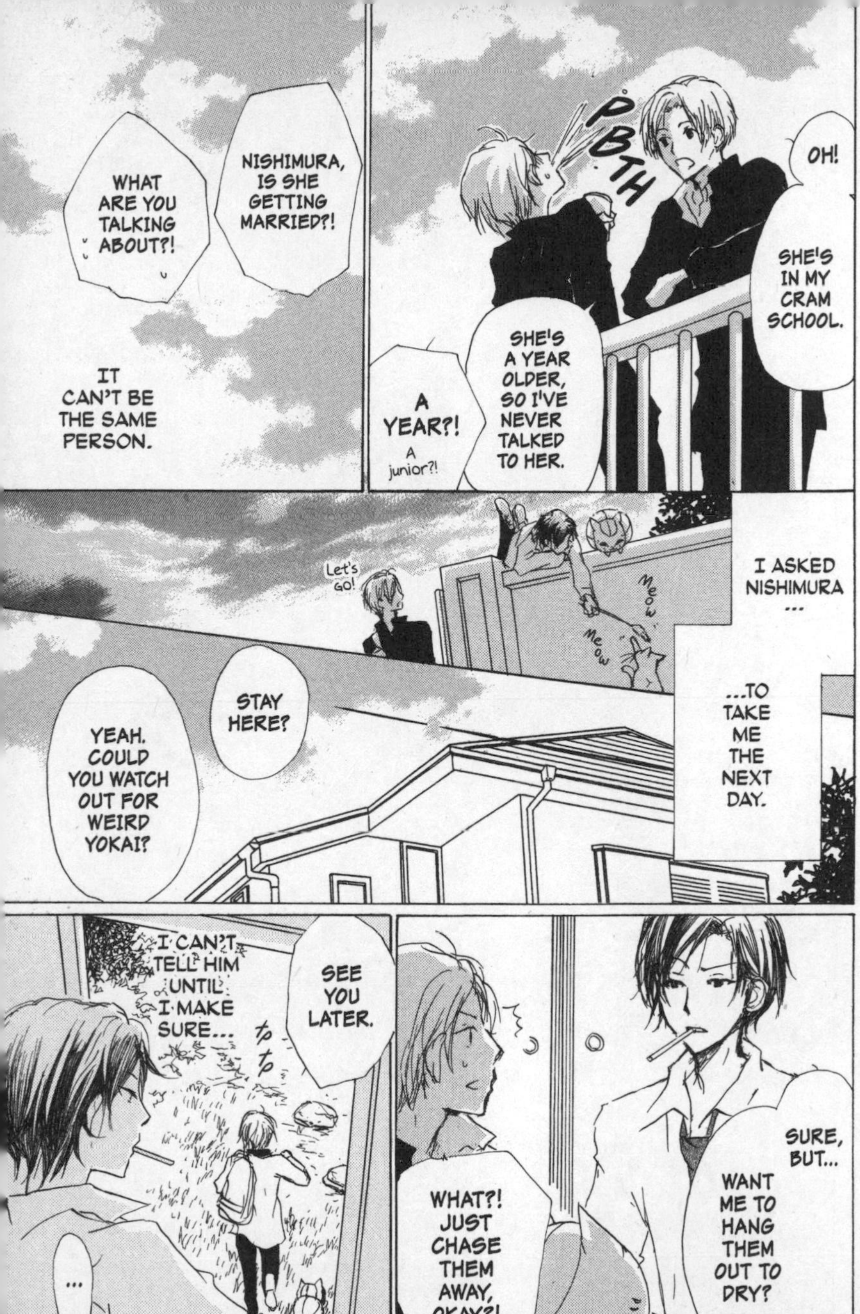
OH!
SHE'S IN MY CRAM SCHOOL.
PBTH
SHE'S A YEAR OLDER, SO I'VE NEVER TALKED TO HER.
A YEAR?!
A junior?!
NISHIMURA, IS SHE GETTING MARRIED?!
WHAT ARE YOU TALKING ABOUT?!
IT CAN'T BE THE SAME PERSON.
I ASKED NISHIMURA...
Meow
Meow
Let's GO!
...TO TAKE ME THE NEXT DAY.
STAY HERE?
YEAH. COULD YOU WATCH OUT FOR WEIRD YOKAI?
SURE, BUT...
WANT ME TO HANG THEM OUT TO DRY?
WHAT?! JUST CHASE THEM AWAY, OKAY?!
SEE YOU LATER.
I CAN'T TELL HIM UNTIL I MAKE SURE...
...

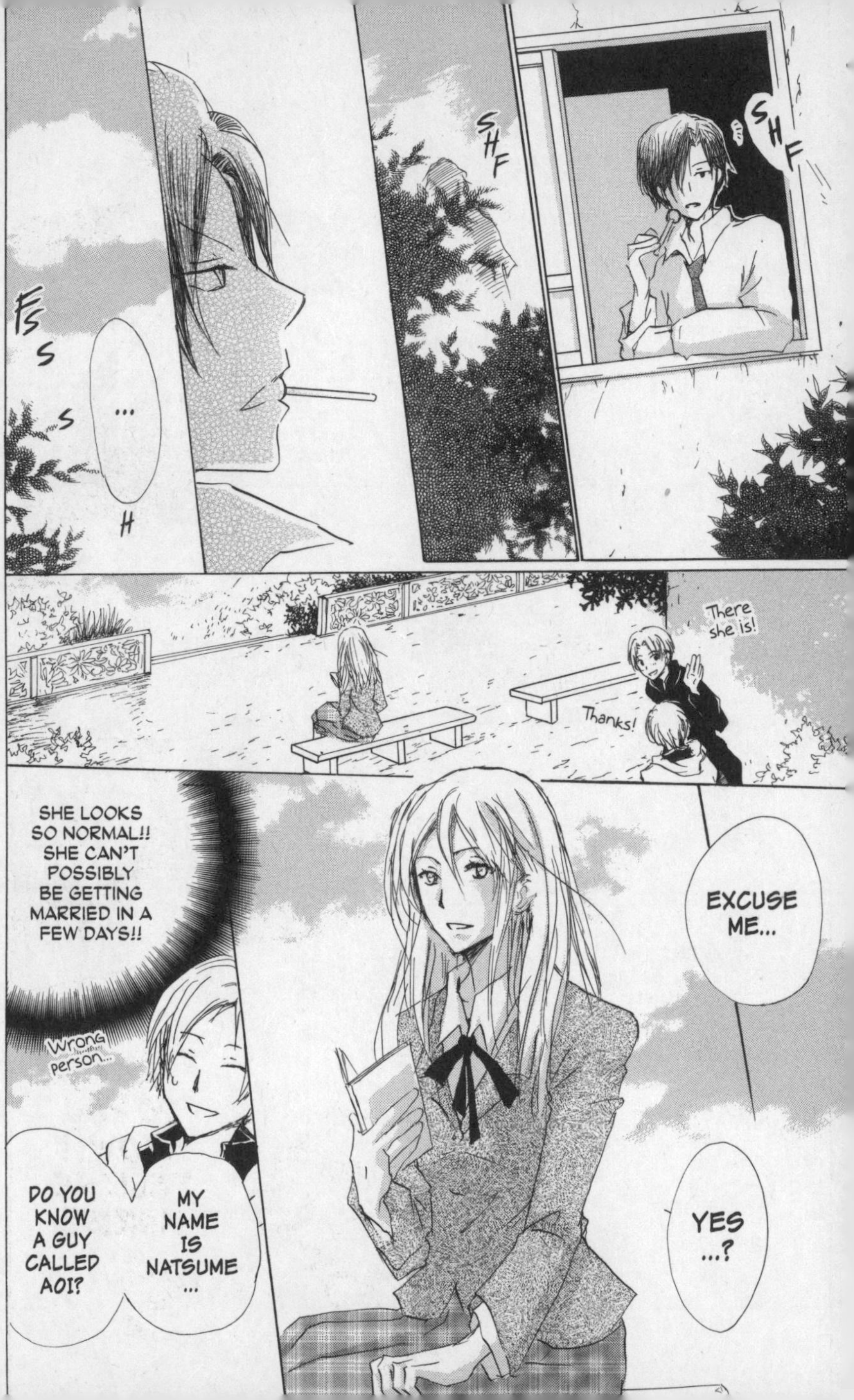
SHF
SHF
FSSSH
...
There she is!
Thanks!
EXCUSE ME...
YES ...?
SHE LOOKS SO NORMAL!! SHE CAN'T POSSIBLY BE GETTING MARRIED IN A FEW DAYS!!
Wrong person...
MY NAME IS NATSUME ...
DO YOU KNOW A GUY CALLED AOI?

02

❋Musical

An original Natsume musical was produced with help from the staff of the anime, Director Ohmori, the voice actors, Mr. Makoto Yoshimori the composer, and Mr. Buno Fujisawa who manages the Sound Theatre project. The beautiful and intricate script and stage direction, the live instrumental performance, the wonderful voice actors who convey the subtleties of emotion... I was moved by them all. Thank you to everyone who came, and to those who helped.

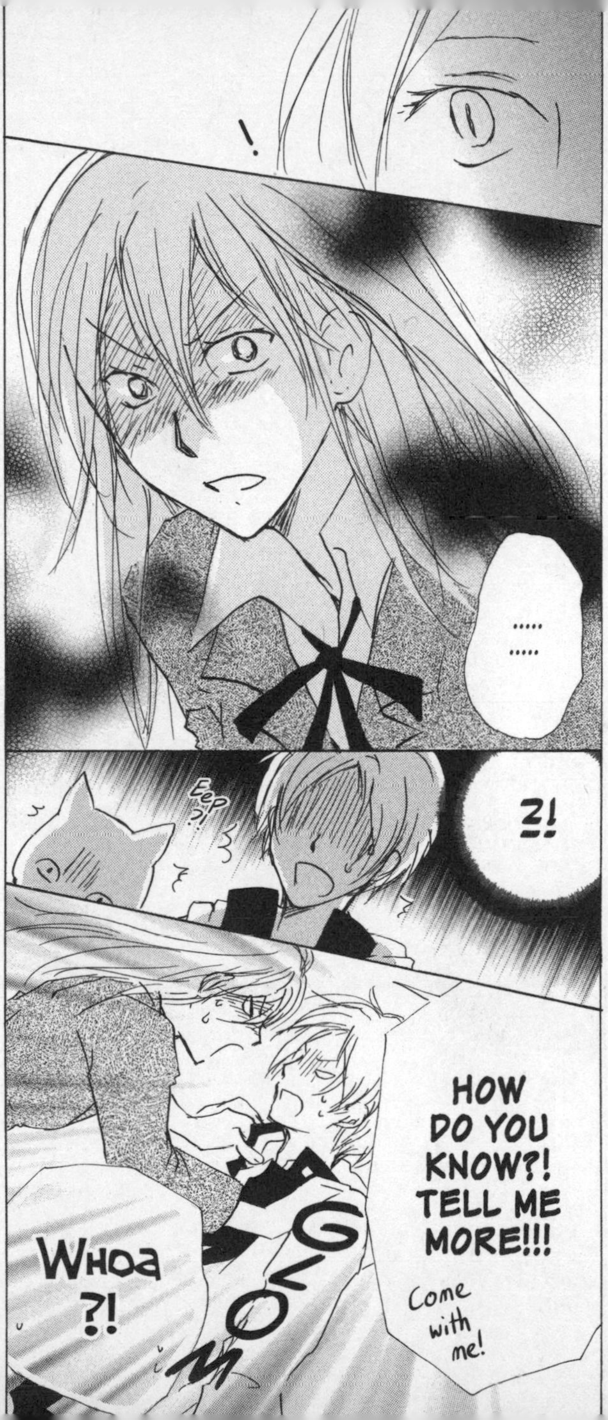
!
......
......
?!
Eep ?!
HOW DO YOU KNOW?! TELL ME MORE!!!
Come with me!
WHOA ?!

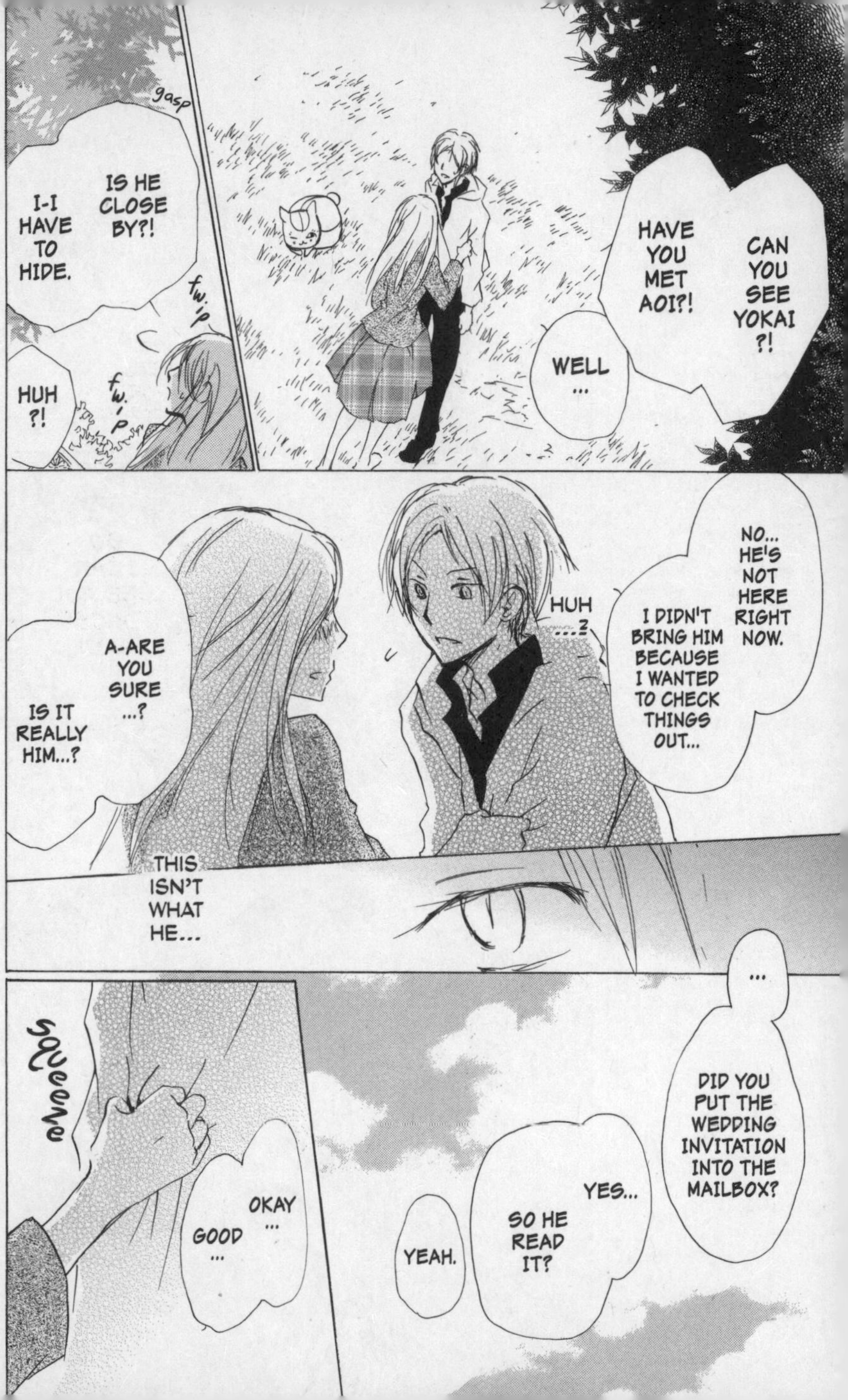
CAN YOU SEE YOKAI?!
HAVE YOU MET AOI?!
WELL ...
gasp
IS HE CLOSE BY?!
I-I HAVE TO HIDE.
fwip
fwip
HUH?!
NO... HE'S NOT HERE RIGHT NOW.
I DIDN'T BRING HIM BECAUSE I WANTED TO CHECK THINGS OUT...
HUH ...?
A-ARE YOU SURE ...?
IS IT REALLY HIM...?
THIS ISN'T WHAT HE...
...
DID YOU PUT THE WEDDING INVITATION INTO THE MAILBOX?
YES...
SO HE READ IT?
YEAH.
OKAY ...
GOOD ...
squeeze

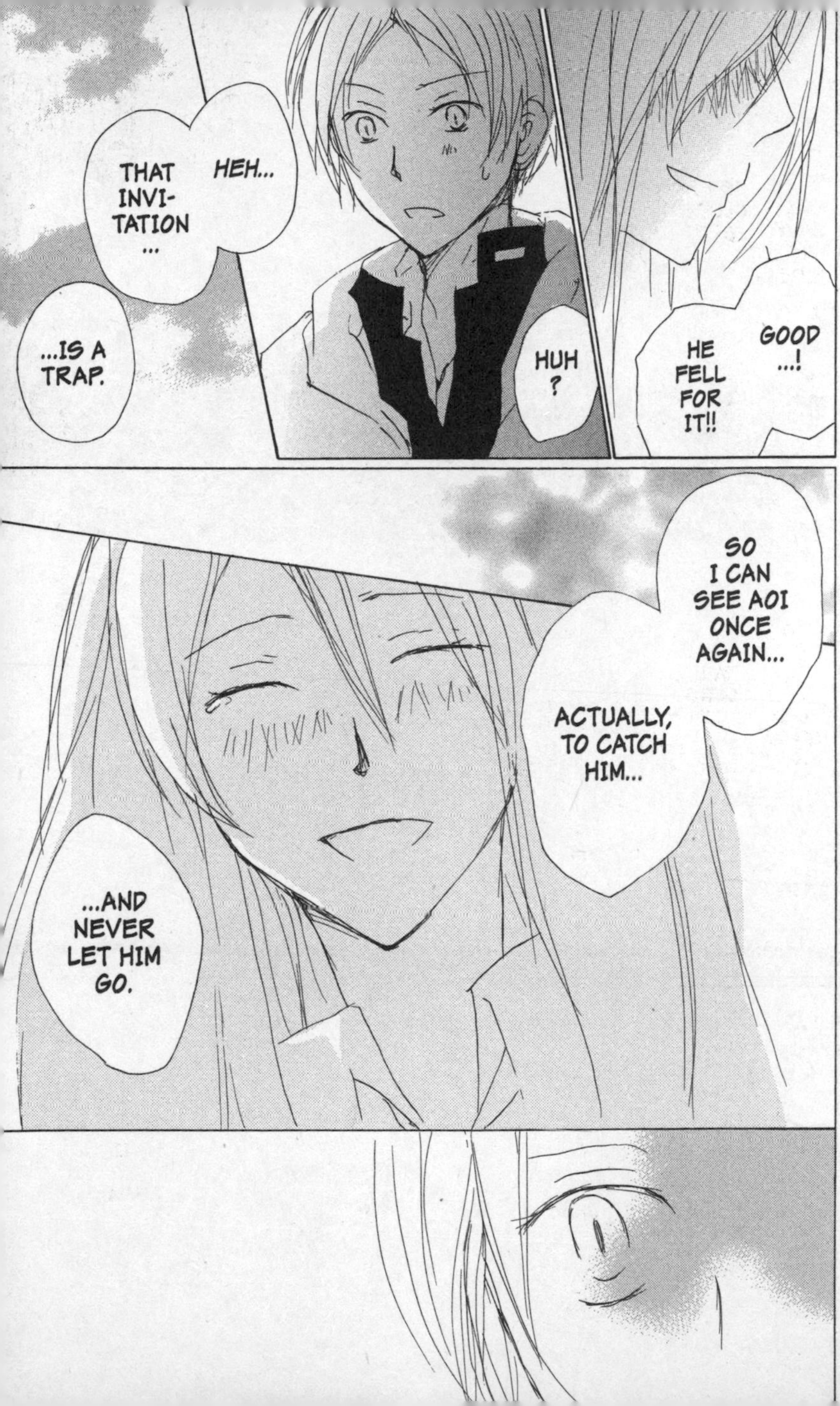
GOOD ...!
HE FELL FOR IT!!
HEH...
THAT INVITATION ...
...IS A TRAP.
HUH ?
SO I CAN SEE AOI ONCE AGAIN...
ACTUALLY, TO CATCH HIM...
...AND NEVER LET HIM GO.

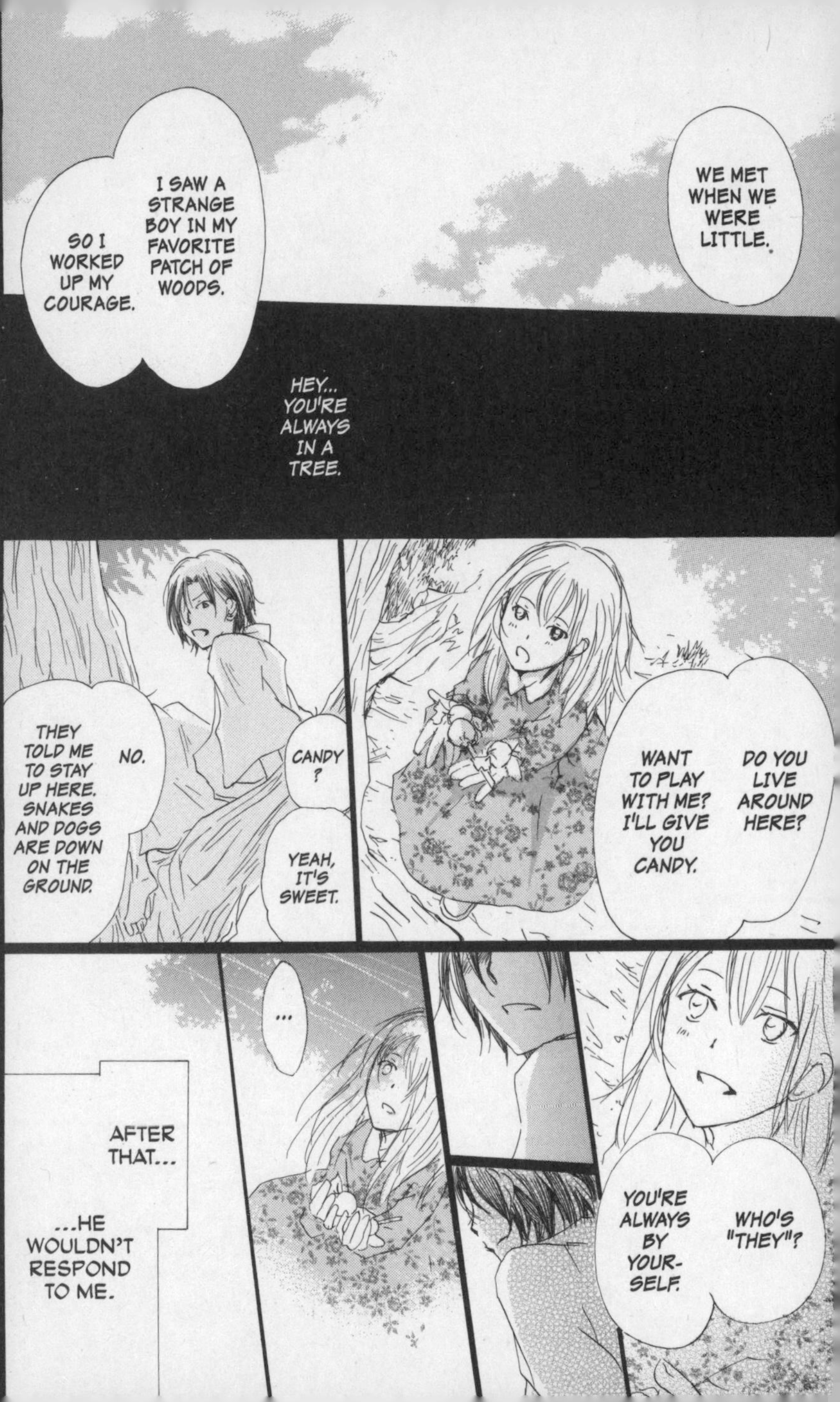
WE MET WHEN WE WERE LITTLE.
I SAW A STRANGE BOY IN MY FAVORITE PATCH OF WOODS. SO I WORKED UP MY COURAGE.
HEY... YOU'RE ALWAYS IN A TREE.
DO YOU LIVE AROUND HERE? WANT TO PLAY WITH ME? I'LL GIVE YOU CANDY.
CANDY?
YEAH, IT'S SWEET.
NO. THEY TOLD ME TO STAY UP HERE. SNAKES AND DOGS ARE DOWN ON THE GROUND.
WHO'S "THEY"? YOU'RE ALWAYS BY YOURSELF.
...
AFTER THAT...
...HE WOULDN'T RESPOND TO ME.

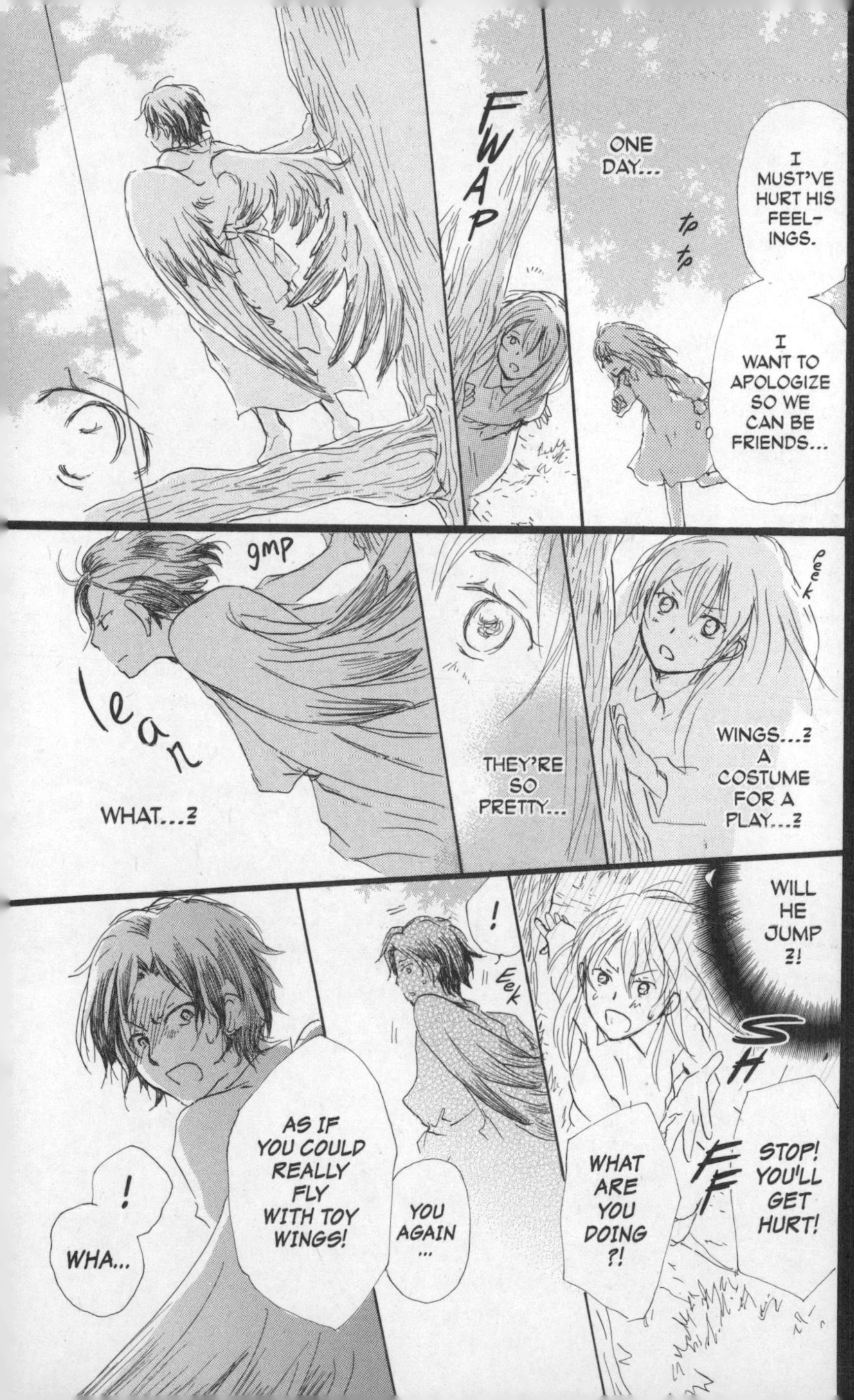
I MUST'VE HURT HIS FEELINGS.
I WANT TO APOLOGIZE SO WE CAN BE FRIENDS...
ONE DAY...
FWAP
peek
WINGS...? A COSTUME FOR A PLAY...?
THEY'RE SO PRETTY...
gmp
lean
WHAT...?
WILL HE JUMP?!
SHFF
STOP! YOU'LL GET HURT!
WHAT ARE YOU DOING?!
!
Eek
YOU AGAIN...
AS IF YOU COULD REALLY FLY WITH TOY WINGS!
!
WHA...

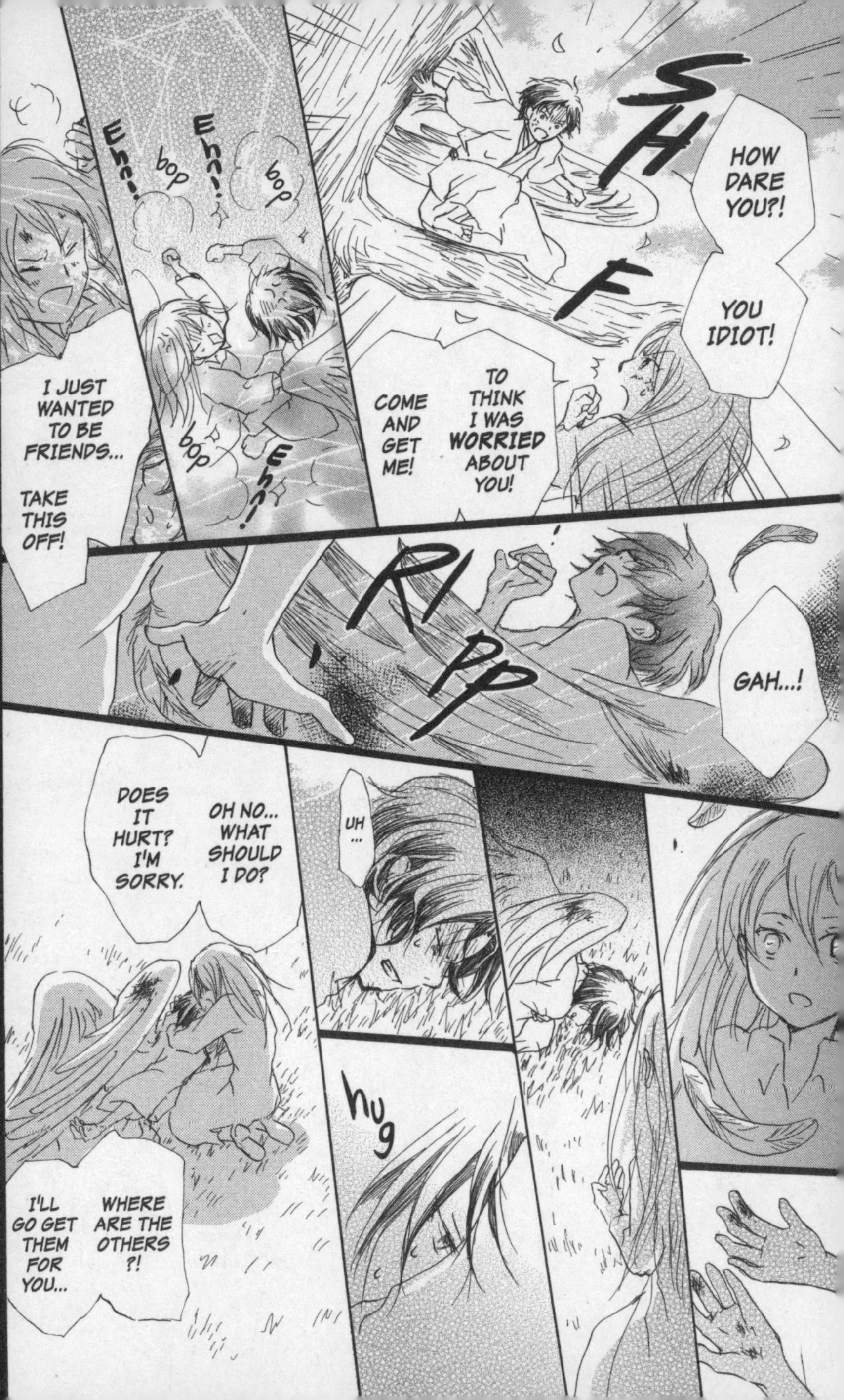
SHF
HOW DARE YOU?!
YOU IDIOT!
TO THINK I WAS WORRIED ABOUT YOU!
COME AND GET ME!
bop
Ehn!
bop
Ehn!
bop
Ehn!
I JUST WANTED TO BE FRIENDS...
TAKE THIS OFF!
RIPP
GAH...!
UH...
OH NO... WHAT SHOULD I DO?
DOES IT HURT? I'M SORRY.
hug
WHERE ARE THE OTHERS?!
I'LL GO GET THEM FOR YOU...

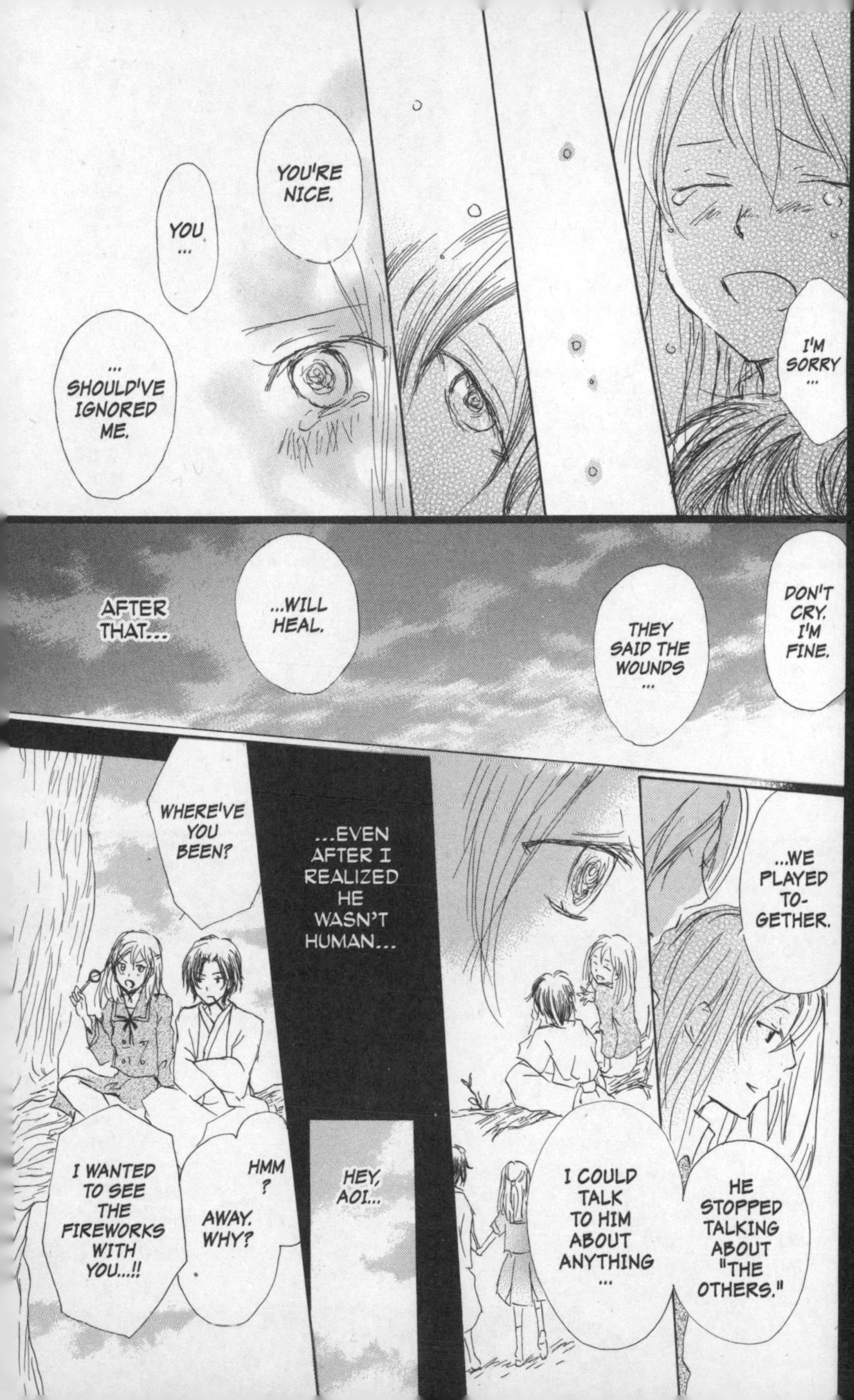
I'M SORRY ...
YOU'RE NICE.
YOU ...
... SHOULD'VE IGNORED ME.
DON'T CRY. I'M FINE.
THEY SAID THE WOUNDS ...
...WILL HEAL.
AFTER THAT...
...WE PLAYED TO-GETHER.
HE STOPPED TALKING ABOUT "THE OTHERS."
I COULD TALK TO HIM ABOUT ANYTHING ...
HEY, AOI...
...EVEN AFTER I REALIZED HE WASN'T HUMAN...
WHERE'VE YOU BEEN?
HMM? AWAY. WHY?
I WANTED TO SEE THE FIREWORKS WITH YOU...!!

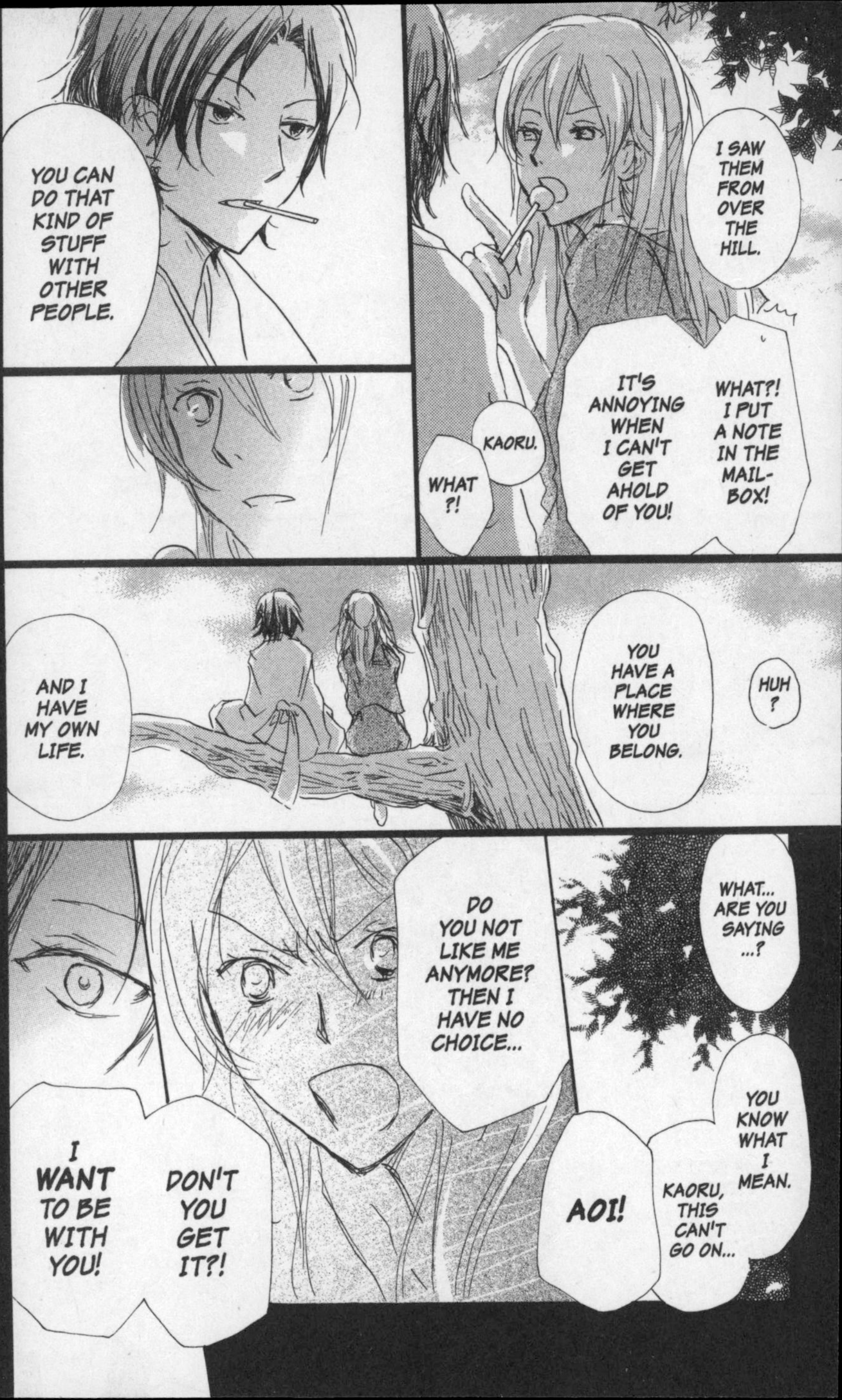
I SAW THEM FROM OVER THE HILL.
WHAT?! I PUT A NOTE IN THE MAIL-BOX!
IT'S ANNOYING WHEN I CAN'T GET AHOLD OF YOU!
KAORU.
WHAT?!
YOU CAN DO THAT KIND OF STUFF WITH OTHER PEOPLE.
HUH?
YOU HAVE A PLACE WHERE YOU BELONG.
AND I HAVE MY OWN LIFE.
WHAT... ARE YOU SAYING...?
YOU KNOW WHAT I MEAN.
KAORU, THIS CAN'T GO ON...
AOI!
DO YOU NOT LIKE ME ANYMORE? THEN I HAVE NO CHOICE...
DON'T YOU GET IT?!
I WANT TO BE WITH YOU!

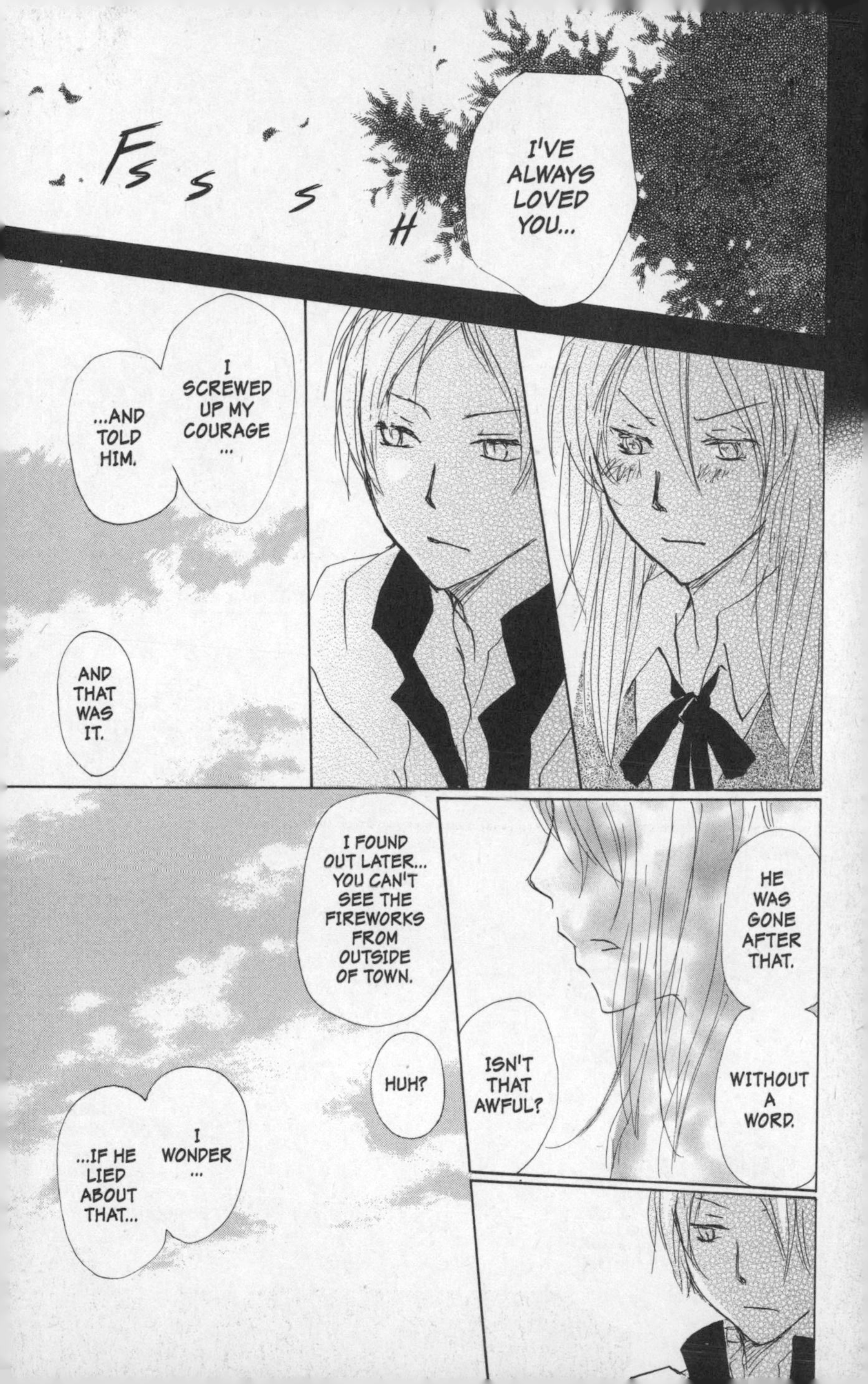
I'VE ALWAYS LOVED YOU...
FSSSH
I SCREWED UP MY COURAGE...
...AND TOLD HIM.
AND THAT WAS IT.
HE WAS GONE AFTER THAT.
WITHOUT A WORD.
ISN'T THAT AWFUL?
HUH?
I FOUND OUT LATER... YOU CAN'T SEE THE FIREWORKS FROM OUTSIDE OF TOWN.
I WONDER...
...IF HE LIED ABOUT THAT...

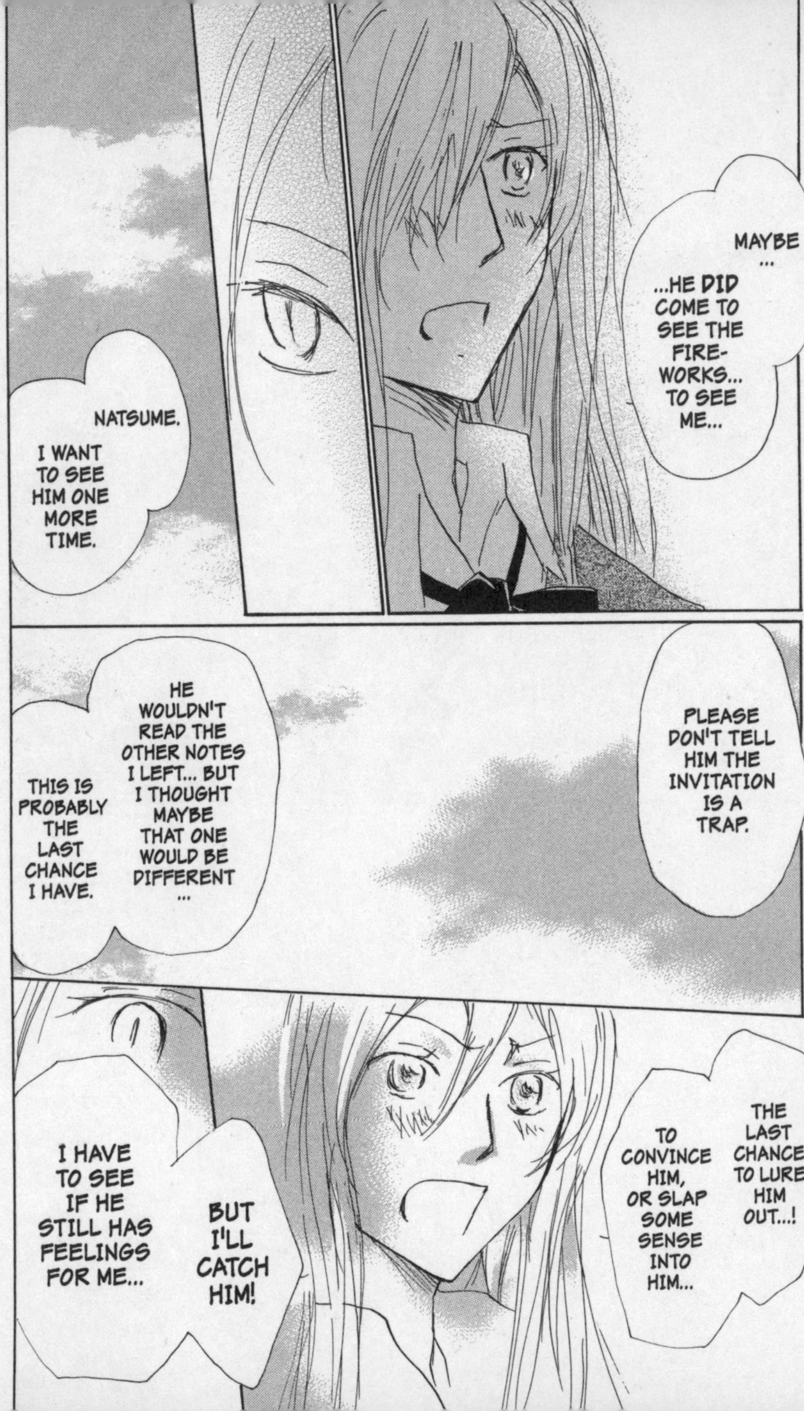
MAYBE ...
...HE DID COME TO SEE THE FIRE-WORKS... TO SEE ME...
NATSUME.
I WANT TO SEE HIM ONE MORE TIME.
PLEASE DON'T TELL HIM THE INVITATION IS A TRAP.
HE WOULDN'T READ THE OTHER NOTES I LEFT... BUT I THOUGHT MAYBE THAT ONE WOULD BE DIFFERENT ...
THIS IS PROBABLY THE LAST CHANCE I HAVE.
THE LAST CHANCE TO LURE HIM OUT...!
TO CONVINCE HIM, OR SLAP SOME SENSE INTO HIM...
BUT I'LL CATCH HIM!
I HAVE TO SEE IF HE STILL HAS FEELINGS FOR ME...

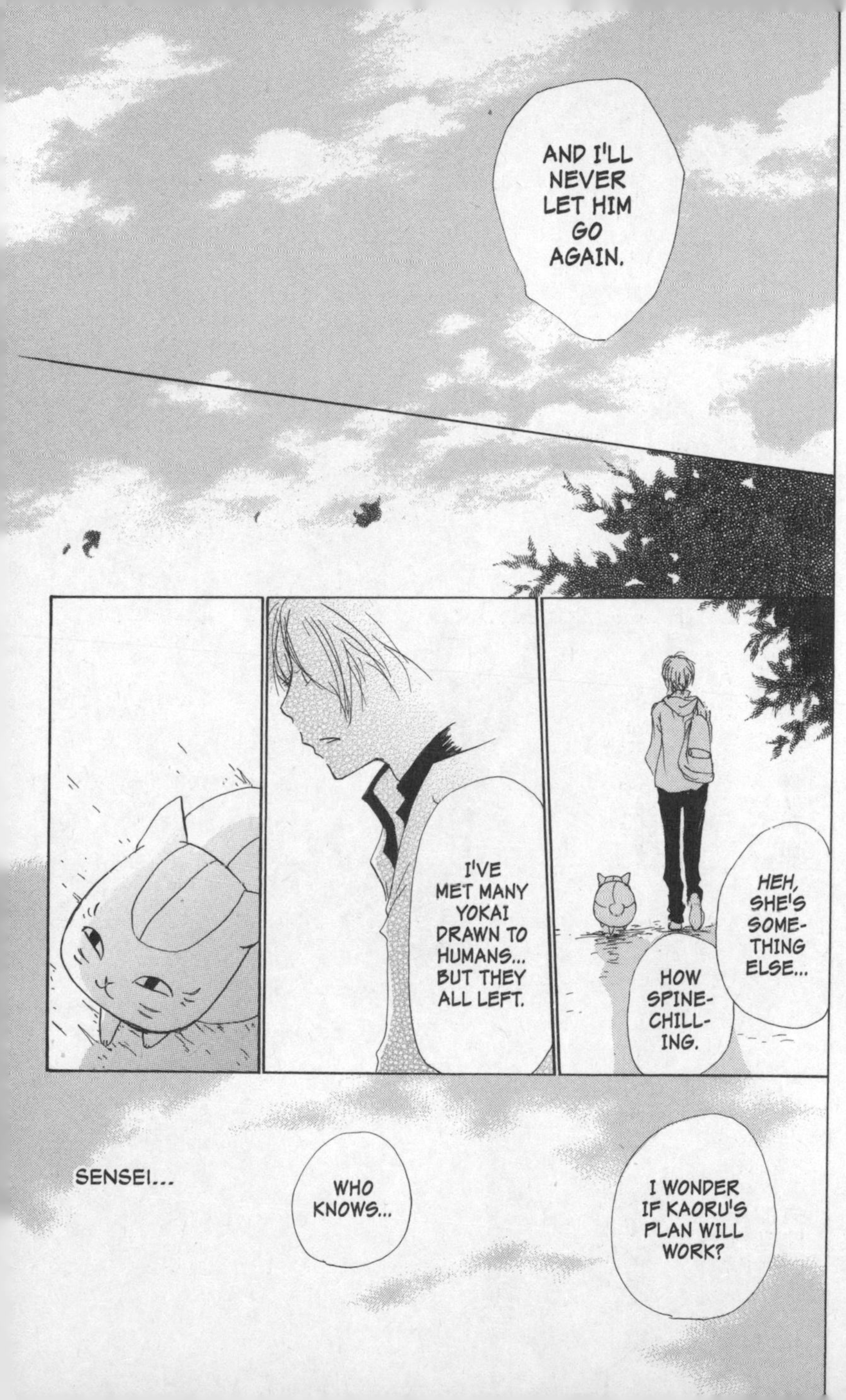
AND I'LL NEVER LET HIM GO AGAIN.
HEH, SHE'S SOME-THING ELSE...
HOW SPINE-CHILL-ING.
I'VE MET MANY YOKAI DRAWN TO HUMANS... BUT THEY ALL LEFT.
I WONDER IF KAORU'S PLAN WILL WORK?
WHO KNOWS...
SENSEI...

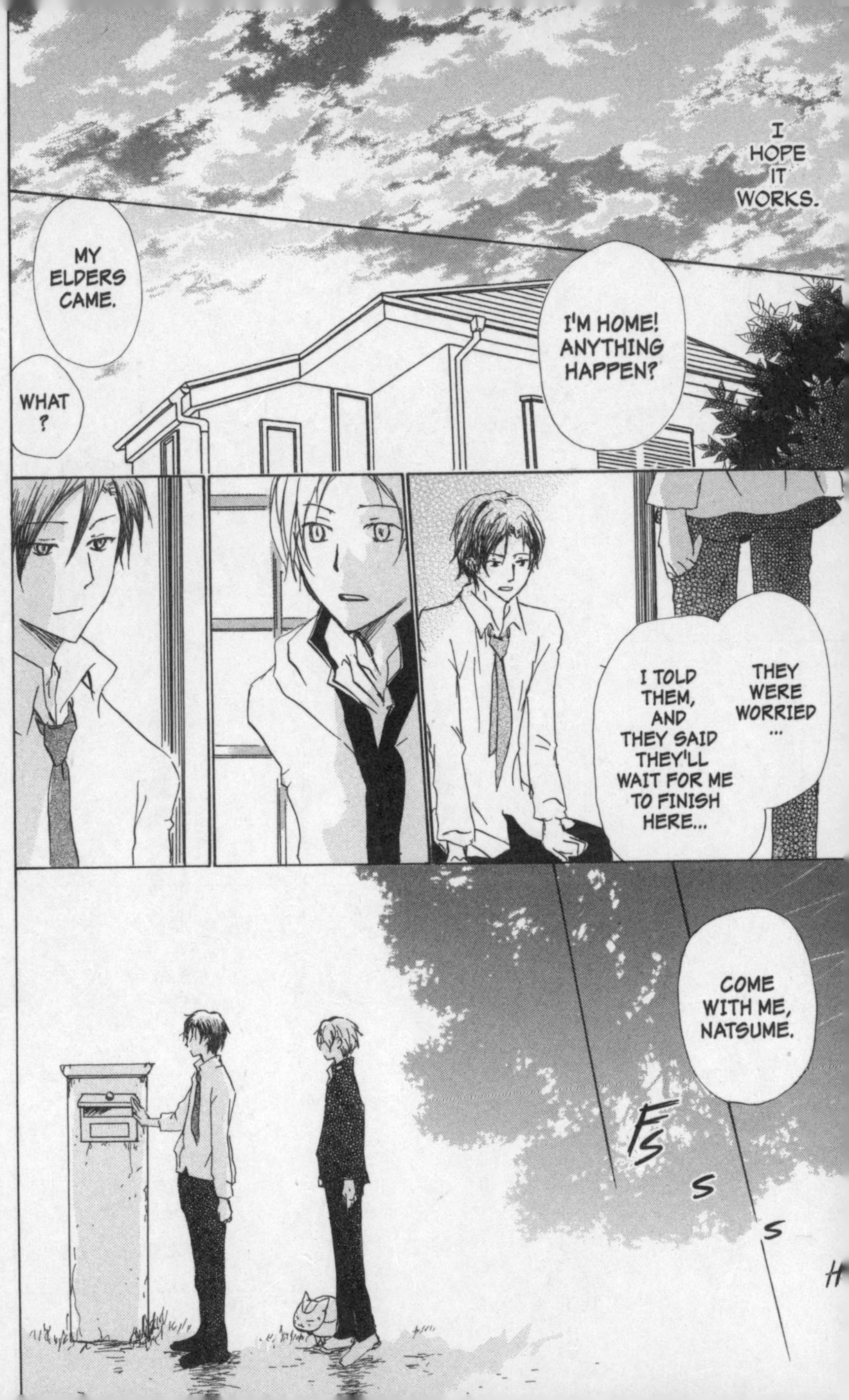
I HOPE IT WORKS.
I'M HOME! ANYTHING HAPPEN?
MY ELDERS CAME.
WHAT?
THEY WERE WORRIED...
I TOLD THEM, AND THEY SAID THEY'LL WAIT FOR ME TO FINISH HERE...
COME WITH ME, NATSUME.
FSSSH

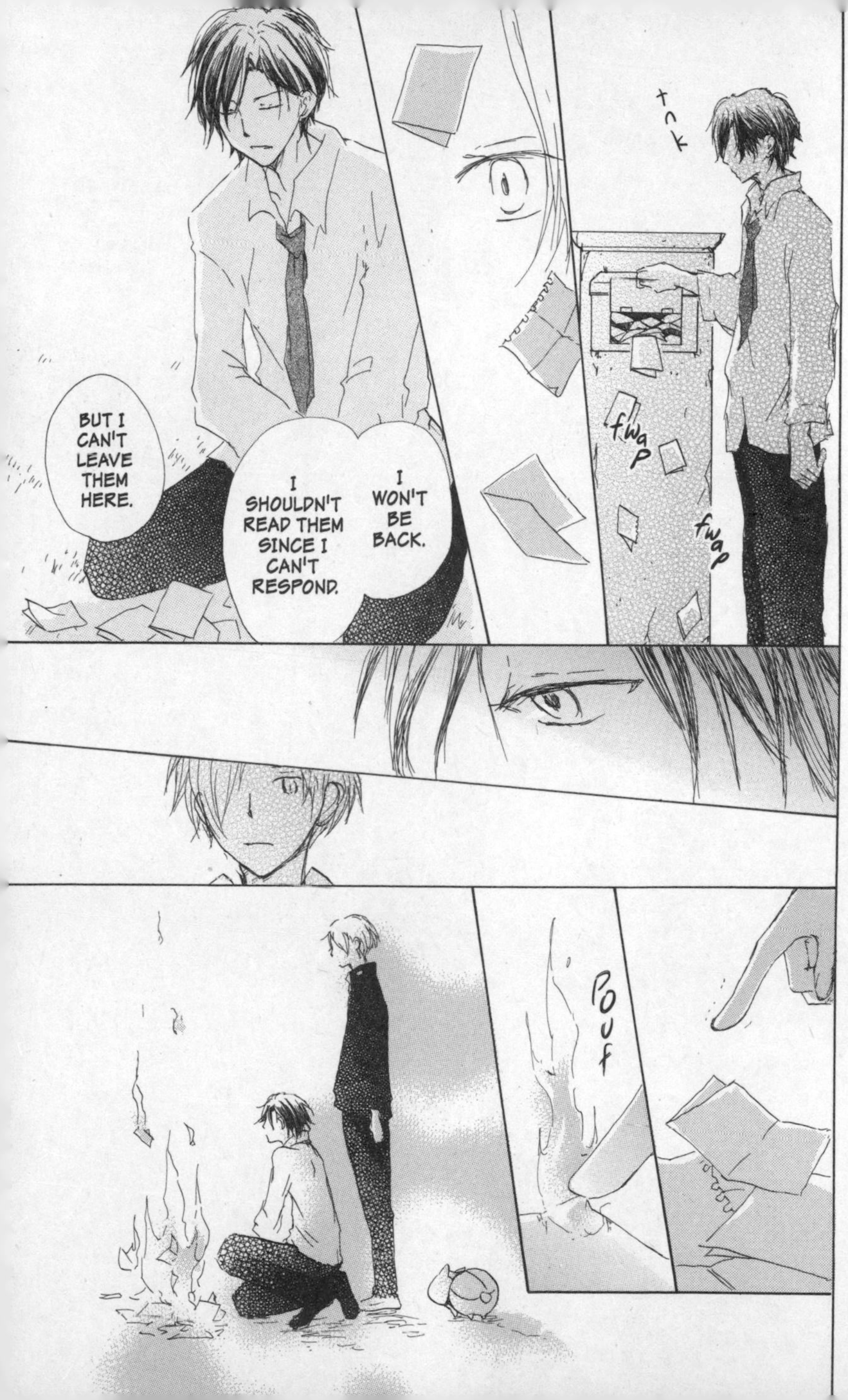
tnk
fwap
fwap
I WON'T BE BACK.
I SHOULDN'T READ THEM SINCE I CAN'T RESPOND.
BUT I CAN'T LEAVE THEM HERE.
POUF

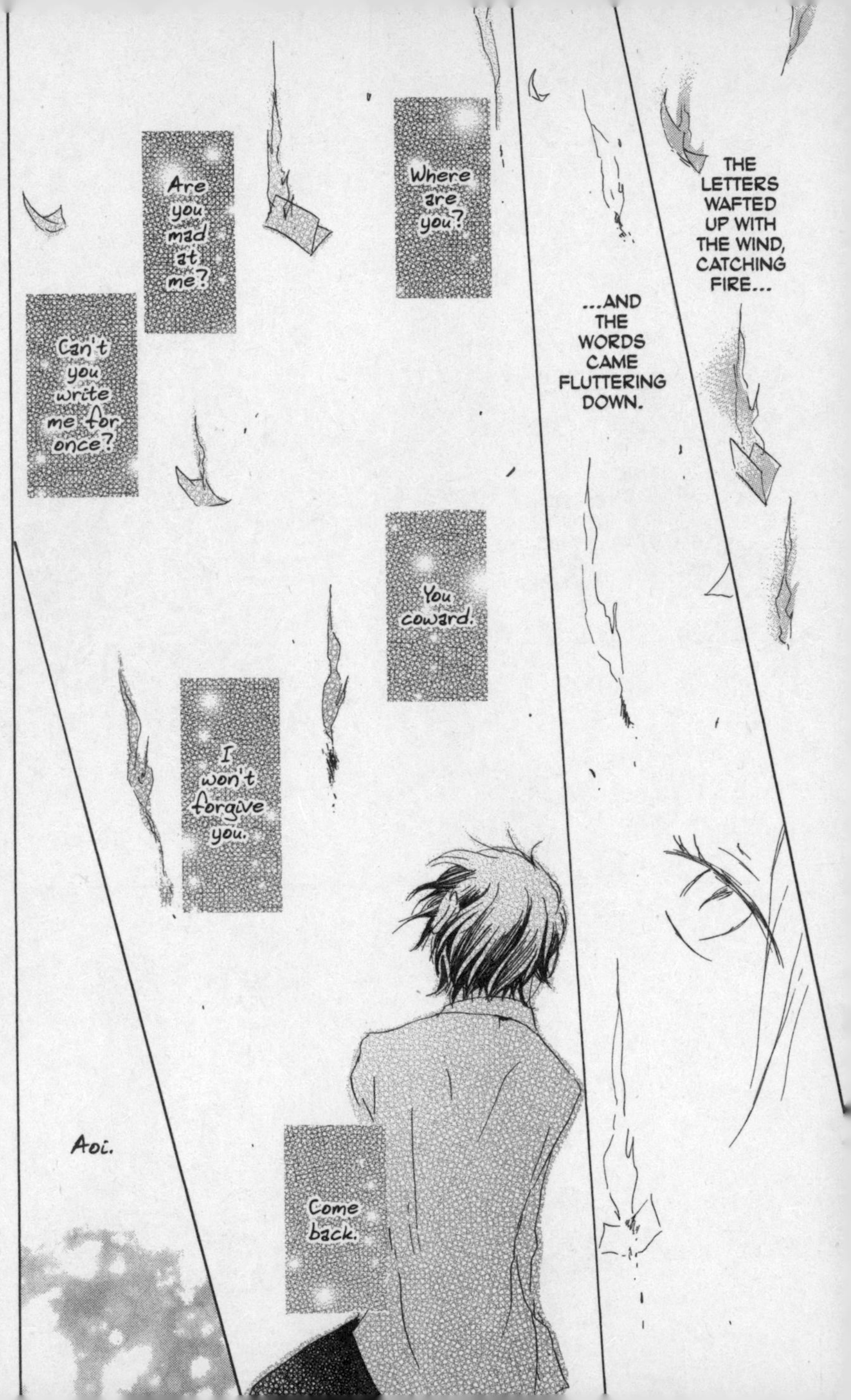
THE LETTERS WAFTED UP WITH THE WIND, CATCHING FIRE...
...AND THE WORDS CAME FLUTTERING DOWN.
Where are you?
Are you mad at me?
Can't you write me for once?
You coward.
I won't forgive you.
Come back.
Aoi.

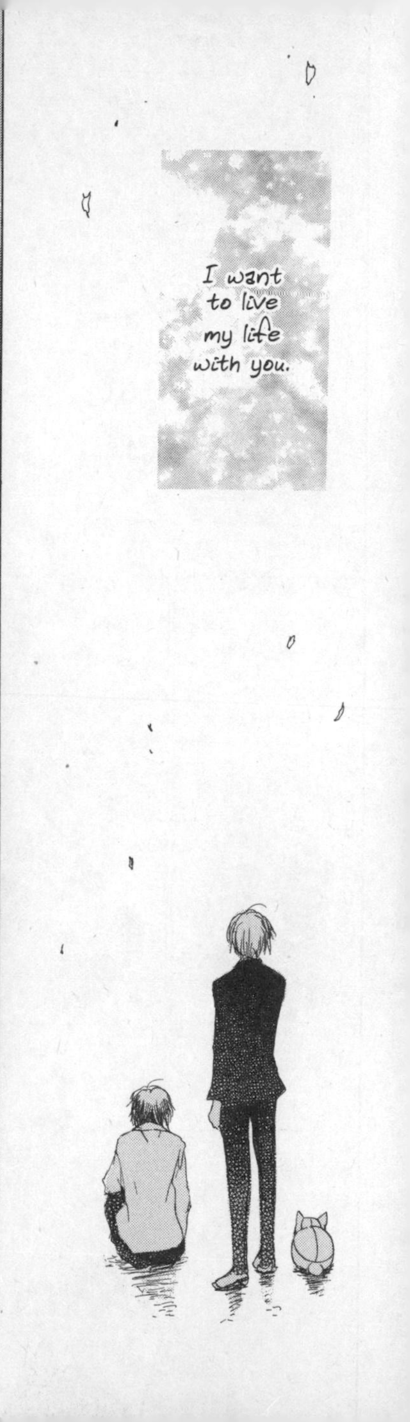
I want to live my life with you.

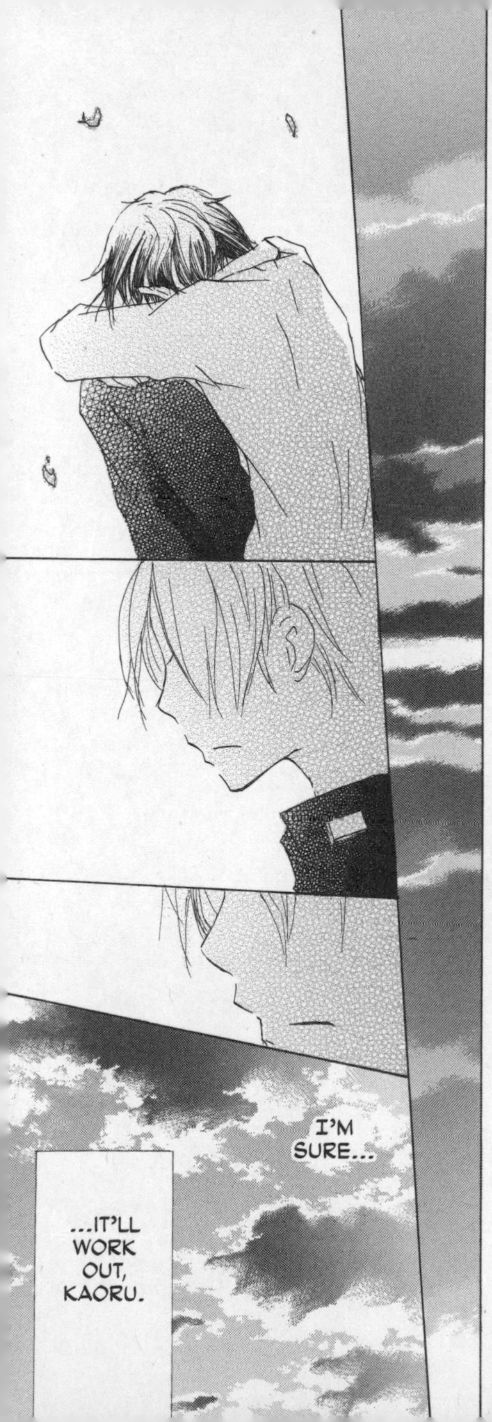
I'M SURE...
...IT'LL WORK OUT, KAORU.

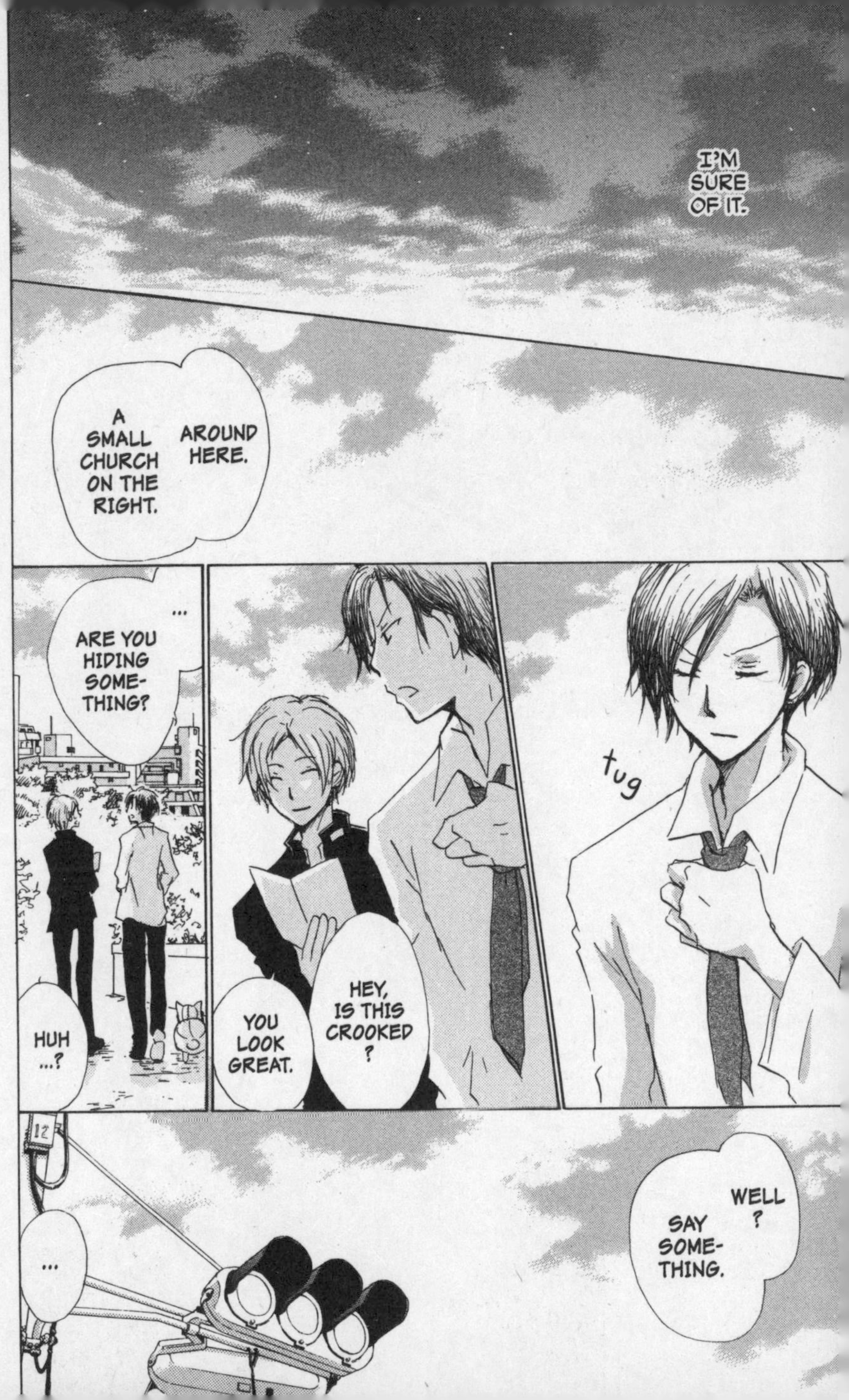
I'M SURE OF IT.
AROUND HERE.
A SMALL CHURCH ON THE RIGHT.
tug
HEY, IS THIS CROOKED?
YOU LOOK GREAT.
... ARE YOU HIDING SOMETHING?
HUH ...?
WELL? SAY SOMETHING.
...

03

❋ Tokyo Gallery

Amazingly, they held an art exhibition and autograph session in Tokyo. Thank you to everyone who came. I received valuable feedback, delightful comments, and adorable gifts. There were many who came all the way out in the summer heat that I couldn't get to meet. It's frustrating that I couldn't do anything for them in return.

The gallery hall had fun, detailed touches like creepy areas and beautiful sections for the enjoyment of the guests. I got pretty emotional. I got to keep the guestbook they had for everyone to leave their comments in. The adorable drawings and messages have become my treasure. Thank you so much.

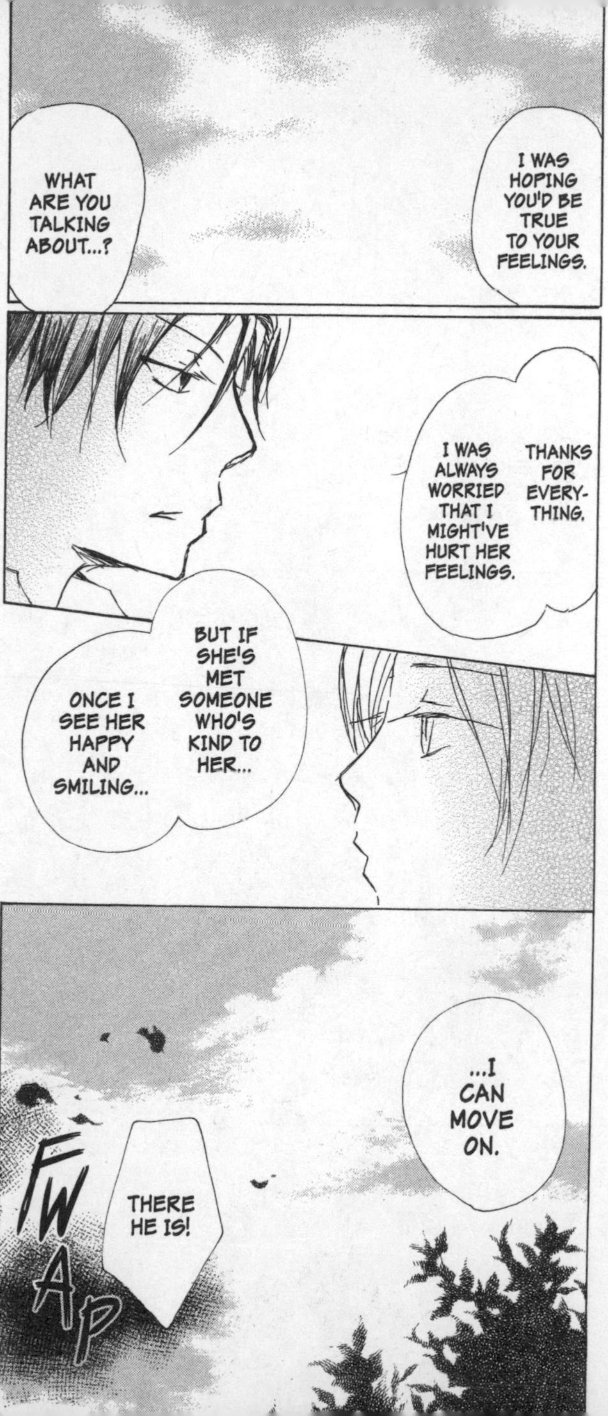
I WAS HOPING YOU'D BE TRUE TO YOUR FEELINGS.
WHAT ARE YOU TALKING ABOUT...?
THANKS FOR EVERYTHING.
I WAS ALWAYS WORRIED THAT I MIGHT'VE HURT HER FEELINGS.
BUT IF SHE'S MET SOMEONE WHO'S KIND TO HER...
ONCE I SEE HER HAPPY AND SMILING...
...I CAN MOVE ON.
THERE HE IS!
FWAP

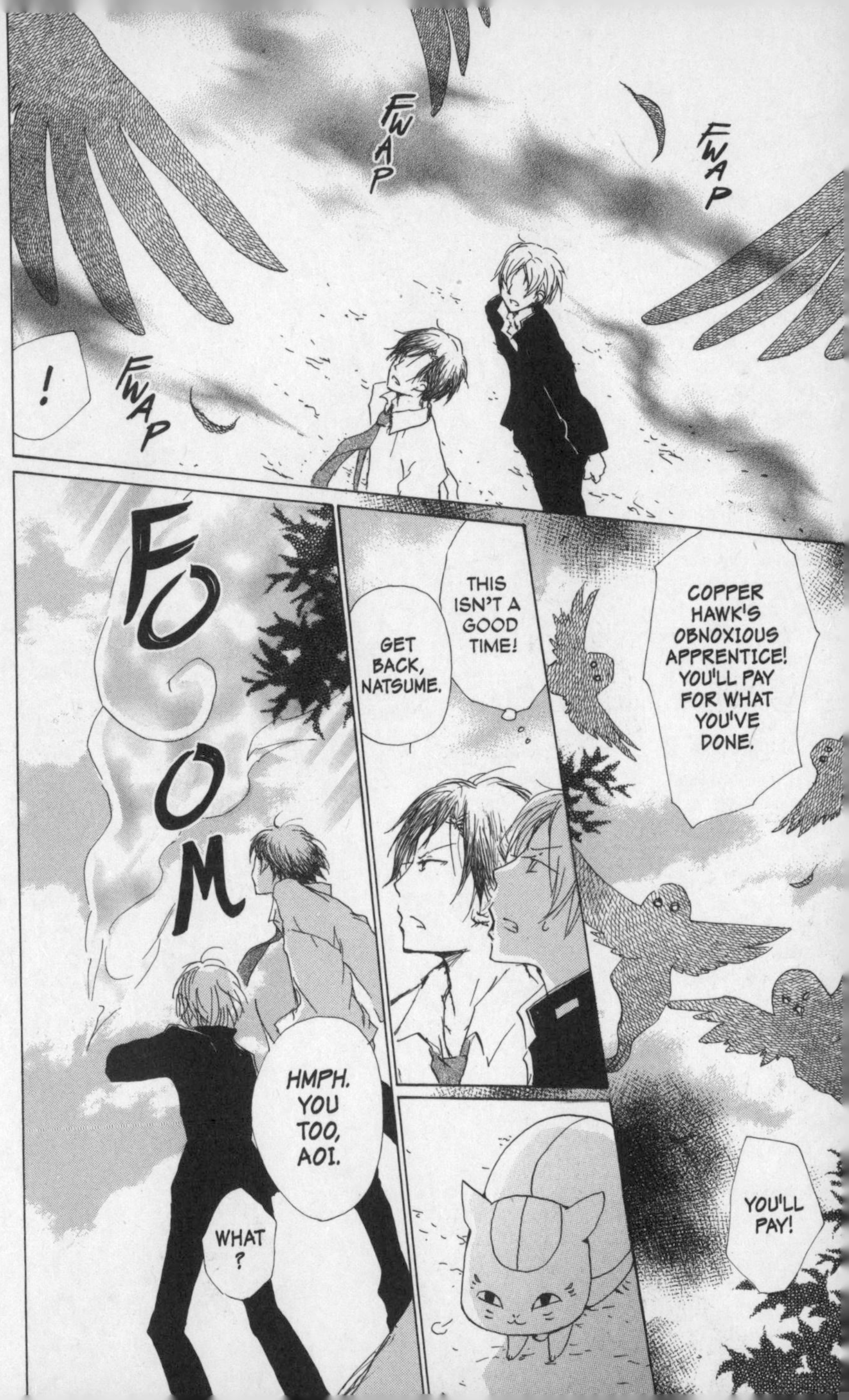
FWAP
FWAP
FWAP
!
COPPER HAWK'S OBNOXIOUS APPRENTICE! YOU'LL PAY FOR WHAT YOU'VE DONE.
THIS ISN'T A GOOD TIME!
GET BACK, NATSUME.
YOU'LL PAY!
FOOM
HMPH. YOU TOO, AOI.
WHAT?

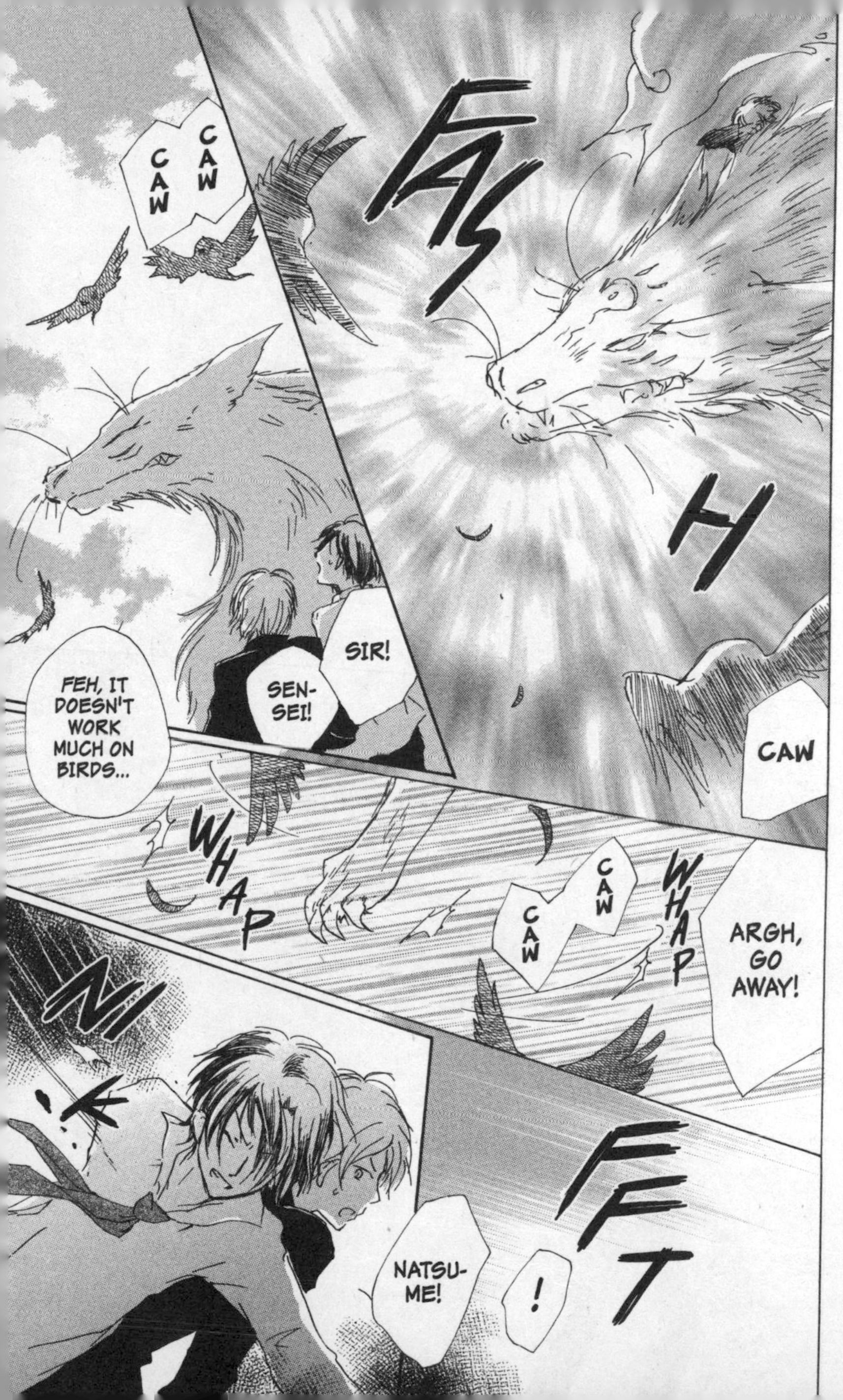
FASH
CAW
CAW CAW
SIR!
SEN-SEI!
FEH, IT DOESN'T WORK MUCH ON BIRDS...
ARGH, GO AWAY!
WHAP
CAW CAW
WHAP
FFT
!
NATSU-ME!

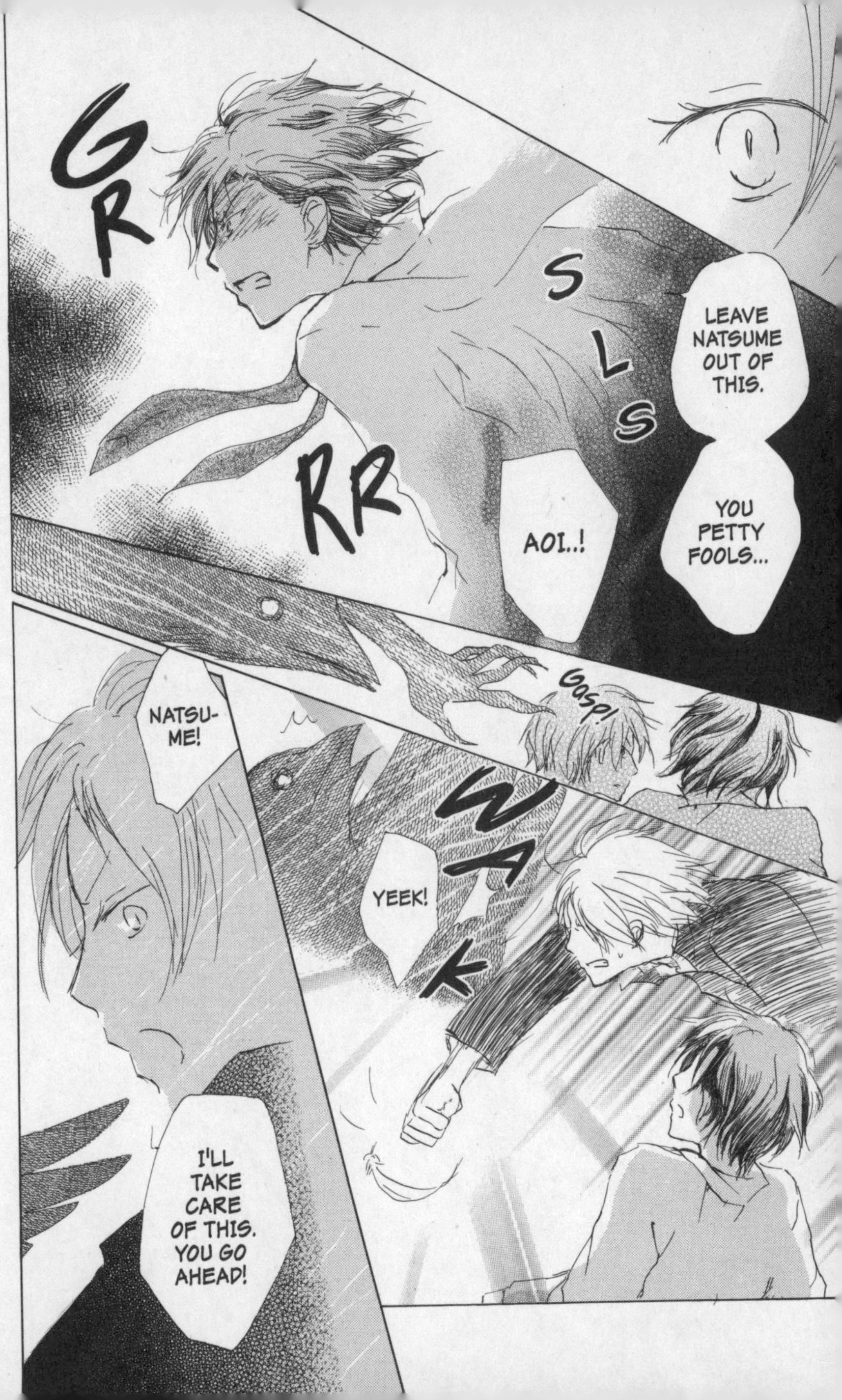
LEAVE NATSUME OUT OF THIS.
YOU PETTY FOOLS...
SLS
AOI..!
GRRR
Gasp!
WAK
YEEK!
NATSU-ME!
I'LL TAKE CARE OF THIS. YOU GO AHEAD!

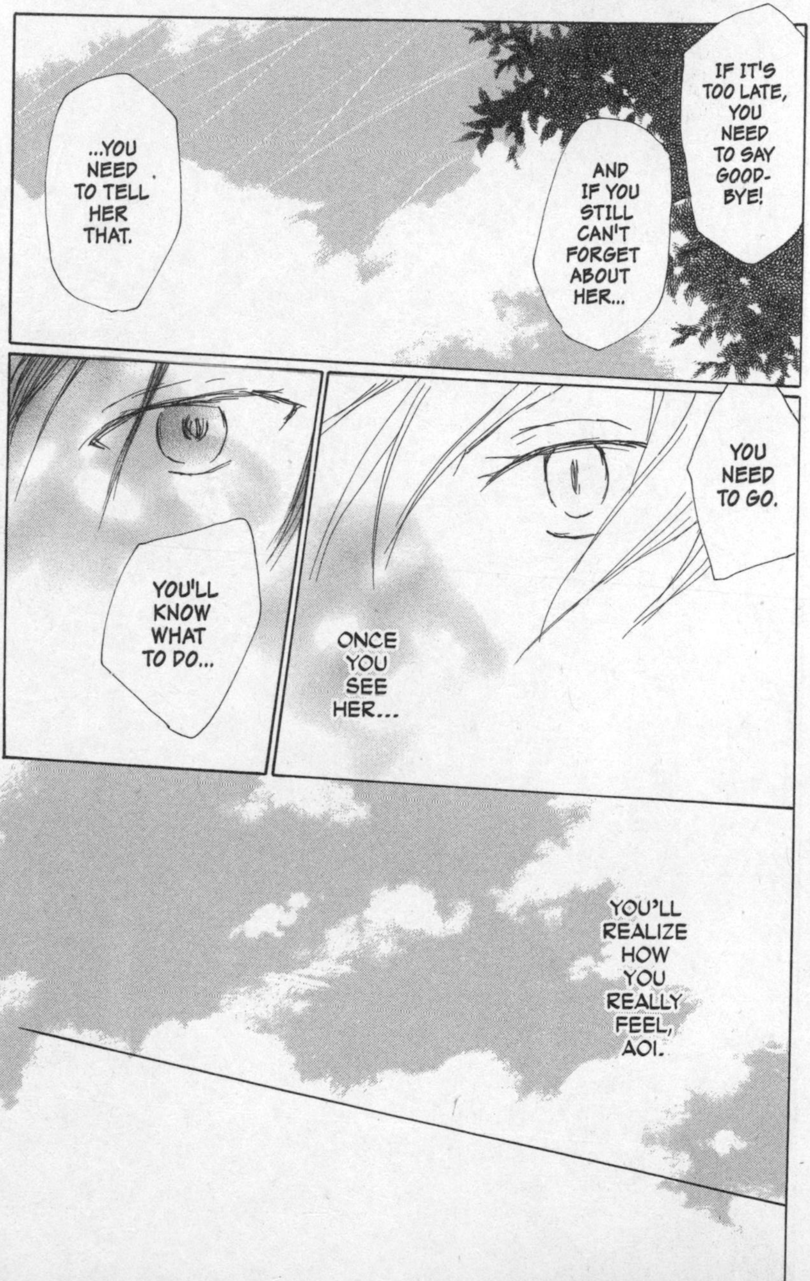
IF IT'S TOO LATE, YOU NEED TO SAY GOOD-BYE!
AND IF YOU STILL CAN'T FORGET ABOUT HER...
...YOU NEED TO TELL HER THAT.
YOU NEED TO GO.
ONCE YOU SEE HER...
YOU'LL KNOW WHAT TO DO...
YOU'LL REALIZE HOW YOU REALLY FEEL, AOI.

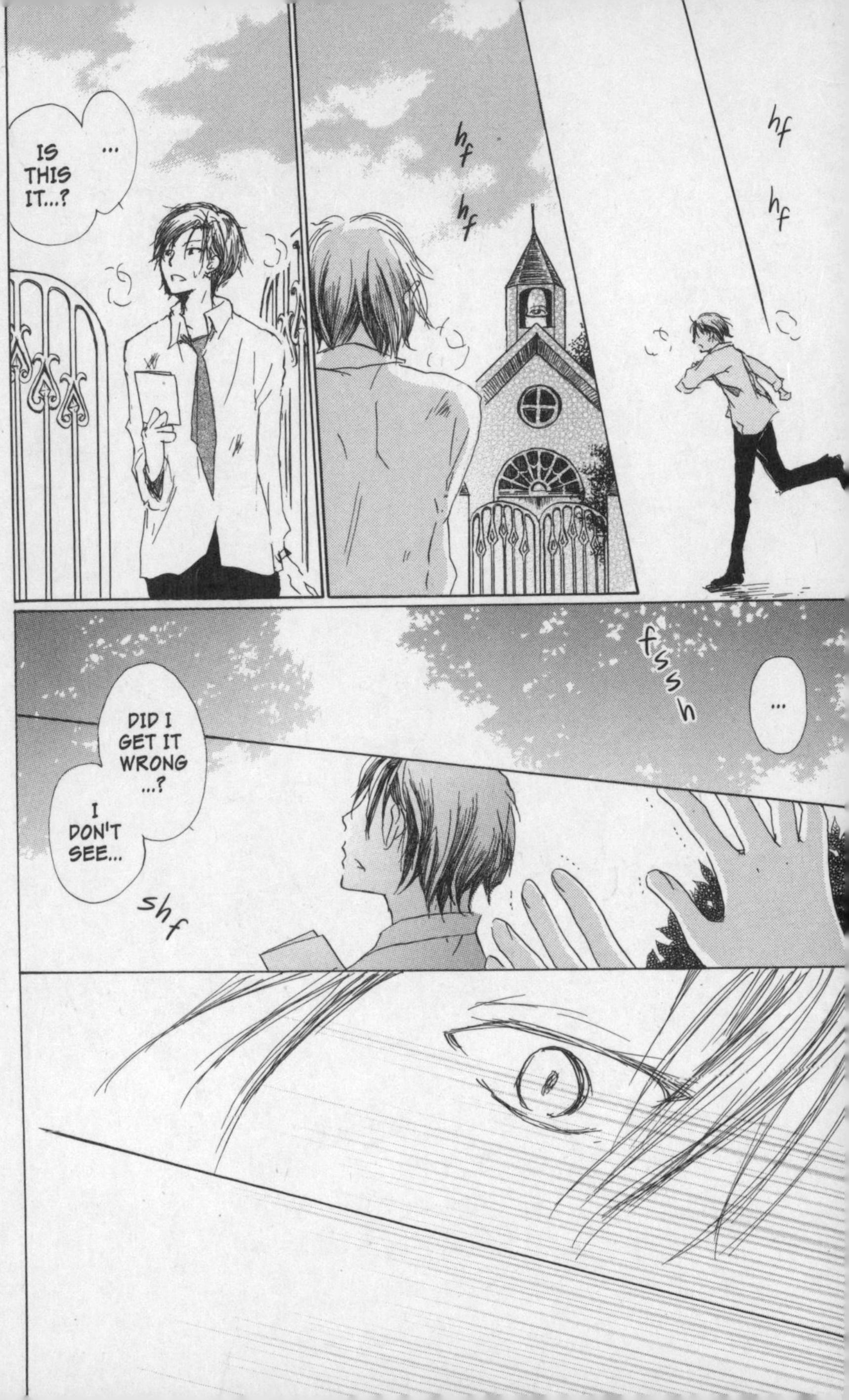
hf
hf
hf
hf
...
IS THIS IT...?
fssh
...
DID I GET IT WRONG...?
I DON'T SEE...
shf

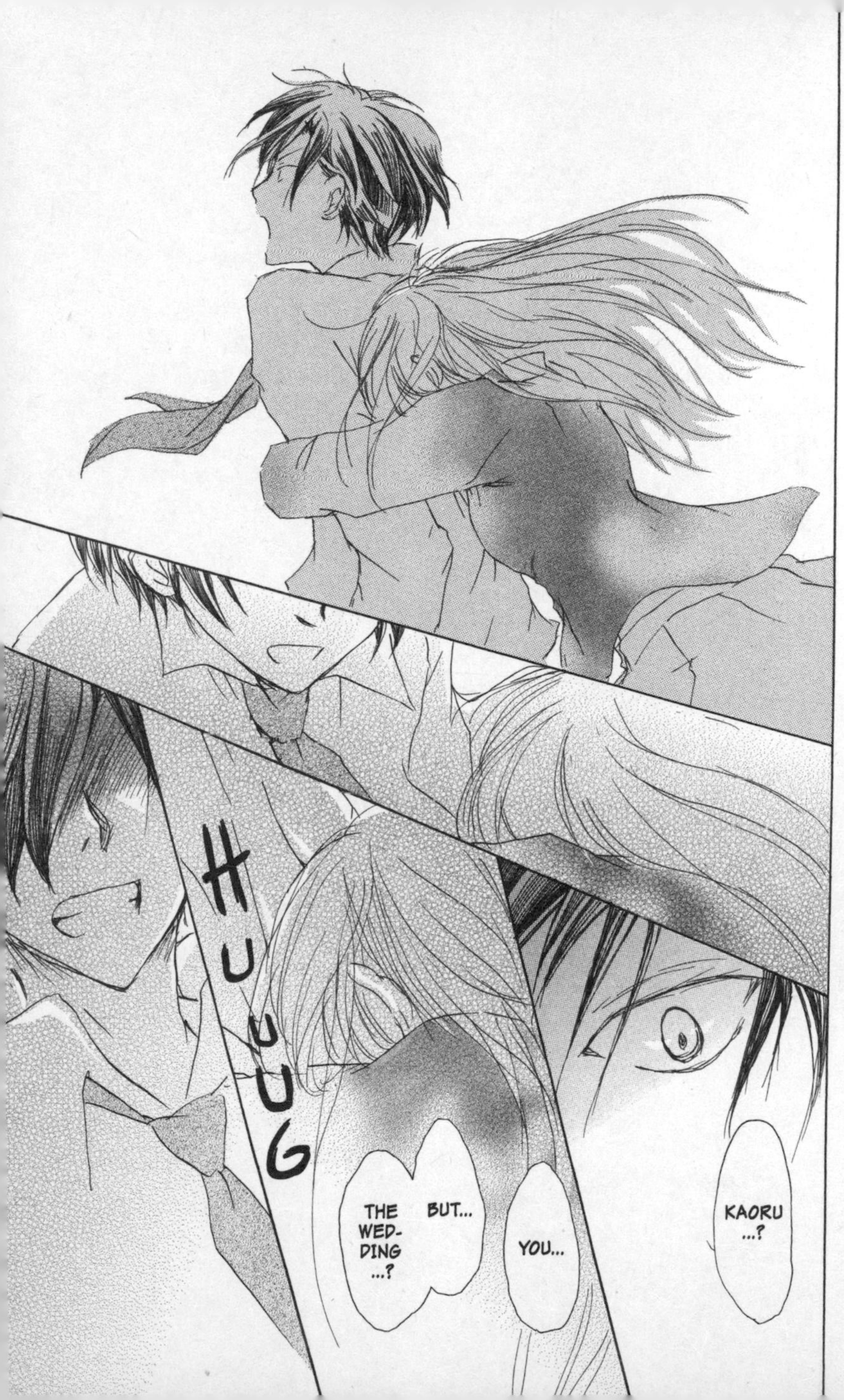
KAORU ...?
YOU...
BUT...
THE WED-DING ...?
HUUUG

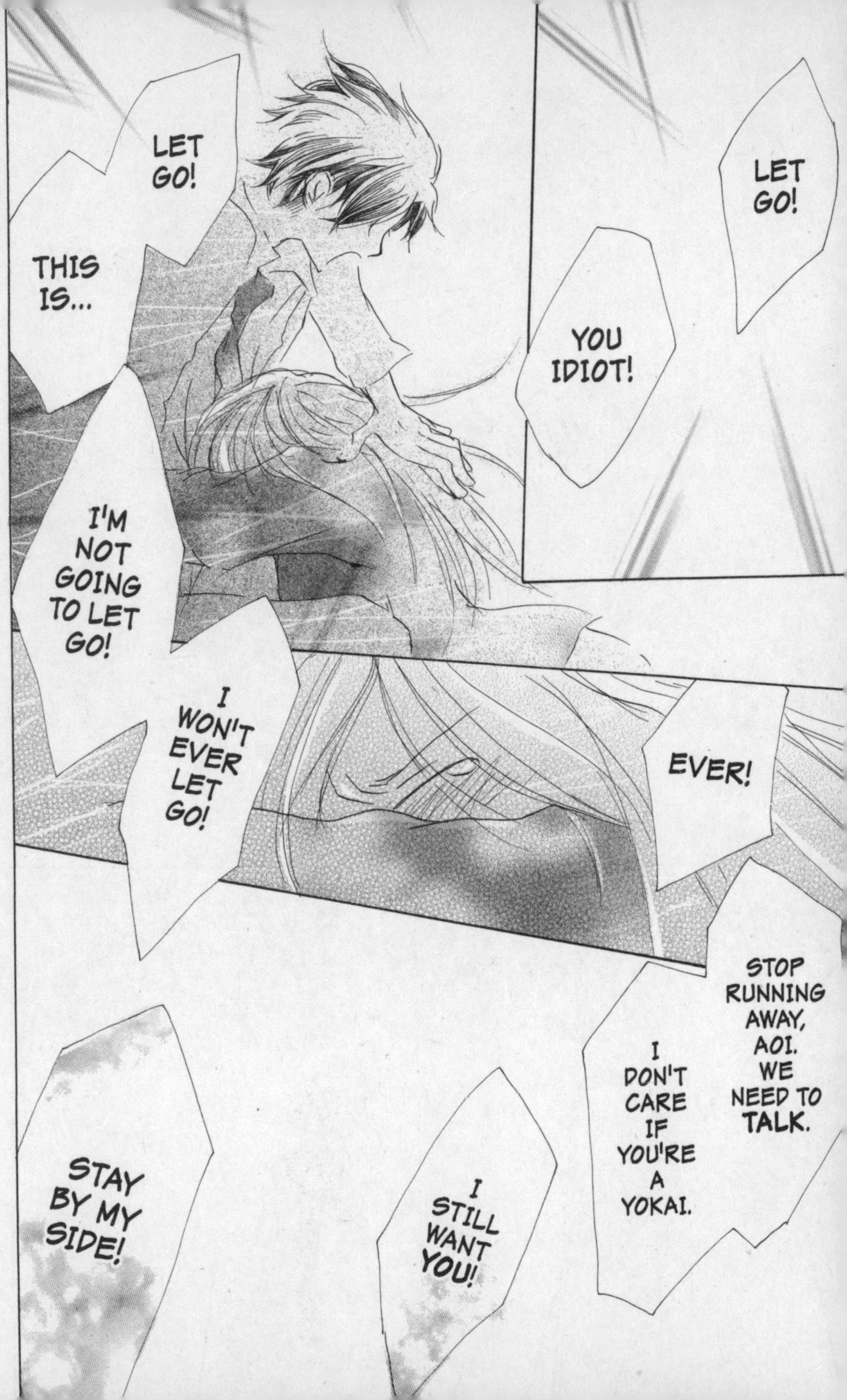
LET GO!
YOU IDIOT!
LET GO!
THIS IS...
I'M NOT GOING TO LET GO!
EVER!
I WON'T EVER LET GO!
STOP RUNNING AWAY, AOI. WE NEED TO TALK.
I DON'T CARE IF YOU'RE A YOKAI.
I STILL WANT YOU!
STAY BY MY SIDE!

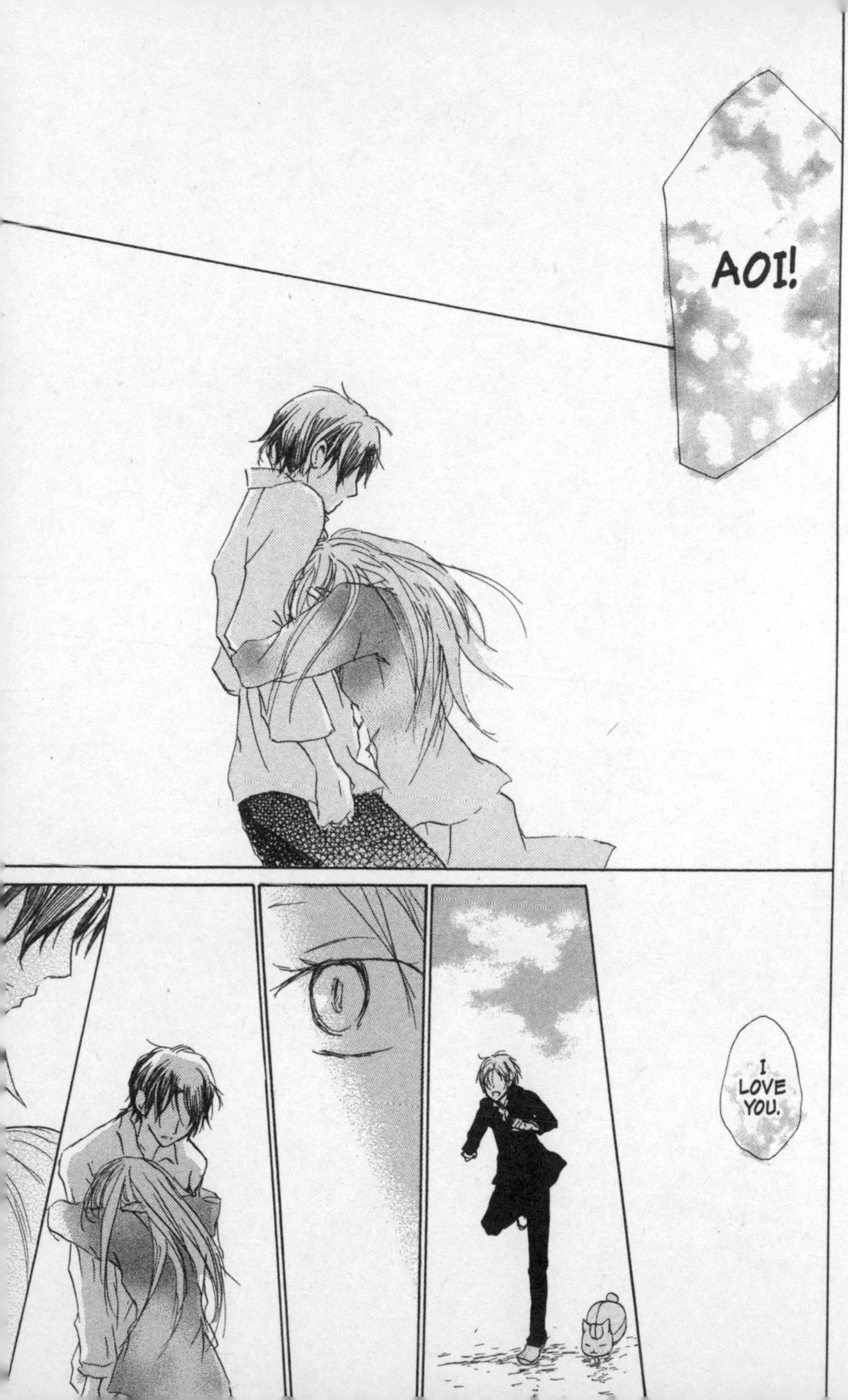
AOI!
I LOVE YOU.

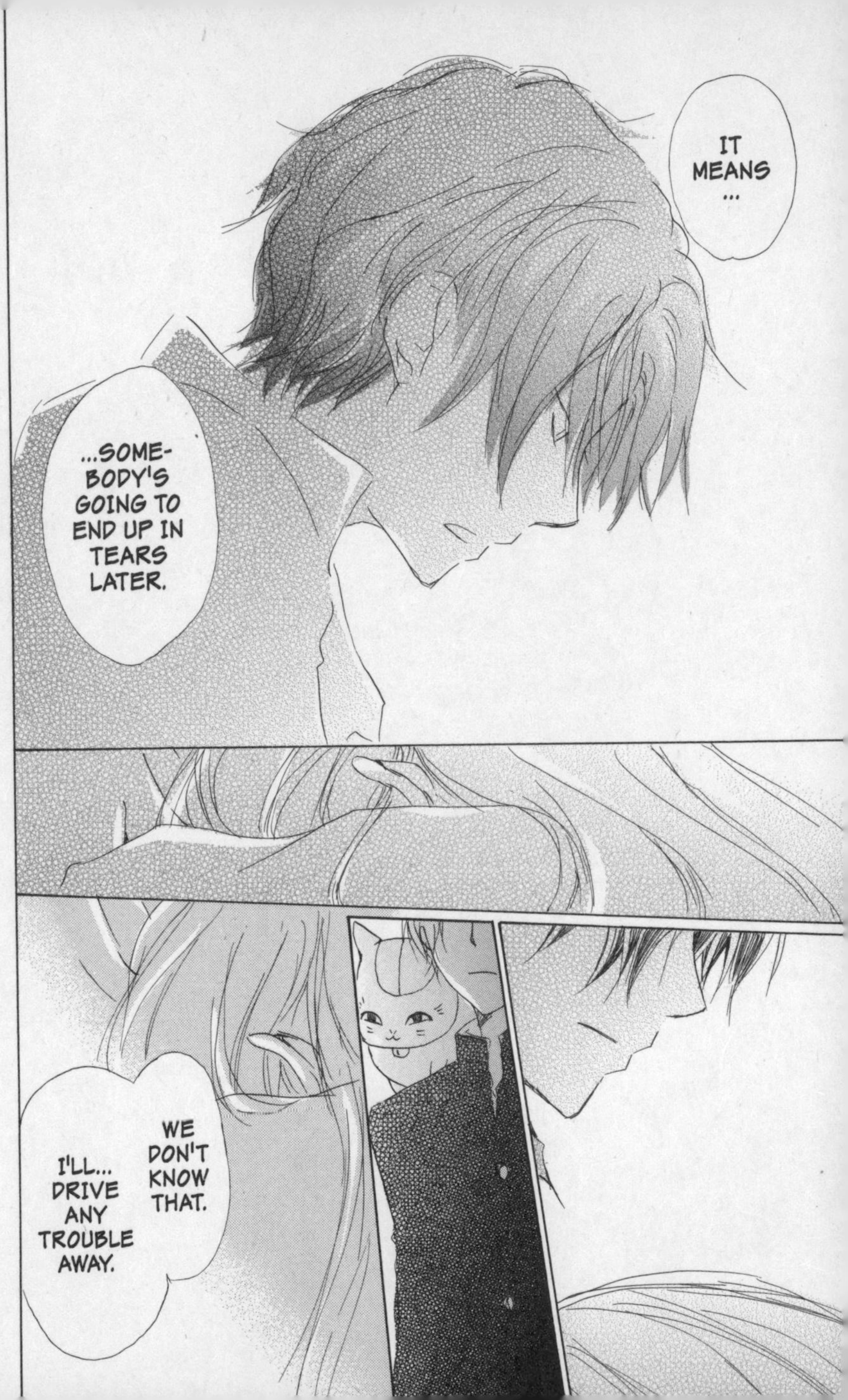
IT MEANS ...
...SOME-BODY'S GOING TO END UP IN TEARS LATER.
WE DON'T KNOW THAT.
I'LL... DRIVE ANY TROUBLE AWAY.

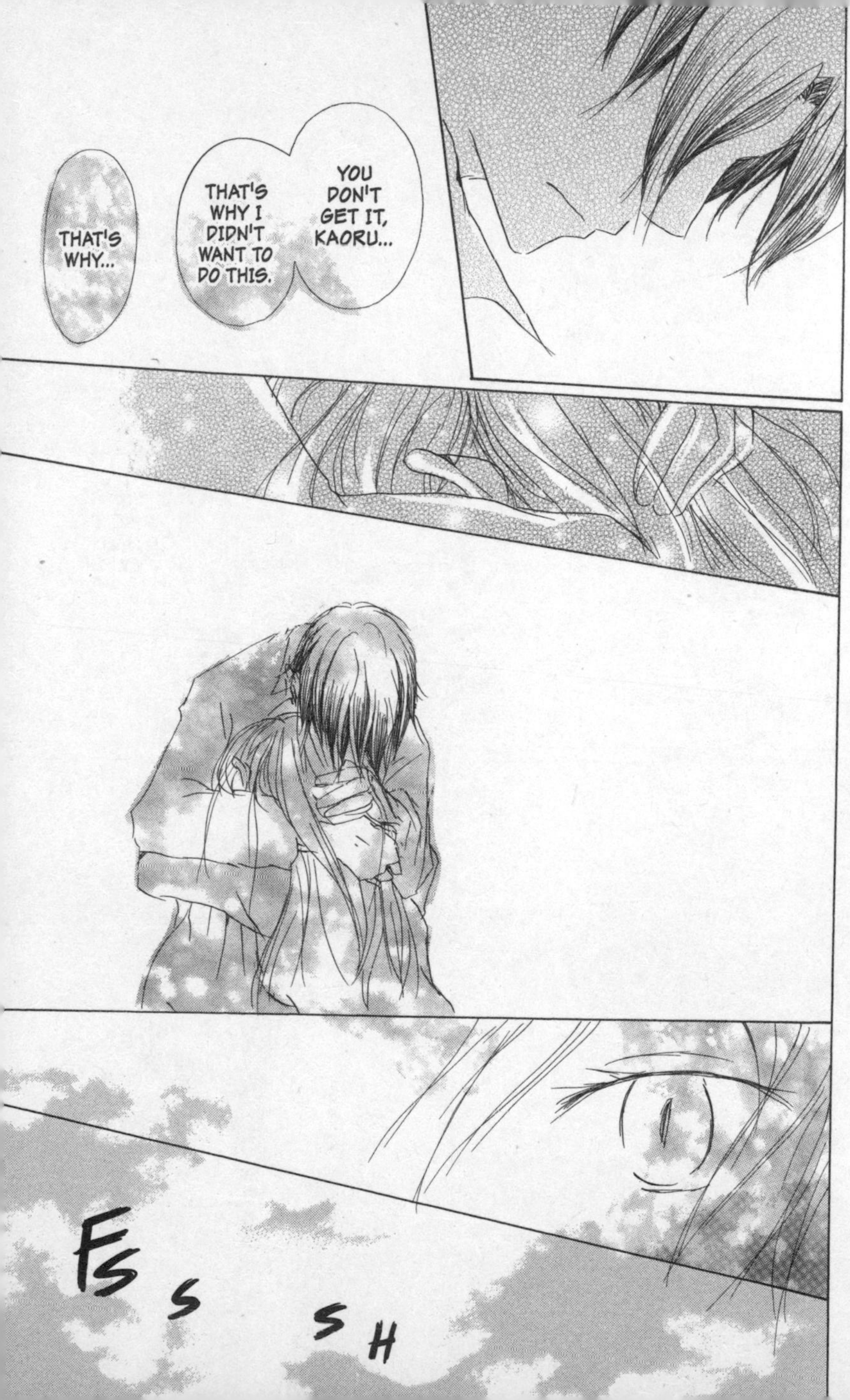
YOU DON'T GET IT, KAORU...
THAT'S WHY I DIDN'T WANT TO DO THIS.
THAT'S WHY...
FS S S H

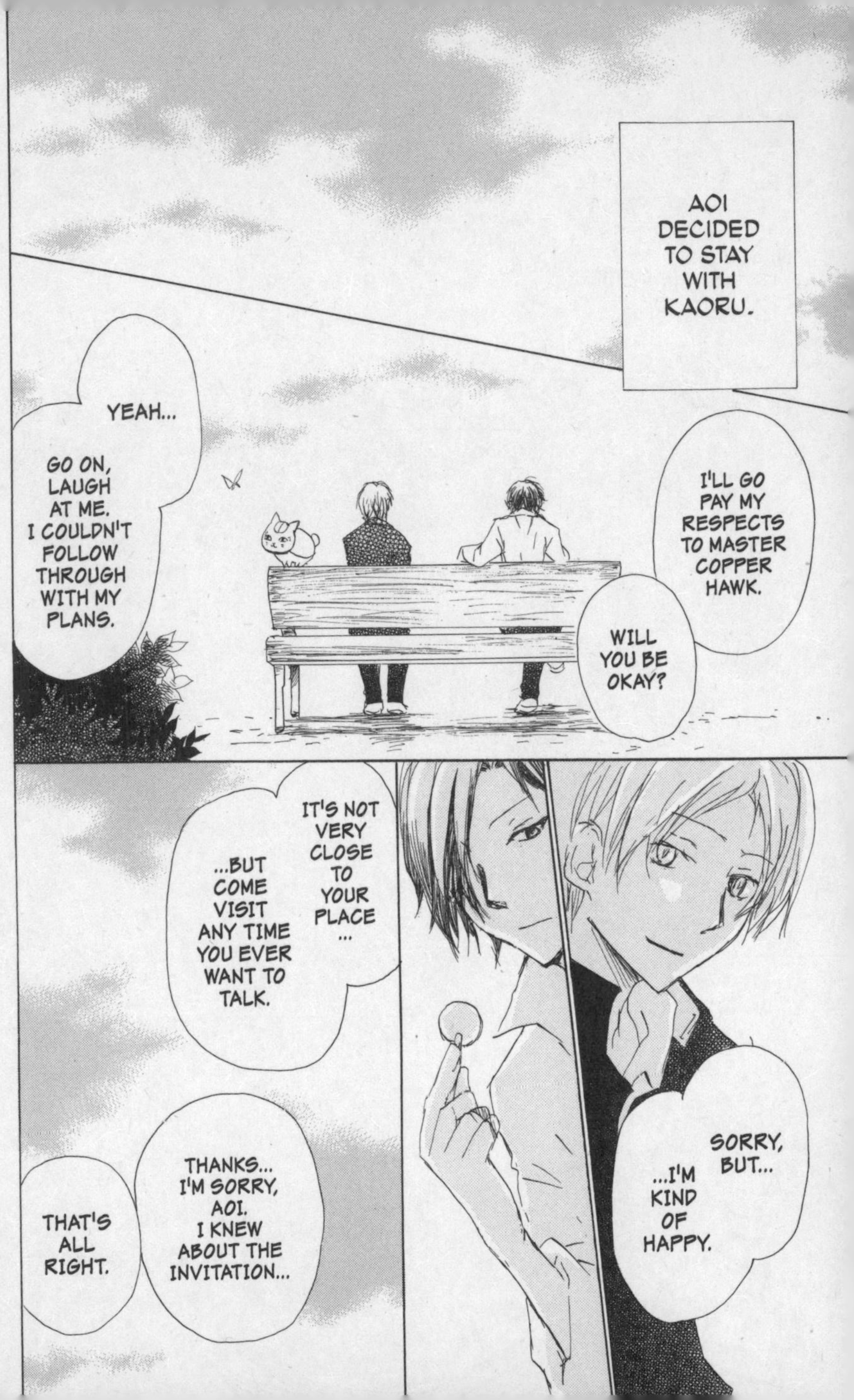
AOI DECIDED TO STAY WITH KAORU.
I'LL GO PAY MY RESPECTS TO MASTER COPPER HAWK.
WILL YOU BE OKAY?
YEAH...
GO ON, LAUGH AT ME. I COULDN'T FOLLOW THROUGH WITH MY PLANS.
SORRY, BUT...
...I'M KIND OF HAPPY.
IT'S NOT VERY CLOSE TO YOUR PLACE ...
...BUT COME VISIT ANY TIME YOU EVER WANT TO TALK.
THANKS... I'M SORRY, AOI. I KNEW ABOUT THE INVITATION...
THAT'S ALL RIGHT.

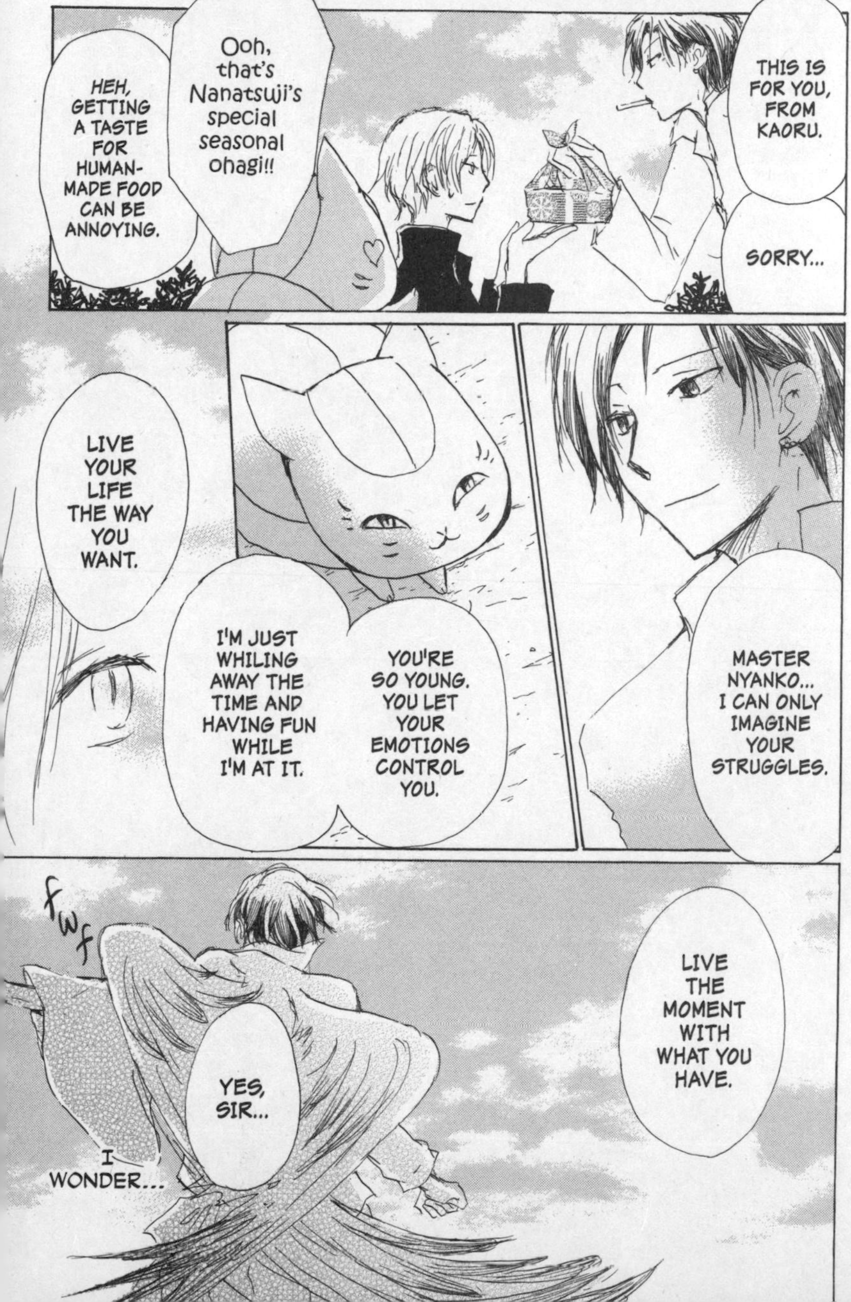
THIS IS FOR YOU, FROM KAORU.
SORRY...
Ooh, that's Nanatsuji's special seasonal ohagi!!
HEH, GETTING A TASTE FOR HUMAN-MADE FOOD CAN BE ANNOYING.
MASTER NYANKO... I CAN ONLY IMAGINE YOUR STRUGGLES.
YOU'RE SO YOUNG. YOU LET YOUR EMOTIONS CONTROL YOU.
I'M JUST WHILING AWAY THE TIME AND HAVING FUN WHILE I'M AT IT.
LIVE YOUR LIFE THE WAY YOU WANT.
LIVE THE MOMENT WITH WHAT YOU HAVE.
fwf
YES, SIR...
I WONDER...

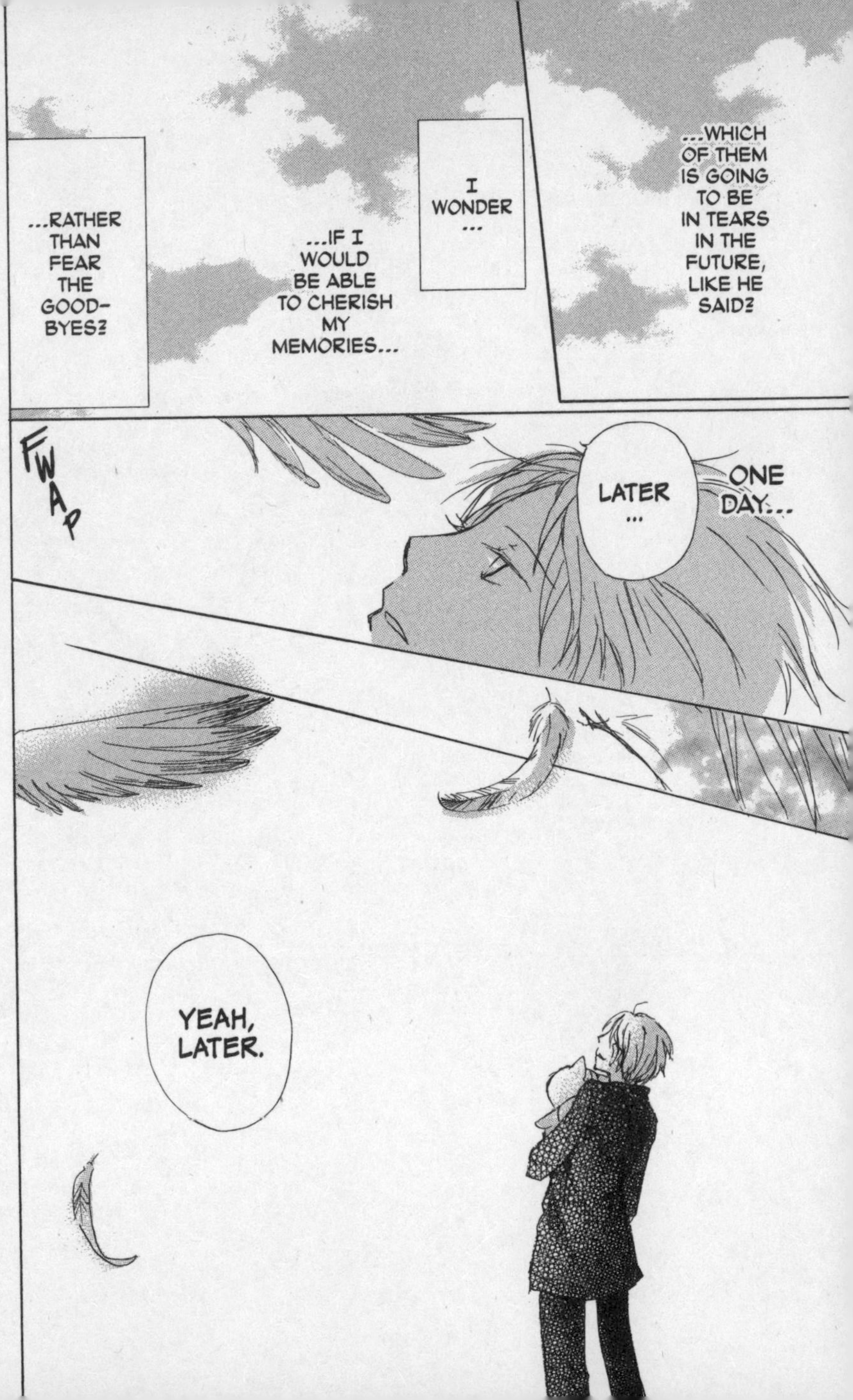
...WHICH OF THEM IS GOING TO BE IN TEARS IN THE FUTURE, LIKE HE SAID?
I WONDER ...
...IF I WOULD BE ABLE TO CHERISH MY MEMORIES...
...RATHER THAN FEAR THE GOOD-BYES?
ONE DAY...
LATER ...
FWAP
YEAH, LATER.

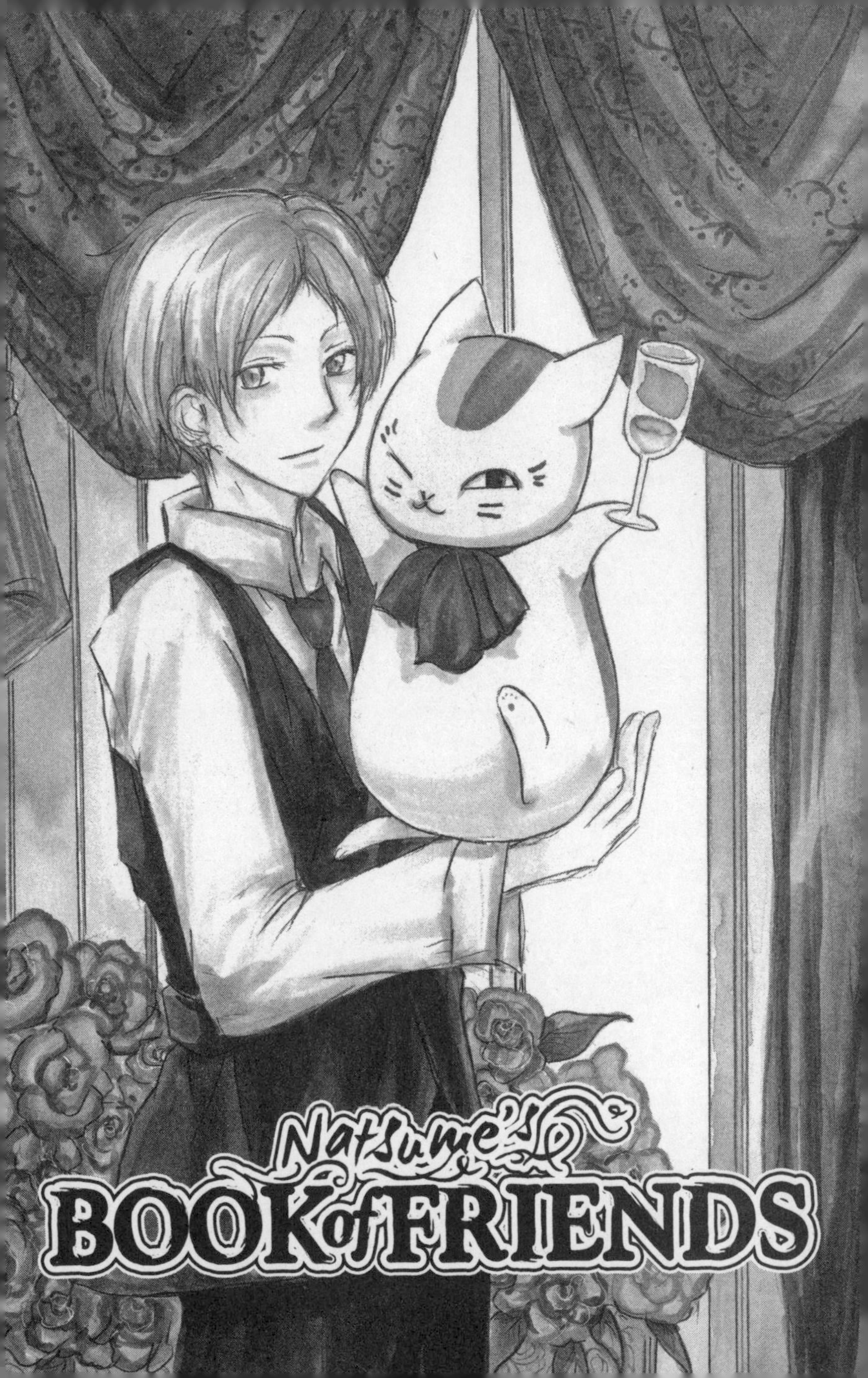
Natsume's
BOOK of FRIENDS

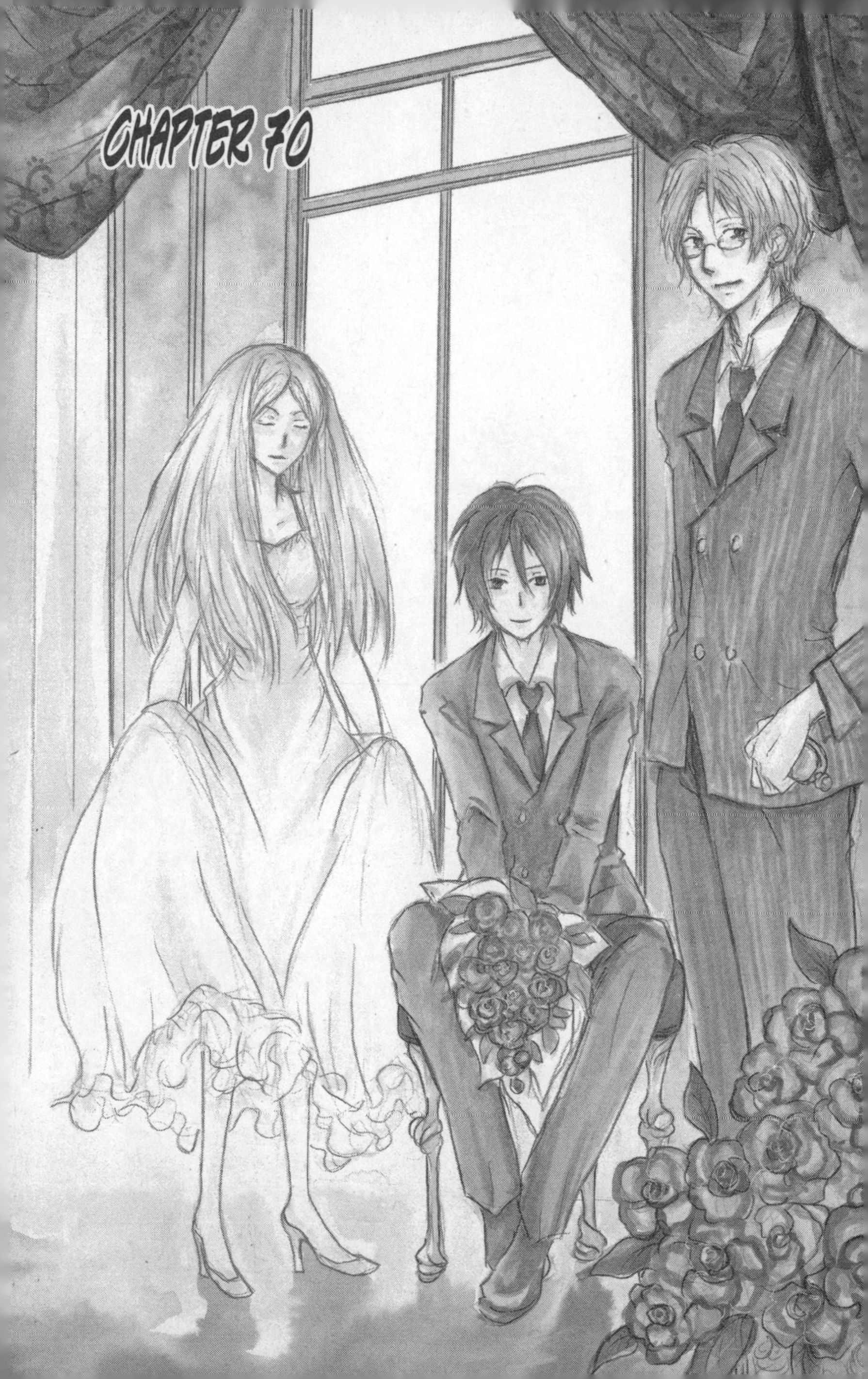
CHAPTER 70

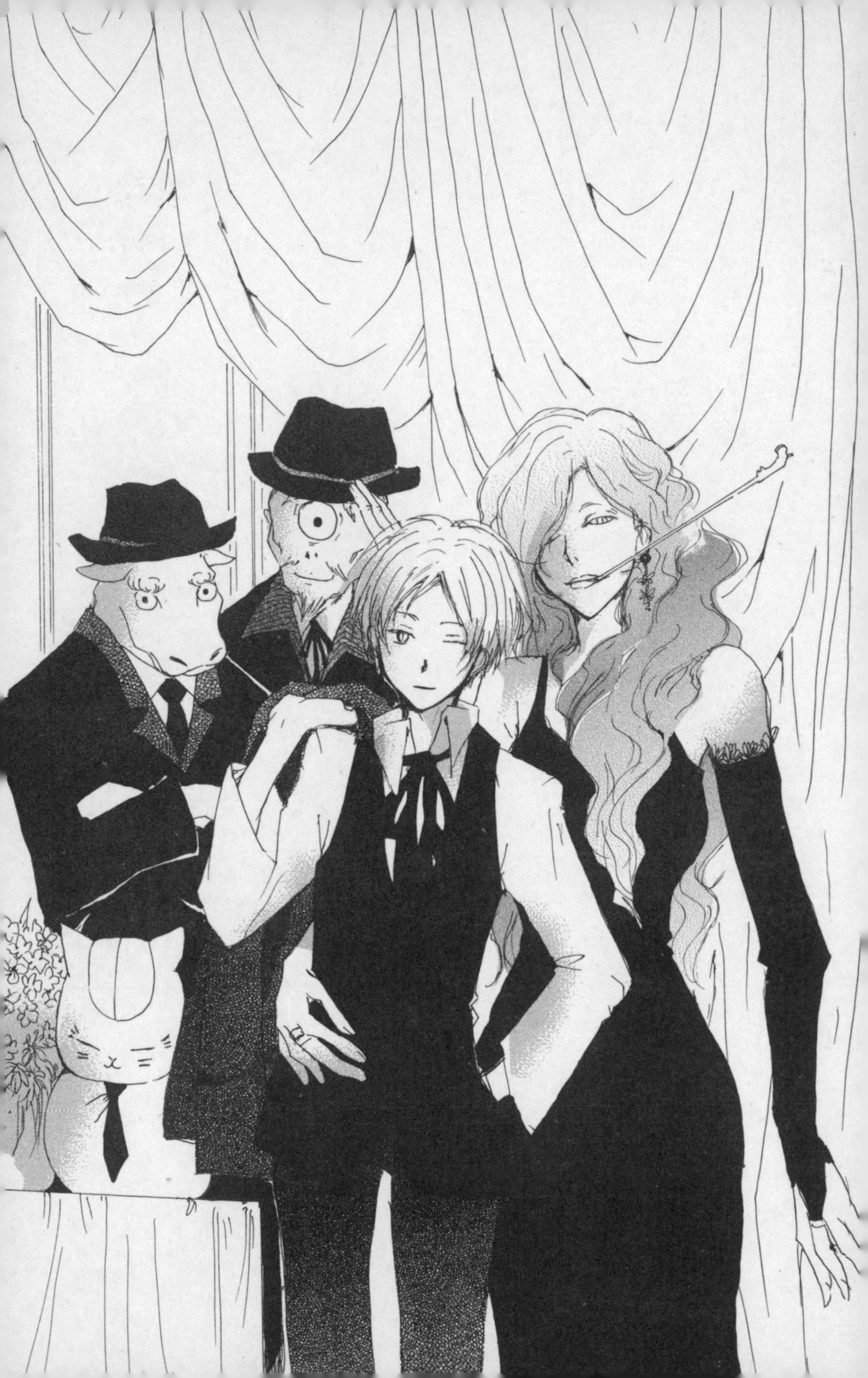

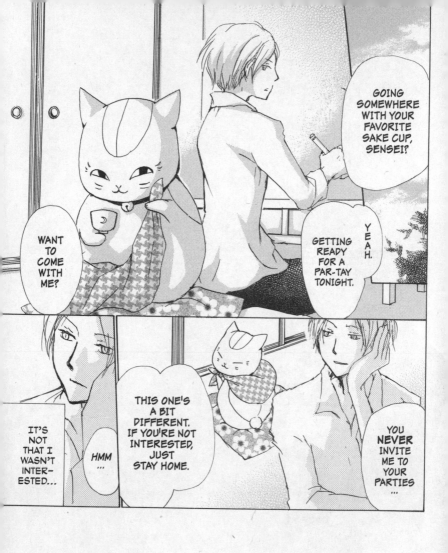

GOING SOMEWHERE WITH YOUR FAVORITE SAKE CUP, SENSEI?
YEAH.
GETTING READY FOR A PAR-TAY TONIGHT.
WANT TO COME WITH ME?
YOU **NEVER** INVITE ME TO YOUR PARTIES...
THIS ONE'S A BIT DIFFERENT. IF YOU'RE NOT INTERESTED, JUST STAY HOME.
HMM...
IT'S NOT THAT I WASN'T INTER-ESTED...

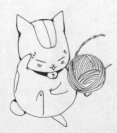

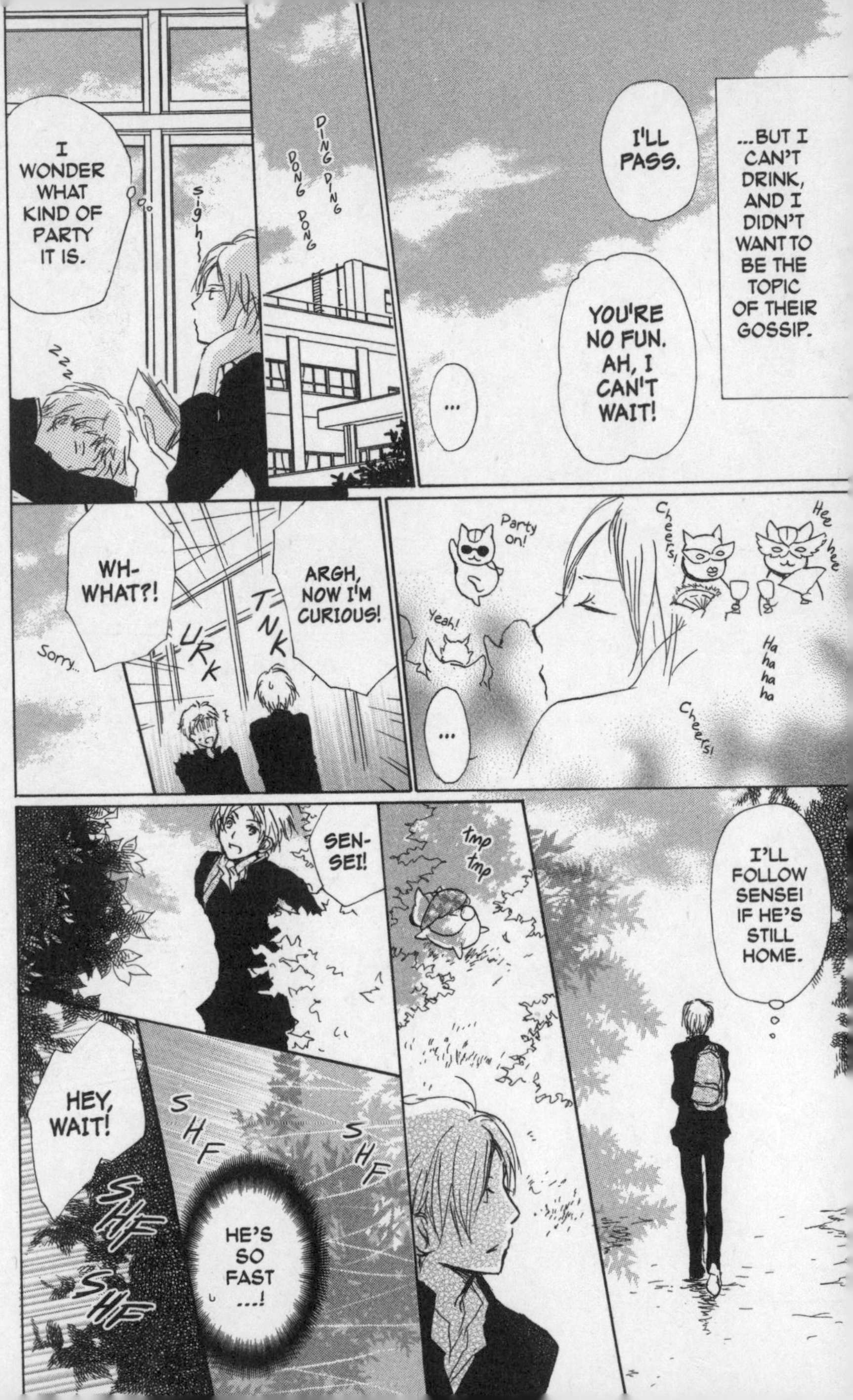
...BUT I CAN'T DRINK, AND I DIDN'T WANT TO BE THE TOPIC OF THEIR GOSSIP.
I'LL PASS.
YOU'RE NO FUN. AH, I CAN'T WAIT!
...
DING DING DONG DONG
sigh
I WONDER WHAT KIND OF PARTY IT IS.
zzz
Hee hee
Cheers!
Party on!
Yeah!
Ha ha ha ha
Cheers!
...
ARGH, NOW I'M CURIOUS!
TNK
URK
WH-WHAT?!
Sorry...
I'LL FOLLOW SENSEI IF HE'S STILL HOME.
tmp tmp
SEN-SEI!
SHF
HEY, WAIT!
SHF
SHF
SHF
HE'S SO FAST...!

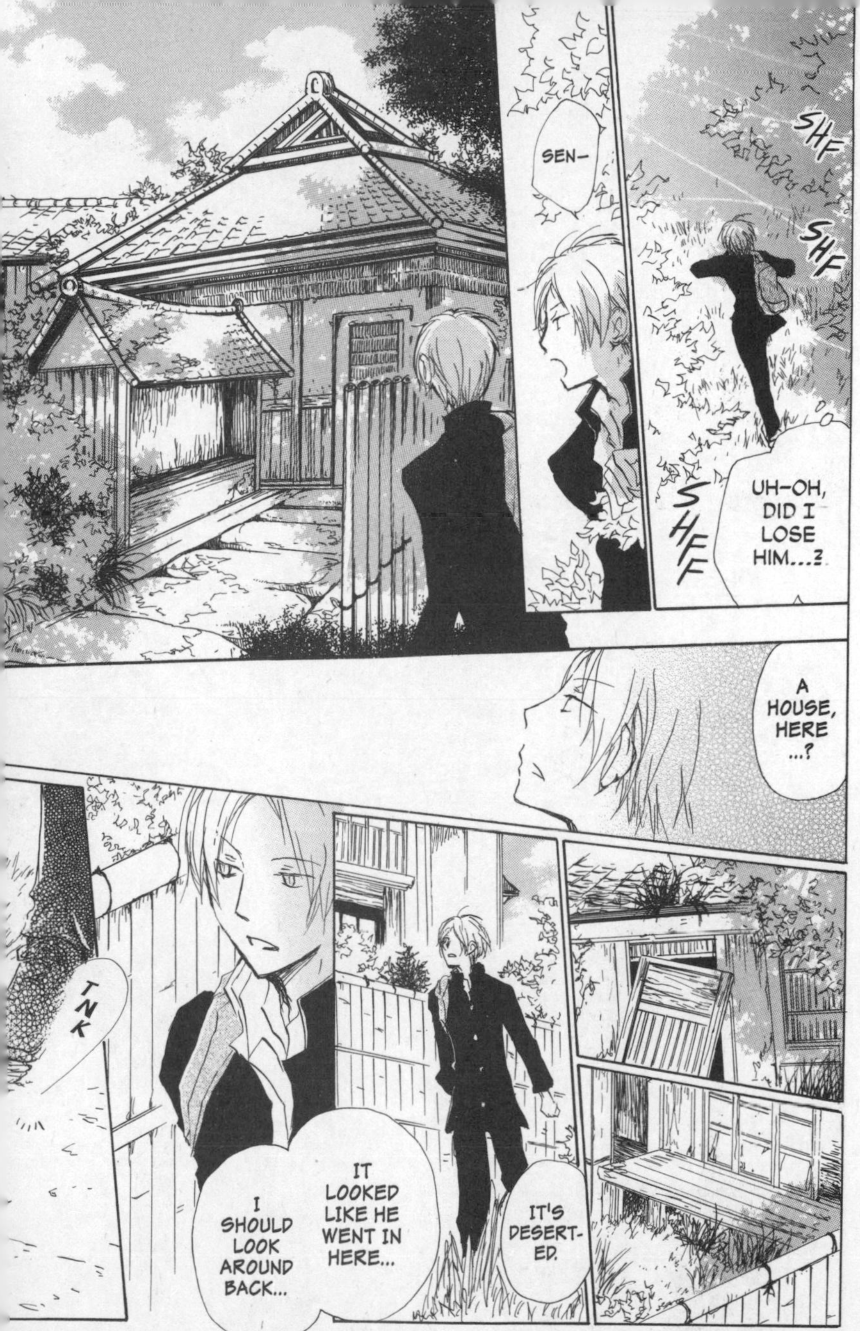
SHF
SHF
UH-OH, DID I LOSE HIM...?
SHFF
SEN-
A HOUSE, HERE ...?
IT'S DESERTED.
IT LOOKED LIKE HE WENT IN HERE...
I SHOULD LOOK AROUND BACK...
TNK

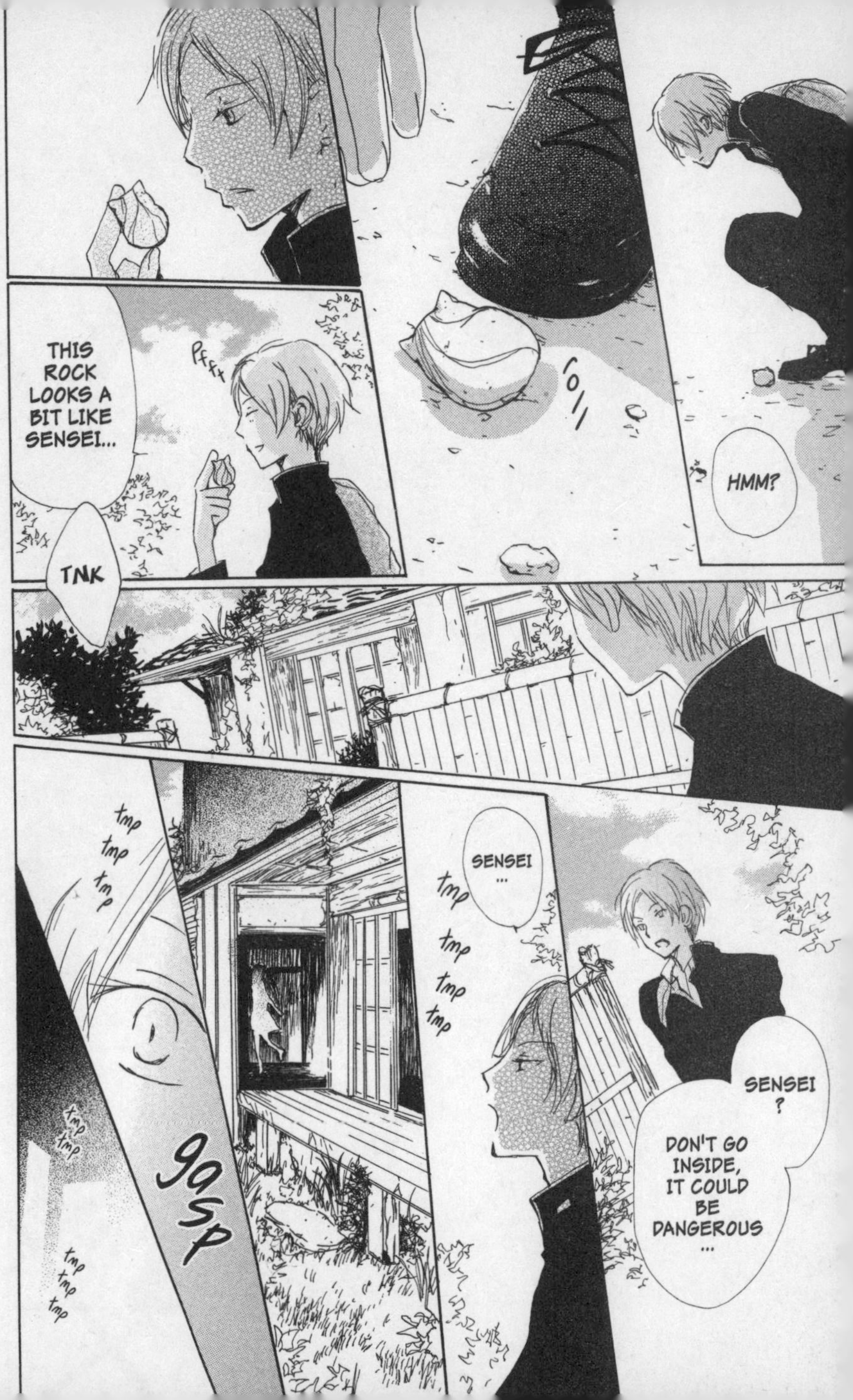

HMM?
Pffft
THIS ROCK LOOKS A BIT LIKE SENSEI...
TNK
SENSEI?
DON'T GO INSIDE, IT COULD BE DANGEROUS...
SENSEI...
tmp tmp tmp tmp
tmp tmp tmp
gasp
tmp tmp
tmp tmp tmp

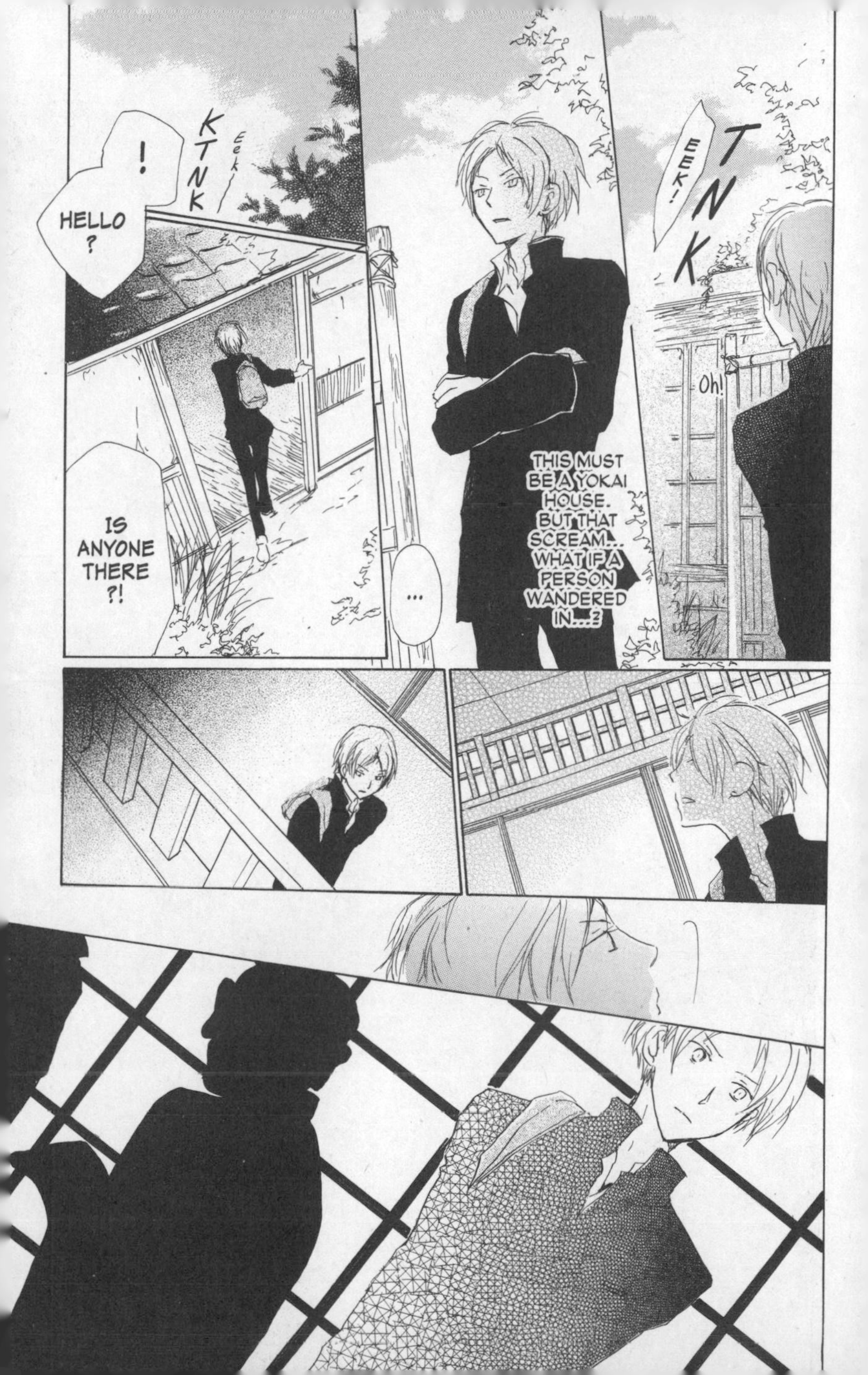
TNK
EEK!
Oh!
THIS MUST BE A YOKAI HOUSE. BUT THAT SCREAM... WHAT IF A PERSON WANDERED IN...?
...
KTNK
Eek
!
HELLO?
IS ANYONE THERE?!

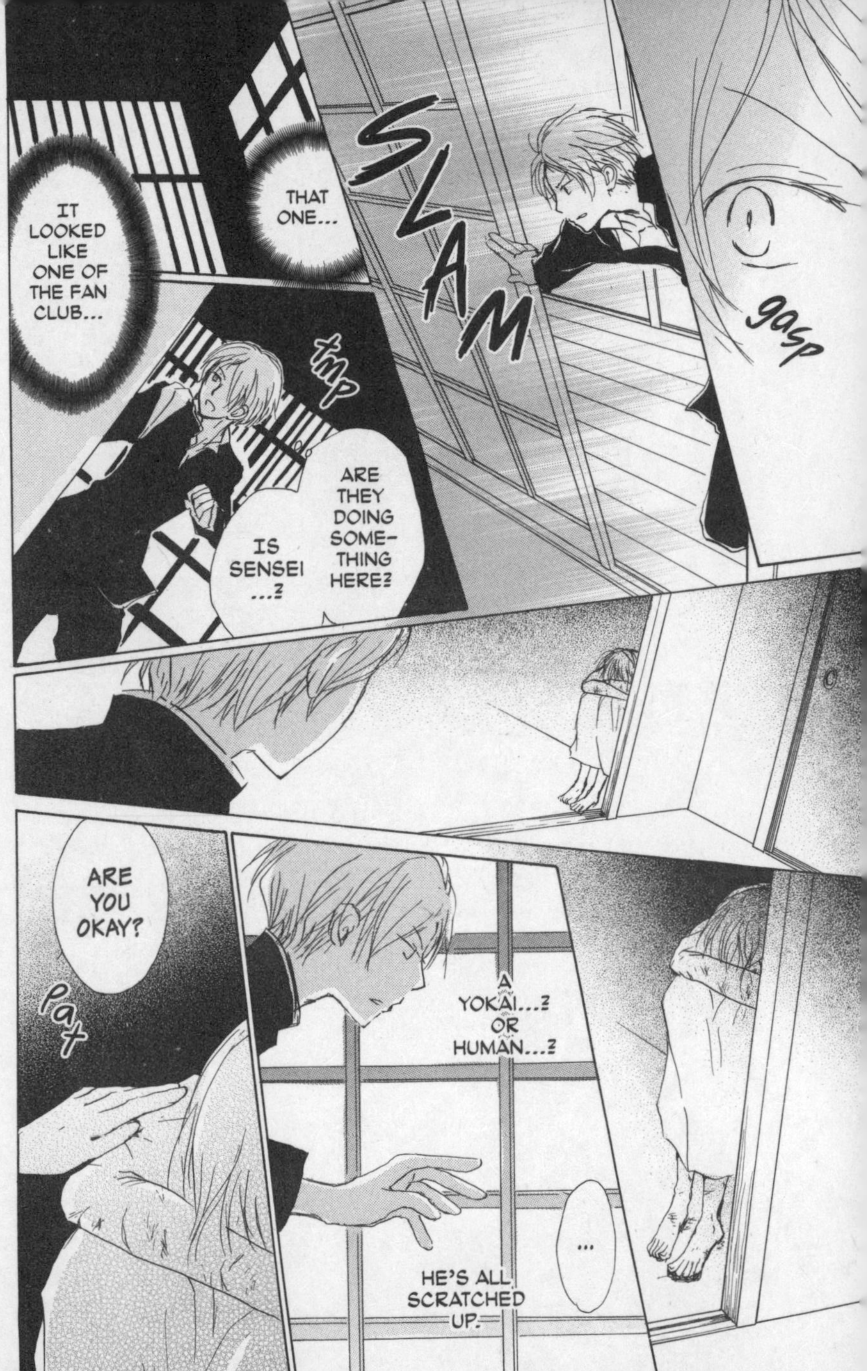
gasp
SLAM
THAT ONE...
IT LOOKED LIKE ONE OF THE FAN CLUB...
tmp
ARE THEY DOING SOME-THING HERE?
IS SENSEI...?
A YOKAI...? OR HUMAN...?
...
HE'S ALL SCRATCHED UP.
ARE YOU OKAY?
pat

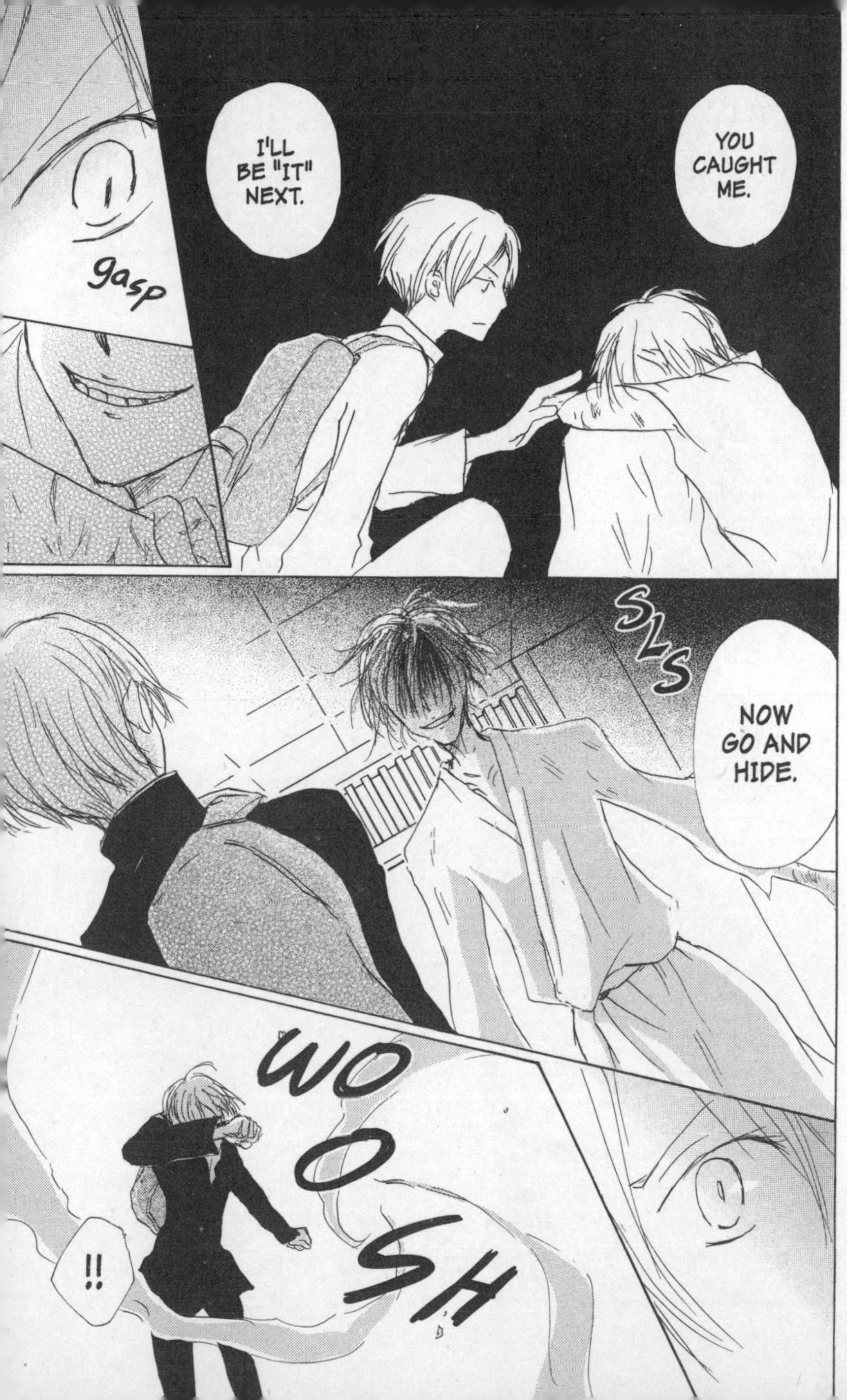
YOU CAUGHT ME.
I'LL BE "IT" NEXT.
gasp
SLS
NOW GO AND HIDE.
WOOSH
!!

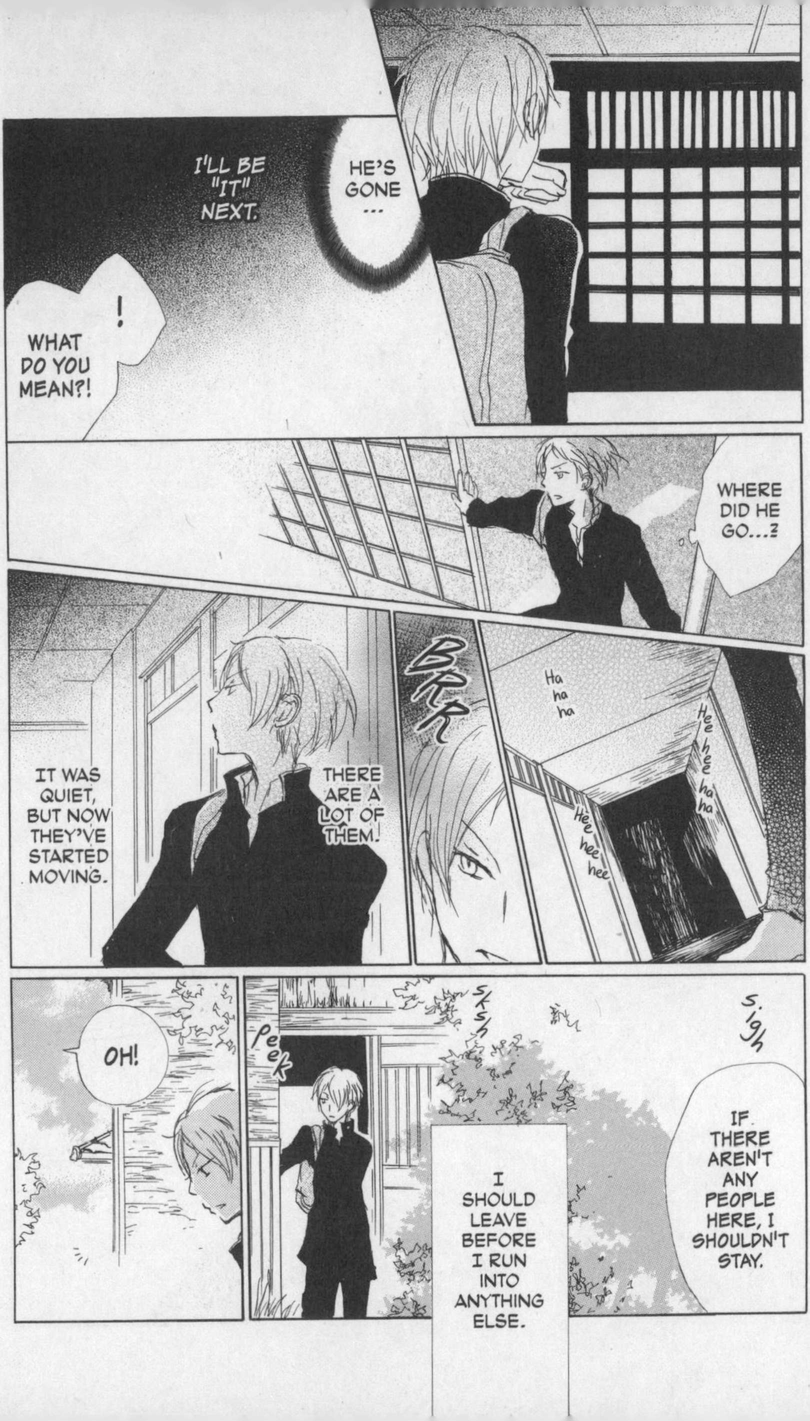
HE'S GONE ...
I'LL BE "IT" NEXT.
!
WHAT DO YOU MEAN?!
WHERE DID HE GO...?
BRR
Ha ha ha
Hee hee ha ha
Hee hee hee
THERE ARE A LOT OF THEM!
IT WAS QUIET, BUT NOW THEY'VE STARTED MOVING.
sigh
IF THERE AREN'T ANY PEOPLE HERE, I SHOULDN'T STAY.
I SHOULD LEAVE BEFORE I RUN INTO ANYTHING ELSE.
sksh
Peek
OH!

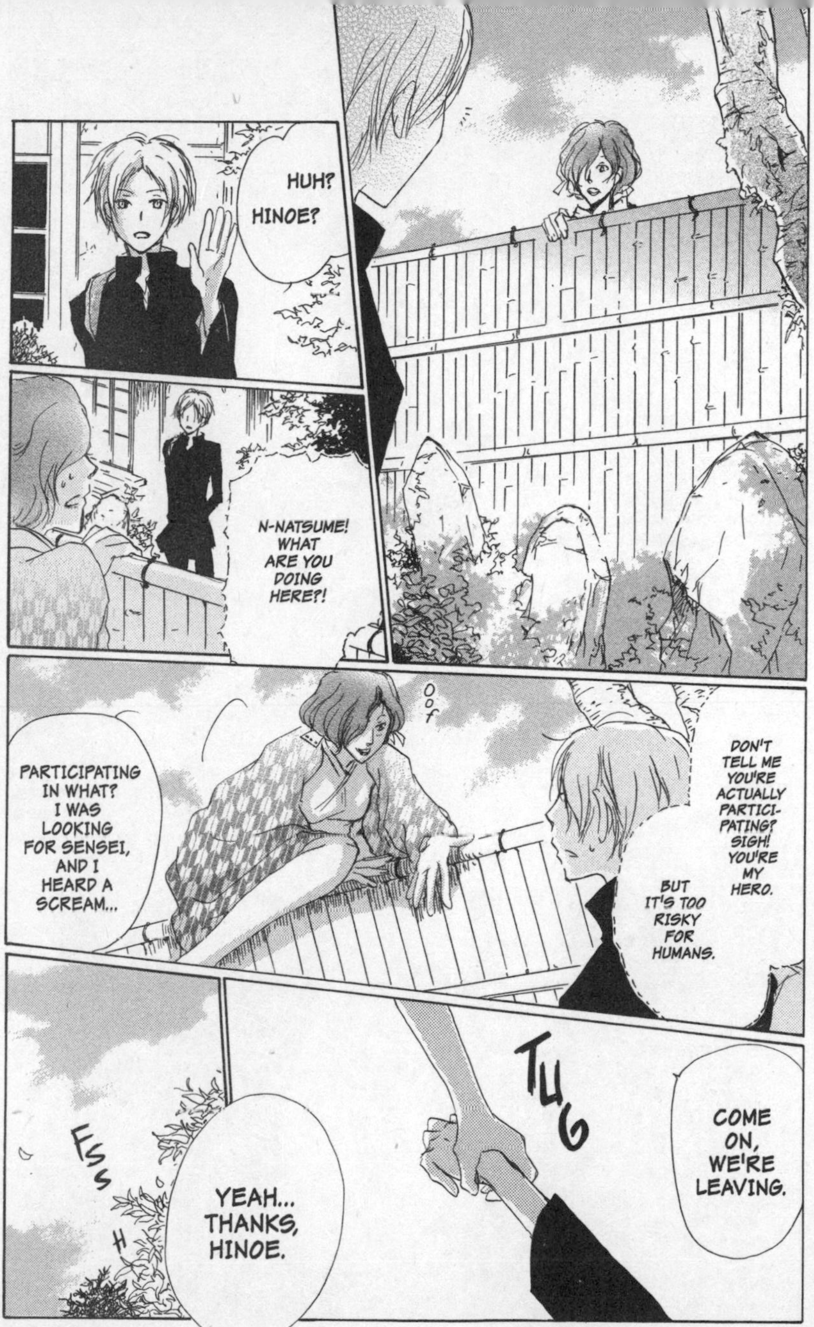
HUH?
HINOE?
N-NATSUME! WHAT ARE YOU DOING HERE?!
Oof
DON'T TELL ME YOU'RE ACTUALLY PARTICI-PATING? SIGH! YOU'RE MY HERO.
BUT IT'S TOO RISKY FOR HUMANS.
PARTICIPATING IN WHAT? I WAS LOOKING FOR SENSEI, AND I HEARD A SCREAM...
TUG
COME ON, WE'RE LEAVING.
FSSH
YEAH... THANKS, HINOE.

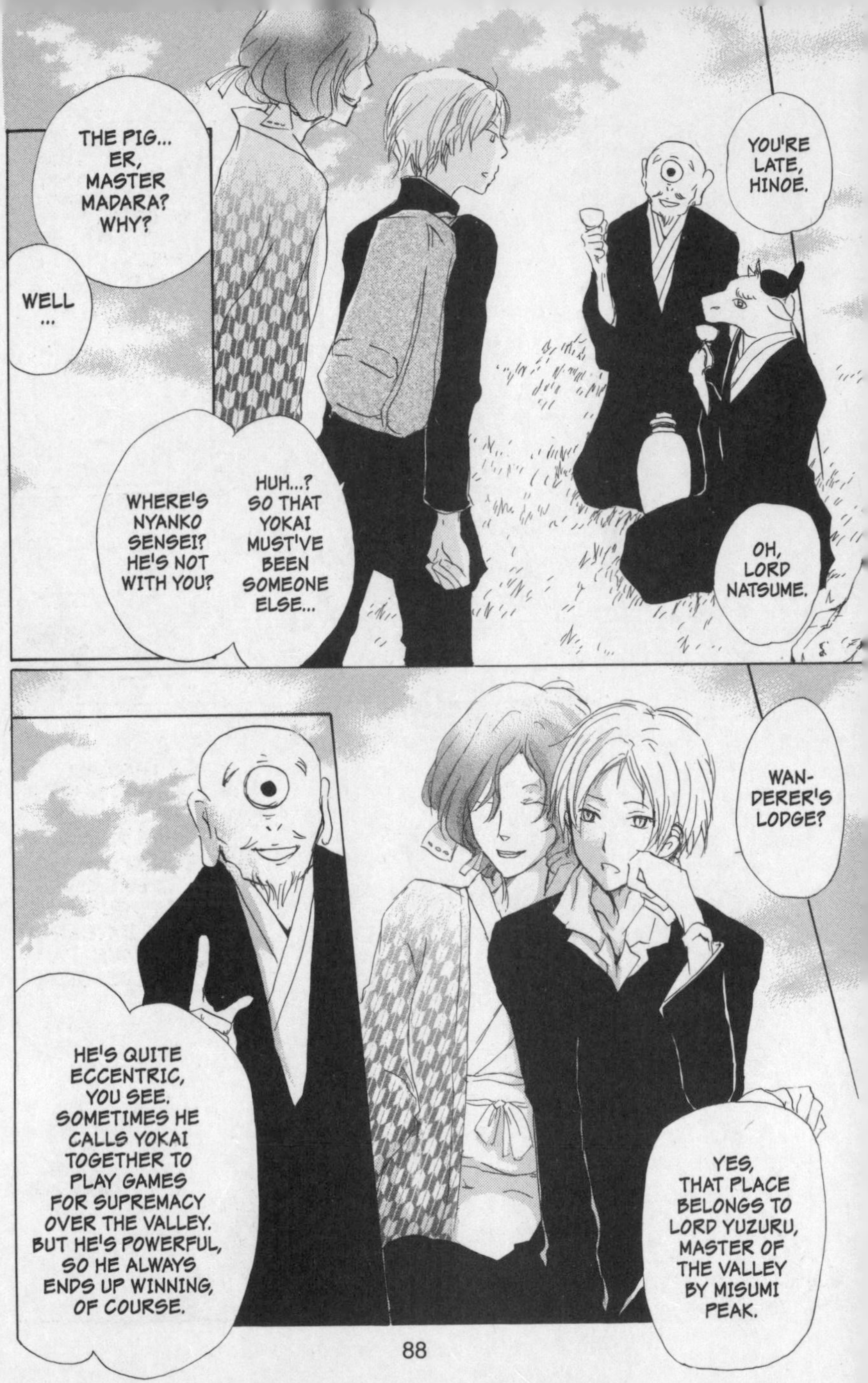
YOU'RE LATE, HINOE.
OH, LORD NATSUME.
HUH...? SO THAT YOKAI MUST'VE BEEN SOMEONE ELSE...
WHERE'S NYANKO SENSEI? HE'S NOT WITH YOU?
THE PIG... ER, MASTER MADARA? WHY?
WELL ...
WAN-DERER'S LODGE?
YES, THAT PLACE BELONGS TO LORD YUZURU, MASTER OF THE VALLEY BY MISUMI PEAK.
HE'S QUITE ECCENTRIC, YOU SEE. SOMETIMES HE CALLS YOKAI TOGETHER TO PLAY GAMES FOR SUPREMACY OVER THE VALLEY. BUT HE'S POWERFUL, SO HE ALWAYS ENDS UP WINNING, OF COURSE.

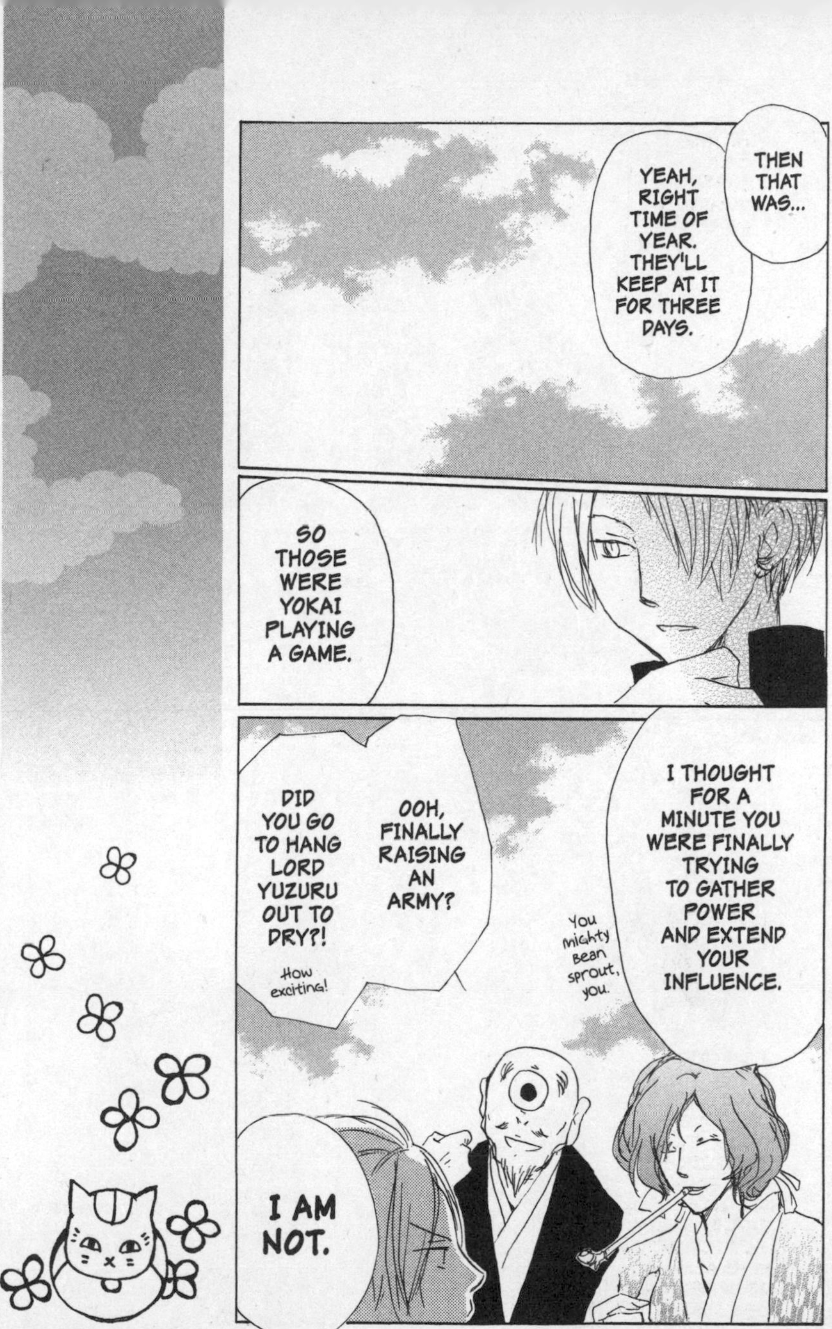
THEN THAT WAS...
YEAH, RIGHT TIME OF YEAR. THEY'LL KEEP AT IT FOR THREE DAYS.
SO THOSE WERE YOKAI PLAYING A GAME.
I THOUGHT FOR A MINUTE YOU WERE FINALLY TRYING TO GATHER POWER AND EXTEND YOUR INFLUENCE.
You mighty bean sprout, you.
OOH, FINALLY RAISING AN ARMY?
DID YOU GO TO HANG LORD YUZURU OUT TO DRY?!
How exciting!
I AM NOT.

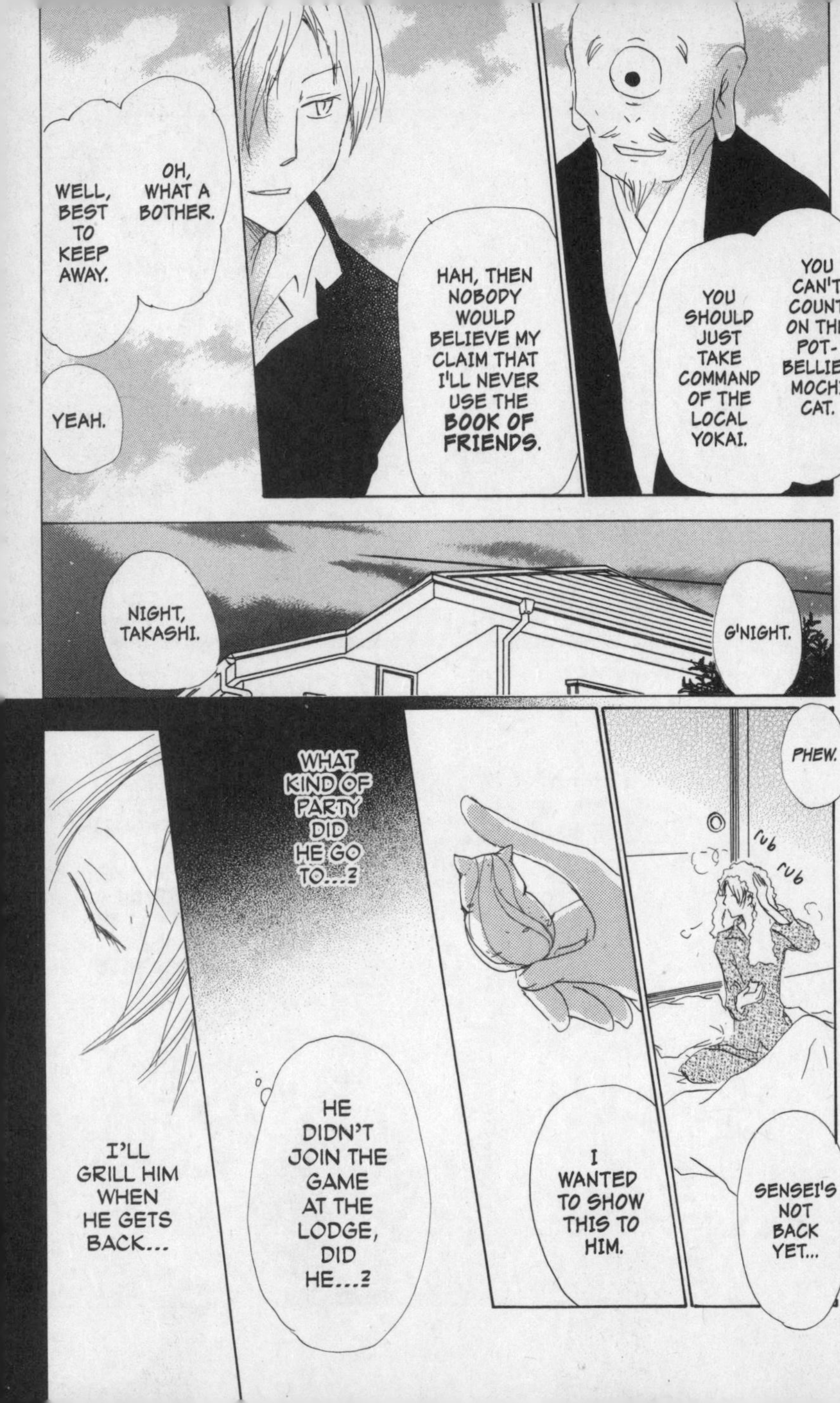
YOU CAN'T COUNT ON THE POT-BELLIED MOCHI CAT.
YOU SHOULD JUST TAKE COMMAND OF THE LOCAL YOKAI.
HAH, THEN NOBODY WOULD BELIEVE MY CLAIM THAT I'LL NEVER USE THE BOOK OF FRIENDS.
OH, WHAT A BOTHER.
WELL, BEST TO KEEP AWAY.
YEAH.
G'NIGHT.
NIGHT, TAKASHI.
PHEW.
rub rub
SENSEI'S NOT BACK YET...
I WANTED TO SHOW THIS TO HIM.
WHAT KIND OF PARTY DID HE GO TO...?
HE DIDN'T JOIN THE GAME AT THE LODGE, DID HE...?
I'LL GRILL HIM WHEN HE GETS BACK...

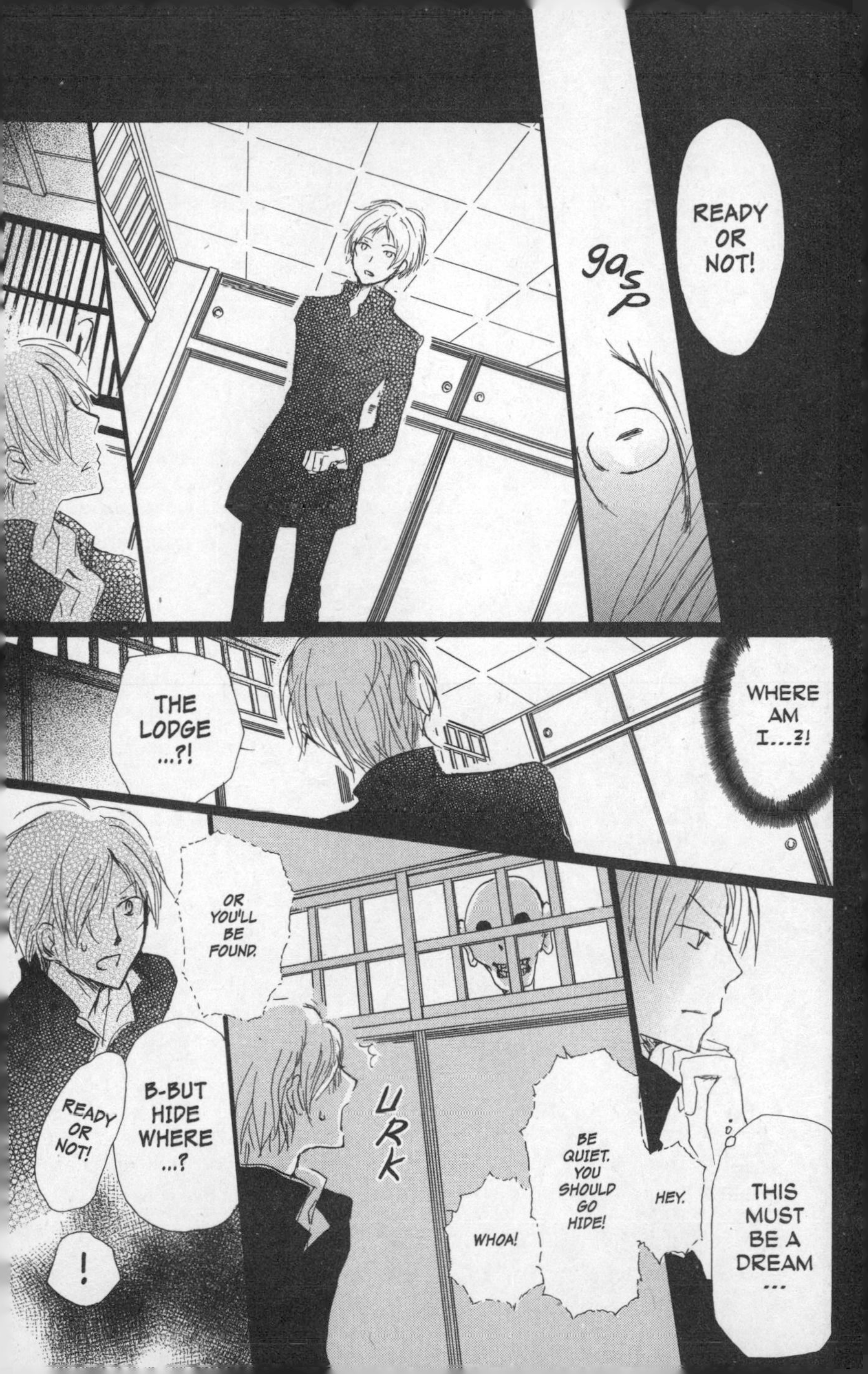
READY OR NOT!
gasp
WHERE AM I...?!
THE LODGE ...?!
THIS MUST BE A DREAM ...
HEY.
BE QUIET. YOU SHOULD GO HIDE!
WHOA!
URK
OR YOU'LL BE FOUND.
B-BUT HIDE WHERE ...?
READY OR NOT!
!

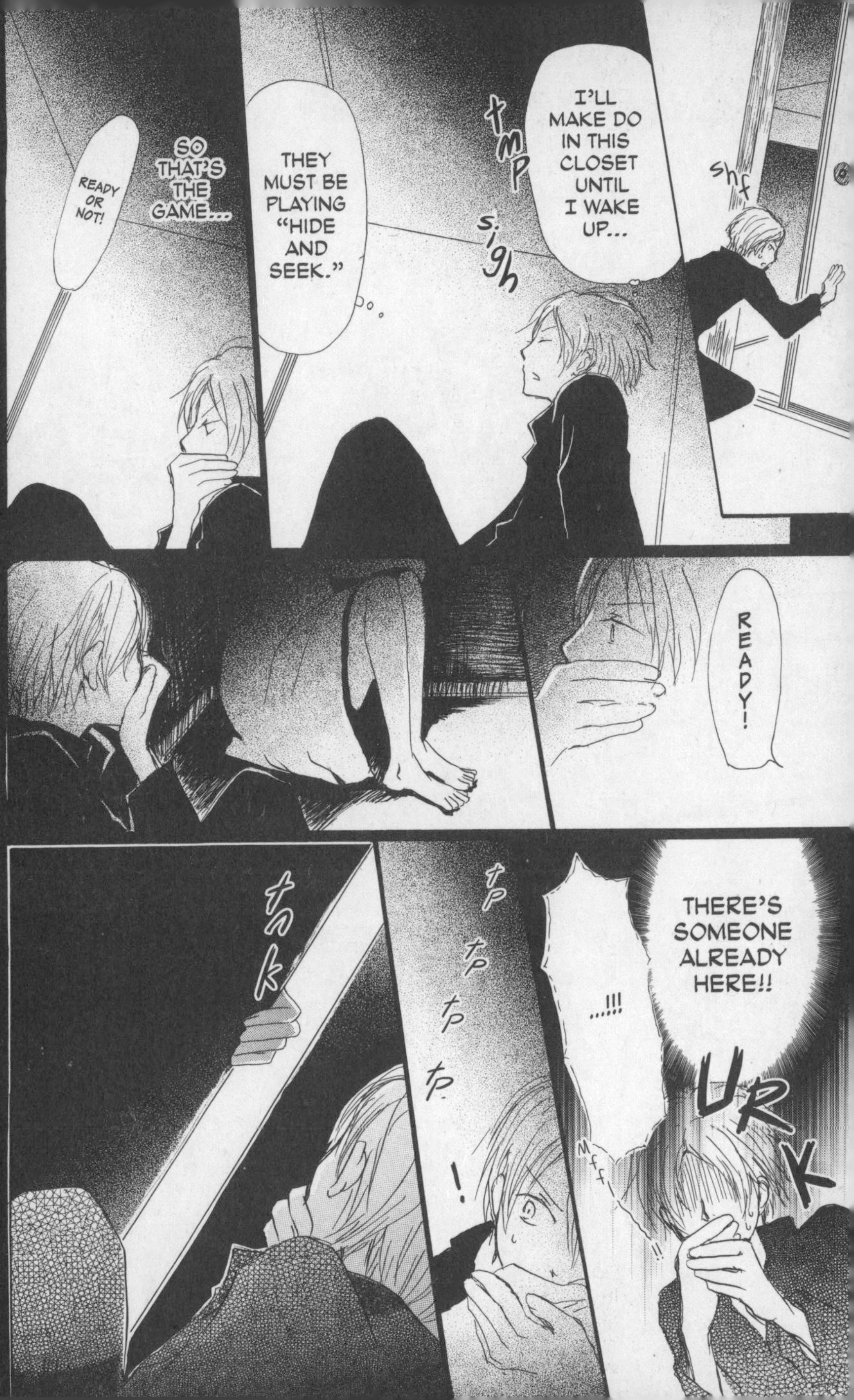
shf
I'LL MAKE DO IN THIS CLOSET UNTIL I WAKE UP...
tmp
sigh
THEY MUST BE PLAYING "HIDE AND SEEK."
SO THAT'S THE GAME...
READY OR NOT!
READY!
THERE'S SOMEONE ALREADY HERE!!
URK
...!!!
Mff!!
tp tp tp tp
!
tnk

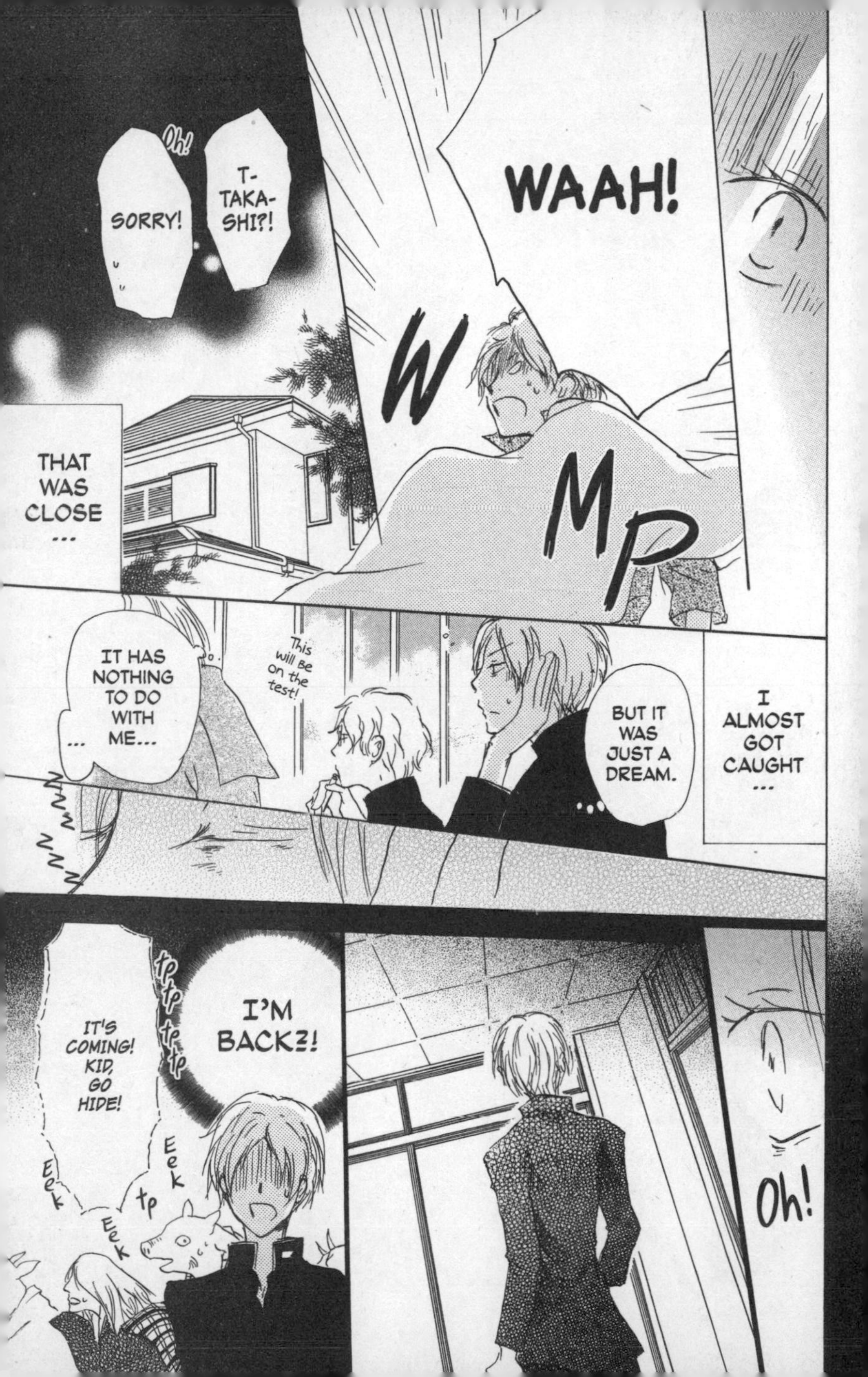
WAAH!
WMP
T-TAKASHI?!
Oh!
SORRY!
THAT WAS CLOSE...
I ALMOST GOT CAUGHT...
BUT IT WAS JUST A DREAM.
This will be on the test!
IT HAS NOTHING TO DO WITH ME... ...
Oh!
I'M BACK~!
tp tp tp tp
IT'S COMING! KID, GO HIDE!
Eek
tp
Eek
Eek

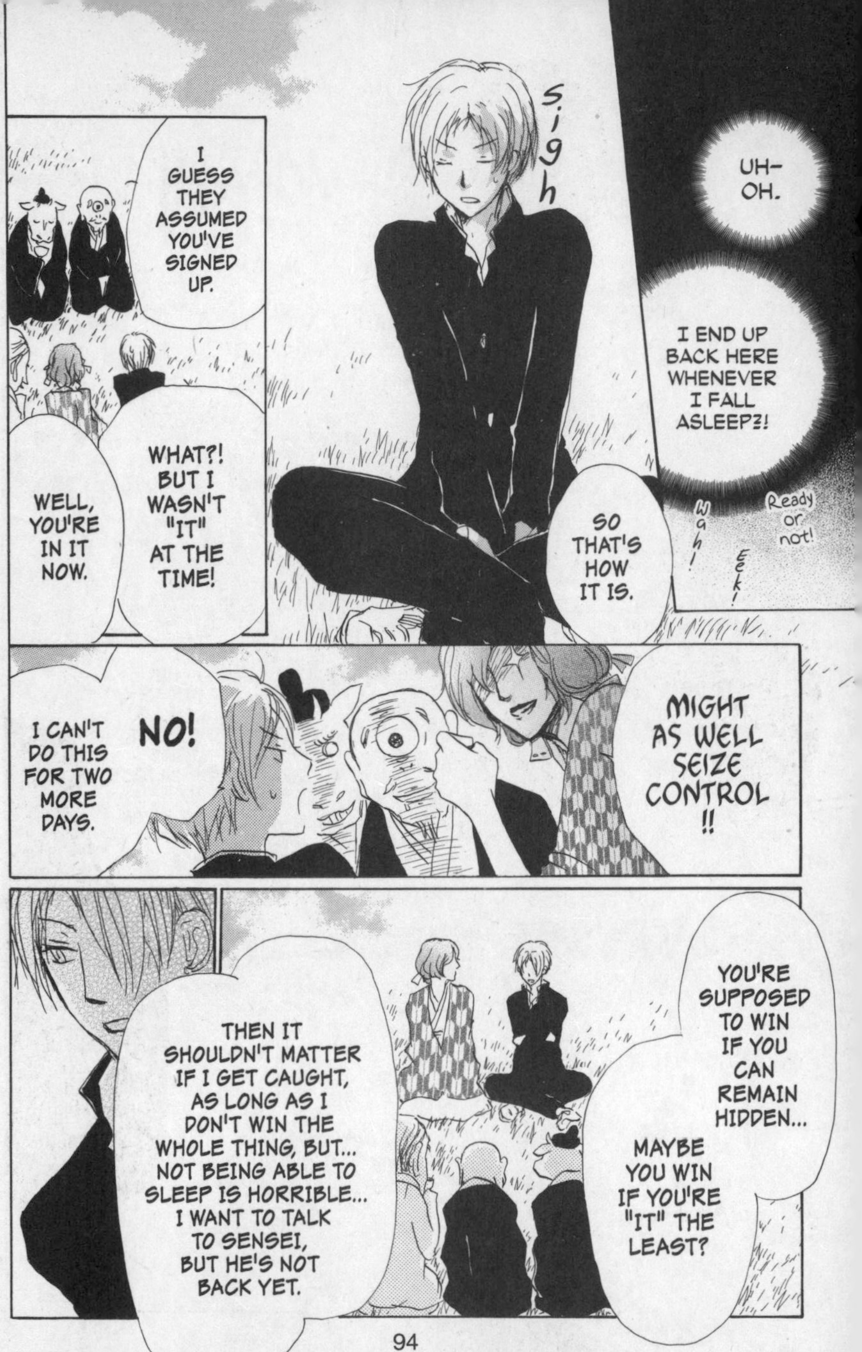
UH-OH.
I END UP BACK HERE WHENEVER I FALL ASLEEP?!
Sigh
Ready or not!
Wah!
Eek!
SO THAT'S HOW IT IS.
I GUESS THEY ASSUMED YOU'VE SIGNED UP.
WHAT?! BUT I WASN'T "IT" AT THE TIME!
WELL, YOU'RE IN IT NOW.
MIGHT AS WELL SEIZE CONTROL!!
NO!
I CAN'T DO THIS FOR TWO MORE DAYS.
YOU'RE SUPPOSED TO WIN IF YOU CAN REMAIN HIDDEN...
MAYBE YOU WIN IF YOU'RE "IT" THE LEAST?
THEN IT SHOULDN'T MATTER IF I GET CAUGHT, AS LONG AS I DON'T WIN THE WHOLE THING, BUT... NOT BEING ABLE TO SLEEP IS HORRIBLE... I WANT TO TALK TO SENSEI, BUT HE'S NOT BACK YET.

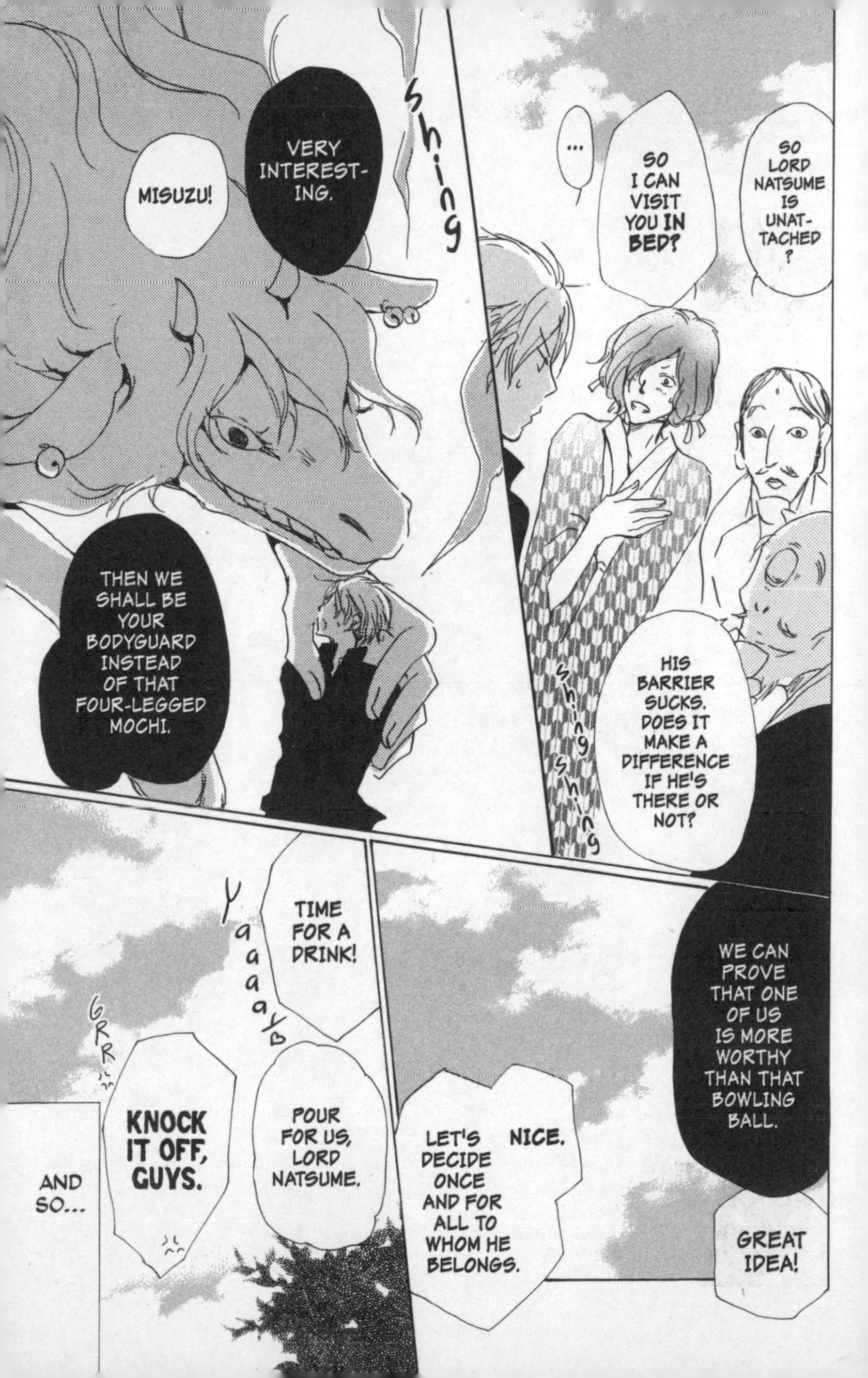
SO LORD NATSUME IS UNATTACHED?
SO I CAN VISIT YOU IN BED?
...
HIS BARRIER SUCKS. DOES IT MAKE A DIFFERENCE IF HE'S THERE OR NOT?
shing shing
shing
VERY INTERESTING.
MISUZU!
THEN WE SHALL BE YOUR BODYGUARD INSTEAD OF THAT FOUR-LEGGED MOCHI.
WE CAN PROVE THAT ONE OF US IS MORE WORTHY THAN THAT BOWLING BALL.
GREAT IDEA!
NICE.
LET'S DECIDE ONCE AND FOR ALL TO WHOM HE BELONGS.
TIME FOR A DRINK!
Yaaaay
POUR FOR US, LORD NATSUME.
KNOCK IT OFF, GUYS.
GRR
AND SO...

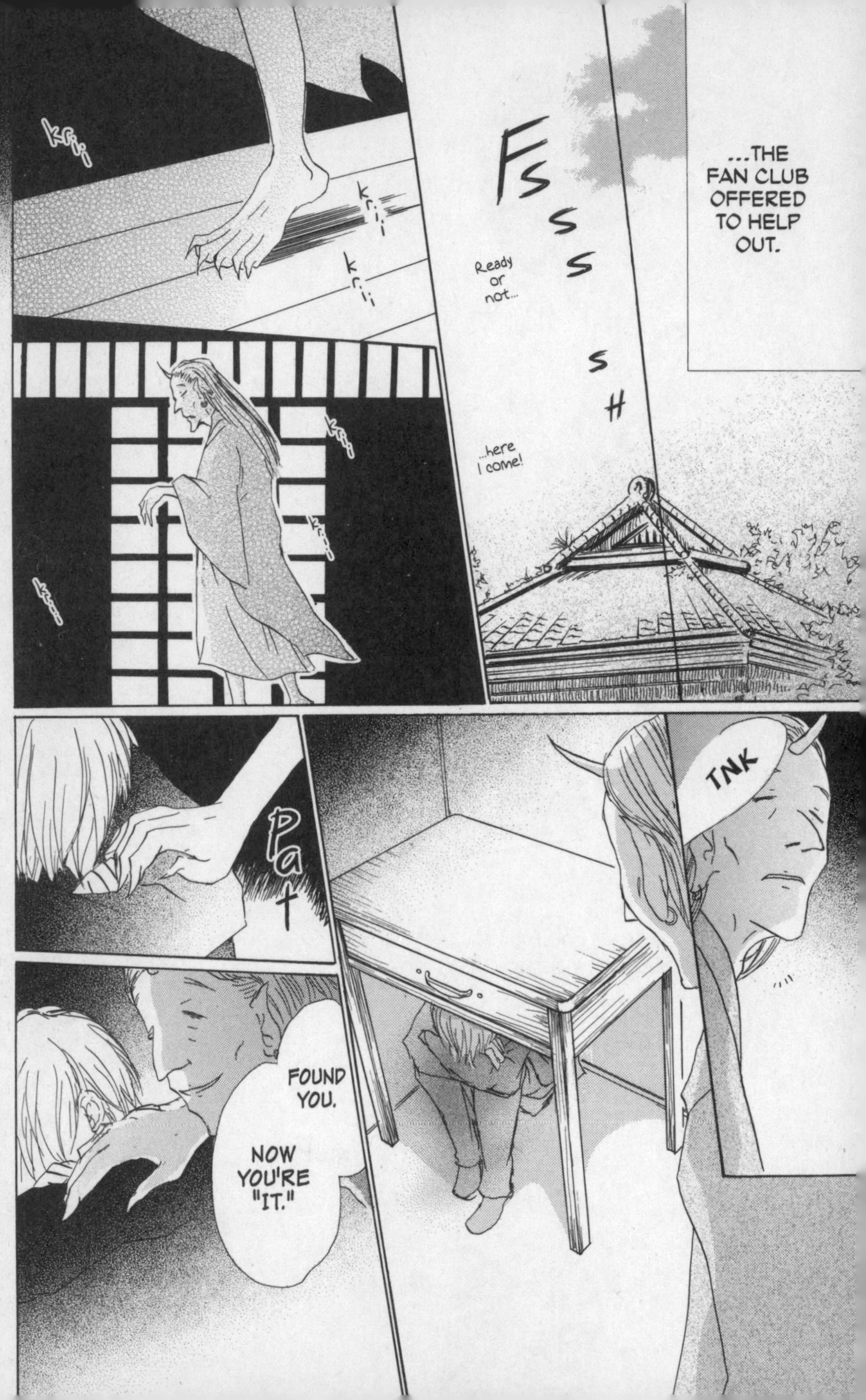
...THE FAN CLUB OFFERED TO HELP OUT.
FSSSSSH
Ready or not...
...here I come!
kri
kri
kri
kri
kri
kri
TNK
Pat
FOUND YOU.
NOW YOU'RE "IT."

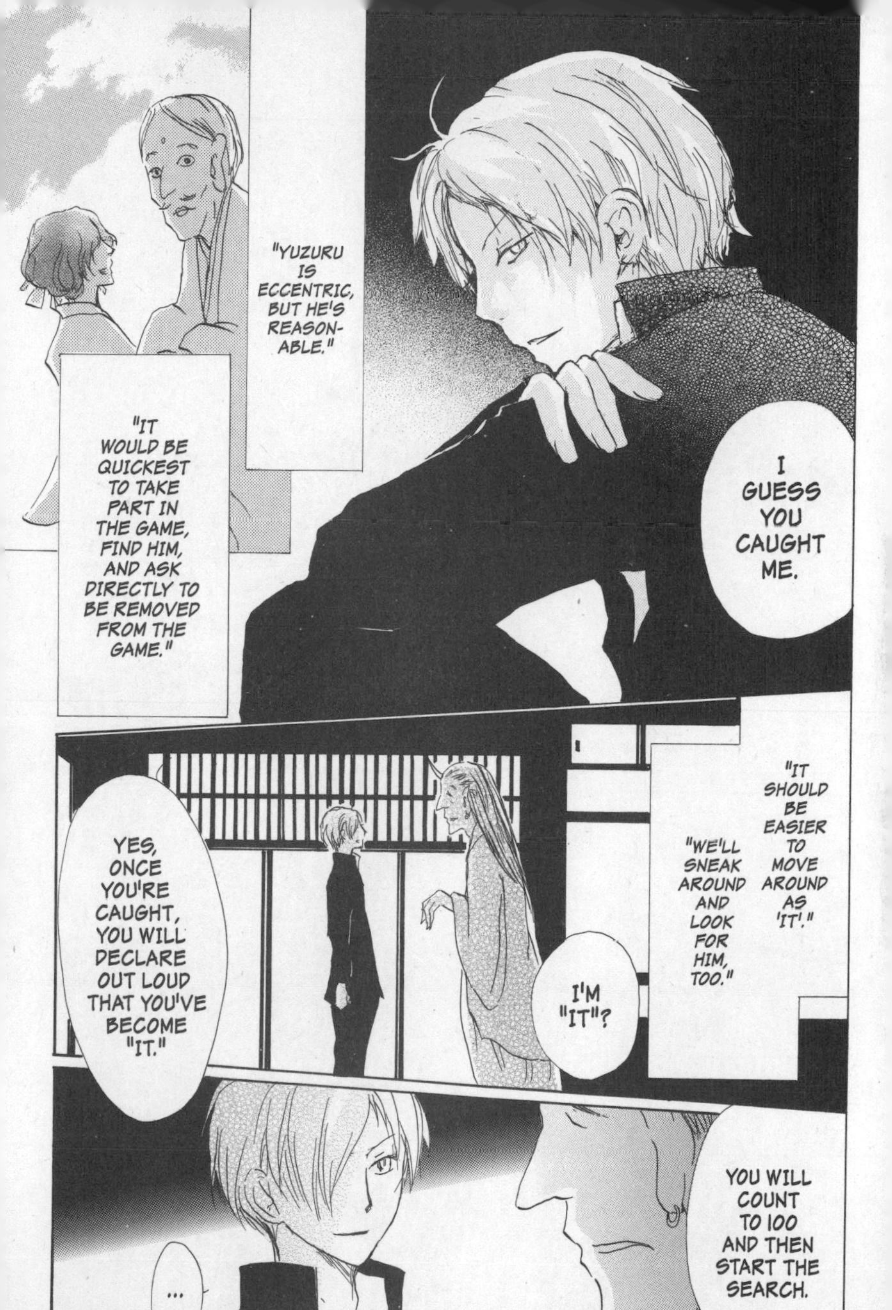
I GUESS YOU CAUGHT ME.
"YUZURU IS ECCENTRIC, BUT HE'S REASONABLE."
"IT WOULD BE QUICKEST TO TAKE PART IN THE GAME, FIND HIM, AND ASK DIRECTLY TO BE REMOVED FROM THE GAME."
"IT SHOULD BE EASIER TO MOVE AROUND AS 'IT'."
"WE'LL SNEAK AROUND AND LOOK FOR HIM, TOO."
I'M "IT"?
YES, ONCE YOU'RE CAUGHT, YOU WILL DECLARE OUT LOUD THAT YOU'VE BECOME "IT."
YOU WILL COUNT TO 100 AND THEN START THE SEARCH.
...

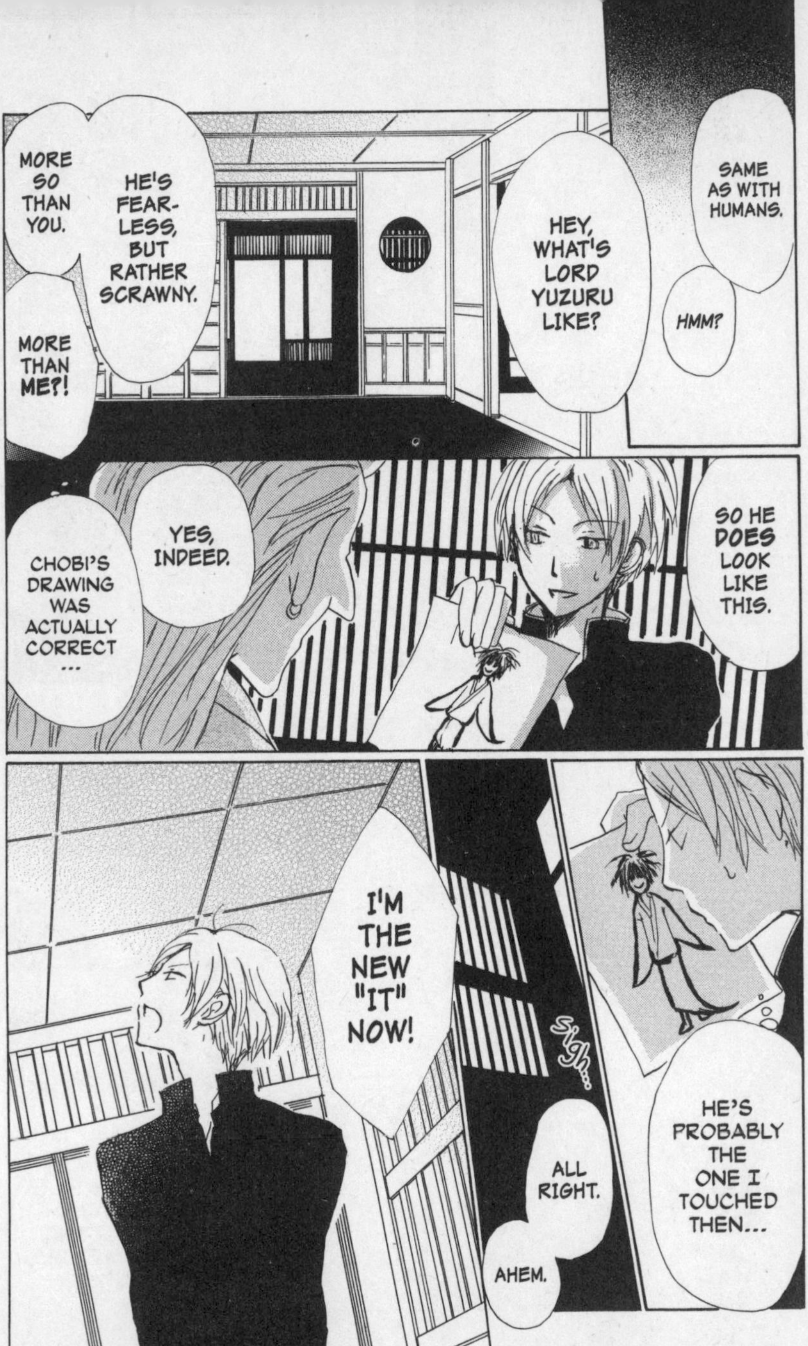
SAME AS WITH HUMANS.
HMM?
HEY, WHAT'S LORD YUZURU LIKE?
HE'S FEAR-LESS, BUT RATHER SCRAWNY.
MORE SO THAN YOU.
MORE THAN ME?!
SO HE DOES LOOK LIKE THIS.
YES, INDEED.
CHOBI'S DRAWING WAS ACTUALLY CORRECT ...
HE'S PROBABLY THE ONE I TOUCHED THEN...
sigh...
ALL RIGHT.
AHEM.
I'M THE NEW "IT" NOW!

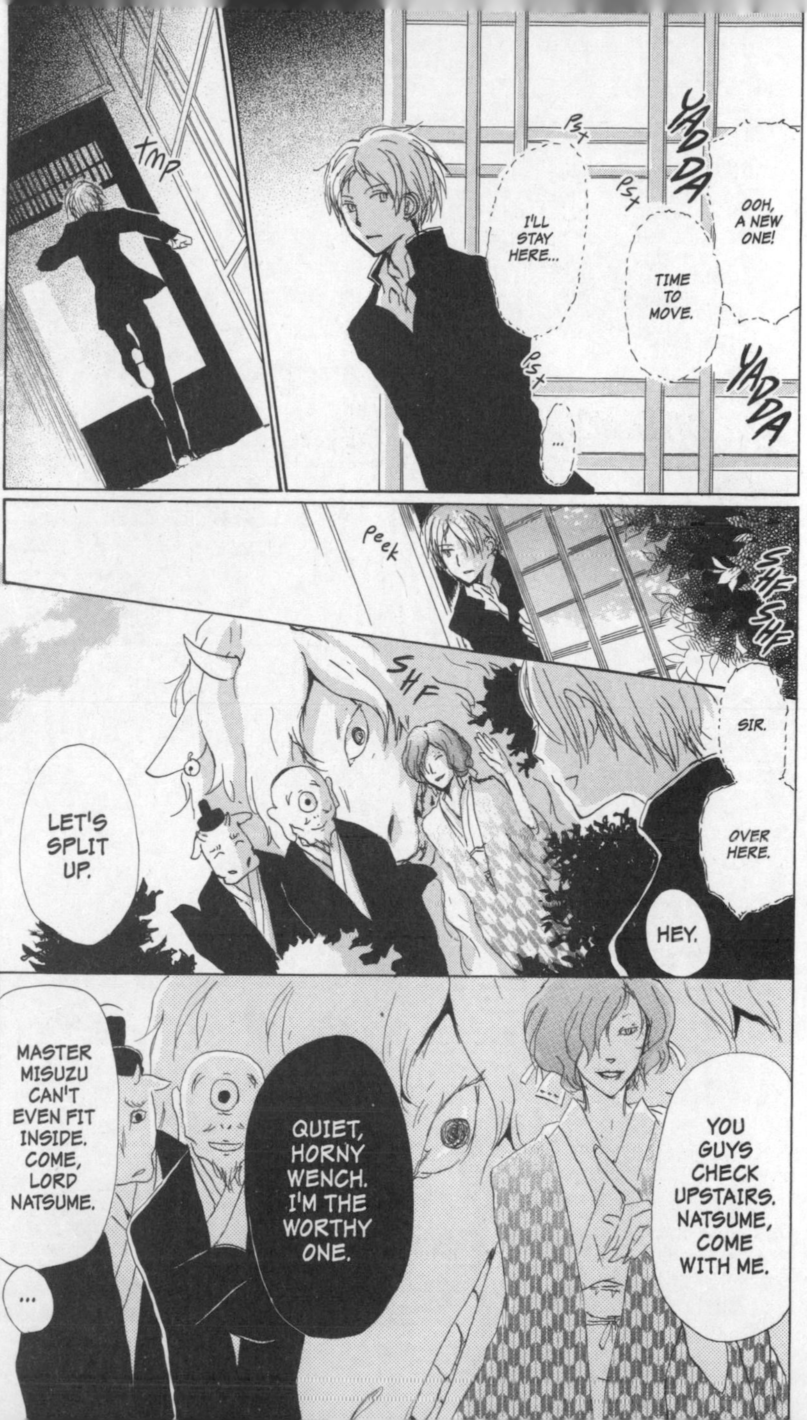
YADDA
OOH, A NEW ONE!
YADDA
Pst
TIME TO MOVE.
Pst
I'LL STAY HERE...
Pst
...
XMP
SHF SHF
Peek
SIR.
OVER HERE.
HEY.
SHF
LET'S SPLIT UP.
YOU GUYS CHECK UPSTAIRS. NATSUME, COME WITH ME.
QUIET, HORNY WENCH. I'M THE WORTHY ONE.
MASTER MISUZU CAN'T EVEN FIT INSIDE. COME, LORD NATSUME.
...

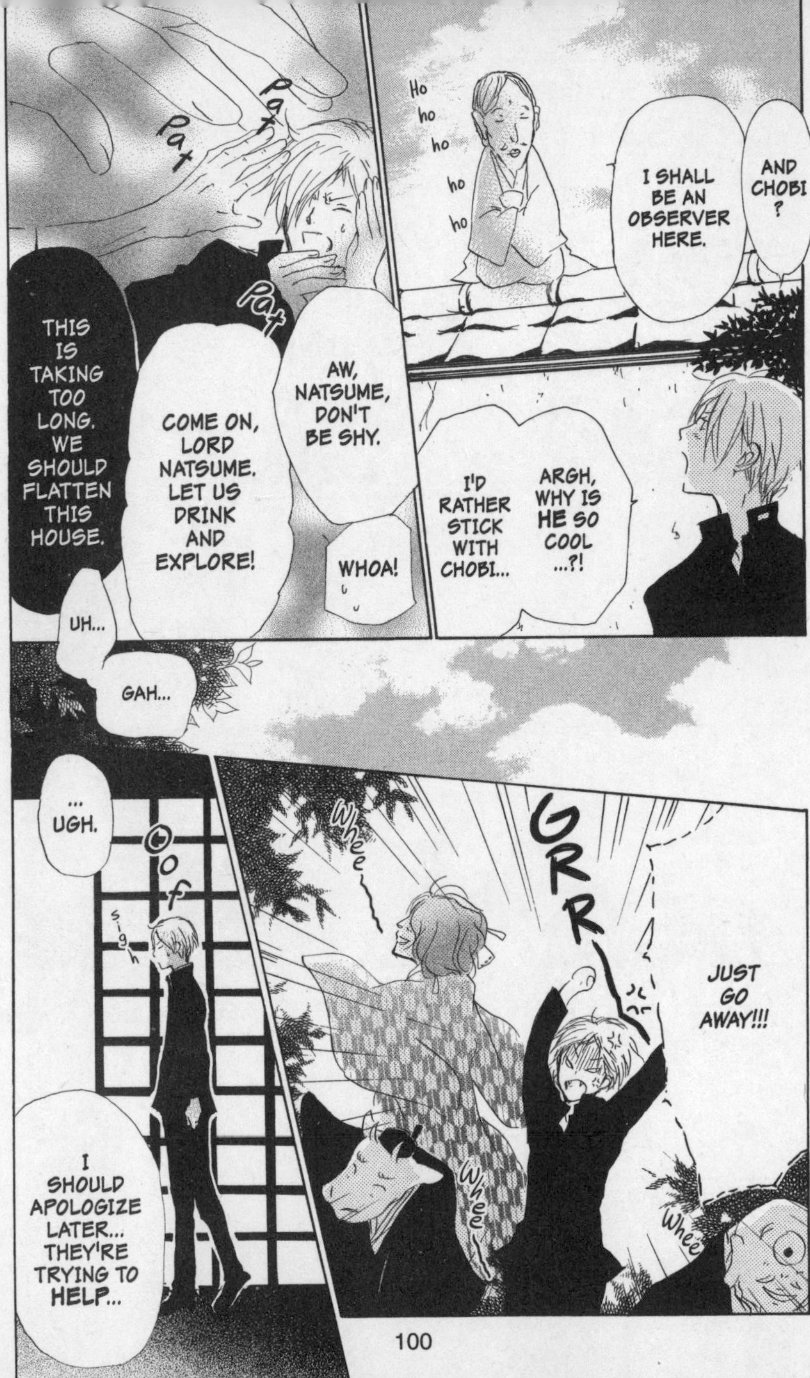
AND CHOBI ?
I SHALL BE AN OBSERVER HERE.
Ho ho ho ho ho
ARGH, WHY IS HE SO COOL ...?!
I'D RATHER STICK WITH CHOBI...
Pat Pat
AW, NATSUME, DON'T BE SHY.
Pat
WHOA!
COME ON, LORD NATSUME. LET US DRINK AND EXPLORE!
THIS IS TAKING TOO LONG. WE SHOULD FLATTEN THIS HOUSE.
UH...
GAH...
GRR
JUST GO AWAY!!!
Whee
Whee
Whee
... UGH.
Oof
sigh
I SHOULD APOLOGIZE LATER... THEY'RE TRYING TO HELP...

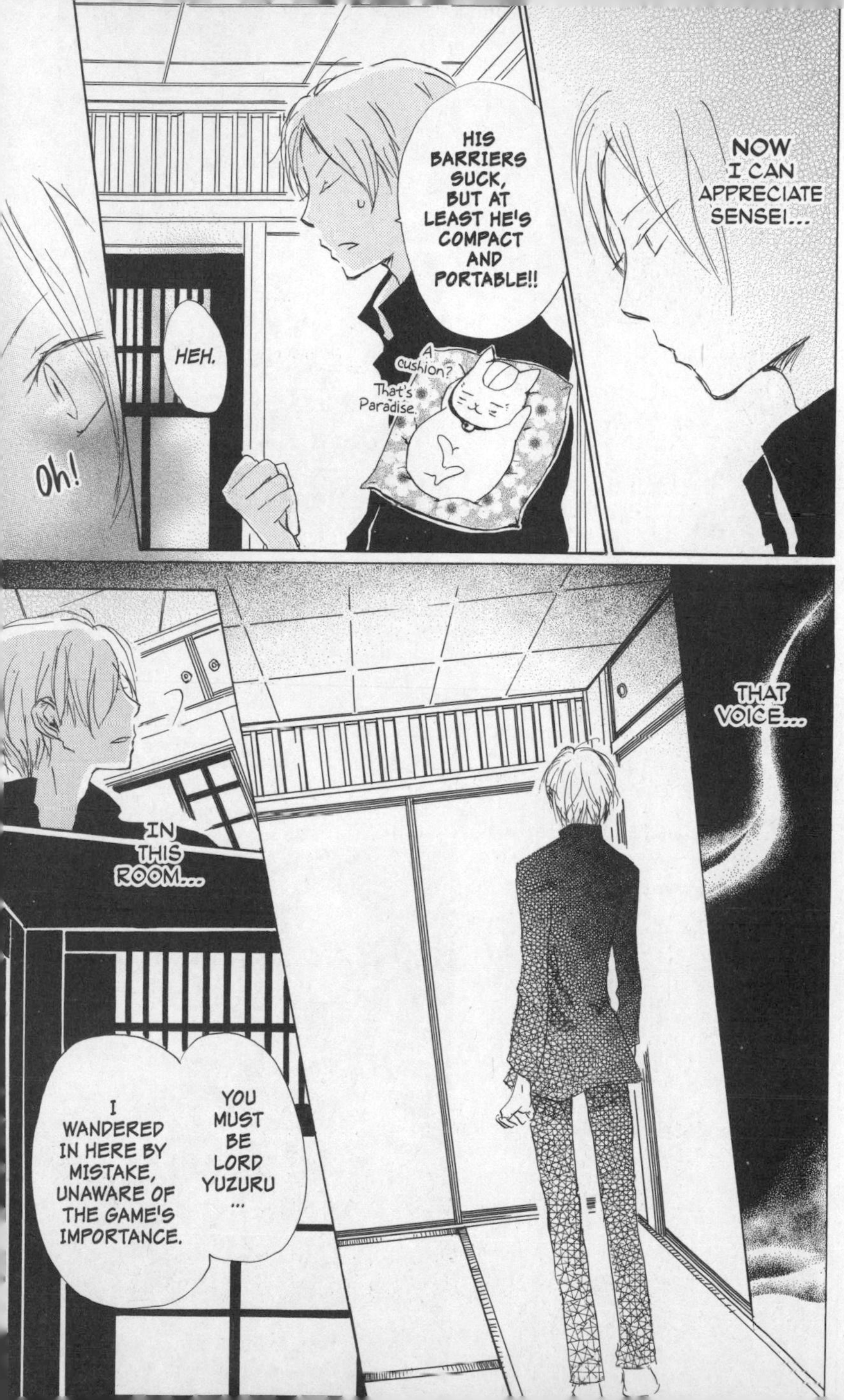
NOW I CAN APPRECIATE SENSEI...
HIS BARRIERS SUCK, BUT AT LEAST HE'S COMPACT AND PORTABLE!!
A cushion? That's Paradise.
HEH.
Oh!
THAT VOICE...
IN THIS ROOM...
YOU MUST BE LORD YUZURU...
I WANDERED IN HERE BY MISTAKE, UNAWARE OF THE GAME'S IMPORTANCE.

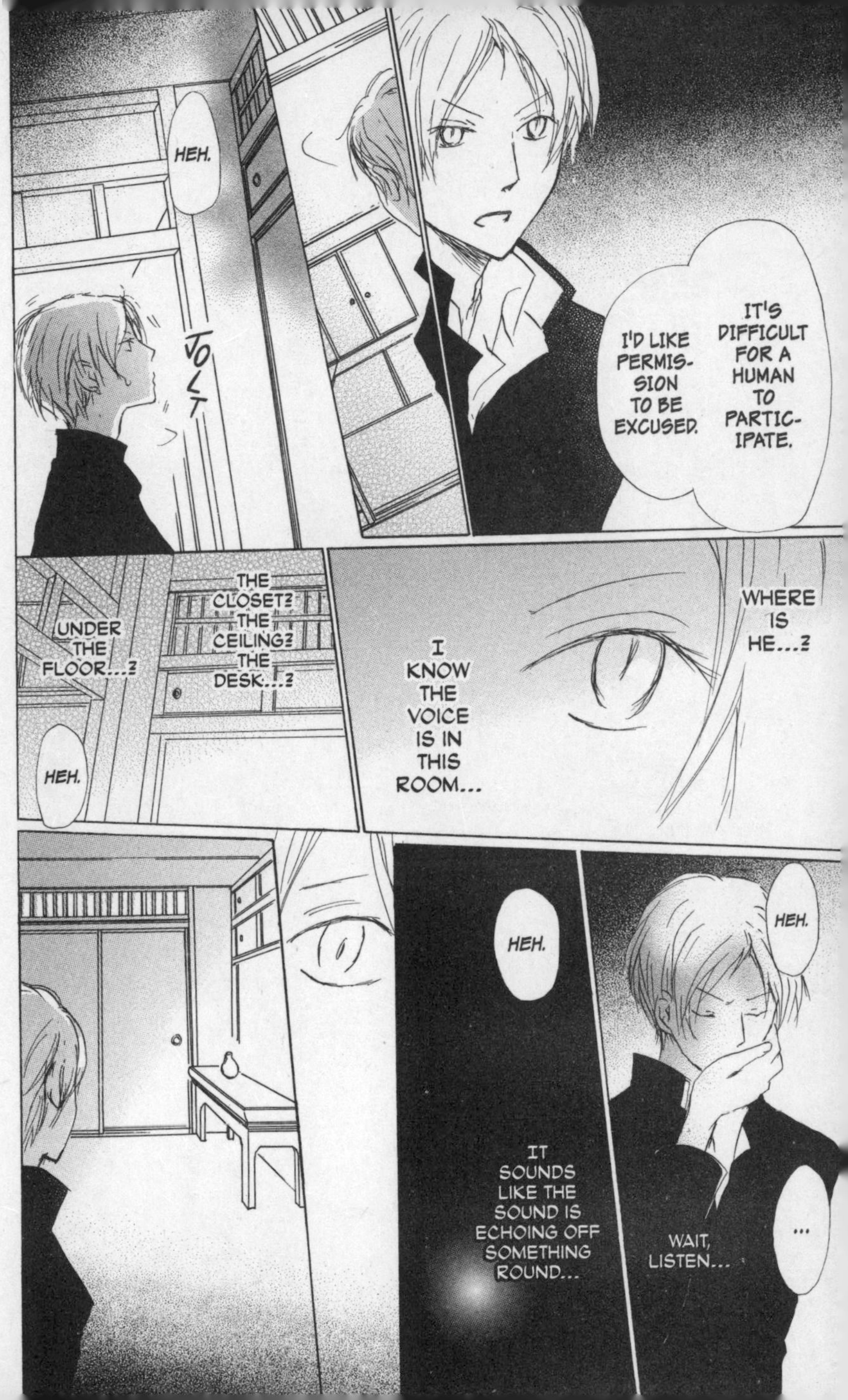
IT'S DIFFICULT FOR A HUMAN TO PARTICIPATE.
I'D LIKE PERMISSION TO BE EXCUSED.
HEH.
JOLT
WHERE IS HE...?
I KNOW THE VOICE IS IN THIS ROOM...
THE CLOSET? THE CEILING? THE DESK...?
UNDER THE FLOOR...?
HEH.
HEH.
...
WAIT, LISTEN...
HEH.
IT SOUNDS LIKE THE SOUND IS ECHOING OFF SOMETHING ROUND...

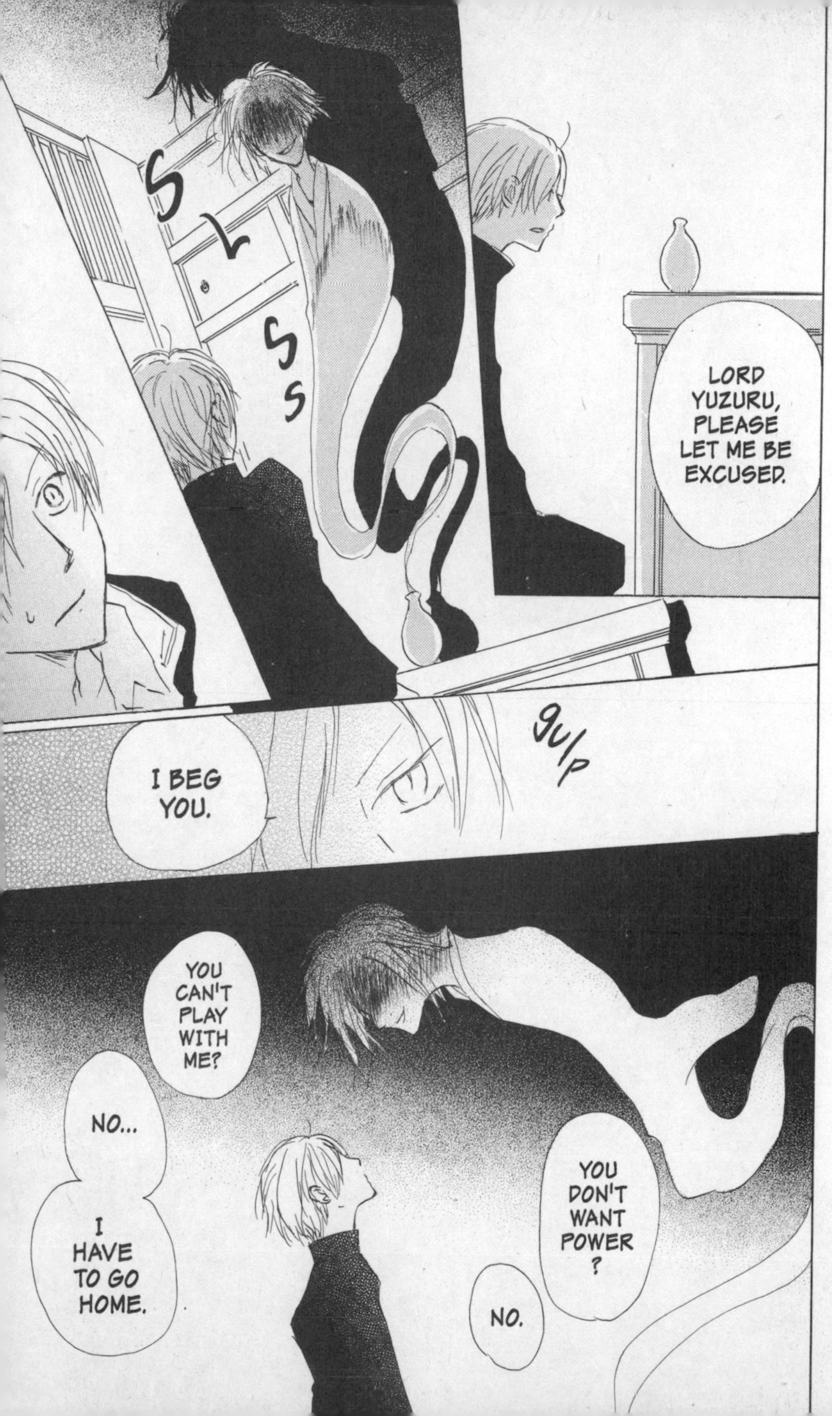
LORD YUZURU, PLEASE LET ME BE EXCUSED.
S S S
gulp
I BEG YOU.
YOU CAN'T PLAY WITH ME?
NO...
I HAVE TO GO HOME.
YOU DON'T WANT POWER?
NO.

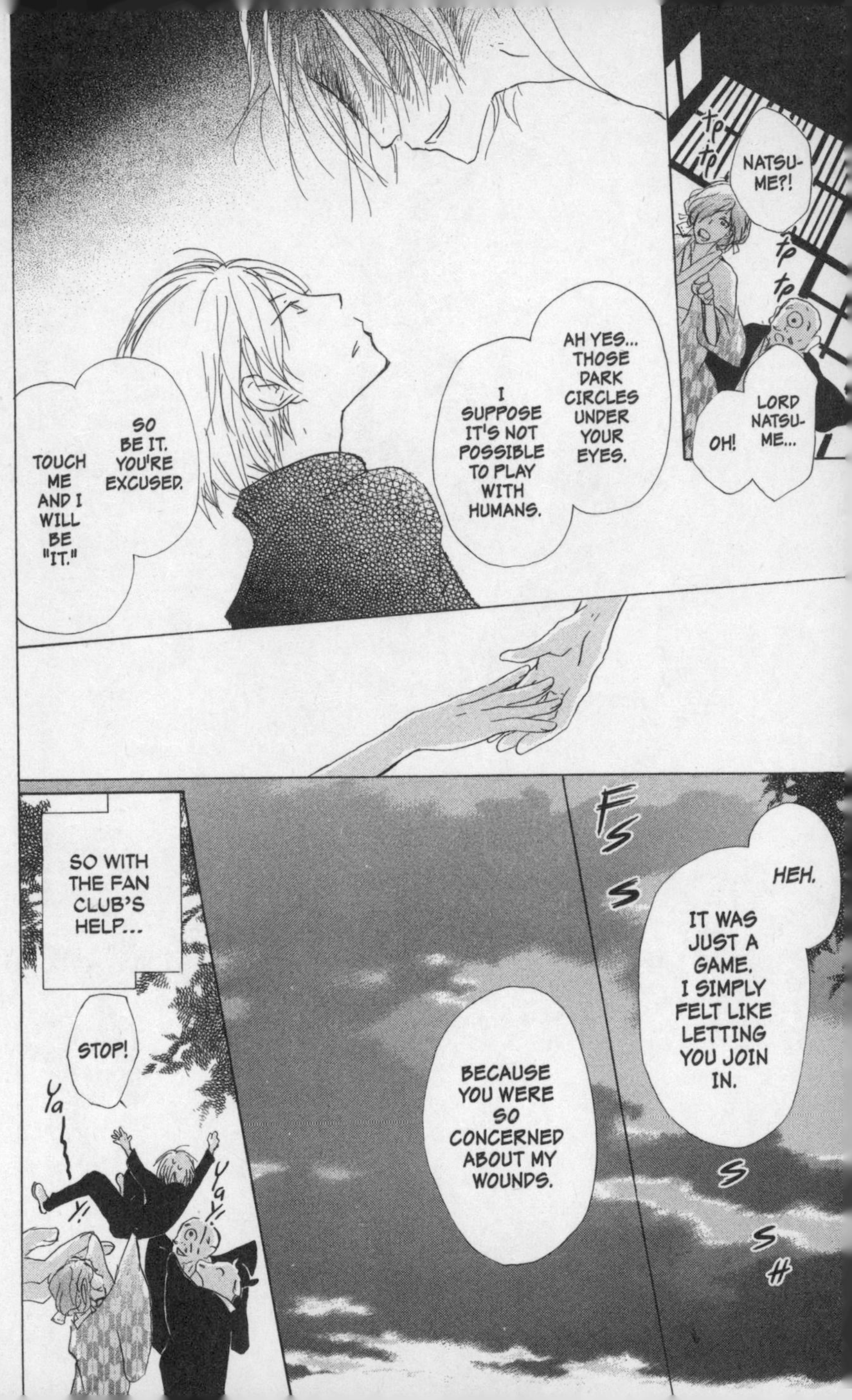
tp tp
NATSU-ME?!
tp tp
LORD NATSU-ME...
OH!
AH YES... THOSE DARK CIRCLES UNDER YOUR EYES.
I SUPPOSE IT'S NOT POSSIBLE TO PLAY WITH HUMANS.
SO BE IT. YOU'RE EXCUSED.
TOUCH ME AND I WILL BE "IT."
FSS
HEH.
IT WAS JUST A GAME. I SIMPLY FELT LIKE LETTING YOU JOIN IN.
SSSH
BECAUSE YOU WERE SO CONCERNED ABOUT MY WOUNDS.
SO WITH THE FAN CLUB'S HELP...
STOP!
Yay!
Yay!

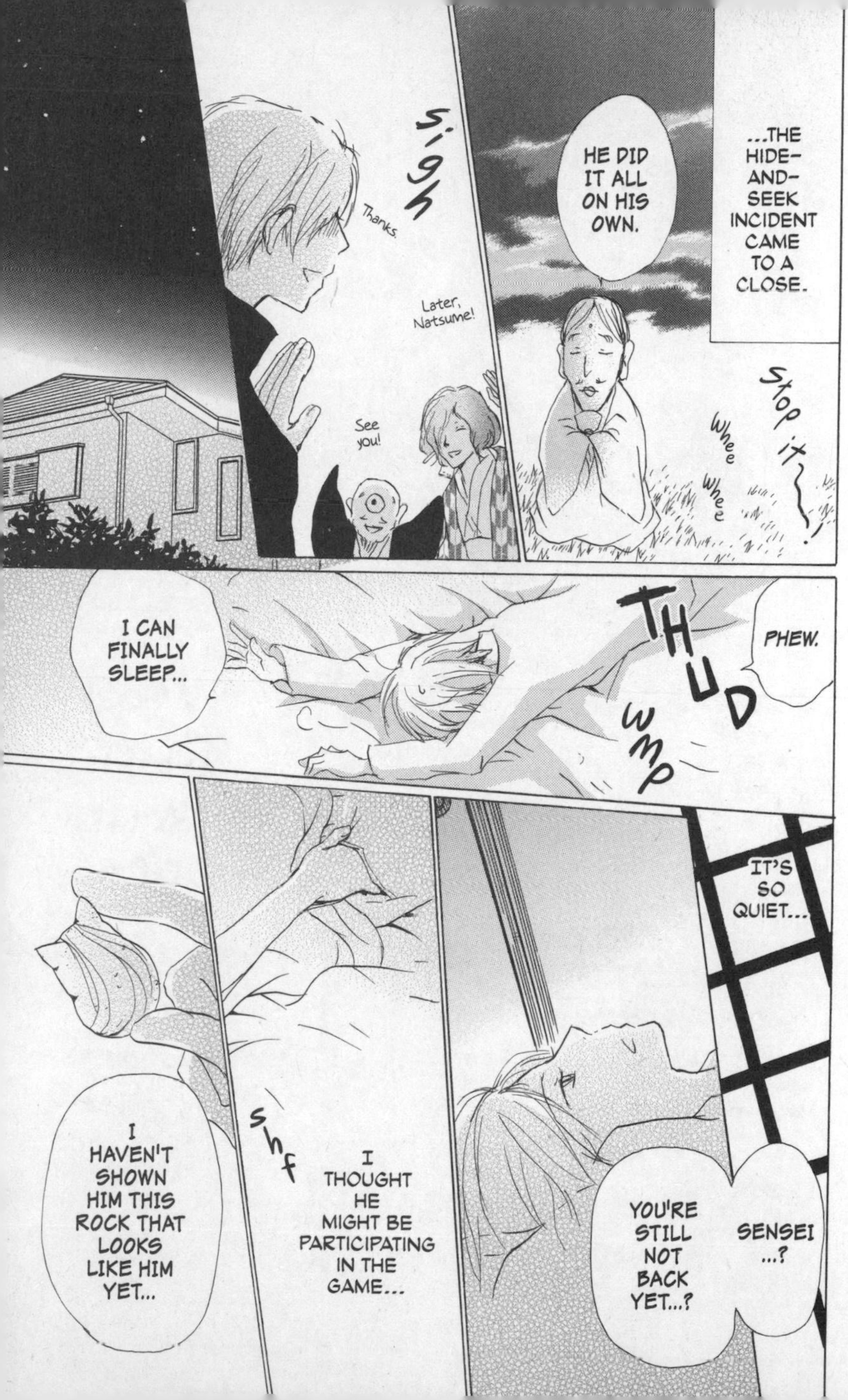
...THE HIDE-AND-SEEK INCIDENT CAME TO A CLOSE.
HE DID IT ALL ON HIS OWN.
Stop it~!
Whee whee
sigh
Thanks.
Later, Natsume!
See you!
PHEW.
THUD
WMP
I CAN FINALLY SLEEP...
IT'S SO QUIET...
SENSEI...?
YOU'RE STILL NOT BACK YET...?
shf
I THOUGHT HE MIGHT BE PARTICIPATING IN THE GAME...
I HAVEN'T SHOWN HIM THIS ROCK THAT LOOKS LIKE HIM YET...

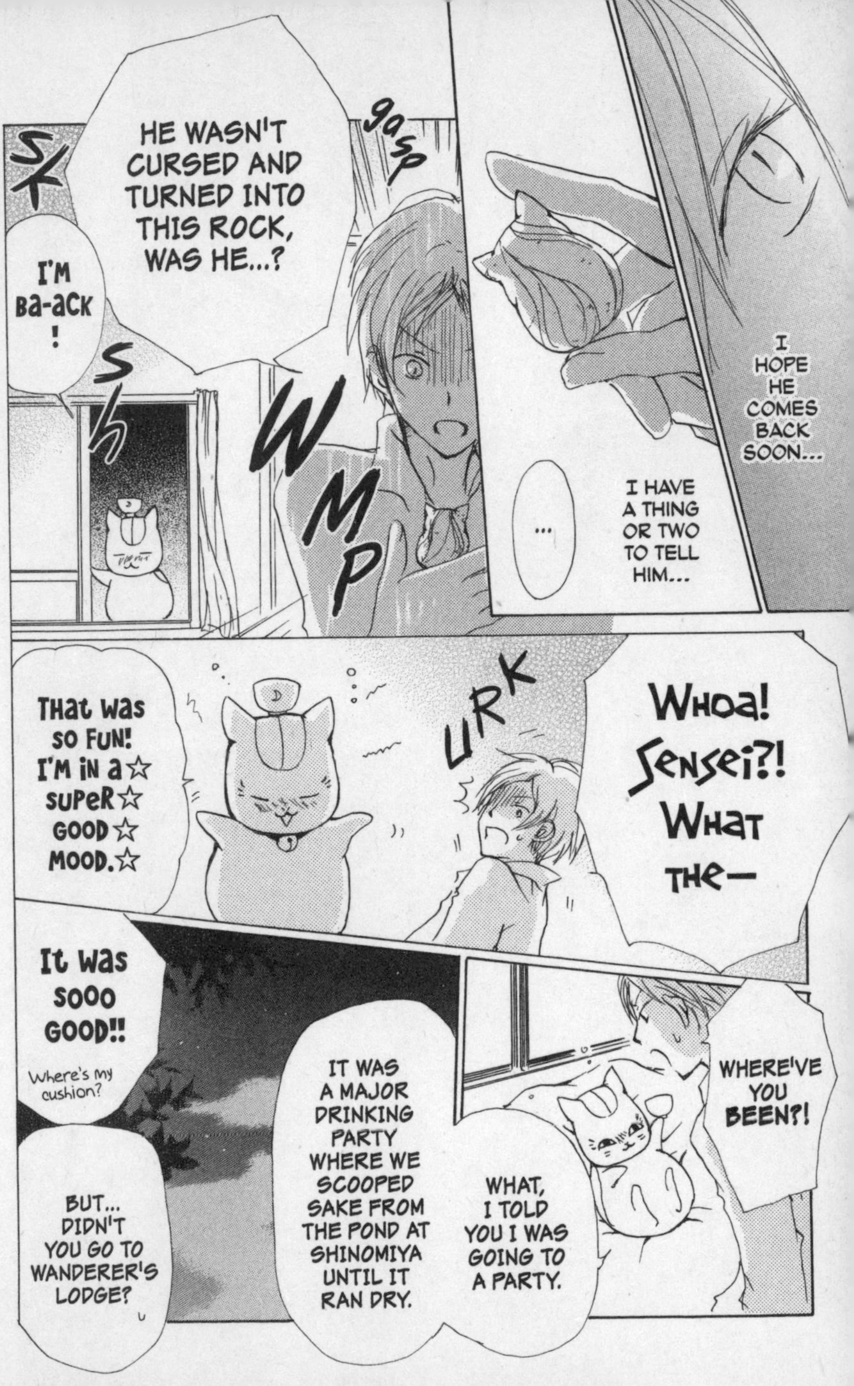
I HOPE HE COMES BACK SOON...
I HAVE A THING OR TWO TO TELL HIM...
...
gasp
HE WASN'T CURSED AND TURNED INTO THIS ROCK, WAS HE...?
SK
I'M BA-ACK!
SH
WMP
Whoa! Sensei?! What the—
URK
That was so fun! I'm in a☆ super☆ good☆ mood.☆
WHERE'VE YOU BEEN?!
WHAT, I TOLD YOU I WAS GOING TO A PARTY.
IT WAS A MAJOR DRINKING PARTY WHERE WE SCOOPED SAKE FROM THE POND AT SHINOMIYA UNTIL IT RAN DRY.
It was sooo good!!
Where's my cushion?
BUT... DIDN'T YOU GO TO WANDERER'S LODGE?

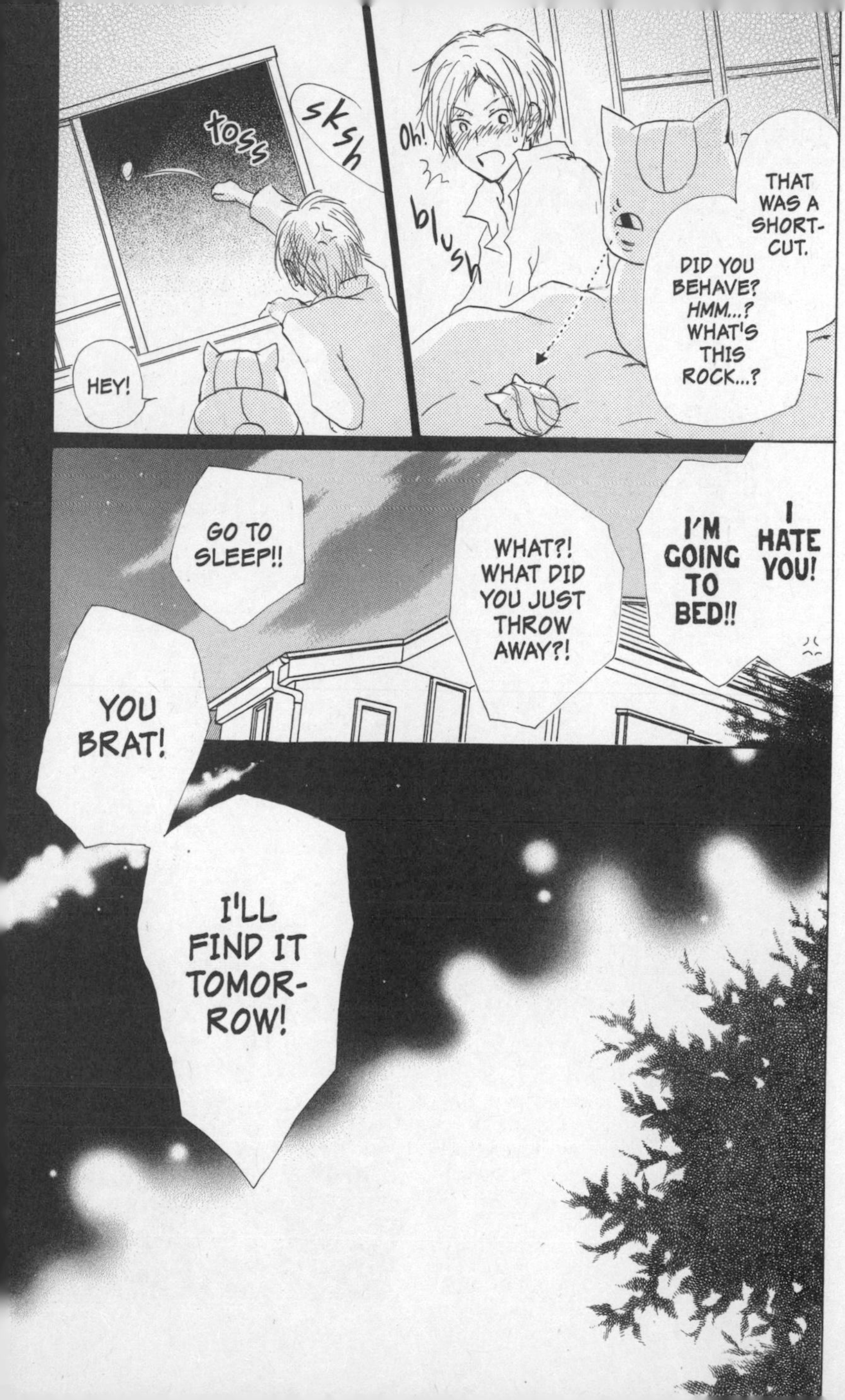
THAT WAS A SHORT-CUT.
DID YOU BEHAVE? HMM...? WHAT'S THIS ROCK...?
Oh!
blush
sksh
toss
HEY!
I HATE YOU!
I'M GOING TO BED!!
WHAT?! WHAT DID YOU JUST THROW AWAY?!
GO TO SLEEP!!
YOU BRAT!
I'LL FIND IT TOMOR-ROW!

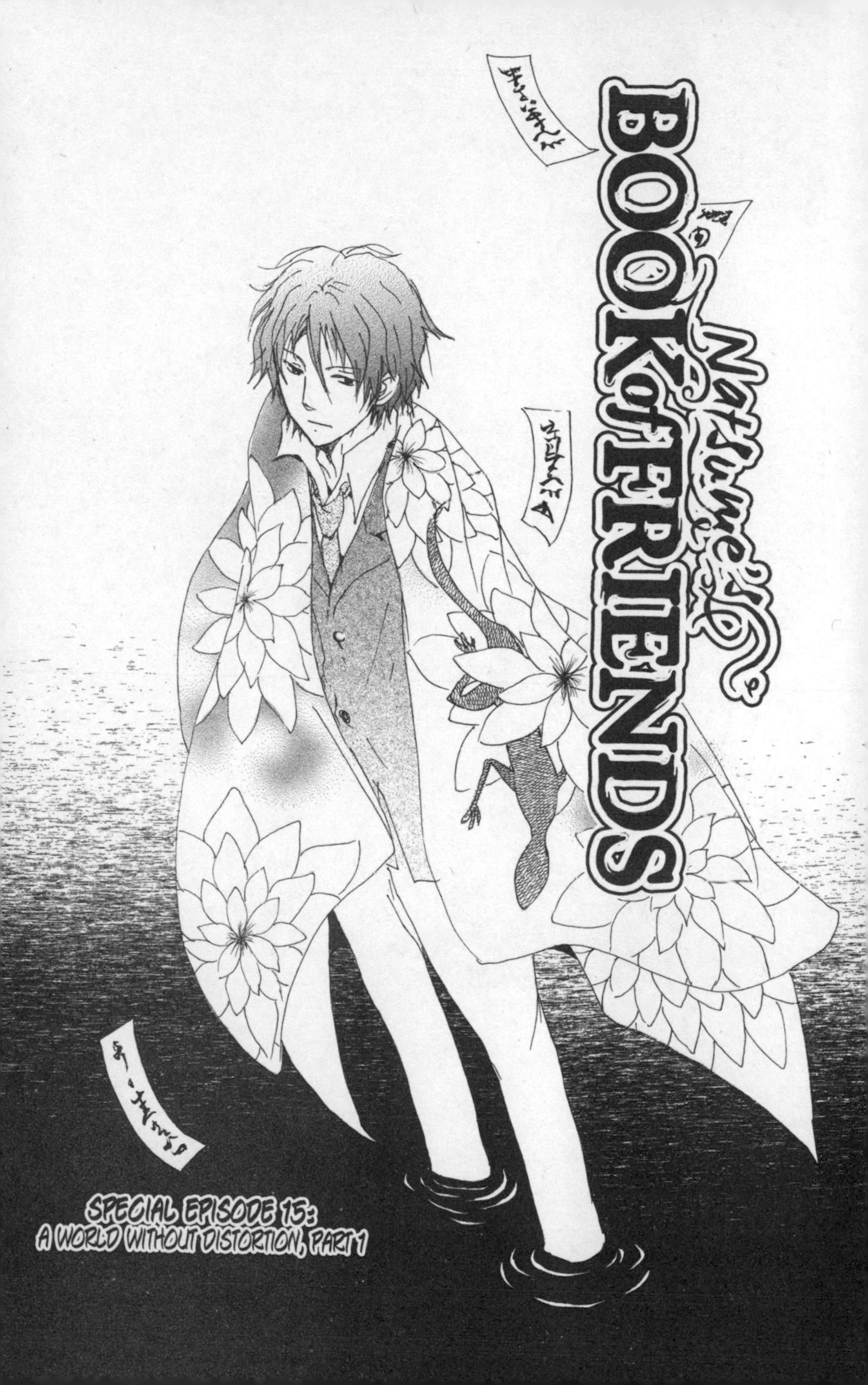
Natsume's BOOK of FRIENDS
SPECIAL EPISODE 15:
A WORLD WITHOUT DISTORTION, PART 1

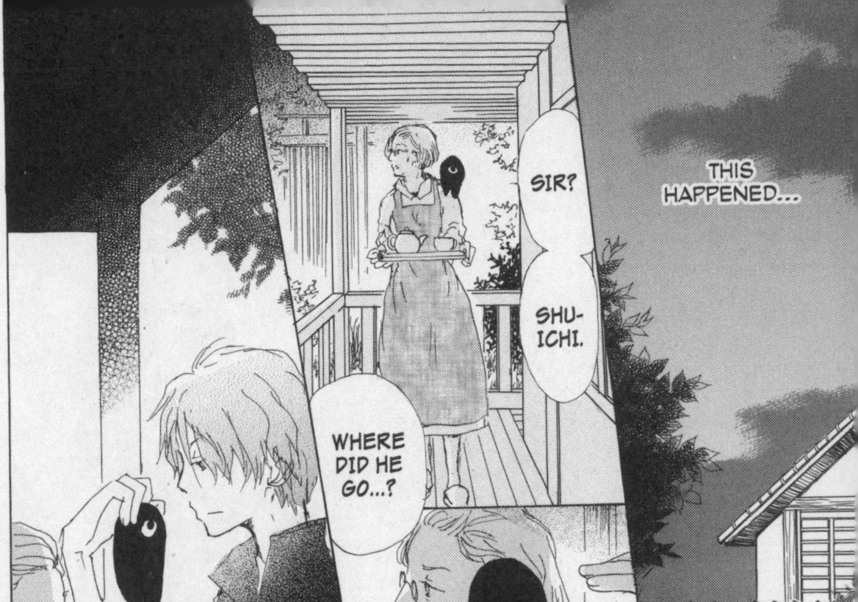
THIS HAPPENED...
...WHEN I WAS A JUNIOR IN HIGH SCHOOL.
...ICHI?
SIR?
SHU-ICHI.
WHERE DID HE GO...?
Yoink
OH, THERE YOU ARE.

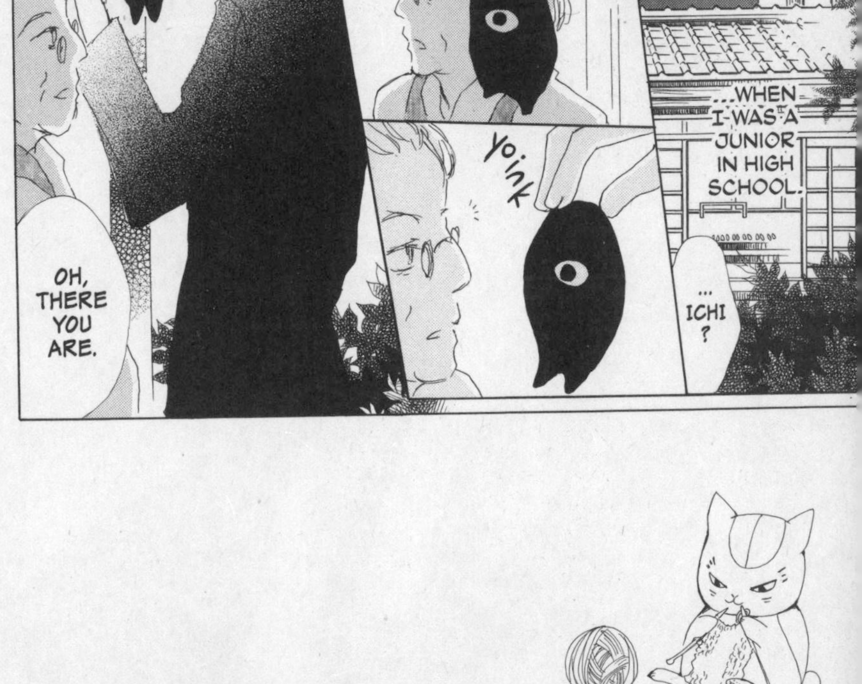

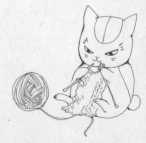

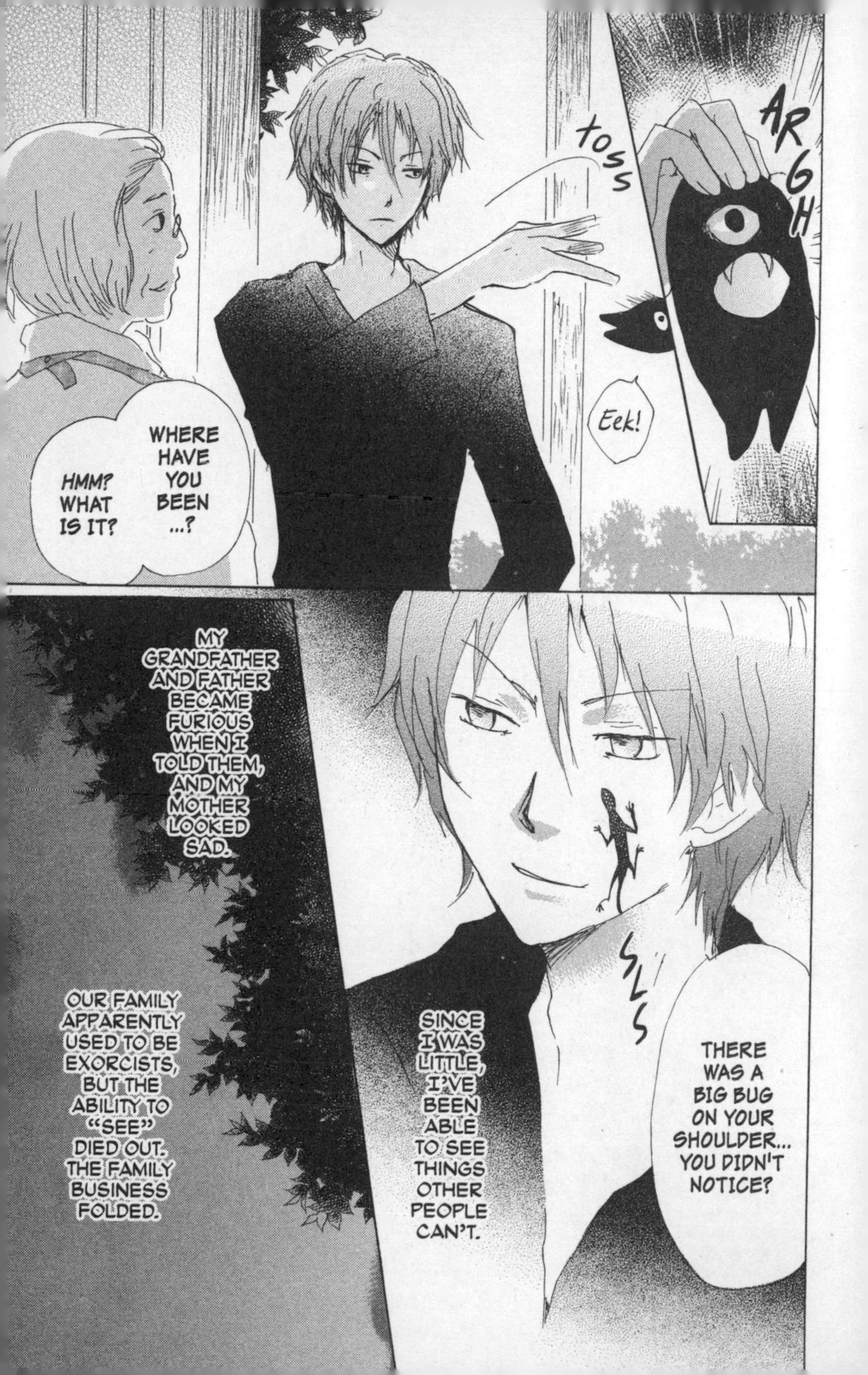
ARGH
Eek!
TOSS
WHERE HAVE YOU BEEN ...?
HMM? WHAT IS IT?
THERE WAS A BIG BUG ON YOUR SHOULDER... YOU DIDN'T NOTICE?
SLS
SINCE I WAS LITTLE, I'VE BEEN ABLE TO SEE THINGS OTHER PEOPLE CAN'T.
MY GRANDFATHER AND FATHER BECAME FURIOUS WHEN I TOLD THEM, AND MY MOTHER LOOKED SAD.
OUR FAMILY APPARENTLY USED TO BE EXORCISTS, BUT THE ABILITY TO "SEE" DIED OUT. THE FAMILY BUSINESS FOLDED.

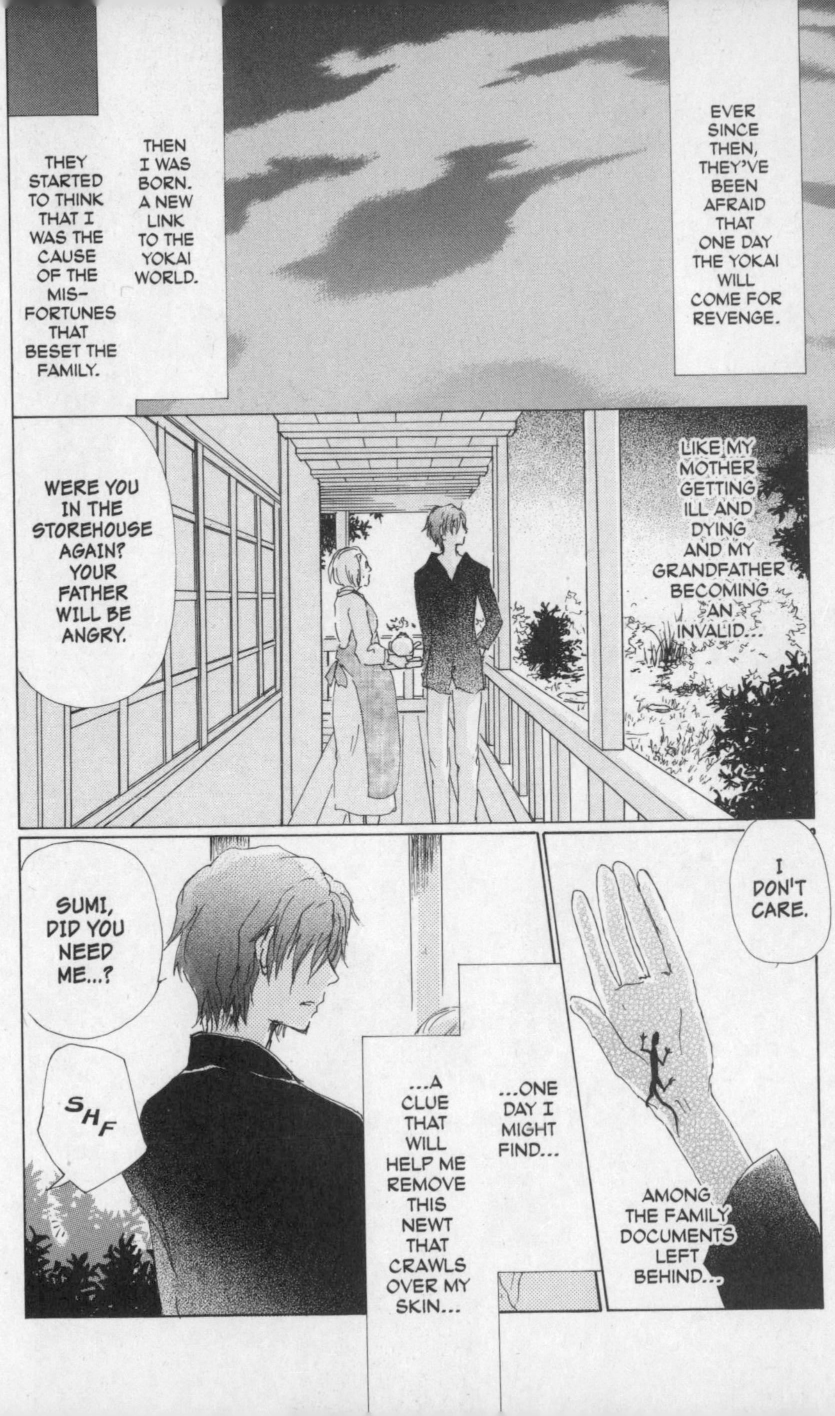
EVER SINCE THEN, THEY'VE BEEN AFRAID THAT ONE DAY THE YOKAI WILL COME FOR REVENGE.
THEN I WAS BORN. A NEW LINK TO THE YOKAI WORLD.
THEY STARTED TO THINK THAT I WAS THE CAUSE OF THE MIS-FORTUNES THAT BESET THE FAMILY.
LIKE MY MOTHER GETTING ILL AND DYING AND MY GRANDFATHER BECOMING AN INVALID...
WERE YOU IN THE STOREHOUSE AGAIN? YOUR FATHER WILL BE ANGRY.
I DON'T CARE.
AMONG THE FAMILY DOCUMENTS LEFT BEHIND...
...ONE DAY I MIGHT FIND...
...A CLUE THAT WILL HELP ME REMOVE THIS NEWT THAT CRAWLS OVER MY SKIN...
SUMI, DID YOU NEED ME...?
SHF

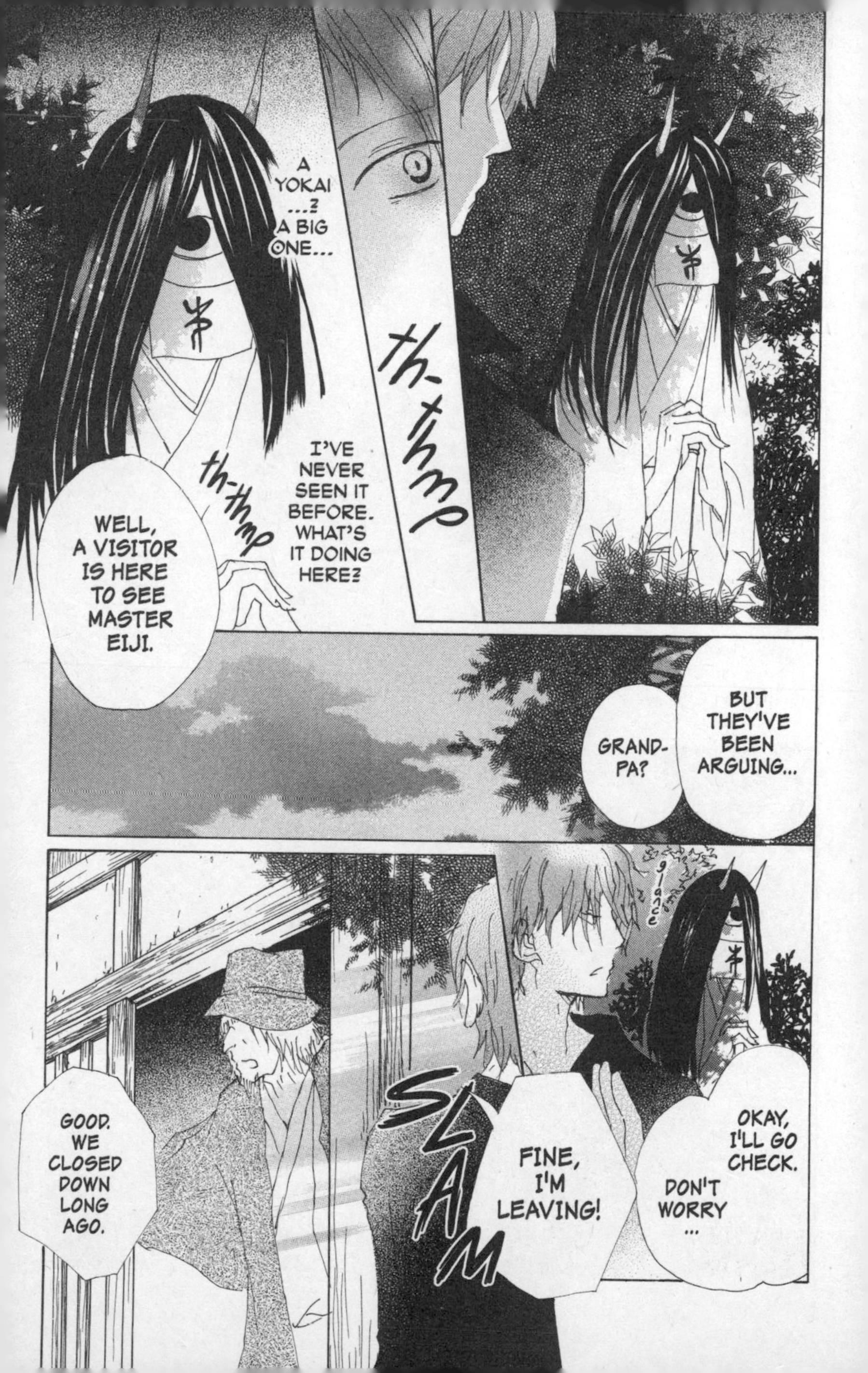
th-thmp
A YOKAI ...? A BIG ONE...
I'VE NEVER SEEN IT BEFORE. WHAT'S IT DOING HERE?
th-thmp
WELL, A VISITOR IS HERE TO SEE MASTER EIJI.
BUT THEY'VE BEEN ARGUING...
GRAND-PA?
glance
OKAY, I'LL GO CHECK.
DON'T WORRY ...
FINE, I'M LEAVING!
SLAM
GOOD. WE CLOSED DOWN LONG AGO.

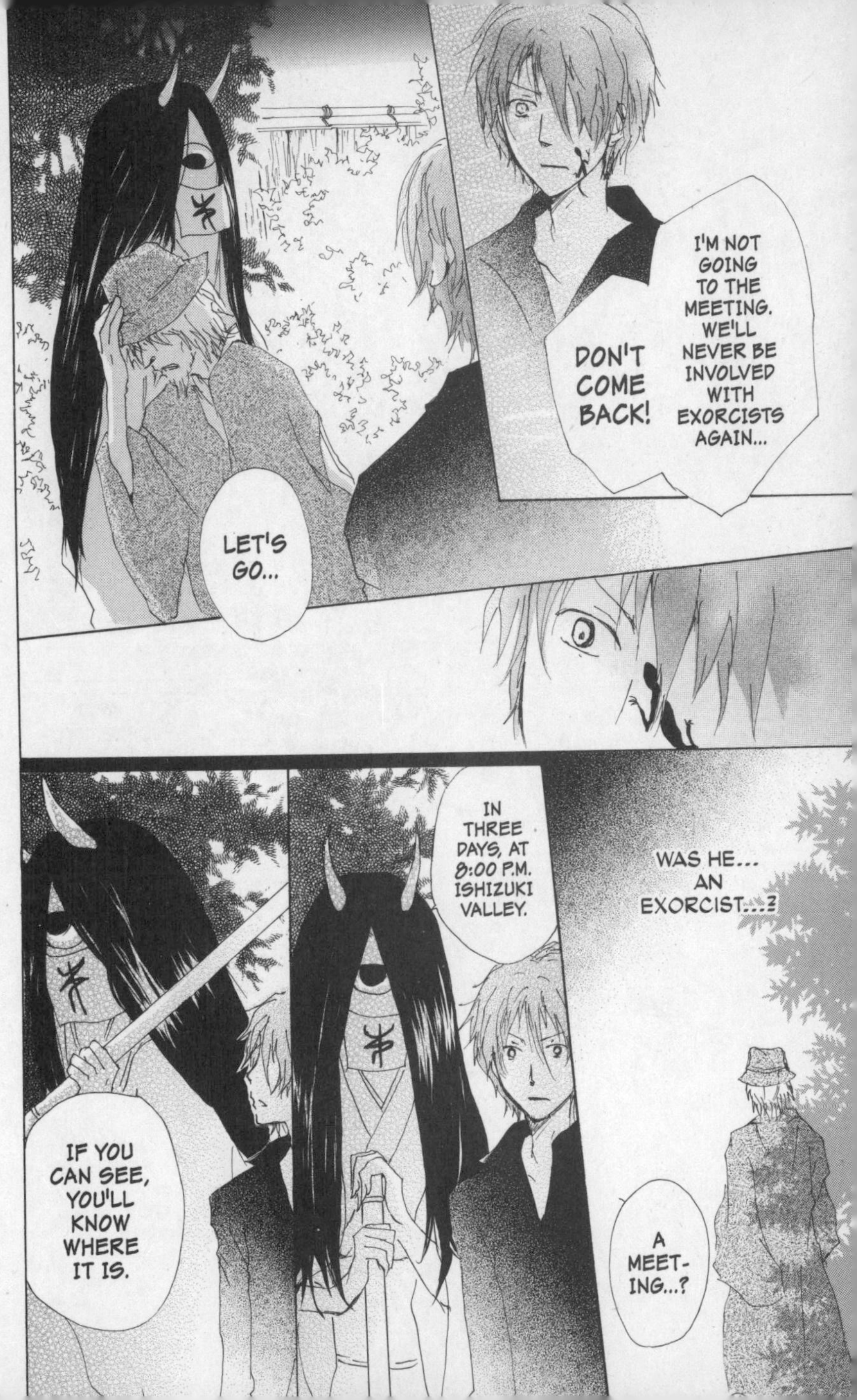
I'M NOT GOING TO THE MEETING. WE'LL NEVER BE INVOLVED WITH EXORCISTS AGAIN...
DON'T COME BACK!
LET'S GO...
WAS HE... AN EXORCIST...?
A MEET-ING...?
IN THREE DAYS, AT 8:00 P.M. ISHIZUKI VALLEY.
IF YOU CAN SEE, YOU'LL KNOW WHERE IT IS.

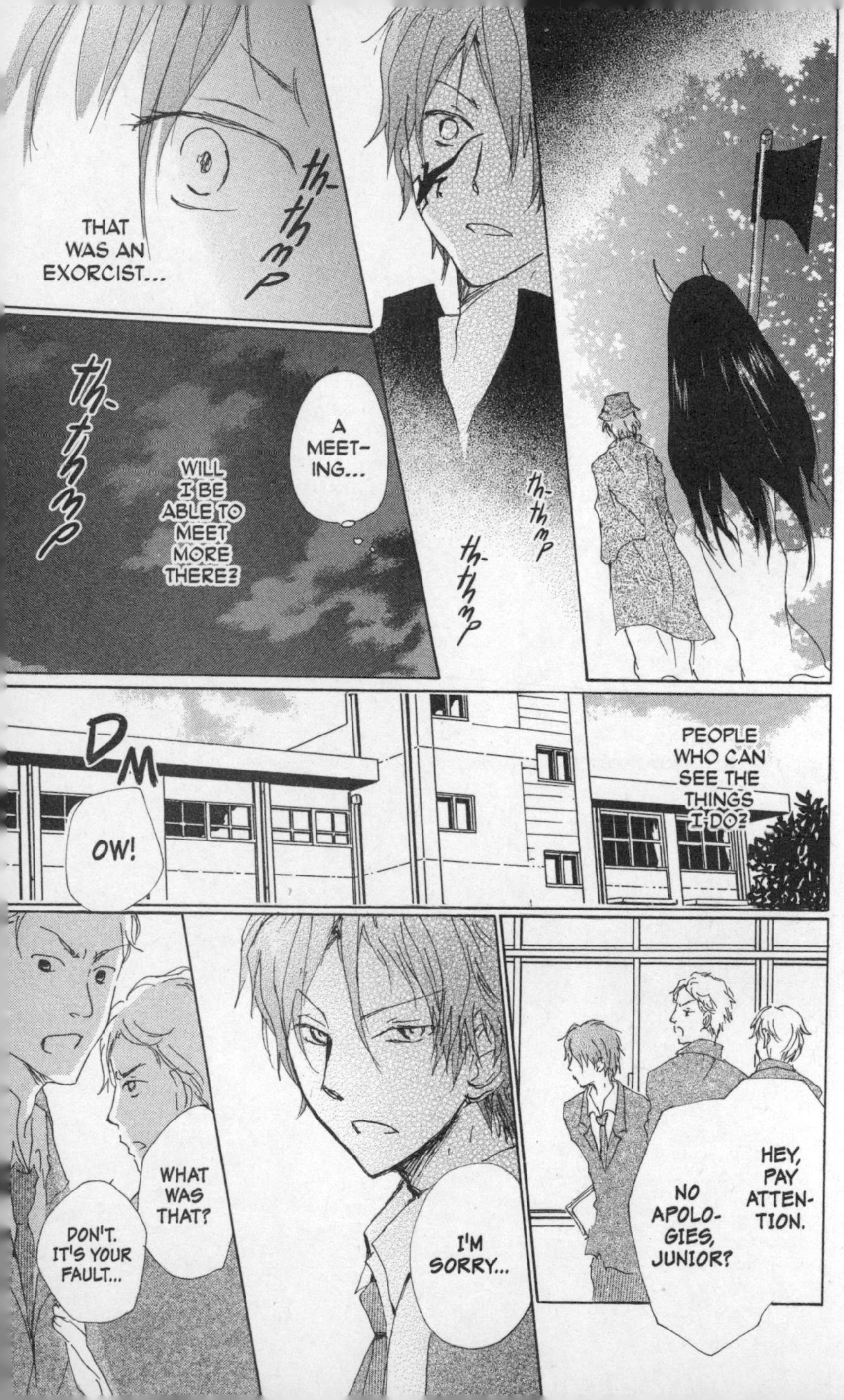
th-thmp
th-thmp
A MEET-ING...
THAT WAS AN EXORCIST...
th-thmp
WILL I BE ABLE TO MEET MORE THERE?
th-thmp
PEOPLE WHO CAN SEE THE THINGS I DO?
DM
OW!
HEY, PAY ATTEN-TION.
NO APOLO-GIES, JUNIOR?
I'M SORRY...
WHAT WAS THAT?
DON'T. IT'S YOUR FAULT...

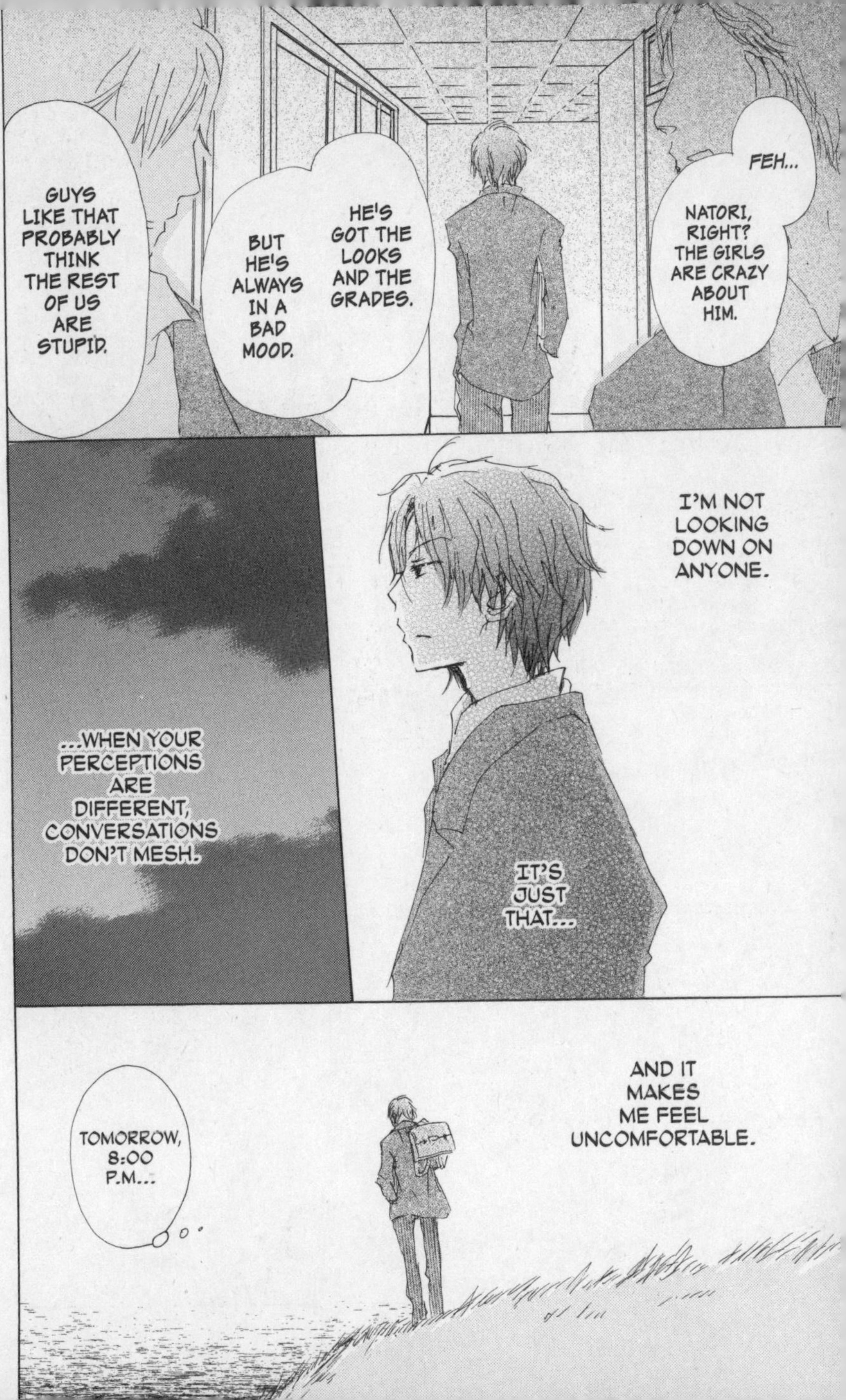
FEH...
NATORI, RIGHT? THE GIRLS ARE CRAZY ABOUT HIM.
HE'S GOT THE LOOKS AND THE GRADES.
BUT HE'S ALWAYS IN A BAD MOOD.
GUYS LIKE THAT PROBABLY THINK THE REST OF US ARE STUPID.
I'M NOT LOOKING DOWN ON ANYONE.
IT'S JUST THAT...
...WHEN YOUR PERCEPTIONS ARE DIFFERENT, CONVERSATIONS DON'T MESH.
AND IT MAKES ME FEEL UNCOMFORTABLE.
TOMORROW, 8:00 P.M...

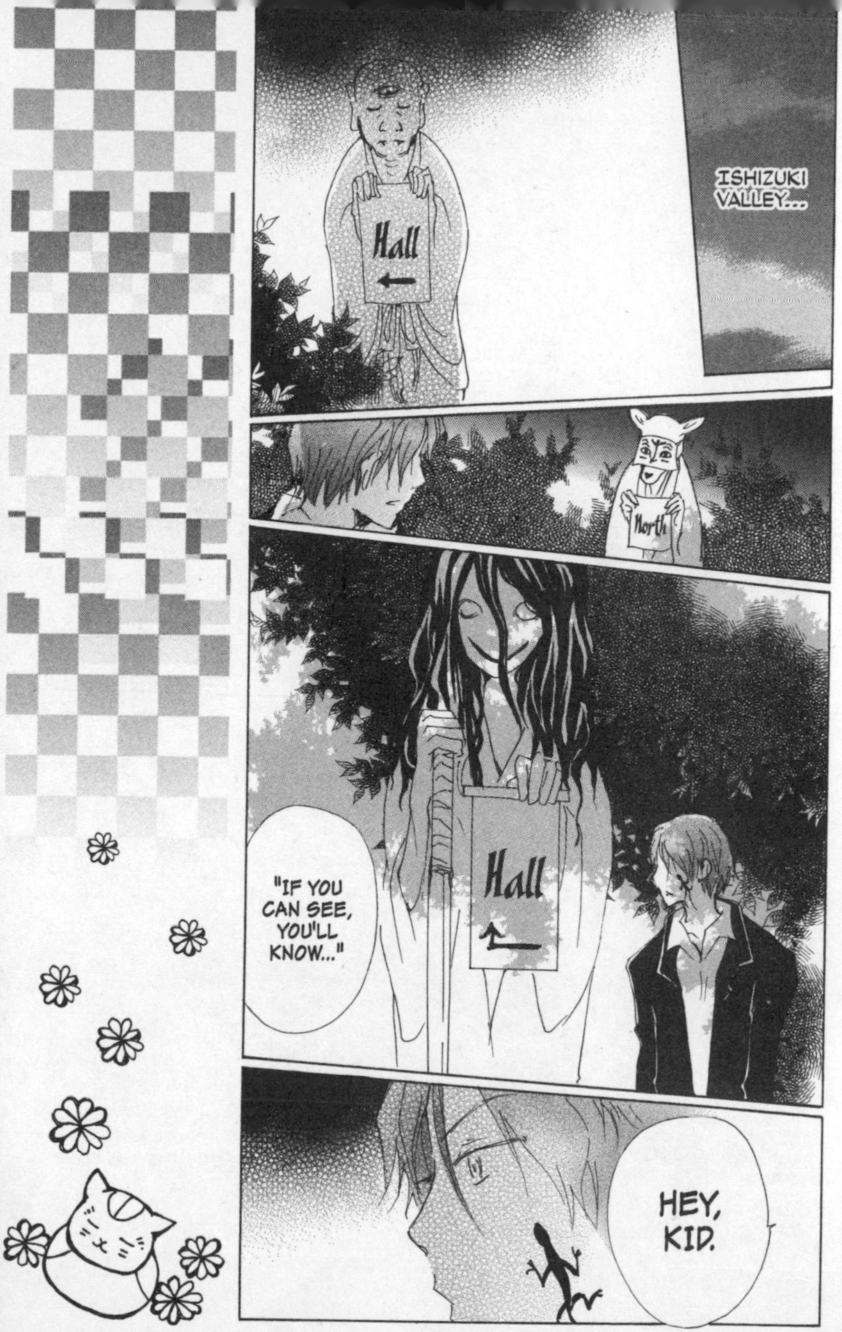
ISHIZUKI VALLEY...
Hall
North
Hall
"IF YOU CAN SEE, YOU'LL KNOW..."
HEY, KID.

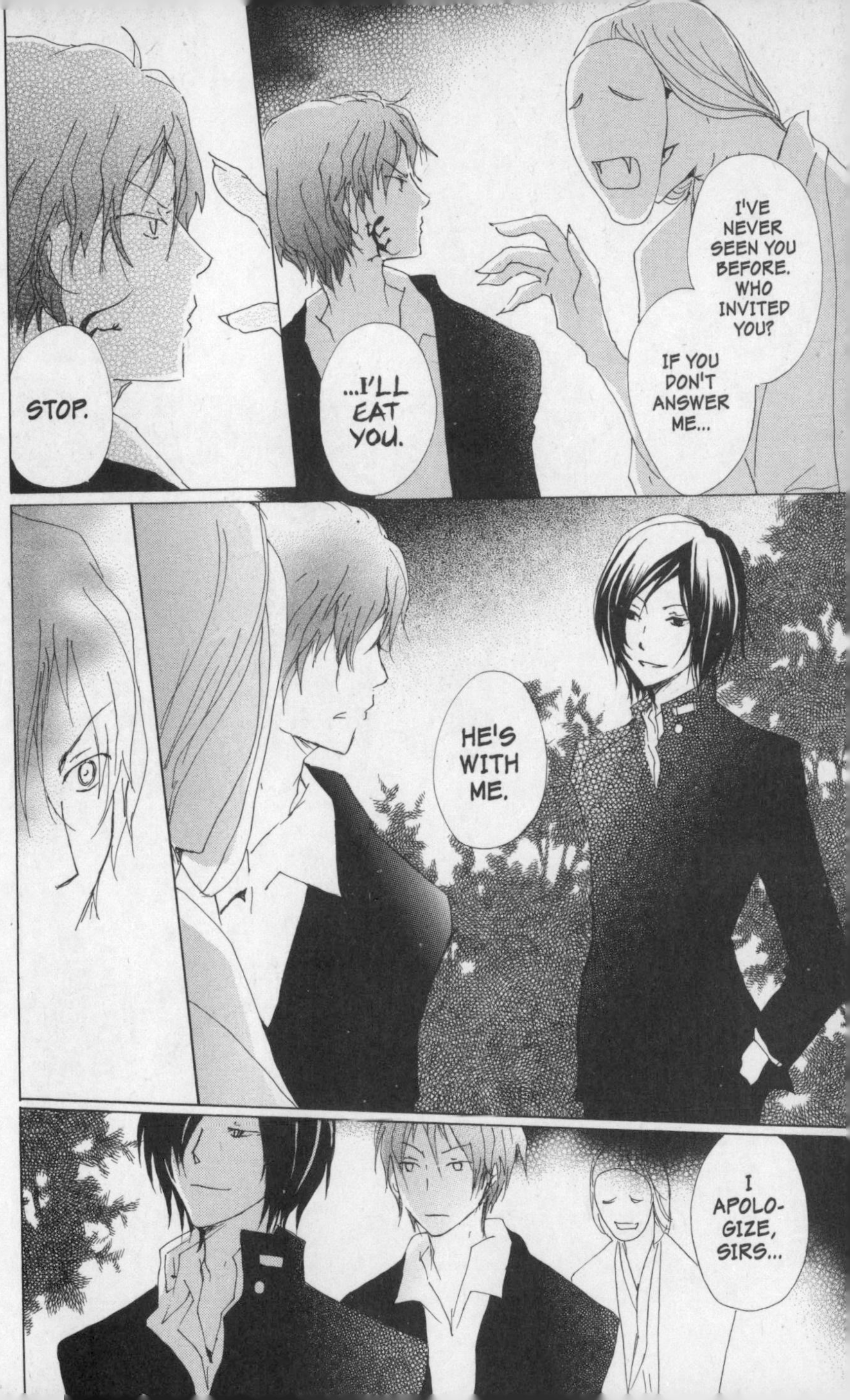
I'VE NEVER SEEN YOU BEFORE. WHO INVITED YOU?
IF YOU DON'T ANSWER ME...
...I'LL EAT YOU.
STOP.
HE'S WITH ME.
I APOLO-GIZE, SIRS...

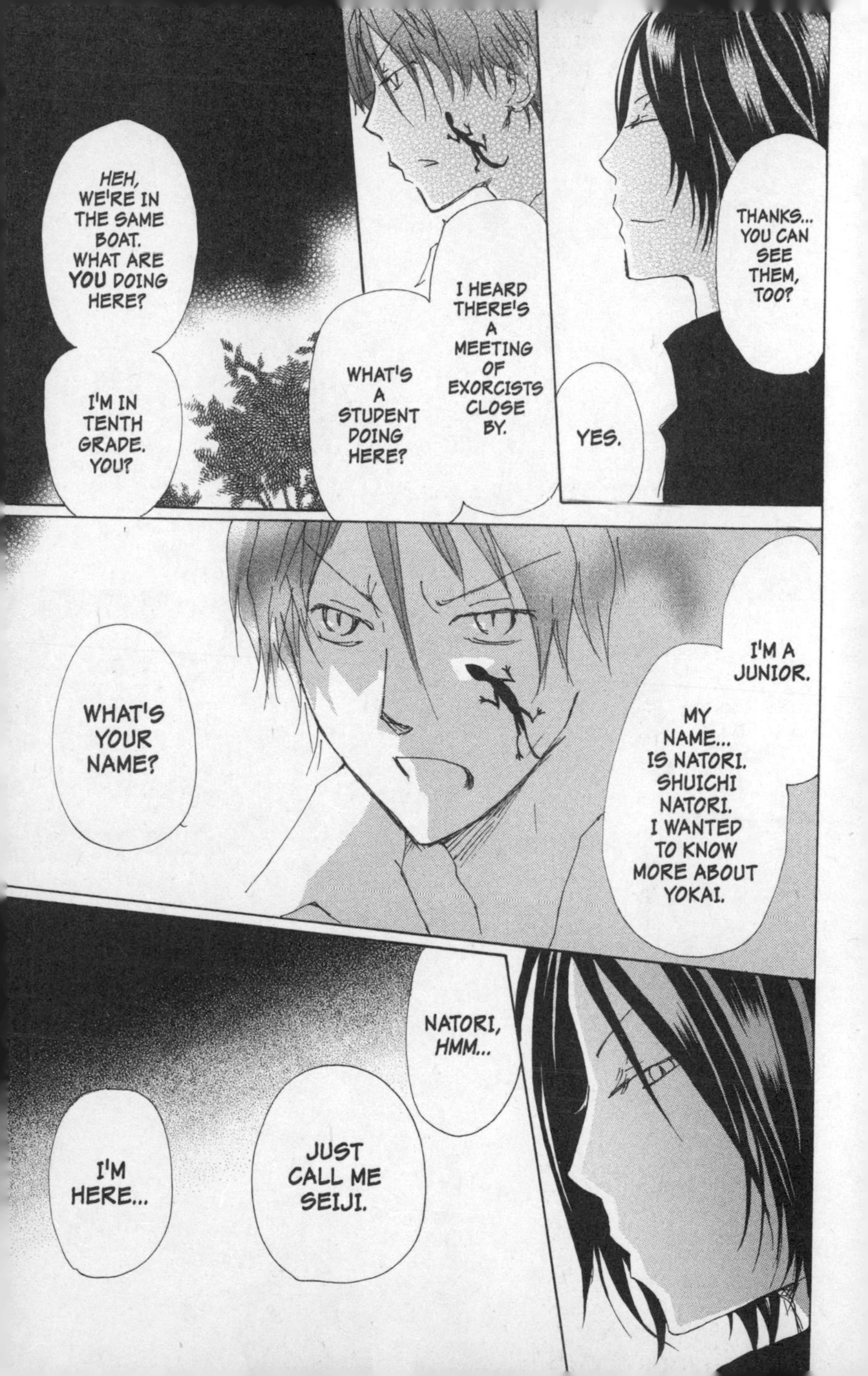
THANKS... YOU CAN SEE THEM, TOO?
YES.
I HEARD THERE'S A MEETING OF EXORCISTS CLOSE BY.
WHAT'S A STUDENT DOING HERE?
HEH, WE'RE IN THE SAME BOAT. WHAT ARE YOU DOING HERE?
I'M IN TENTH GRADE. YOU?
I'M A JUNIOR.
MY NAME... IS NATORI. SHUICHI NATORI. I WANTED TO KNOW MORE ABOUT YOKAI.
WHAT'S YOUR NAME?
NATORI, HMM...
JUST CALL ME SEIJI.
I'M HERE...

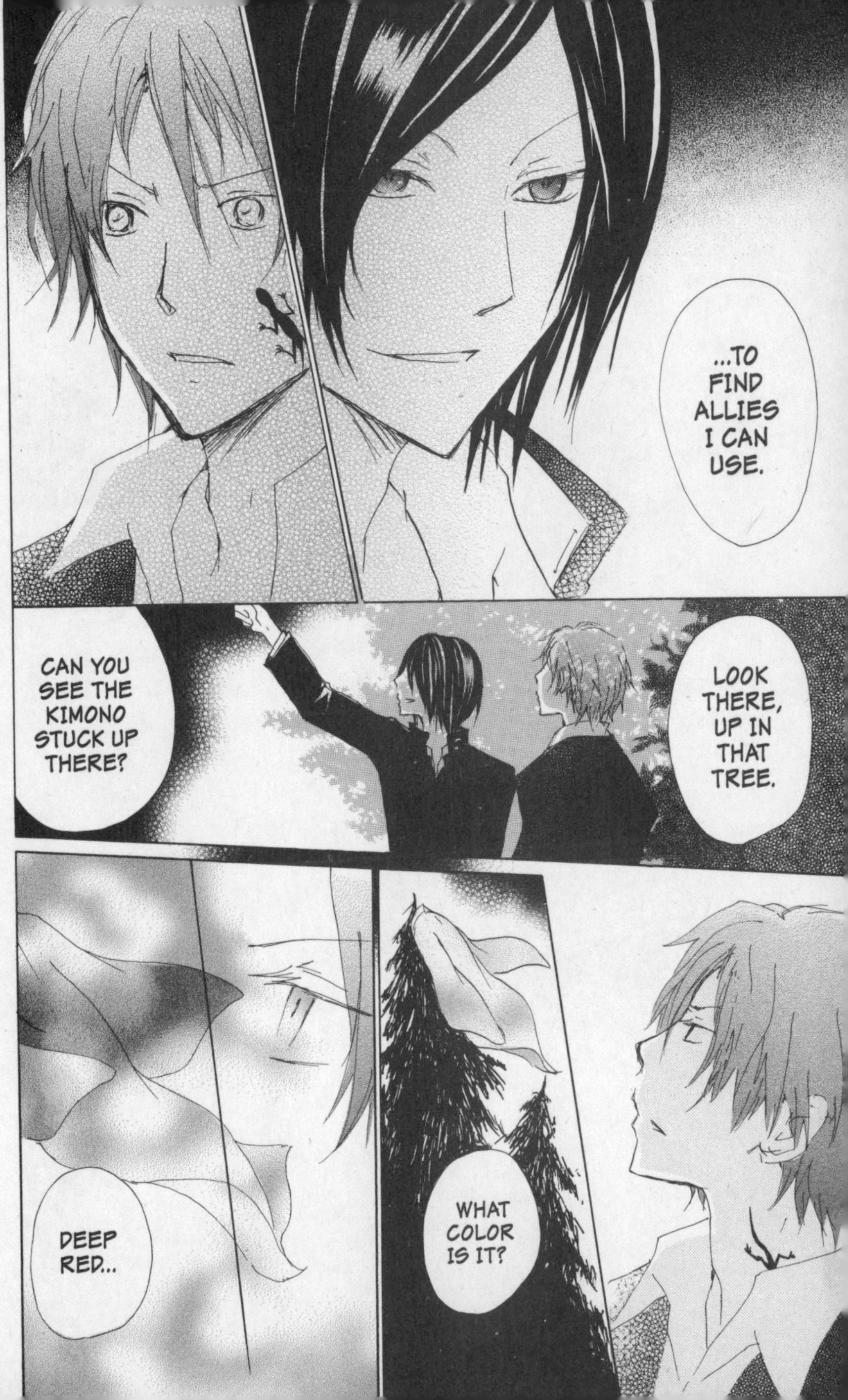
...TO FIND ALLIES I CAN USE.
LOOK THERE, UP IN THAT TREE.
CAN YOU SEE THE KIMONO STUCK UP THERE?
WHAT COLOR IS IT?
DEEP RED...

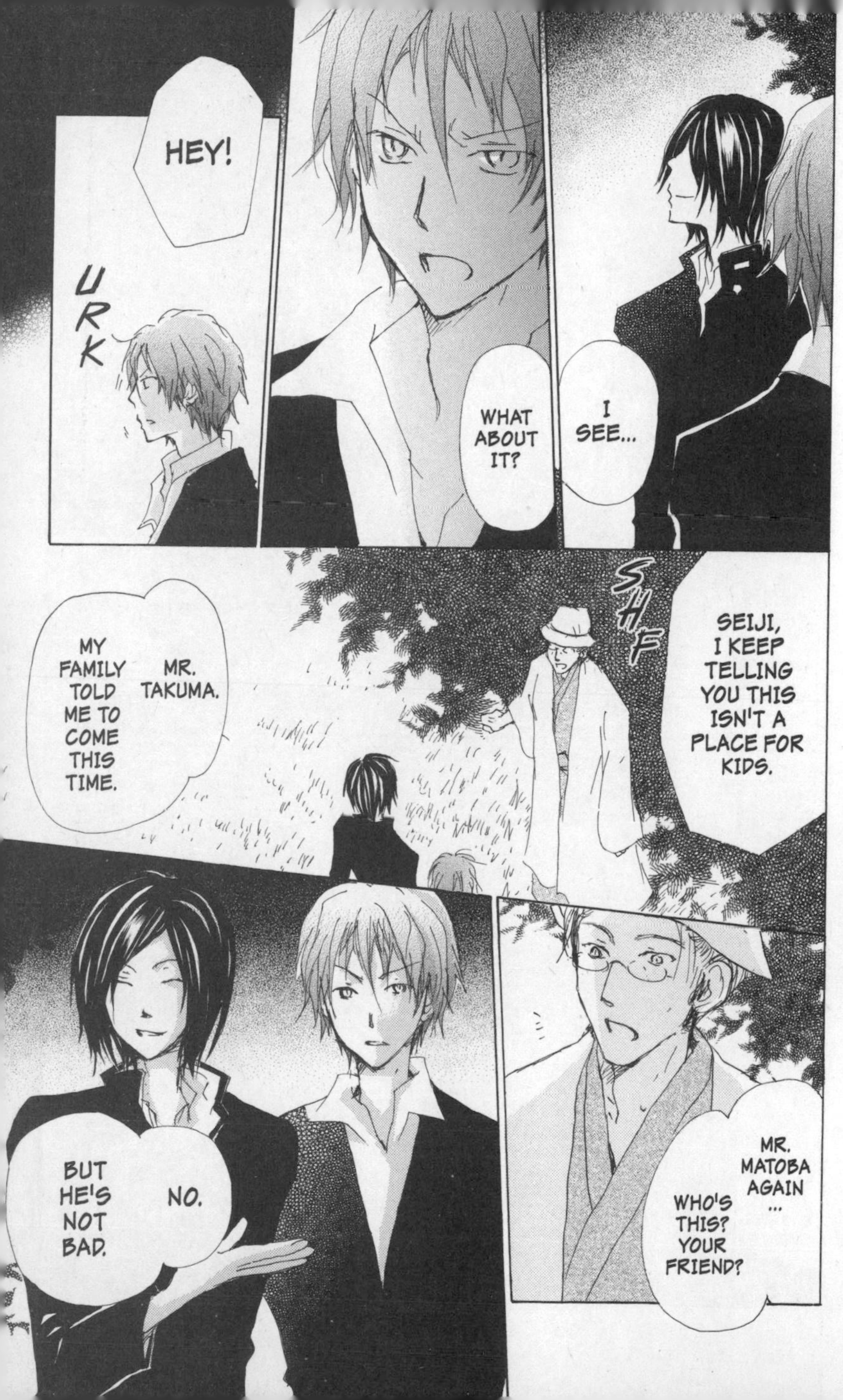
I SEE...
WHAT ABOUT IT?
HEY!
URK
SHF
SEIJI, I KEEP TELLING YOU THIS ISN'T A PLACE FOR KIDS.
MR. TAKUMA.
MY FAMILY TOLD ME TO COME THIS TIME.
MR. MATOBA AGAIN...
WHO'S THIS? YOUR FRIEND?
NO.
BUT HE'S NOT BAD.

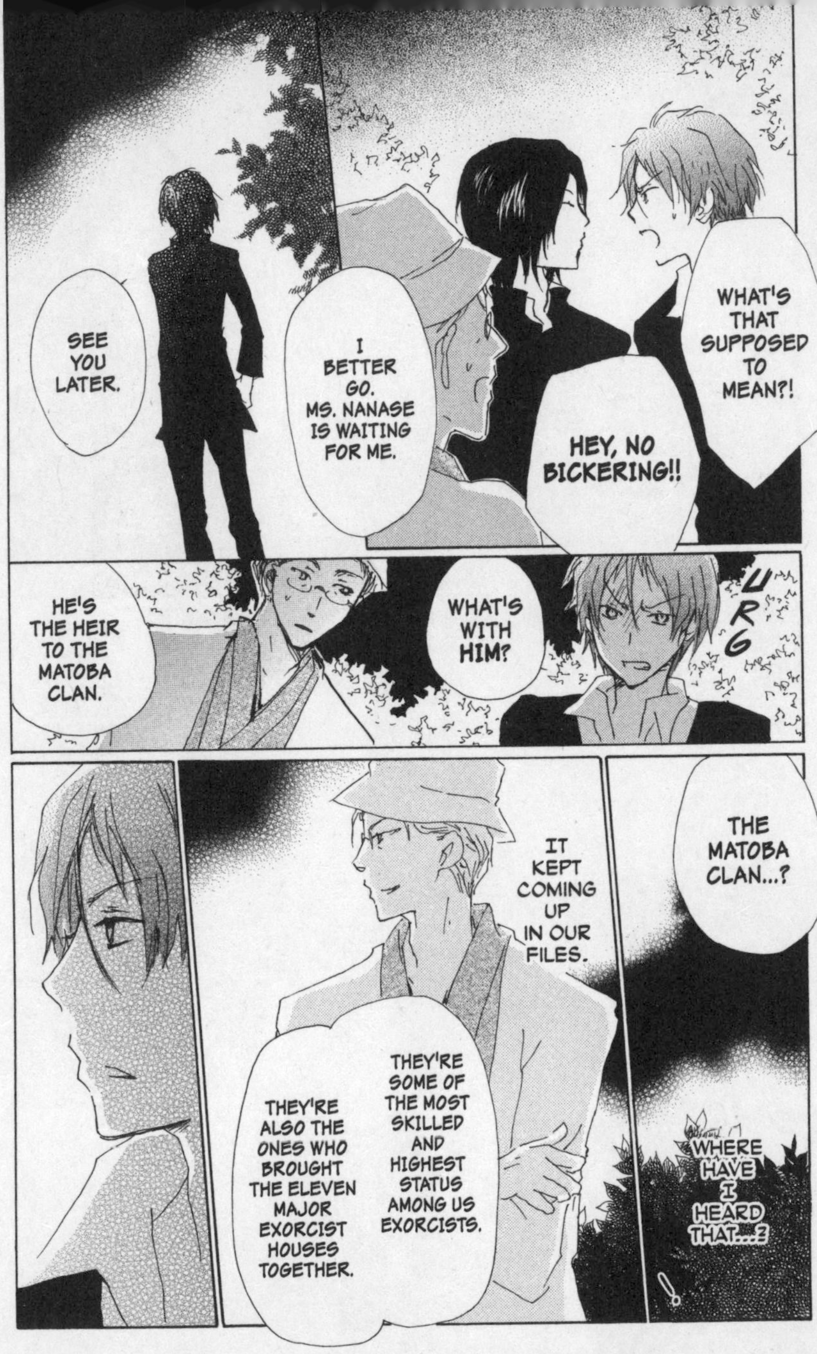
WHAT'S THAT SUPPOSED TO MEAN?!
HEY, NO BICKERING!!
I BETTER GO. MS. NANASE IS WAITING FOR ME.
SEE YOU LATER.
URG
WHAT'S WITH HIM?
HE'S THE HEIR TO THE MATOBA CLAN.
THE MATOBA CLAN...?
WHERE HAVE I HEARD THAT...?
!
IT KEPT COMING UP IN OUR FILES.
THEY'RE SOME OF THE MOST SKILLED AND HIGHEST STATUS AMONG US EXORCISTS.
THEY'RE ALSO THE ONES WHO BROUGHT THE ELEVEN MAJOR EXORCIST HOUSES TOGETHER.

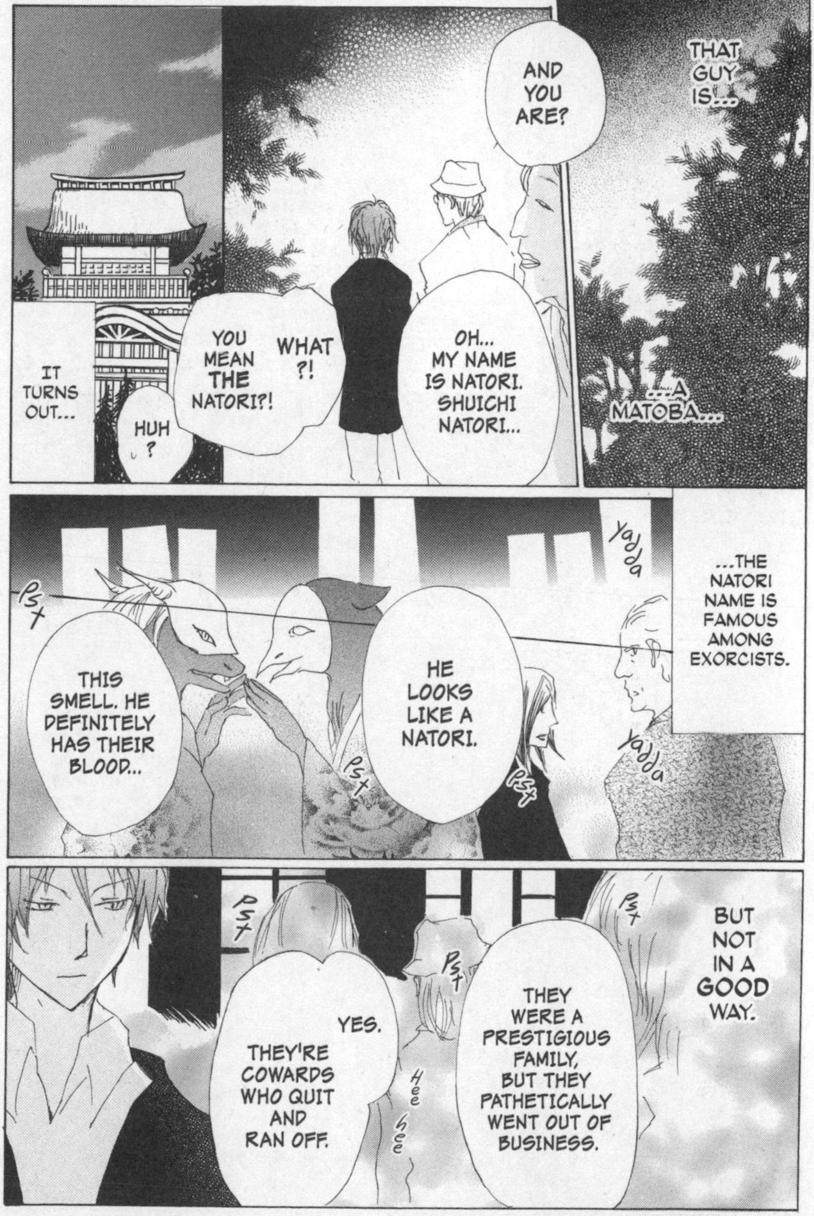
THAT GUY IS...
...A MATOBA...
AND YOU ARE?
OH... MY NAME IS NATORI. SHUICHI NATORI...
WHAT?!
YOU MEAN THE NATORI?!
IT TURNS OUT...
HUH?
...THE NATORI NAME IS FAMOUS AMONG EXORCISTS.
Yadda
Yadda
Pst
HE LOOKS LIKE A NATORI.
Pst
Pst
THIS SMELL. HE DEFINITELY HAS THEIR BLOOD...
BUT NOT IN A GOOD WAY.
Pst
THEY WERE A PRESTIGIOUS FAMILY, BUT THEY PATHETICALLY WENT OUT OF BUSINESS.
Pst
Hee hee
YES.
THEY'RE COWARDS WHO QUIT AND RAN OFF.
Pst

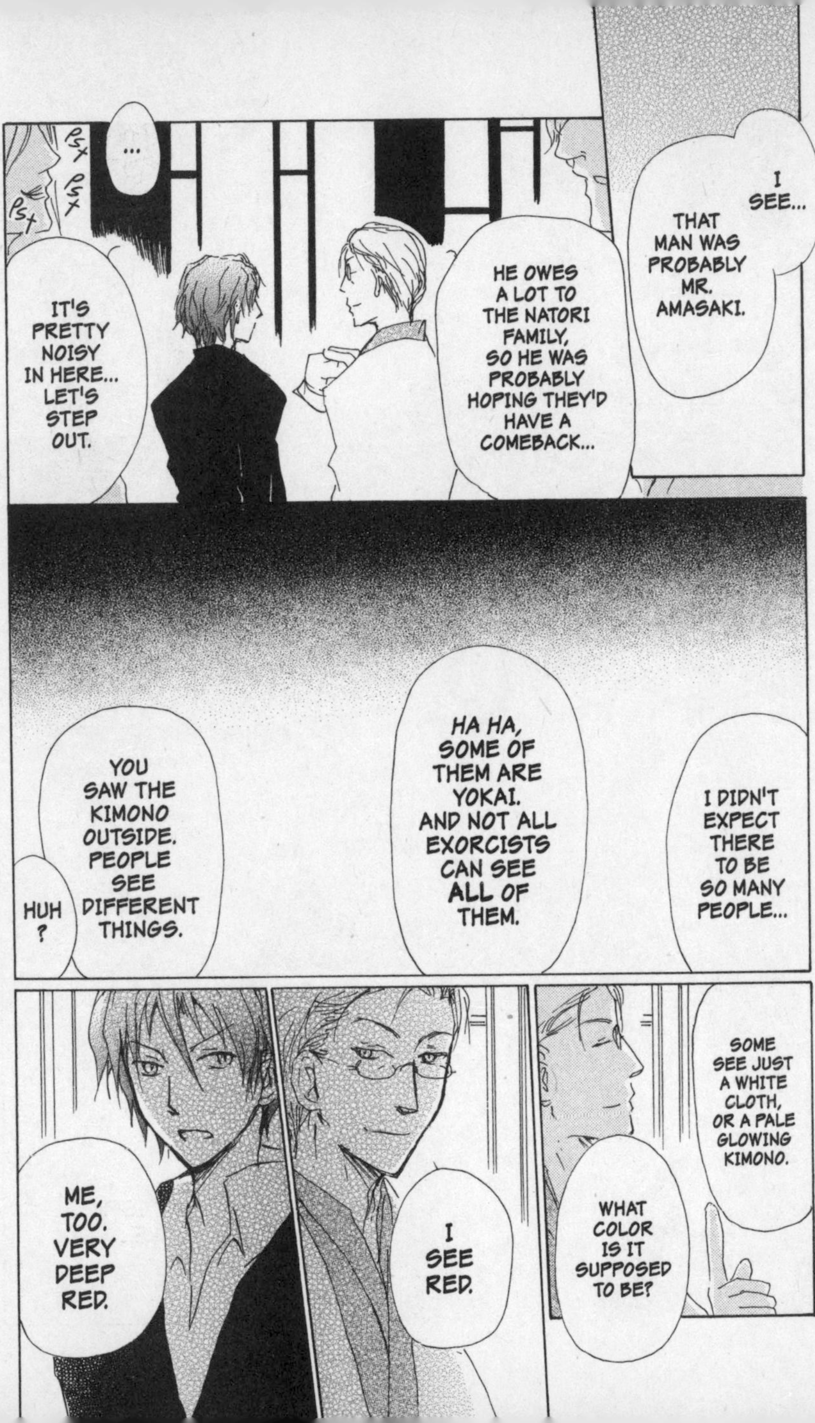
I SEE...
THAT MAN WAS PROBABLY MR. AMASAKI.
HE OWES A LOT TO THE NATORI FAMILY, SO HE WAS PROBABLY HOPING THEY'D HAVE A COMEBACK...
...
Psst psst psst
IT'S PRETTY NOISY IN HERE... LET'S STEP OUT.
I DIDN'T EXPECT THERE TO BE SO MANY PEOPLE...
HA HA, SOME OF THEM ARE YOKAI. AND NOT ALL EXORCISTS CAN SEE ALL OF THEM.
YOU SAW THE KIMONO OUTSIDE. PEOPLE SEE DIFFERENT THINGS.
HUH?
SOME SEE JUST A WHITE CLOTH, OR A PALE GLOWING KIMONO.
WHAT COLOR IS IT SUPPOSED TO BE?
I SEE RED.
ME, TOO. VERY DEEP RED.

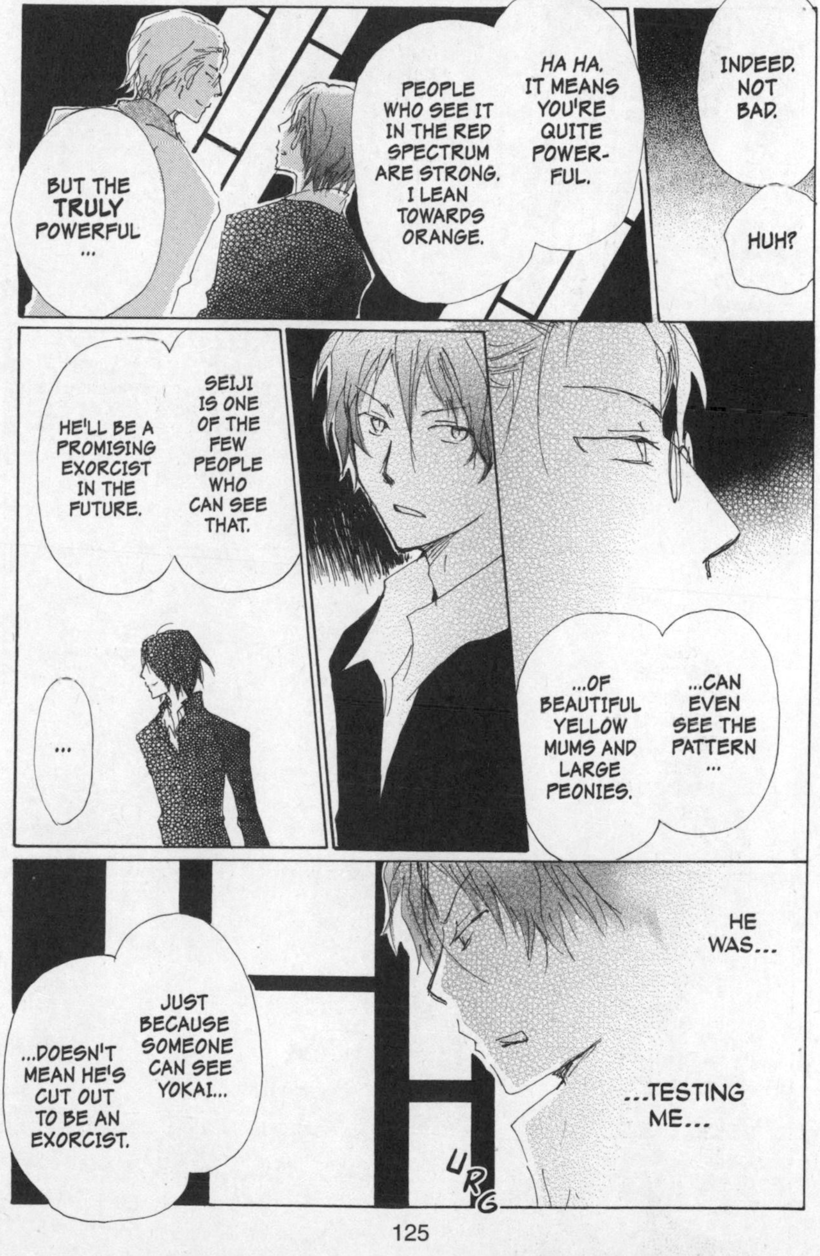
INDEED. NOT BAD.
HUH?
HA HA. IT MEANS YOU'RE QUITE POWER-FUL.
PEOPLE WHO SEE IT IN THE RED SPECTRUM ARE STRONG. I LEAN TOWARDS ORANGE.
BUT THE TRULY POWERFUL ...
...CAN EVEN SEE THE PATTERN ...
...OF BEAUTIFUL YELLOW MUMS AND LARGE PEONIES.
SEIJI IS ONE OF THE FEW PEOPLE WHO CAN SEE THAT.
HE'LL BE A PROMISING EXORCIST IN THE FUTURE.
...
HE WAS...
...TESTING ME...
URG
JUST BECAUSE SOMEONE CAN SEE YOKAI...
...DOESN'T MEAN HE'S CUT OUT TO BE AN EXORCIST.

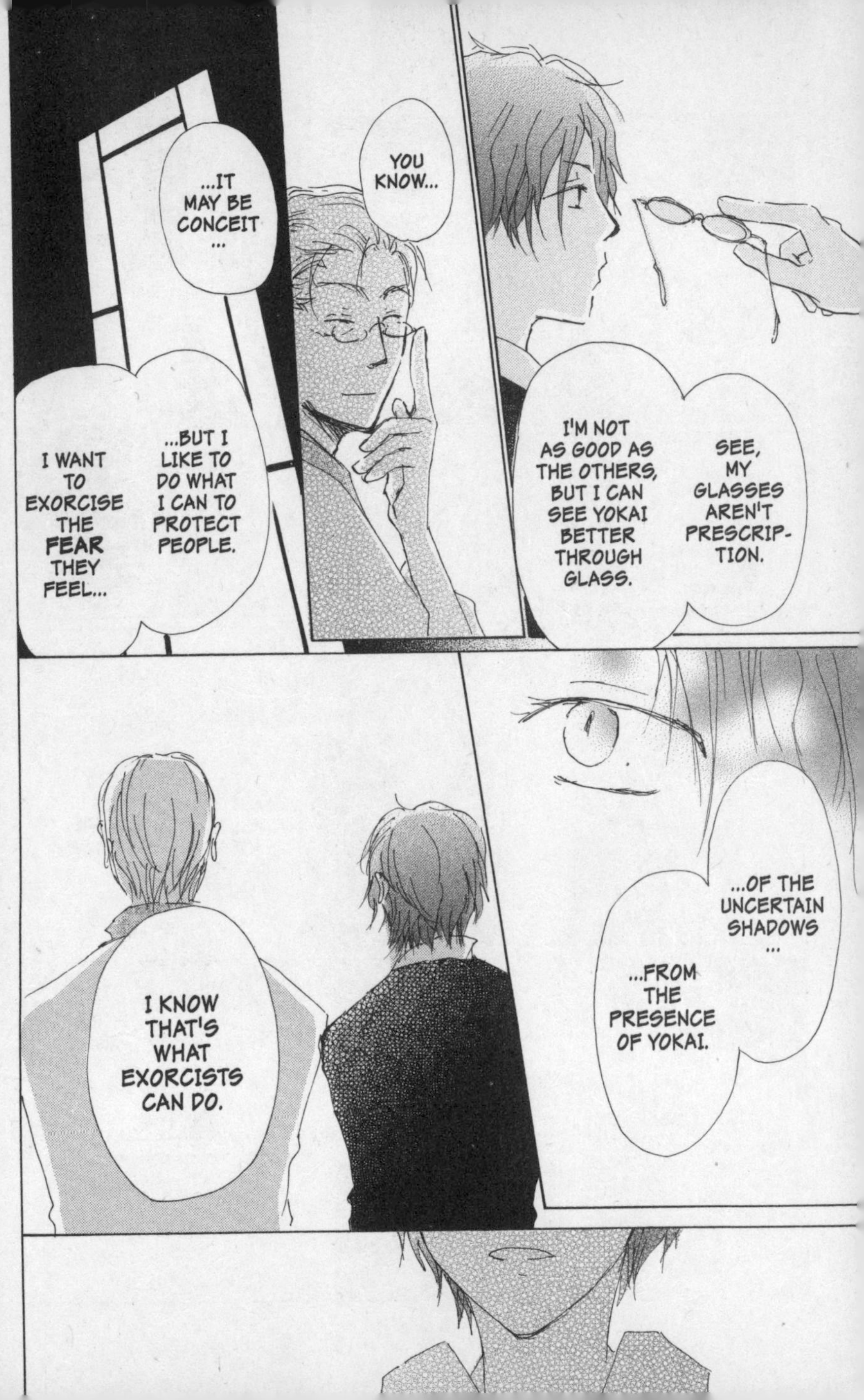
SEE, MY GLASSES AREN'T PRESCRIP-TION.
I'M NOT AS GOOD AS THE OTHERS, BUT I CAN SEE YOKAI BETTER THROUGH GLASS.
YOU KNOW...
...IT MAY BE CONCEIT ...
...BUT I LIKE TO DO WHAT I CAN TO PROTECT PEOPLE.
I WANT TO EXORCISE THE FEAR THEY FEEL...
...OF THE UNCERTAIN SHADOWS ...
...FROM THE PRESENCE OF YOKAI.
I KNOW THAT'S WHAT EXORCISTS CAN DO.

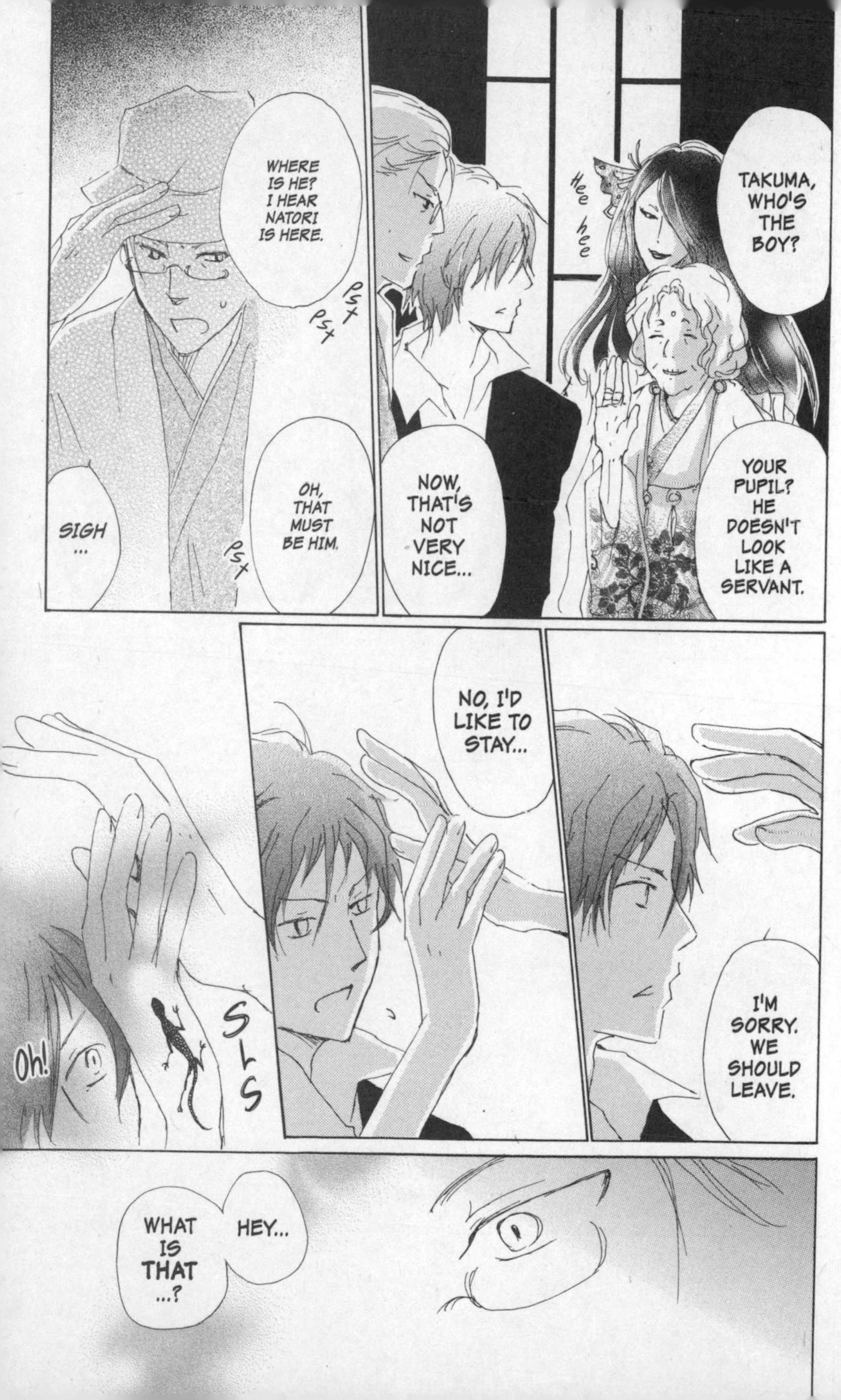
TAKUMA, WHO'S THE BOY?
Hee hee
YOUR PUPIL? HE DOESN'T LOOK LIKE A SERVANT.
NOW, THAT'S NOT VERY NICE...
WHERE IS HE? I HEAR NATORI IS HERE.
Pst Pst
OH, THAT MUST BE HIM.
Pst
SIGH ...
I'M SORRY. WE SHOULD LEAVE.
NO, I'D LIKE TO STAY...
SLS
Oh!
HEY...
WHAT IS THAT ...?

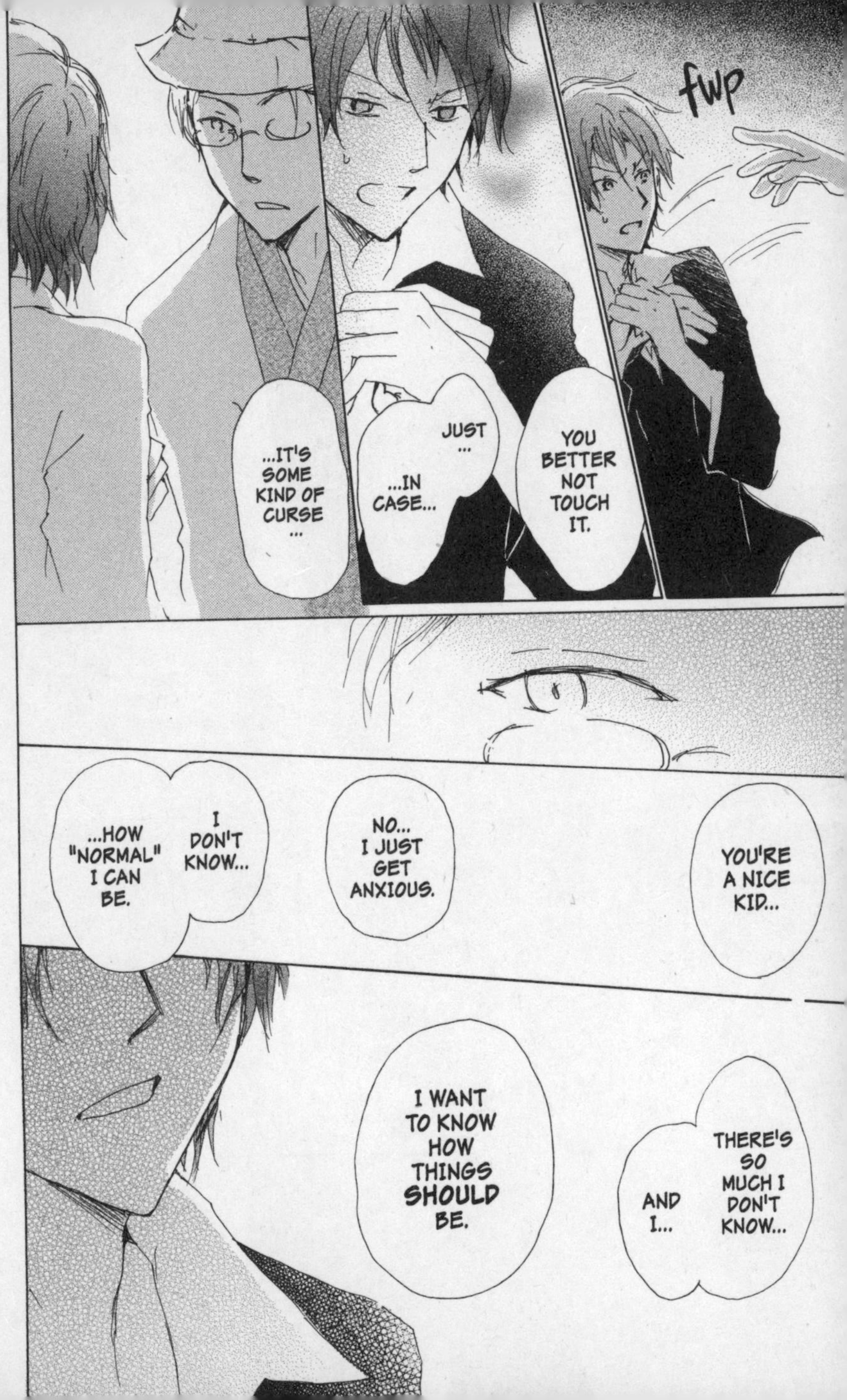
fwp
YOU BETTER NOT TOUCH IT.
JUST ...
...IN CASE...
...IT'S SOME KIND OF CURSE ...
YOU'RE A NICE KID...
NO... I JUST GET ANXIOUS.
I DON'T KNOW...
...HOW "NORMAL" I CAN BE.
THERE'S SO MUCH I DON'T KNOW...
AND I...
I WANT TO KNOW HOW THINGS **SHOULD** BE.

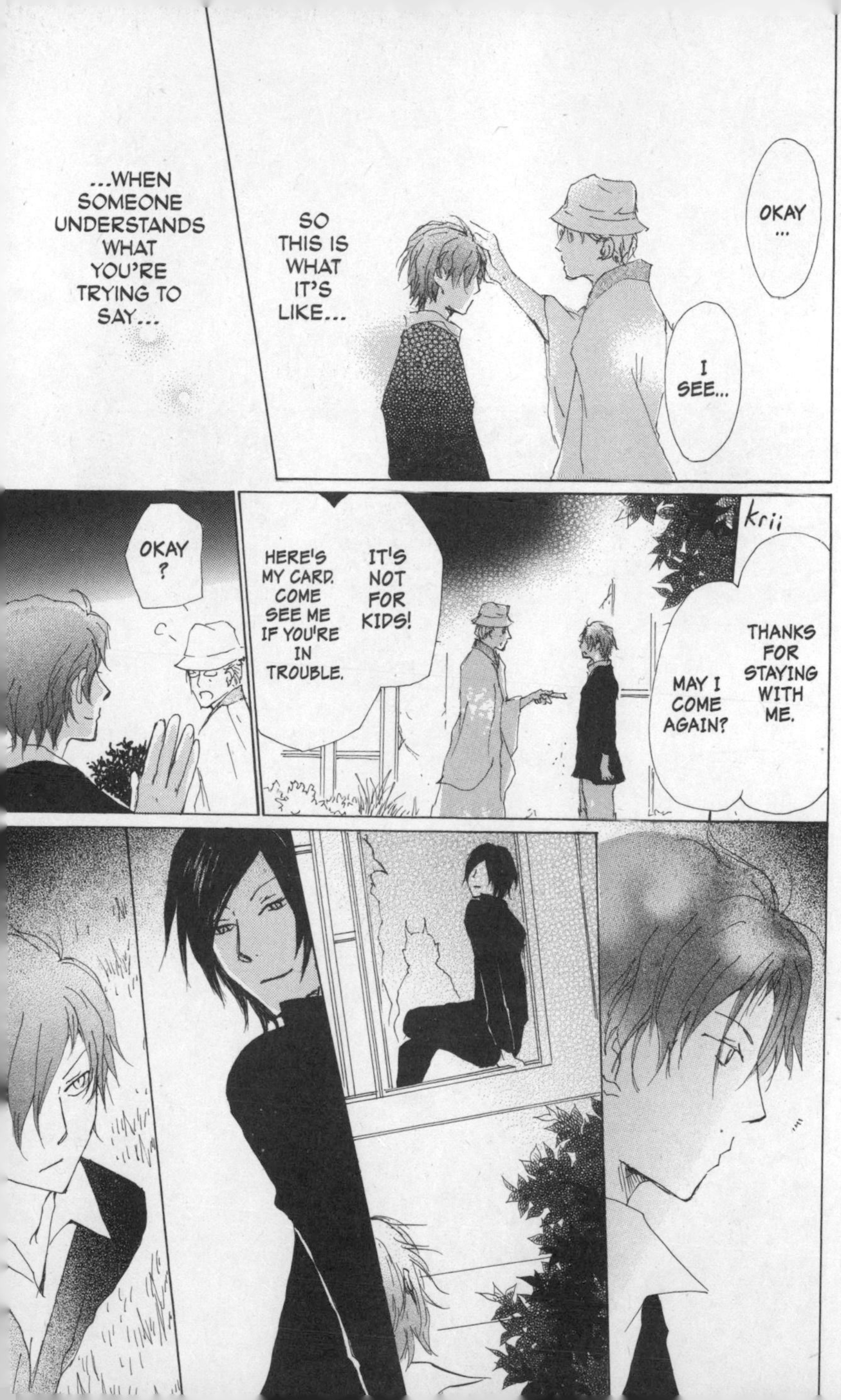
OKAY...
I SEE...
SO THIS IS WHAT IT'S LIKE...
...WHEN SOMEONE UNDERSTANDS WHAT YOU'RE TRYING TO SAY...
krii
THANKS FOR STAYING WITH ME.
MAY I COME AGAIN?
IT'S NOT FOR KIDS!
HERE'S MY CARD. COME SEE ME IF YOU'RE IN TROUBLE.
OKAY?

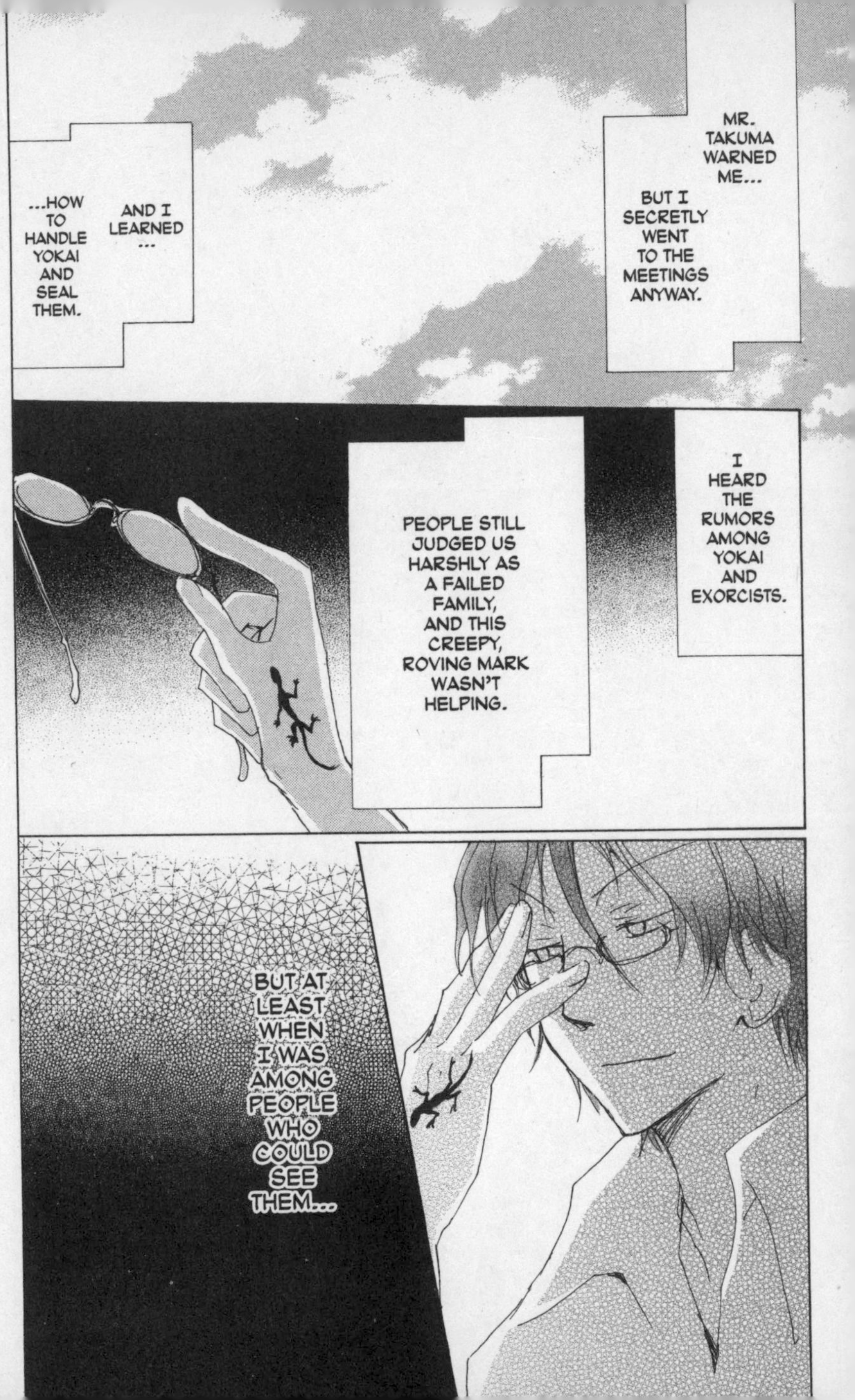
MR. TAKUMA WARNED ME...
BUT I SECRETLY WENT TO THE MEETINGS ANYWAY.
AND I LEARNED...
...HOW TO HANDLE YOKAI AND SEAL THEM.
I HEARD THE RUMORS AMONG YOKAI AND EXORCISTS.
PEOPLE STILL JUDGED US HARSHLY AS A FAILED FAMILY, AND THIS CREEPY, ROVING MARK WASN'T HELPING.
BUT AT LEAST WHEN I WAS AMONG PEOPLE WHO COULD SEE THEM...

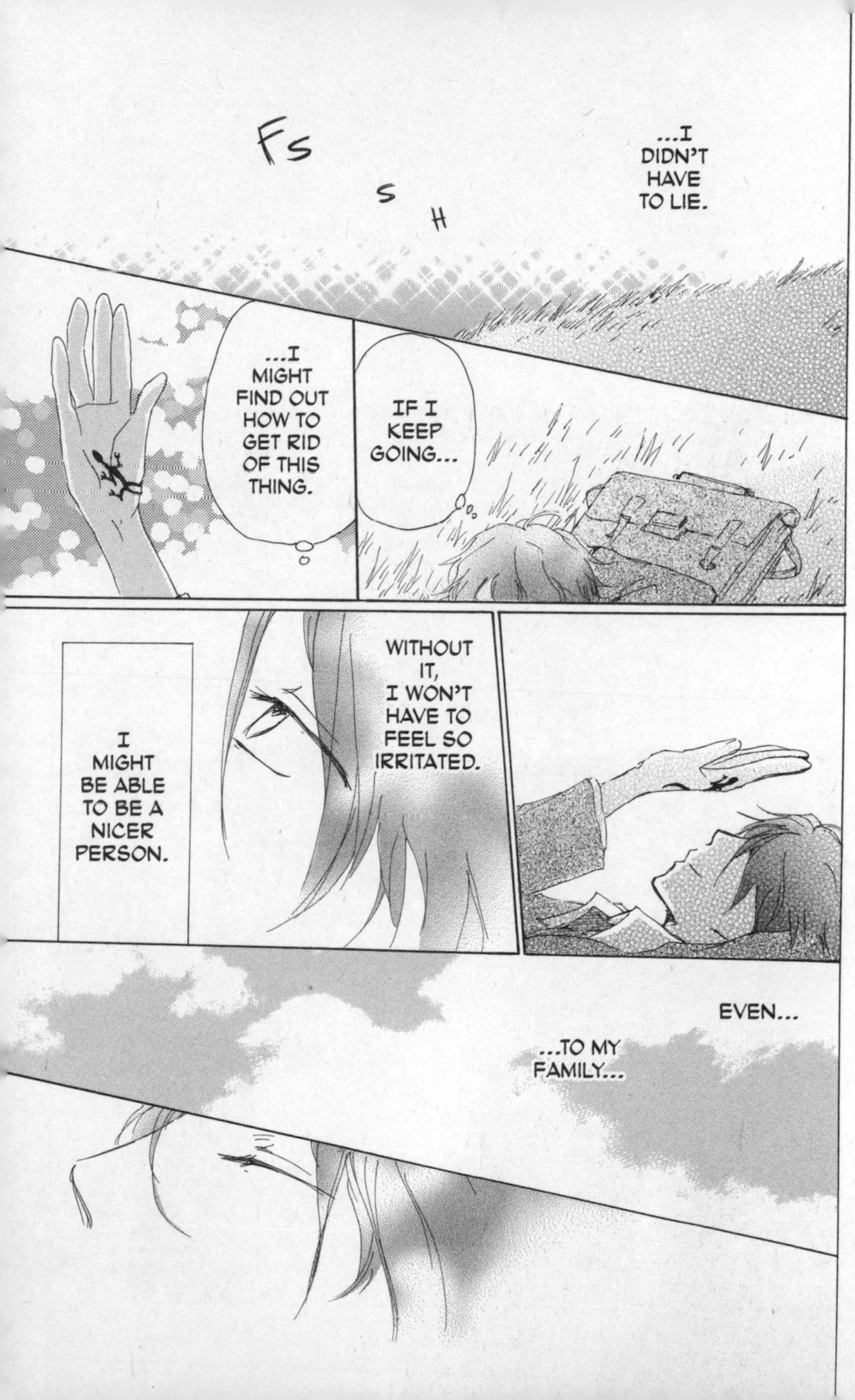
...I DIDN'T HAVE TO LIE.
FSSH
IF I KEEP GOING...
...I MIGHT FIND OUT HOW TO GET RID OF THIS THING.
WITHOUT IT, I WON'T HAVE TO FEEL SO IRRITATED.
I MIGHT BE ABLE TO BE A NICER PERSON.
EVEN...
...TO MY FAMILY...

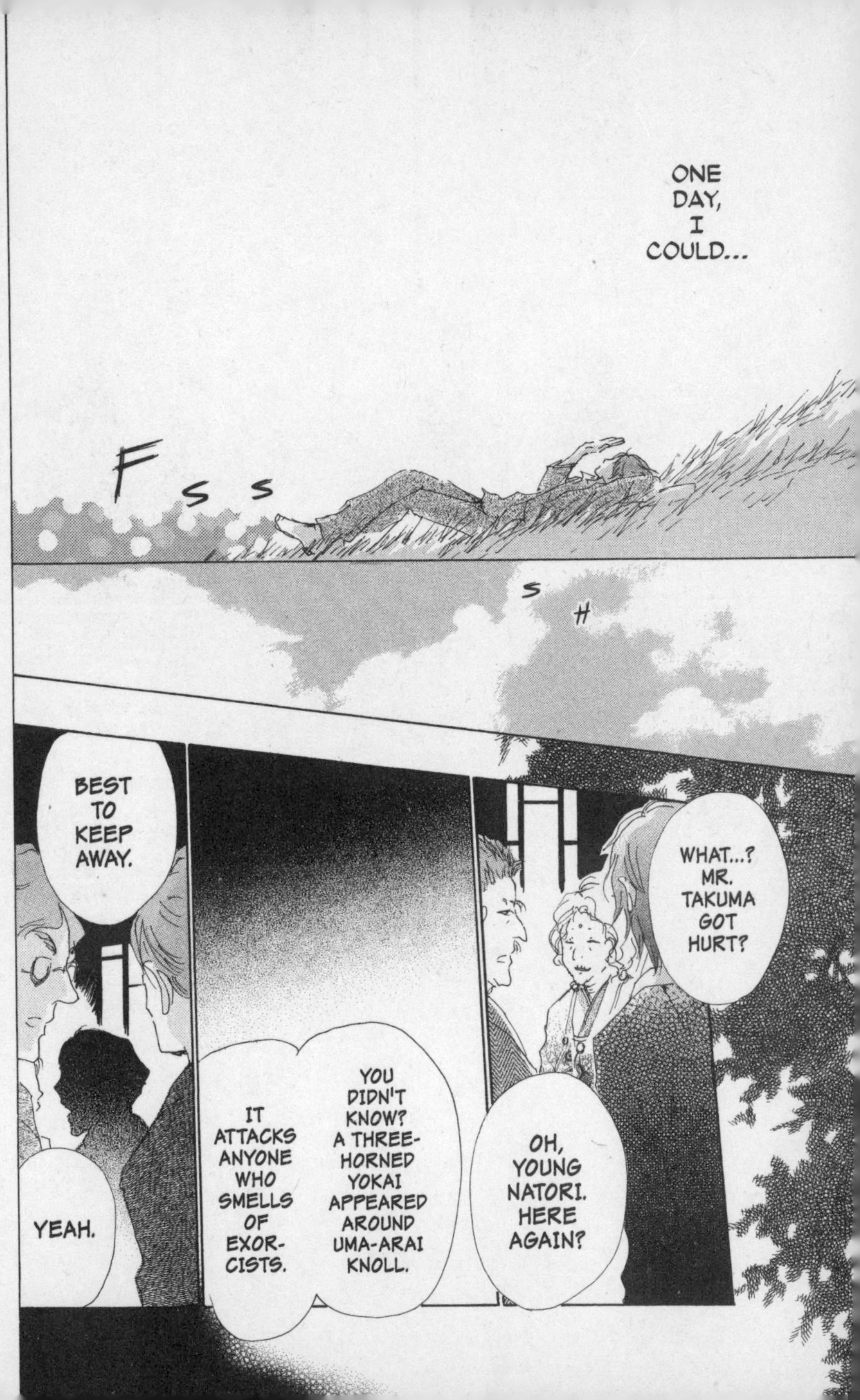
ONE DAY, I COULD...
FSS
SH
WHAT...? MR. TAKUMA GOT HURT?
OH, YOUNG NATORI. HERE AGAIN?
YOU DIDN'T KNOW? A THREE-HORNED YOKAI APPEARED AROUND UMA-ARAI KNOLL.
IT ATTACKS ANYONE WHO SMELLS OF EXORCISTS.
BEST TO KEEP AWAY.
YEAH.

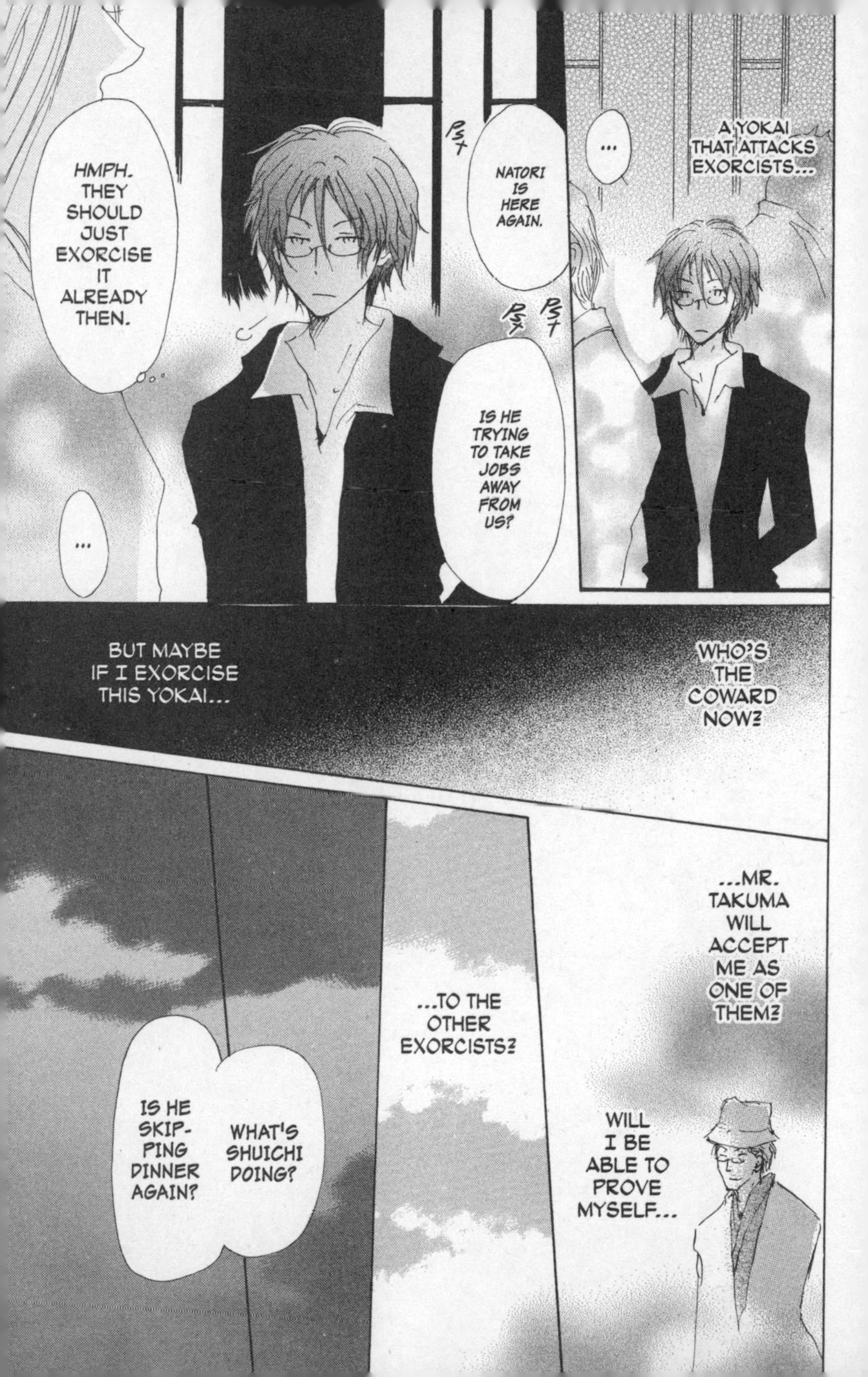
A YOKAI THAT ATTACKS EXORCISTS...
...
PST
NATORI IS HERE AGAIN.
PST
PST
IS HE TRYING TO TAKE JOBS AWAY FROM US?
HMPH. THEY SHOULD JUST EXORCISE IT ALREADY THEN.
...
WHO'S THE COWARD NOW?
BUT MAYBE IF I EXORCISE THIS YOKAI...
...MR. TAKUMA WILL ACCEPT ME AS ONE OF THEM?
WILL I BE ABLE TO PROVE MYSELF...
...TO THE OTHER EXORCISTS?
WHAT'S SHUICHI DOING?
IS HE SKIP-PING DINNER AGAIN?

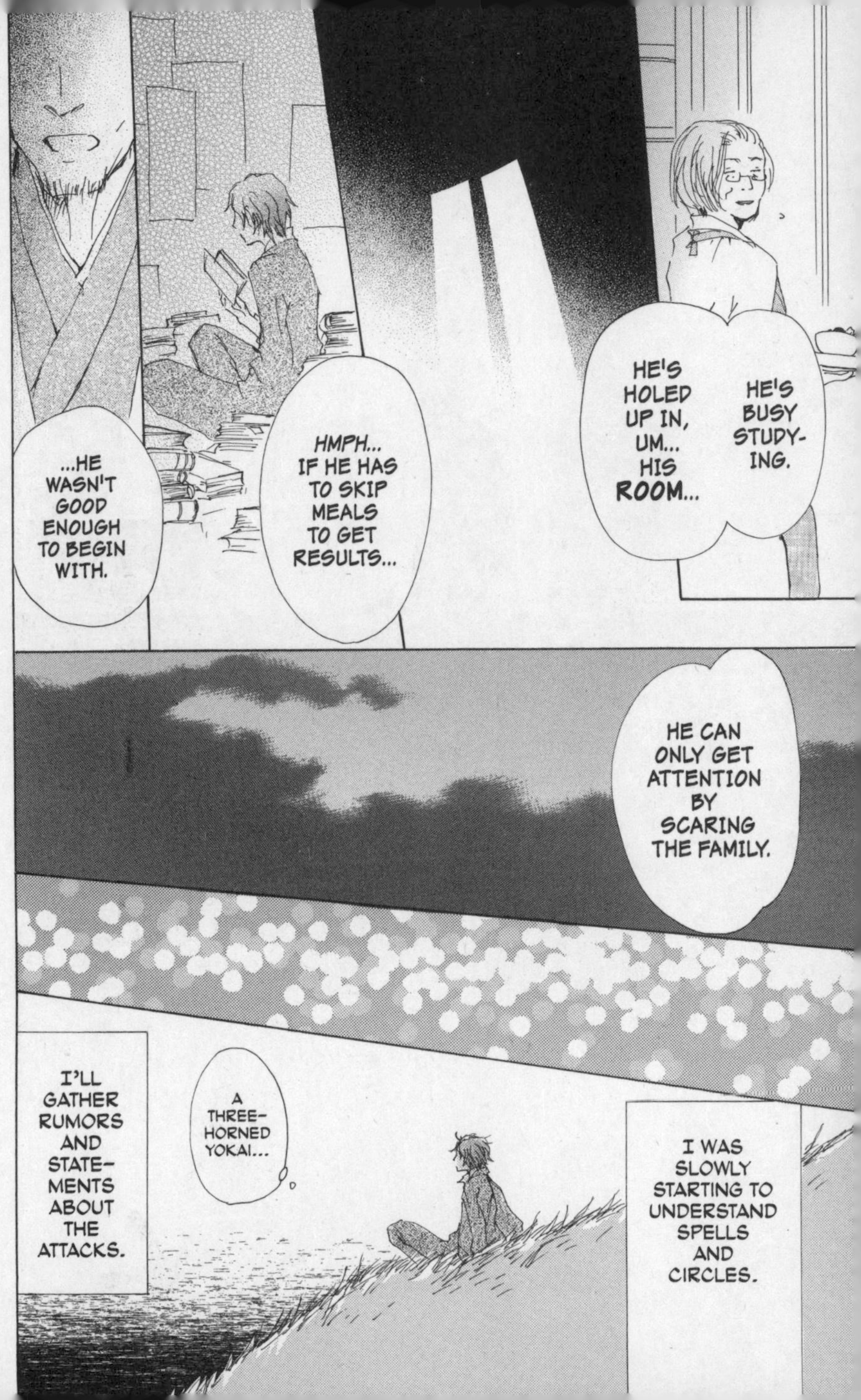
HE'S BUSY STUDYING.
HE'S HOLED UP IN, UM... HIS ROOM...
HMPH... IF HE HAS TO SKIP MEALS TO GET RESULTS...
...HE WASN'T GOOD ENOUGH TO BEGIN WITH.
HE CAN ONLY GET ATTENTION BY SCARING THE FAMILY.
I WAS SLOWLY STARTING TO UNDERSTAND SPELLS AND CIRCLES.
A THREE-HORNED YOKAI...
I'LL GATHER RUMORS AND STATEMENTS ABOUT THE ATTACKS.

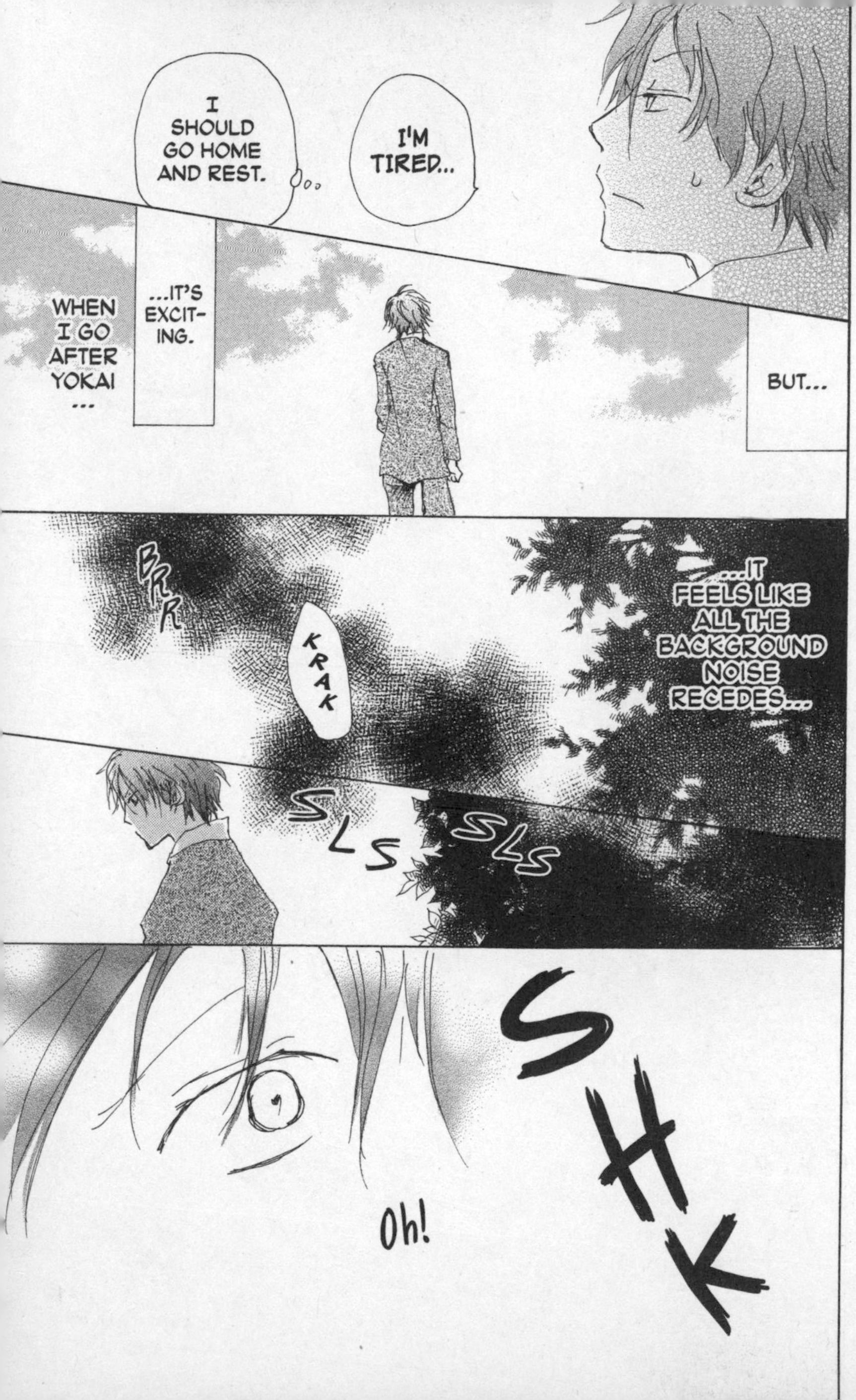
I'M TIRED...
I SHOULD GO HOME AND REST.
BUT...
...IT'S EXCIT-ING.
WHEN I GO AFTER YOKAI...
...IT FEELS LIKE ALL THE BACKGROUND NOISE RECEDES...
KRAK
BRR
SLS
SLS
SHK
Oh!

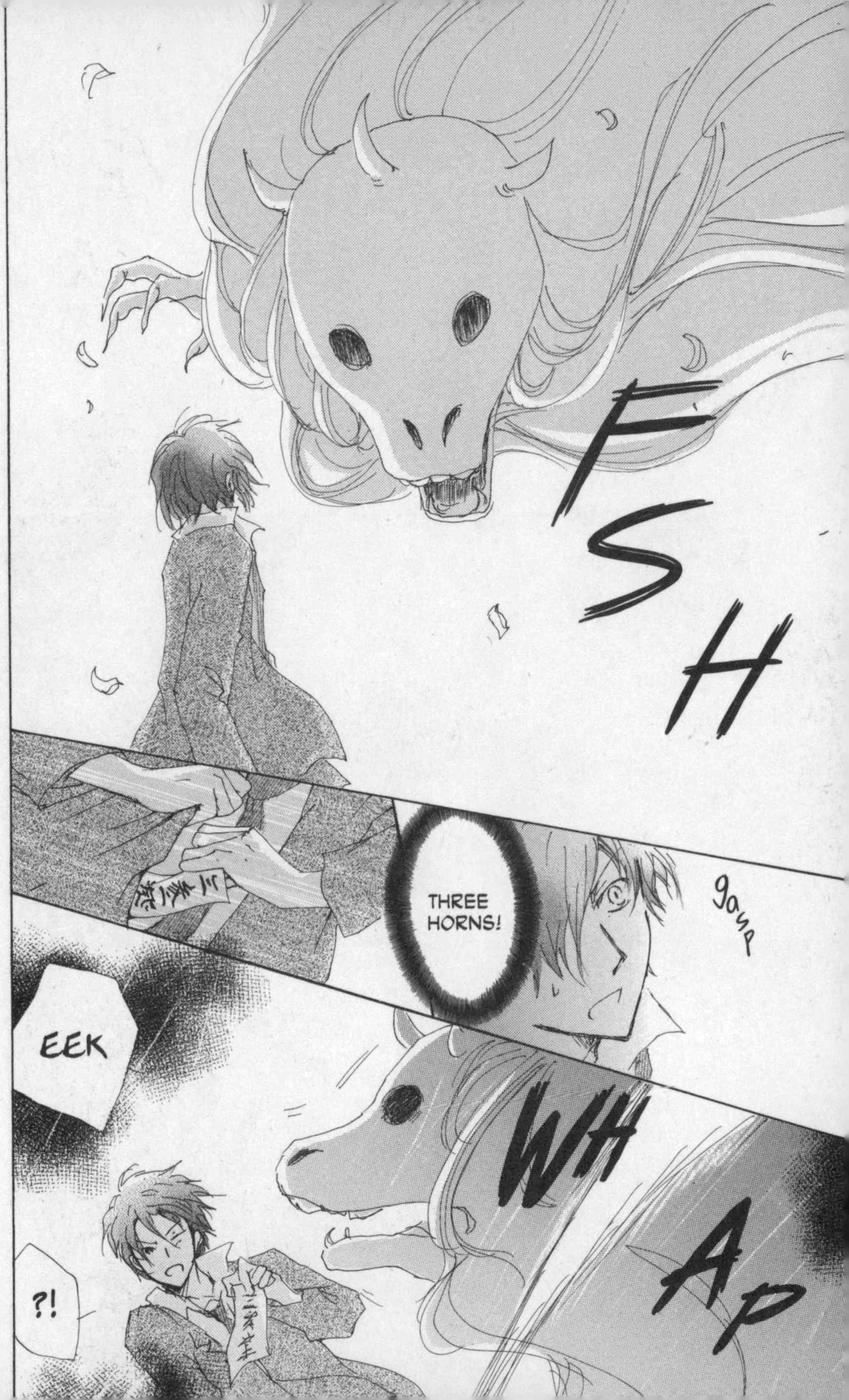
FSH
THREE HORNS!
gasp
WHAP
EEK
?!

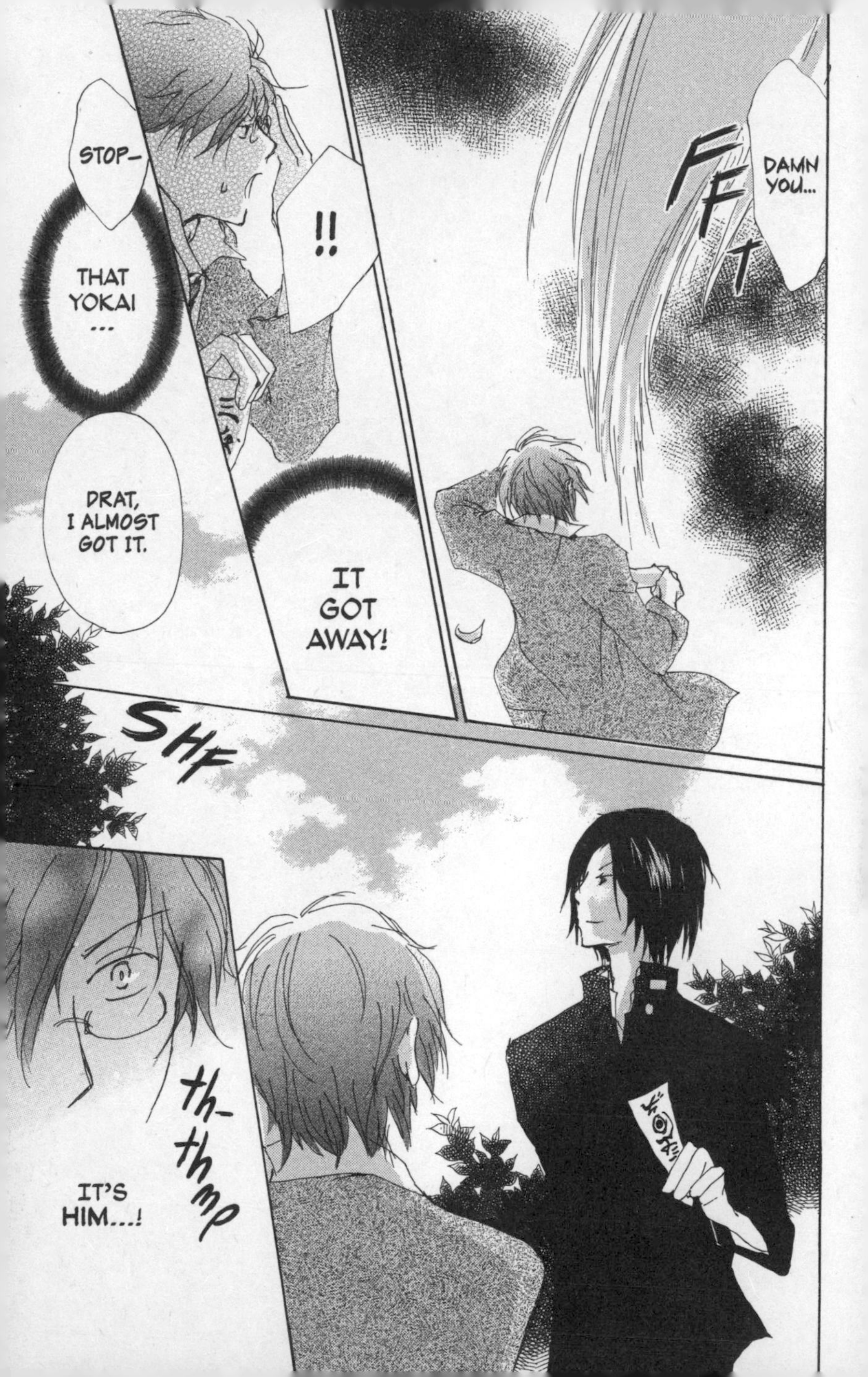
DAMN YOU...
FFT
!!
IT GOT AWAY!
STOP—
THAT YOKAI ...
DRAT, I ALMOST GOT IT.
SHF
th-thmp
IT'S HIM...!

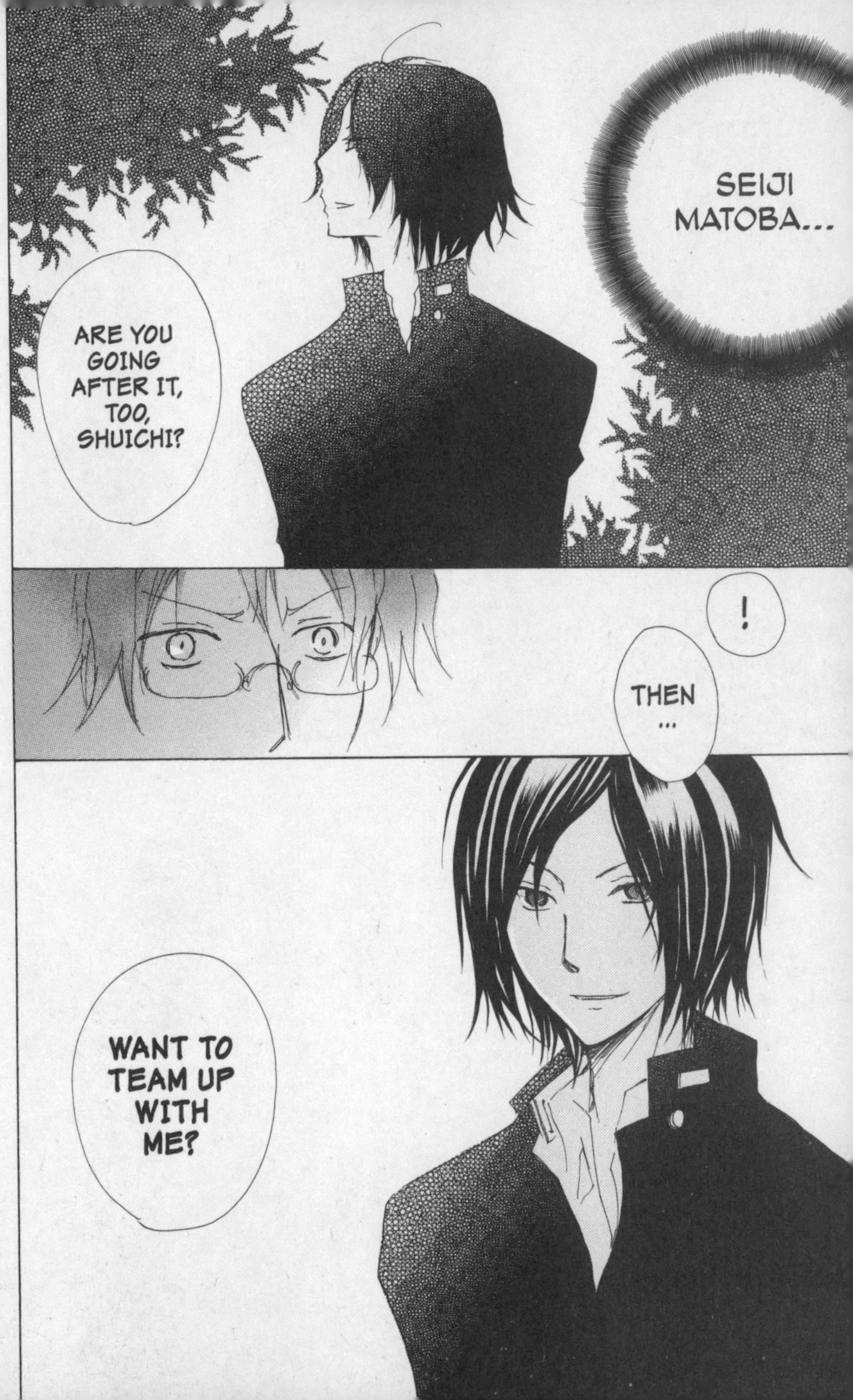
SEIJI MATOBA...
ARE YOU GOING AFTER IT, TOO, SHUICHI?
!
THEN ...
WANT TO TEAM UP WITH ME?

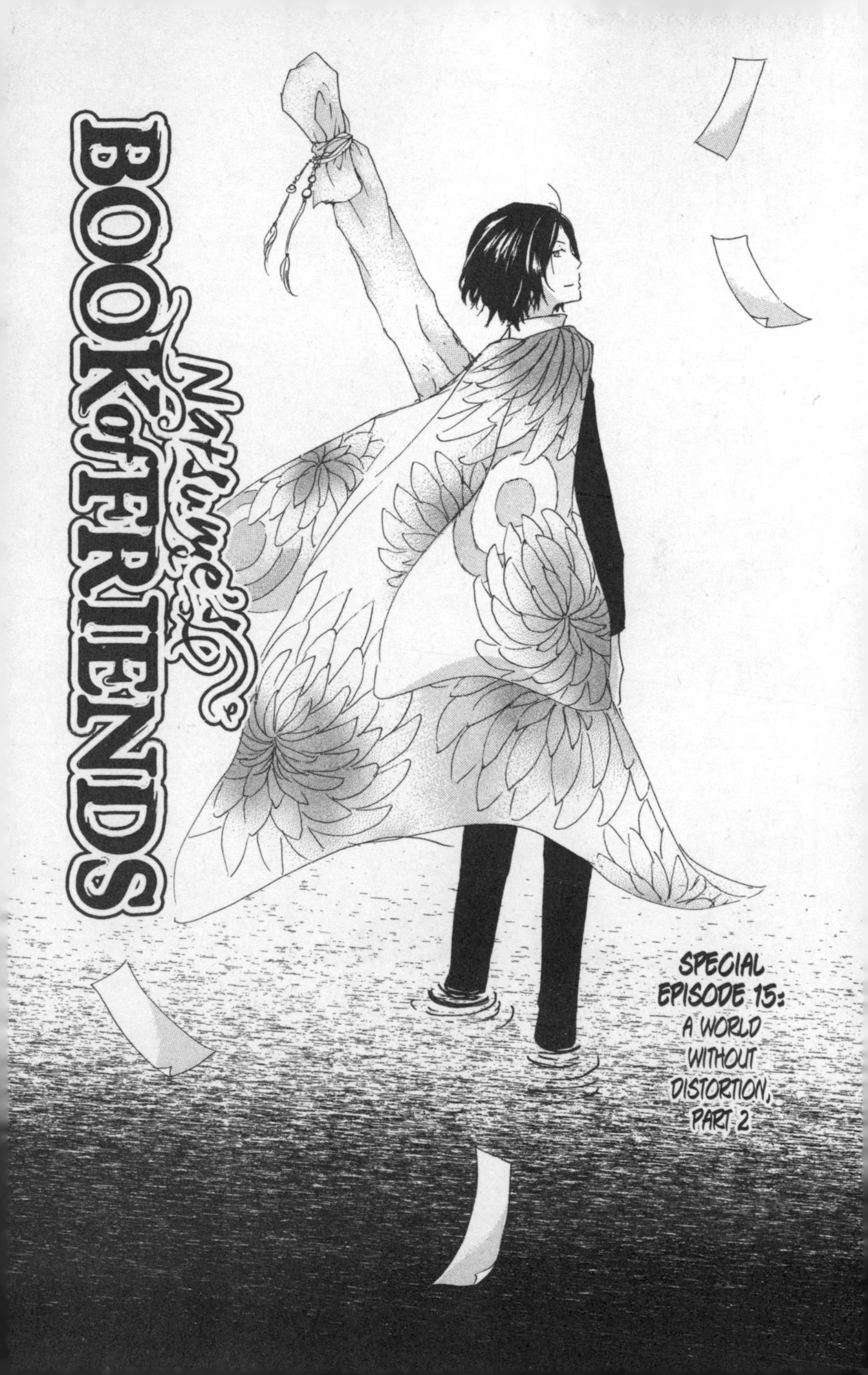
Natsume's BOOK of FRIENDS
SPECIAL EPISODE 15:
A WORLD WITHOUT DISTORTION, PART 2

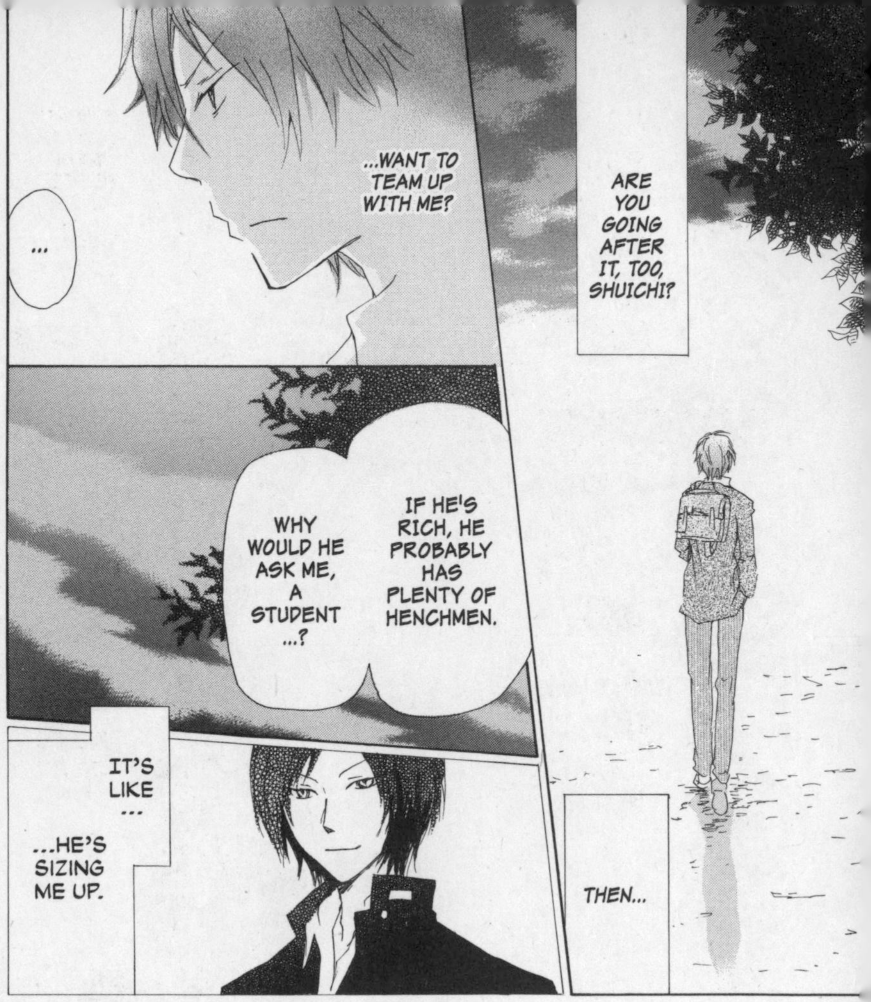
ARE YOU GOING AFTER IT, TOO, SHUICHI?
THEN...
...WANT TO TEAM UP WITH ME?
...
IF HE'S RICH, HE PROBABLY HAS PLENTY OF HENCHMEN.
WHY WOULD HE ASK ME, A STUDENT ...?
IT'S LIKE ...
...HE'S SIZING ME UP.

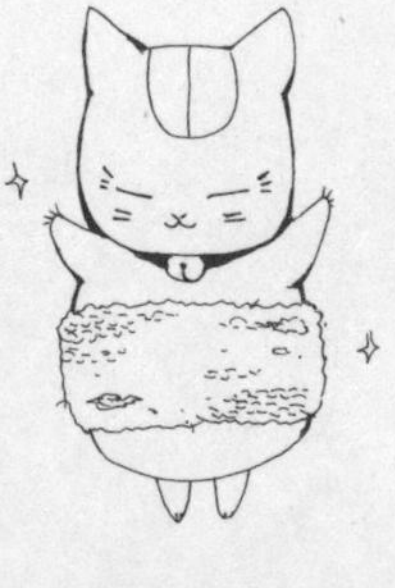

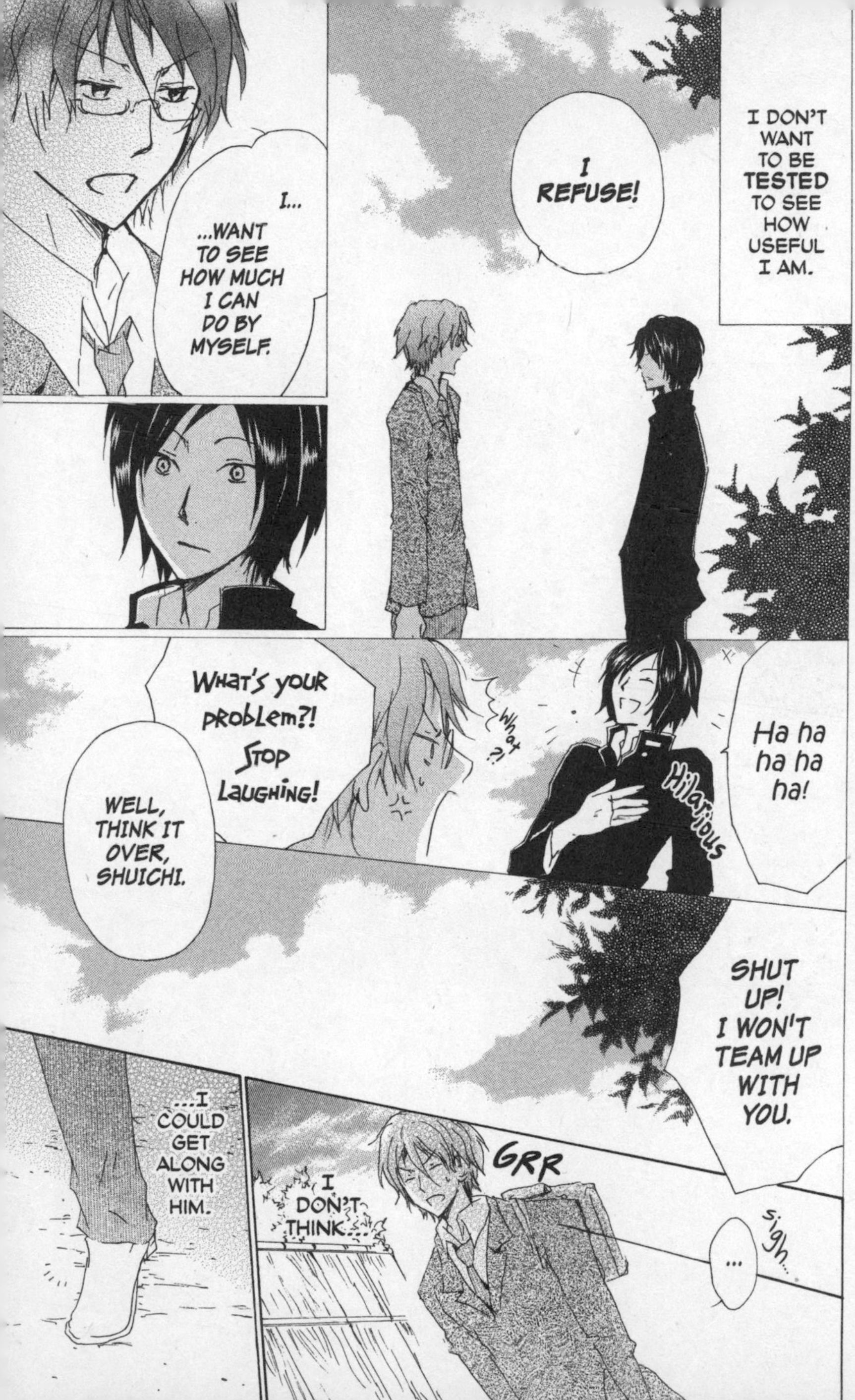
I DON'T WANT TO BE TESTED TO SEE HOW USEFUL I AM.
I REFUSE!
I...
...WANT TO SEE HOW MUCH I CAN DO BY MYSELF.
Ha ha ha ha ha!
Hilarious
What?!
What's your problem?! Stop laughing!
WELL, THINK IT OVER, SHUICHI.
SHUT UP! I WON'T TEAM UP WITH YOU.
sigh...
...
GRR
I DON'T THINK
...I COULD GET ALONG WITH HIM.

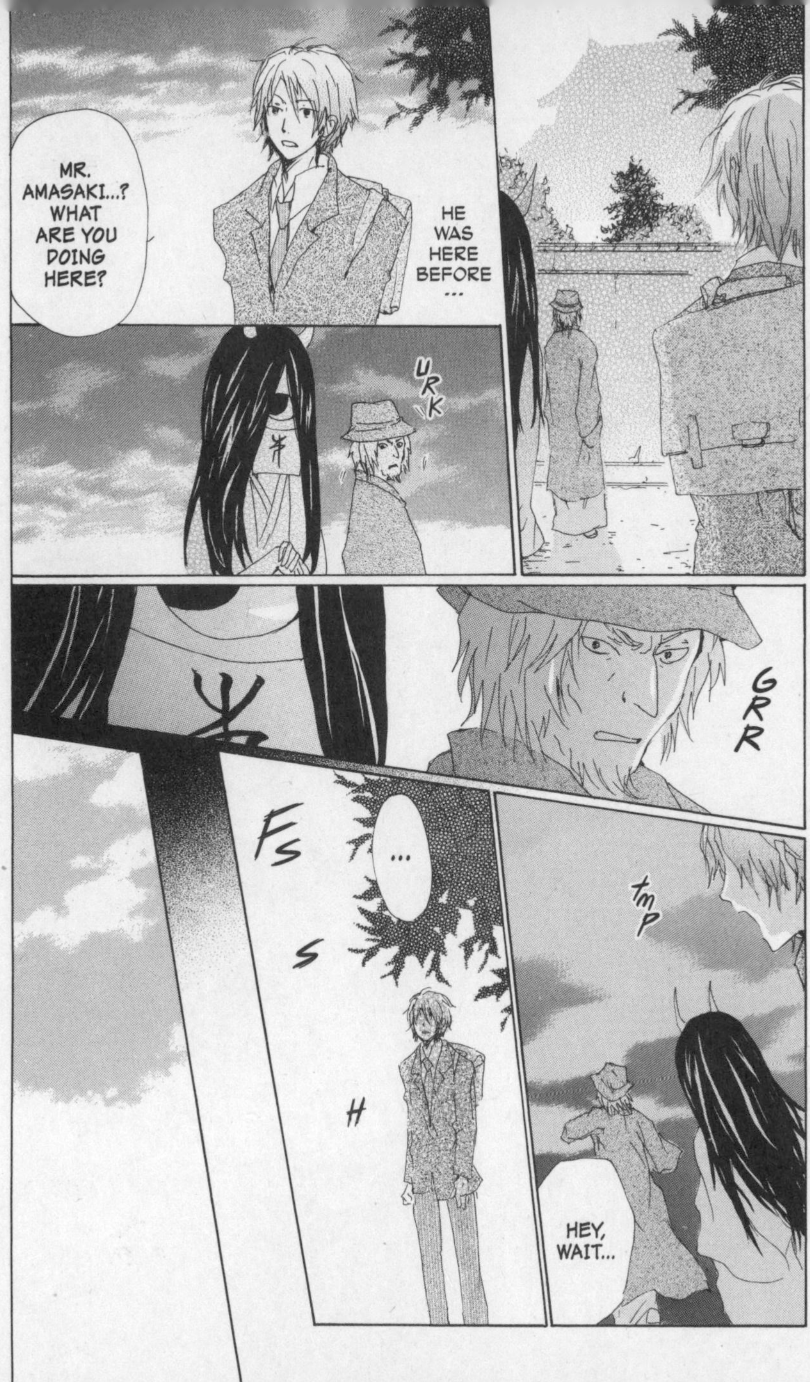
HE WAS HERE BEFORE...
MR. AMASAKI...? WHAT ARE YOU DOING HERE?
URK
GRR
tmp
HEY, WAIT...
...
FS
S
H

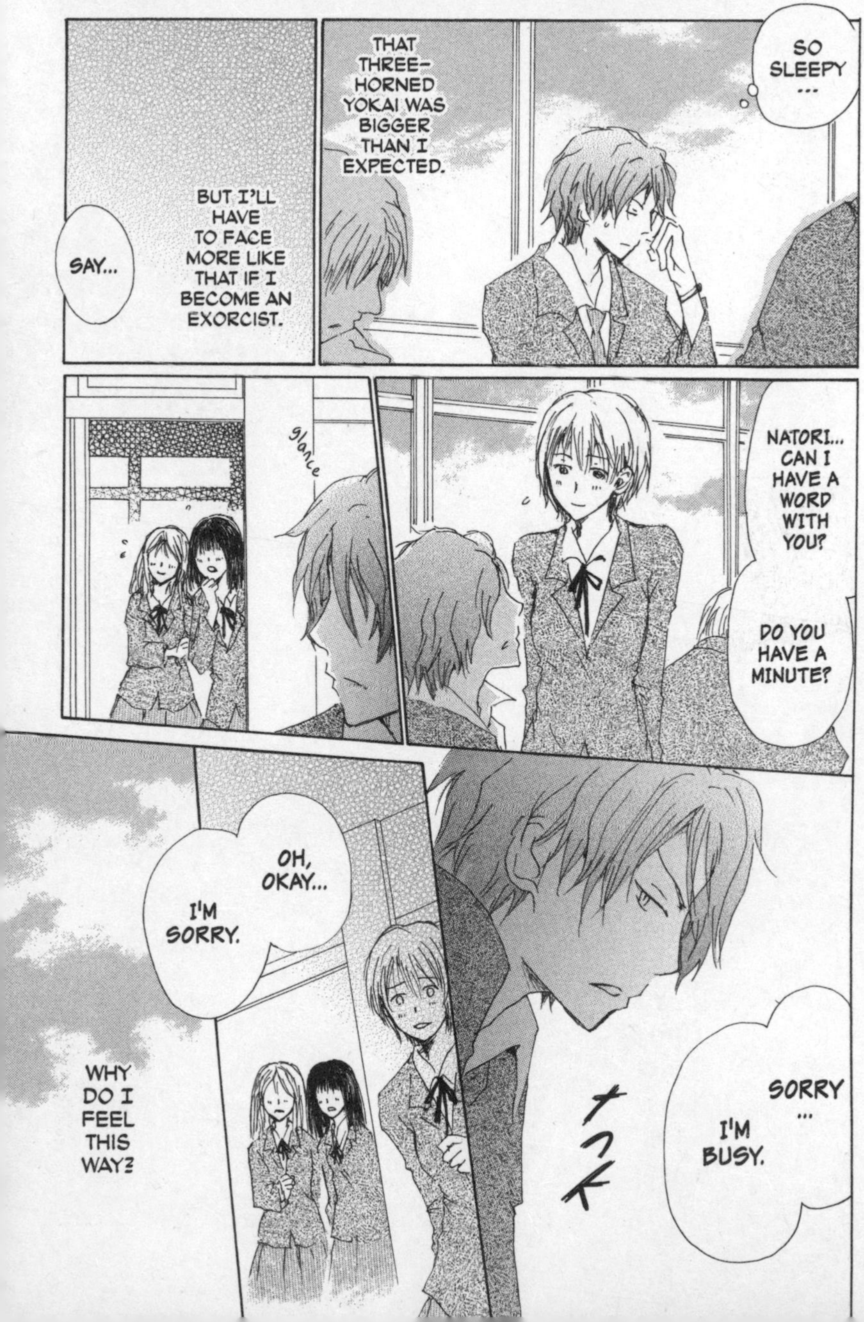
SO SLEEPY...
THAT THREE-HORNED YOKAI WAS BIGGER THAN I EXPECTED.
BUT I'LL HAVE TO FACE MORE LIKE THAT IF I BECOME AN EXORCIST.
SAY...
NATORI... CAN I HAVE A WORD WITH YOU?
DO YOU HAVE A MINUTE?
glance
SORRY... I'M BUSY.
OH, OKAY... I'M SORRY.
WHY DO I FEEL THIS WAY?

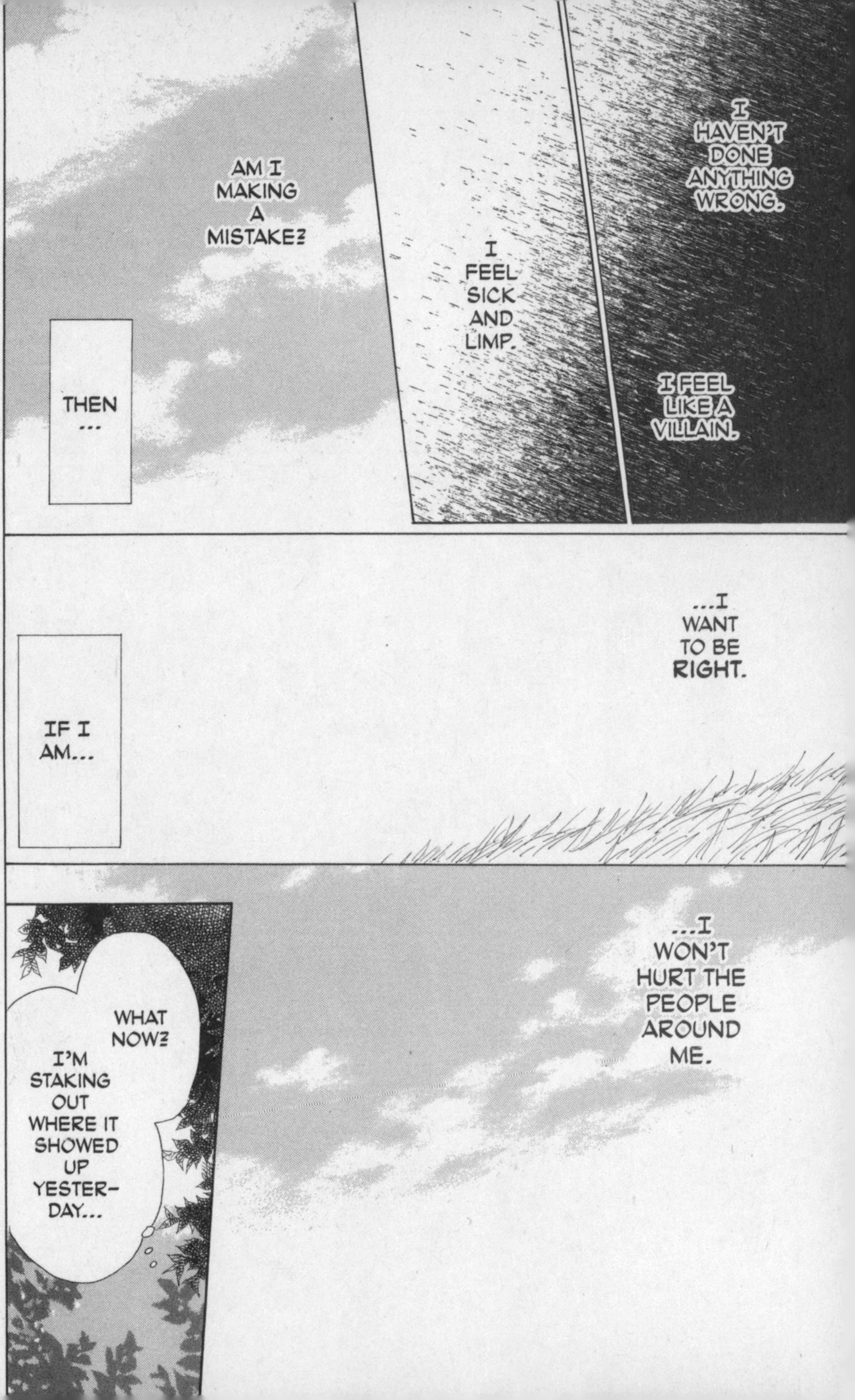
I HAVEN'T DONE ANYTHING WRONG.
I FEEL LIKE A VILLAIN.
I FEEL SICK AND LIMP.
AM I MAKING A MISTAKE?
THEN...
...I WANT TO BE RIGHT.
IF I AM...
...I WON'T HURT THE PEOPLE AROUND ME.
WHAT NOW? I'M STAKING OUT WHERE IT SHOWED UP YESTER-DAY...

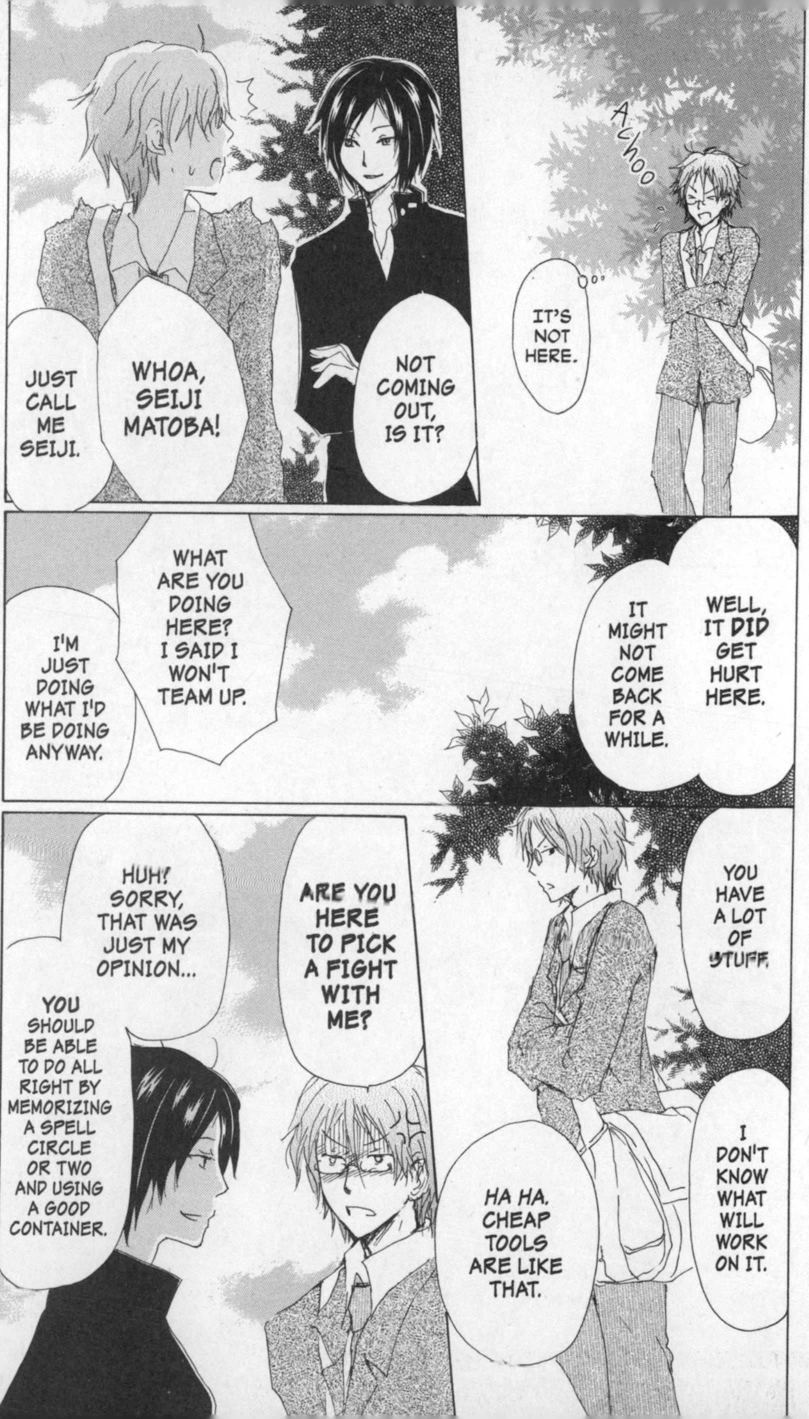
Achoo
IT'S NOT HERE.
NOT COMING OUT, IS IT?
WHOA, SEIJI MATOBA!
JUST CALL ME SEIJI.
WELL, IT DID GET HURT HERE.
IT MIGHT NOT COME BACK FOR A WHILE.
WHAT ARE YOU DOING HERE? I SAID I WON'T TEAM UP.
I'M JUST DOING WHAT I'D BE DOING ANYWAY.
YOU HAVE A LOT OF STUFF.
I DON'T KNOW WHAT WILL WORK ON IT.
HA HA. CHEAP TOOLS ARE LIKE THAT.
ARE YOU HERE TO PICK A FIGHT WITH ME?
HUH! SORRY, THAT WAS JUST MY OPINION...
YOU SHOULD BE ABLE TO DO ALL RIGHT BY MEMORIZING A SPELL CIRCLE OR TWO AND USING A GOOD CONTAINER.

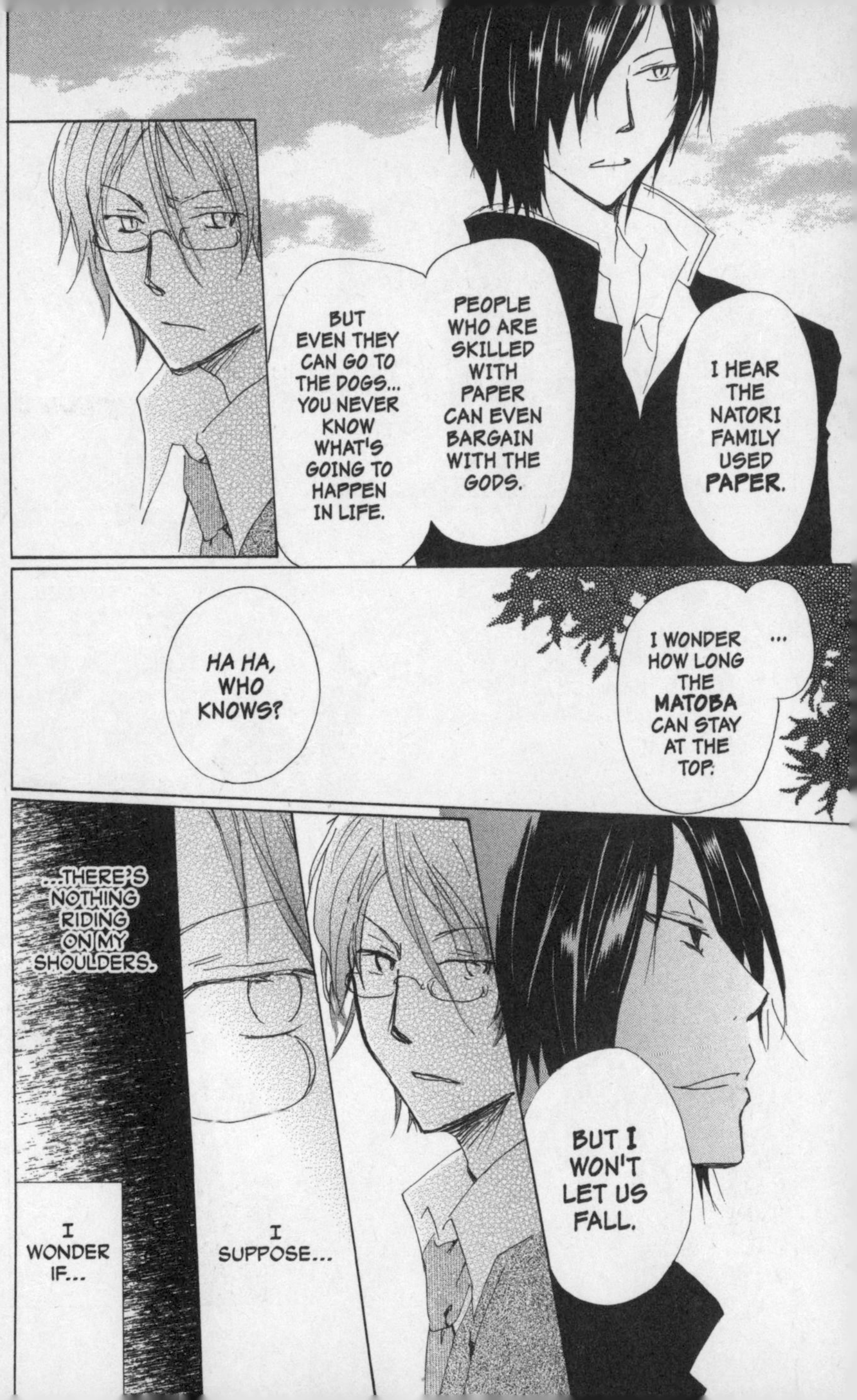
I HEAR THE NATORI FAMILY USED PAPER.
PEOPLE WHO ARE SKILLED WITH PAPER CAN EVEN BARGAIN WITH THE GODS.
BUT EVEN THEY CAN GO TO THE DOGS... YOU NEVER KNOW WHAT'S GOING TO HAPPEN IN LIFE.
...
I WONDER HOW LONG THE MATOBA CAN STAY AT THE TOP.
HA HA, WHO KNOWS?
BUT I WON'T LET US FALL.
I SUPPOSE...
I WONDER IF...
...THERE'S NOTHING RIDING ON MY SHOULDERS.

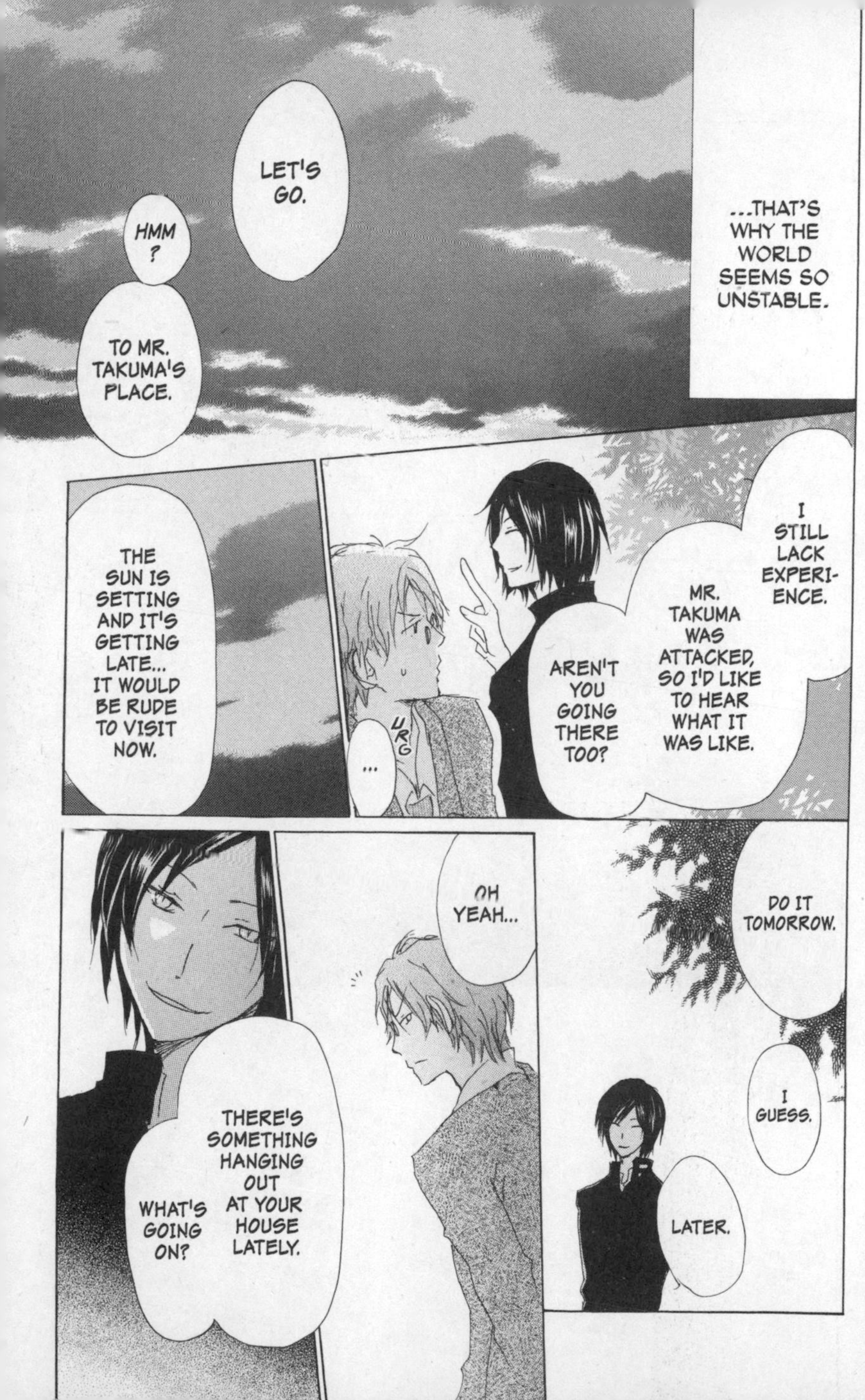
...THAT'S WHY THE WORLD SEEMS SO UNSTABLE.
LET'S GO.
HMM?
TO MR. TAKUMA'S PLACE.
I STILL LACK EXPERIENCE.
MR. TAKUMA WAS ATTACKED, SO I'D LIKE TO HEAR WHAT IT WAS LIKE.
AREN'T YOU GOING THERE TOO?
URG
...
THE SUN IS SETTING AND IT'S GETTING LATE... IT WOULD BE RUDE TO VISIT NOW.
DO IT TOMORROW.
I GUESS.
LATER.
OH YEAH...
THERE'S SOMETHING HANGING OUT AT YOUR HOUSE LATELY.
WHAT'S GOING ON?

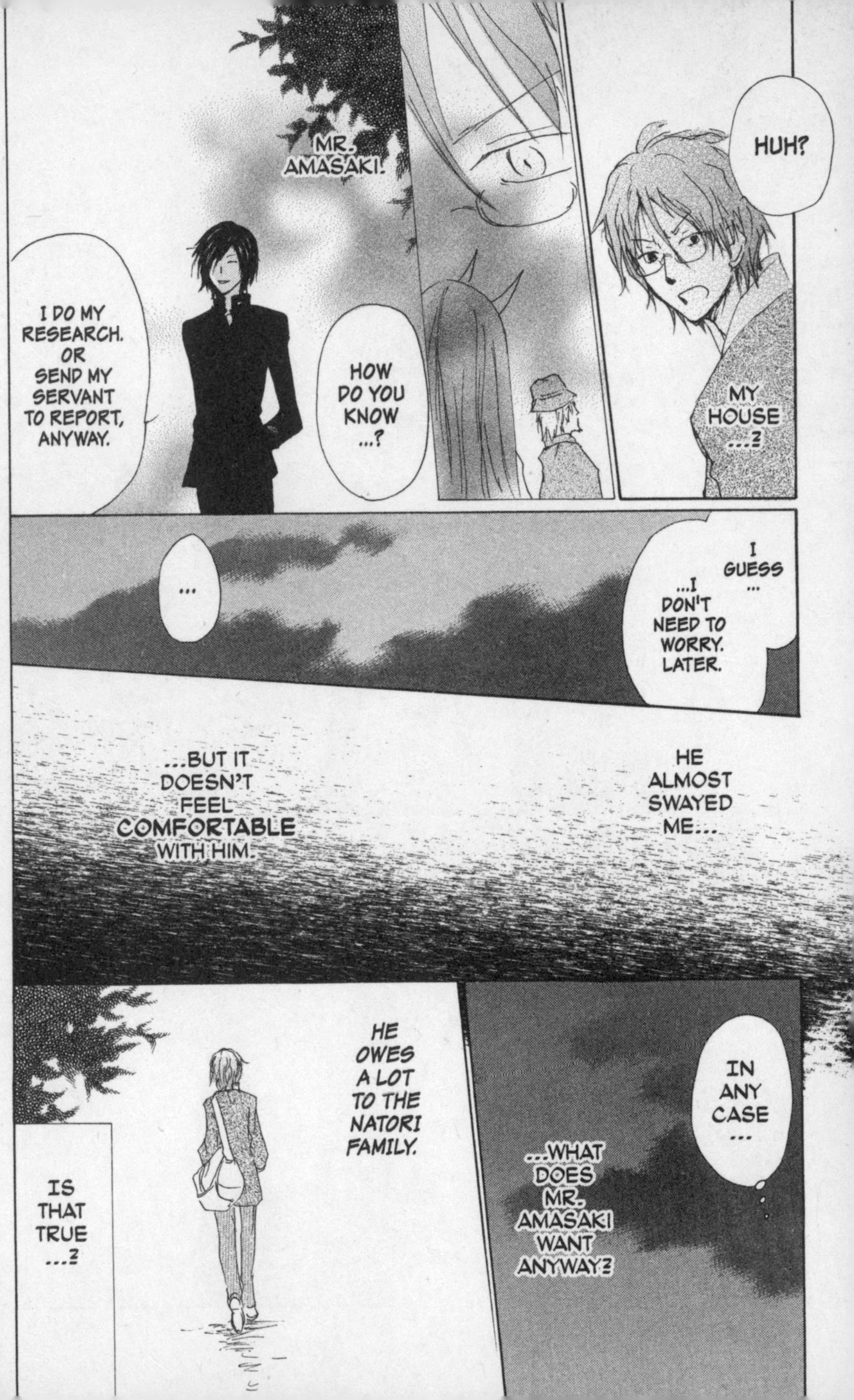
HUH?
MY HOUSE ...?
MR. AMASAKI.
HOW DO YOU KNOW ...?
I DO MY RESEARCH. OR SEND MY SERVANT TO REPORT, ANYWAY.
I GUESS ... ...I DON'T NEED TO WORRY. LATER.
...
HE ALMOST SWAYED ME...
...BUT IT DOESN'T FEEL COMFORTABLE WITH HIM.
IN ANY CASE ...
...WHAT DOES MR. AMASAKI WANT ANYWAY?
HE OWES A LOT TO THE NATORI FAMILY.
IS THAT TRUE ...?

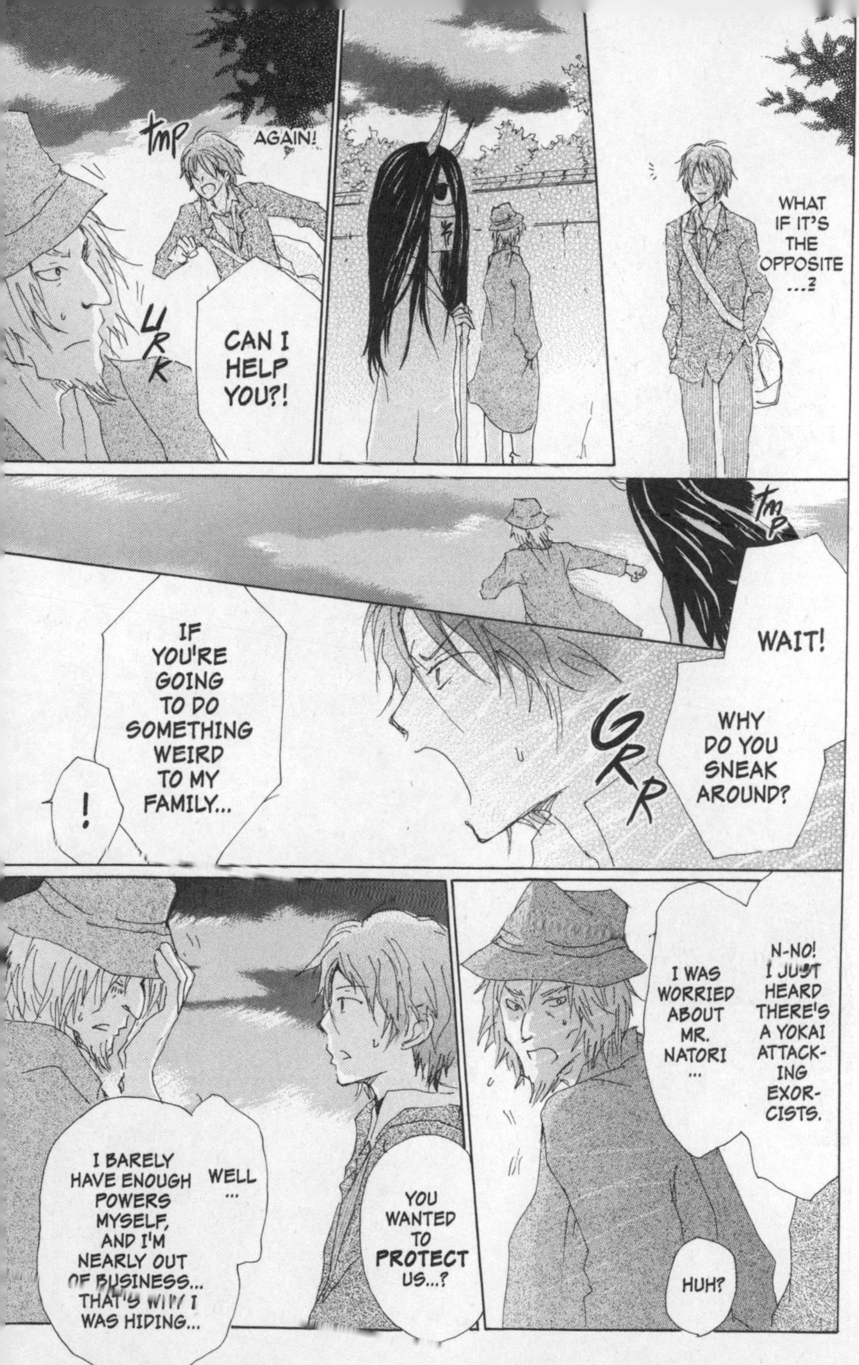
WHAT IF IT'S THE OPPOSITE...?
AGAIN!
tmp
CAN I HELP YOU?!
URK
tmp
WAIT!
WHY DO YOU SNEAK AROUND?
GRR
IF YOU'RE GOING TO DO SOMETHING WEIRD TO MY FAMILY...
!
N-NO! I JUST HEARD THERE'S A YOKAI ATTACKING EXORCISTS.
I WAS WORRIED ABOUT MR. NATORI...
HUH?
YOU WANTED TO PROTECT US...?
WELL...
I BARELY HAVE ENOUGH POWERS MYSELF, AND I'M NEARLY OUT OF BUSINESS... THAT'S WHY I WAS HIDING...

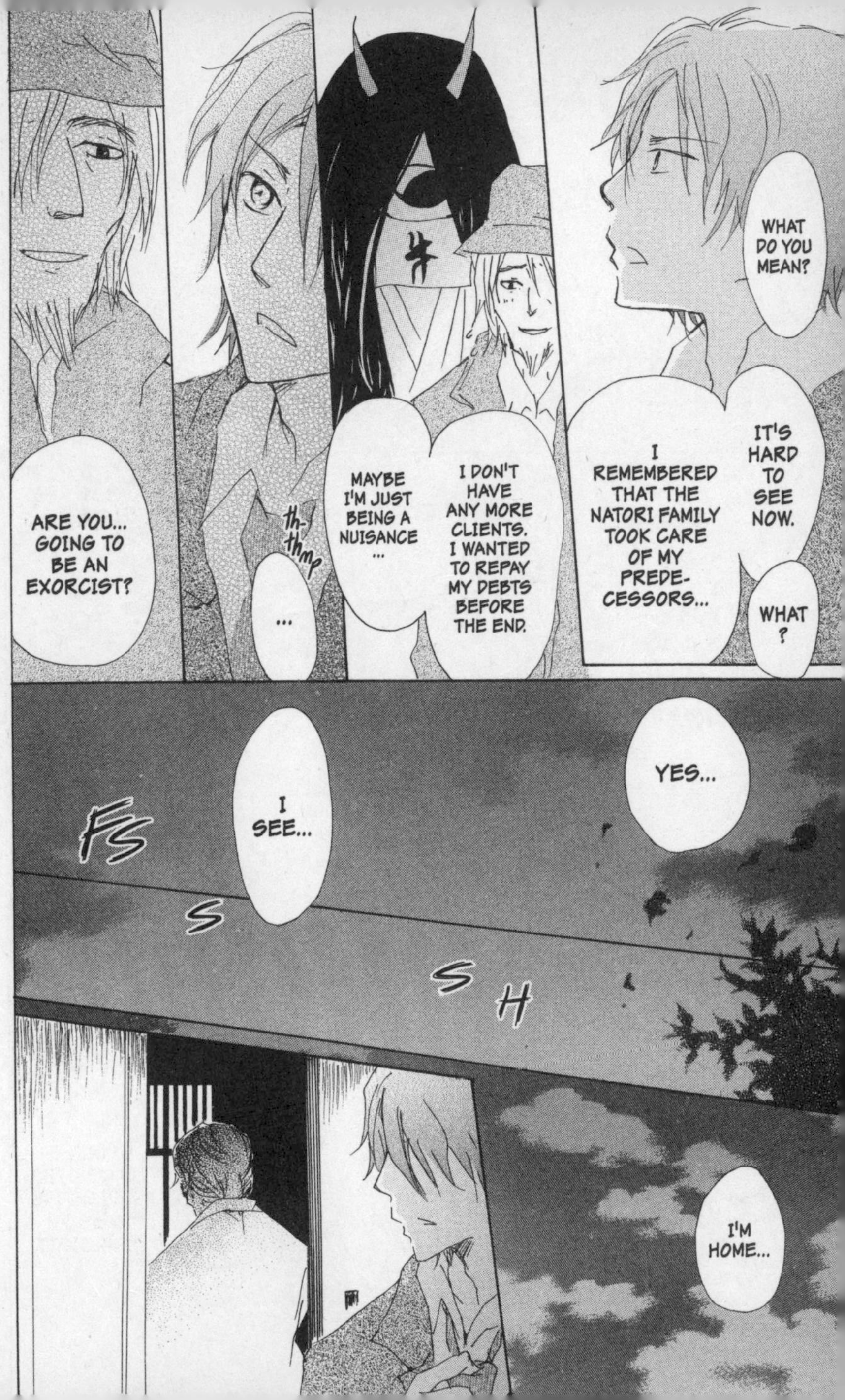
WHAT DO YOU MEAN?
IT'S HARD TO SEE NOW.
WHAT?
I REMEMBERED THAT THE NATORI FAMILY TOOK CARE OF MY PREDE-CESSORS...
I DON'T HAVE ANY MORE CLIENTS. I WANTED TO REPAY MY DEBTS BEFORE THE END.
MAYBE I'M JUST BEING A NUISANCE ...
th-thmp
...
ARE YOU... GOING TO BE AN EXORCIST?
YES...
I SEE...
FS
S
S
H
I'M HOME...

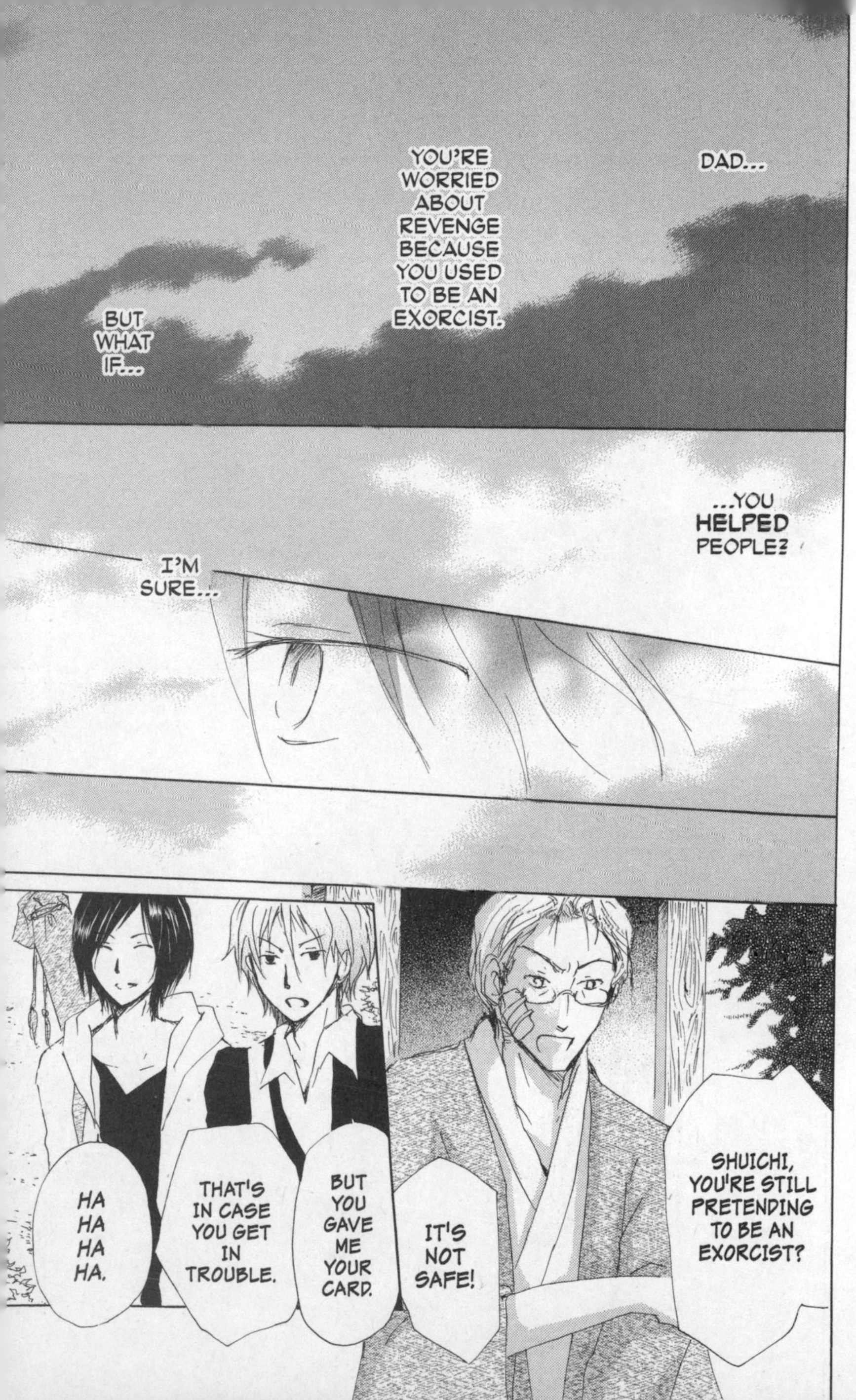
DAD...
YOU'RE WORRIED ABOUT REVENGE BECAUSE YOU USED TO BE AN EXORCIST.
BUT WHAT IF...
...YOU HELPED PEOPLE?
I'M SURE...
SHUICHI, YOU'RE STILL PRETENDING TO BE AN EXORCIST?
IT'S NOT SAFE!
BUT YOU GAVE ME YOUR CARD.
THAT'S IN CASE YOU GET IN TROUBLE.
HA HA HA HA.

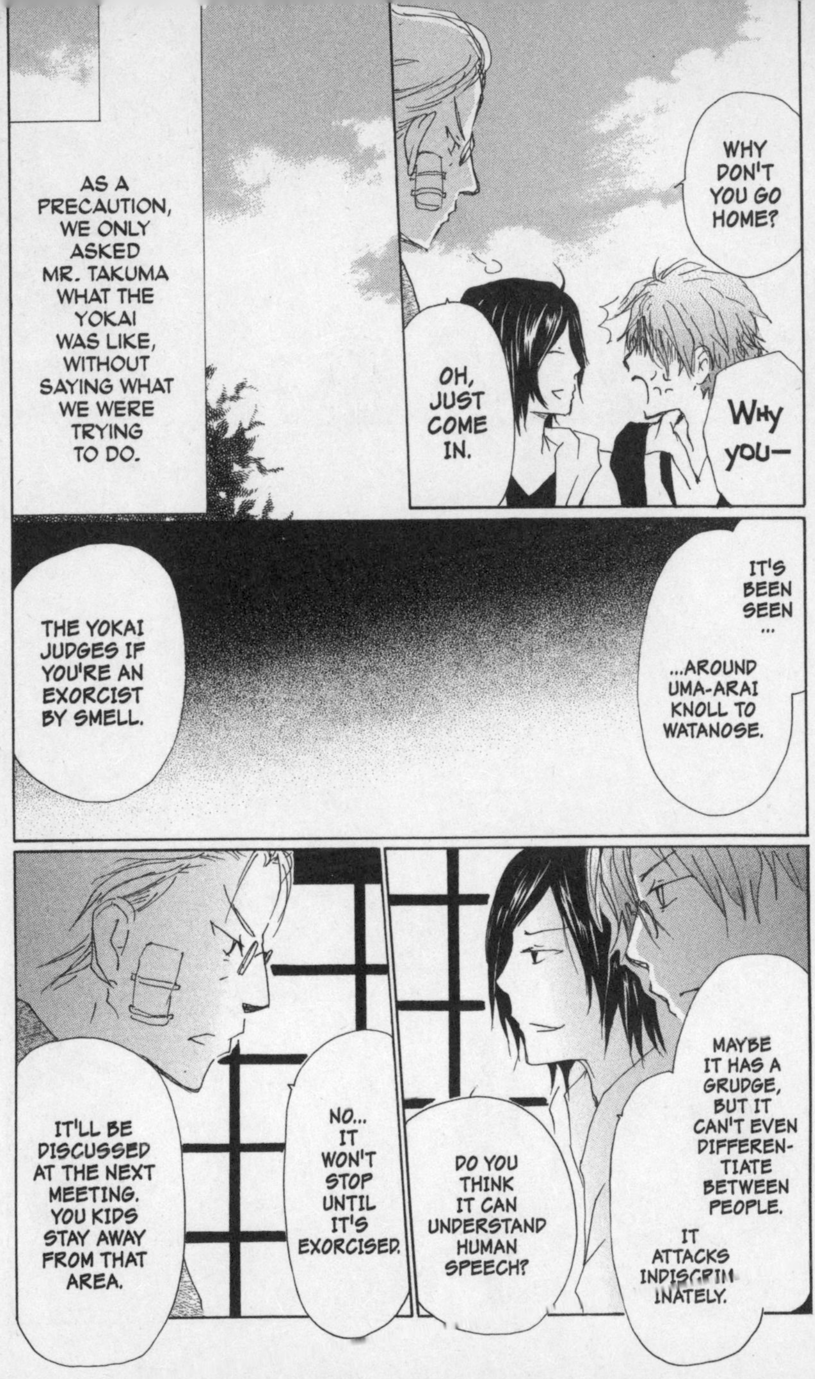
WHY DON'T YOU GO HOME?
Why you—
OH, JUST COME IN.
AS A PRECAUTION, WE ONLY ASKED MR. TAKUMA WHAT THE YOKAI WAS LIKE, WITHOUT SAYING WHAT WE WERE TRYING TO DO.
IT'S BEEN SEEN ...
...AROUND UMA-ARAI KNOLL TO WATANOSE.
THE YOKAI JUDGES IF YOU'RE AN EXORCIST BY SMELL.
MAYBE IT HAS A GRUDGE, BUT IT CAN'T EVEN DIFFEREN-TIATE BETWEEN PEOPLE.
IT ATTACKS INDISCRIMINATELY.
DO YOU THINK IT CAN UNDERSTAND HUMAN SPEECH?
NO... IT WON'T STOP UNTIL IT'S EXORCISED.
IT'LL BE DISCUSSED AT THE NEXT MEETING. YOU KIDS STAY AWAY FROM THAT AREA.

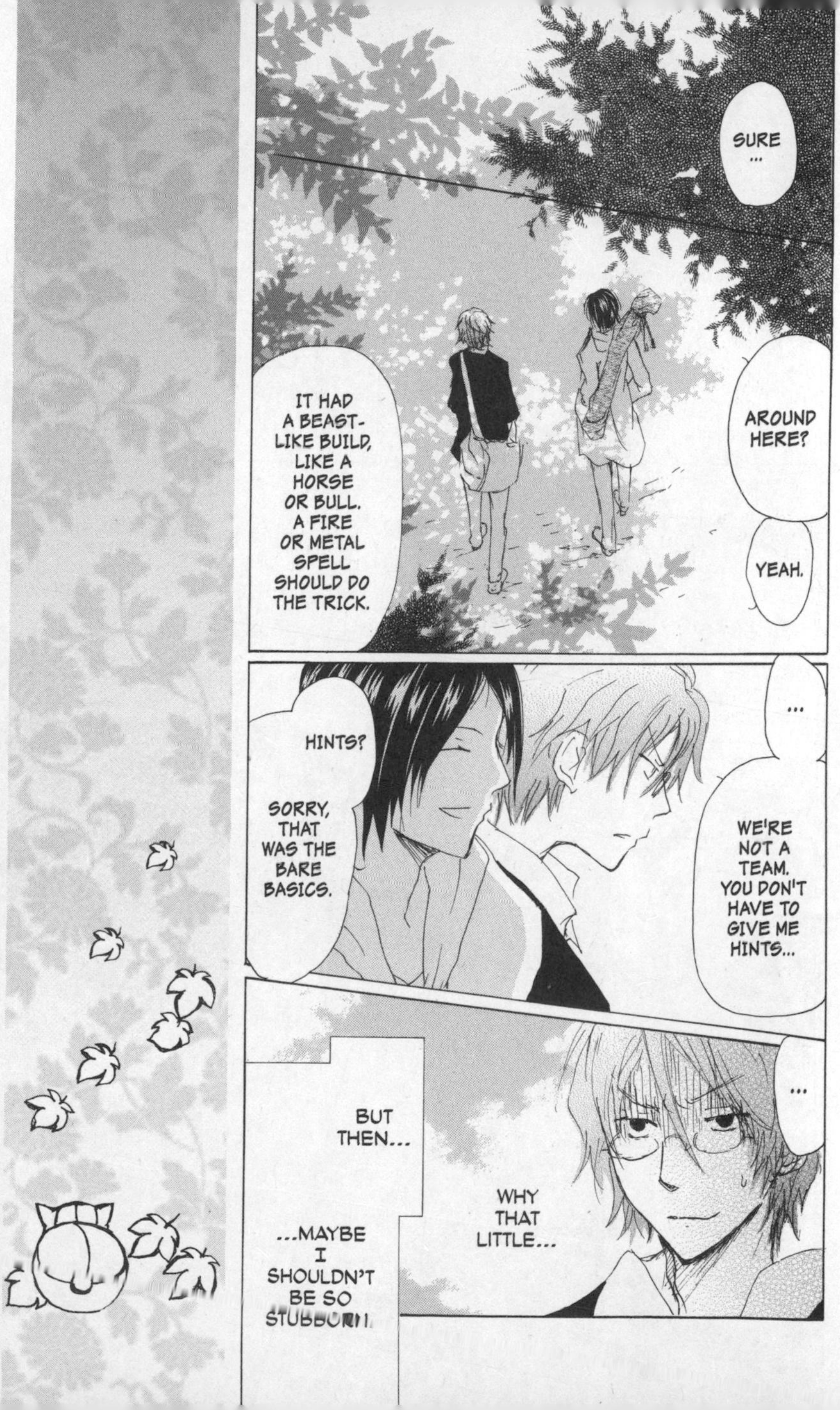
SURE...
AROUND HERE?
YEAH.
IT HAD A BEAST-LIKE BUILD, LIKE A HORSE OR BULL. A FIRE OR METAL SPELL SHOULD DO THE TRICK.
...
WE'RE NOT A TEAM. YOU DON'T HAVE TO GIVE ME HINTS...
HINTS?
SORRY, THAT WAS THE BARE BASICS.
...
WHY THAT LITTLE...
BUT THEN...
...MAYBE I SHOULDN'T BE SO STUBBORN.

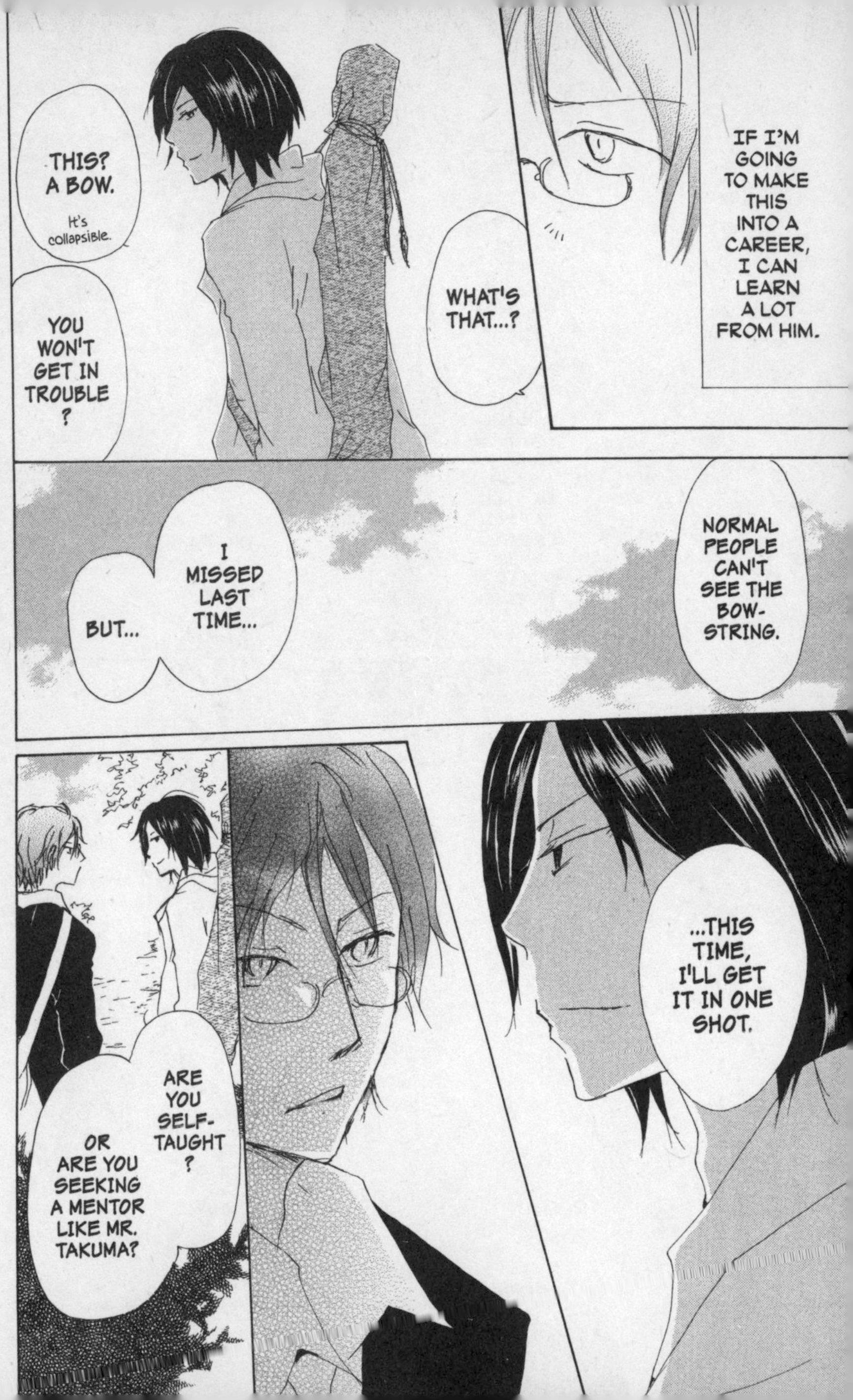
IF I'M GOING TO MAKE THIS INTO A CAREER, I CAN LEARN A LOT FROM HIM.
WHAT'S THAT...?
THIS? A BOW.
It's collapsible.
YOU WON'T GET IN TROUBLE?
NORMAL PEOPLE CAN'T SEE THE BOW-STRING.
I MISSED LAST TIME...
BUT...
...THIS TIME, I'LL GET IT IN ONE SHOT.
ARE YOU SELF-TAUGHT?
OR ARE YOU SEEKING A MENTOR LIKE MR. TAKUMA?

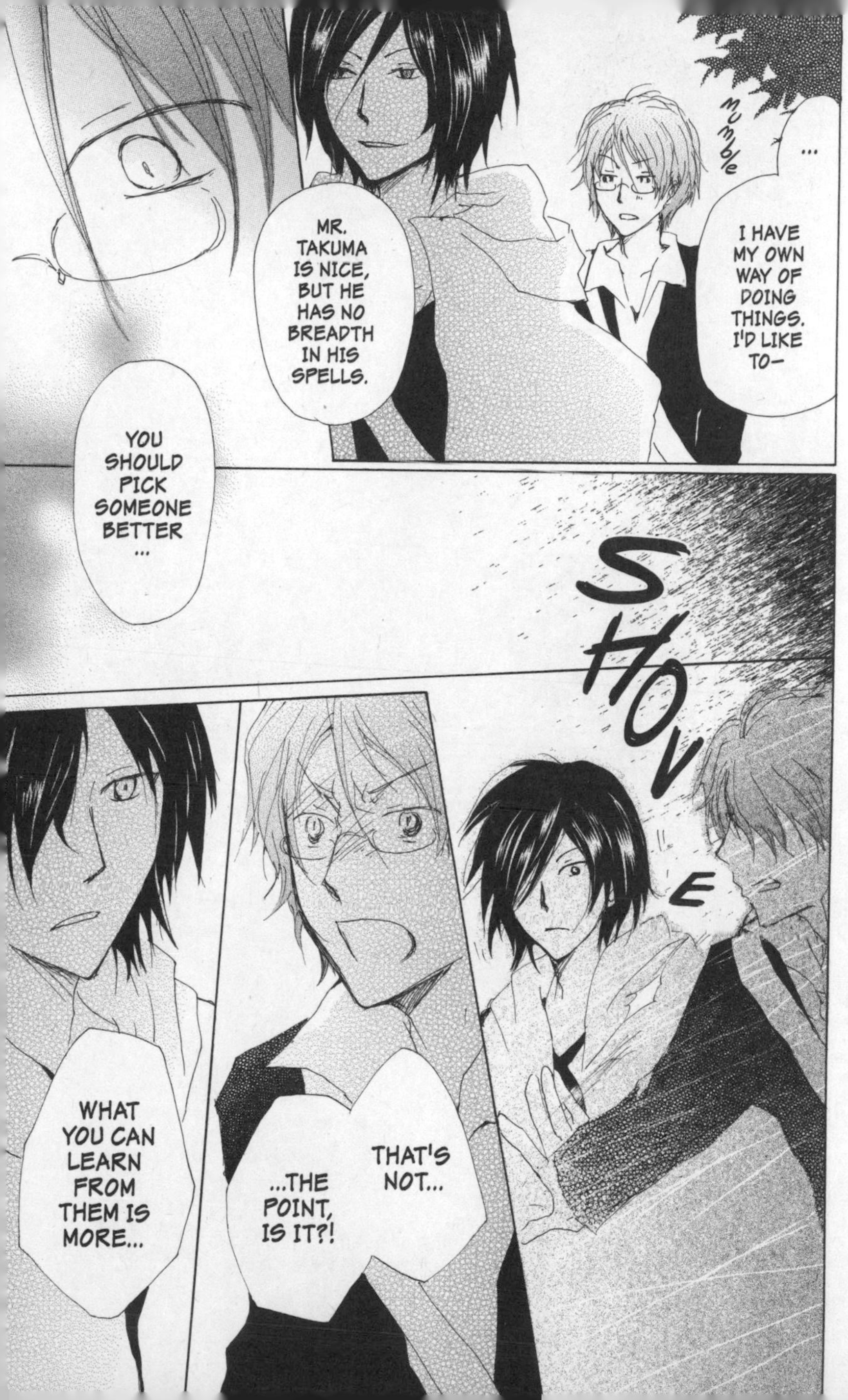
MUMBLE
...
I HAVE MY OWN WAY OF DOING THINGS. I'D LIKE TO—
MR. TAKUMA IS NICE, BUT HE HAS NO BREADTH IN HIS SPELLS.
YOU SHOULD PICK SOMEONE BETTER ...
SHOVE
THAT'S NOT...
...THE POINT, IS IT?!
WHAT YOU CAN LEARN FROM THEM IS MORE...

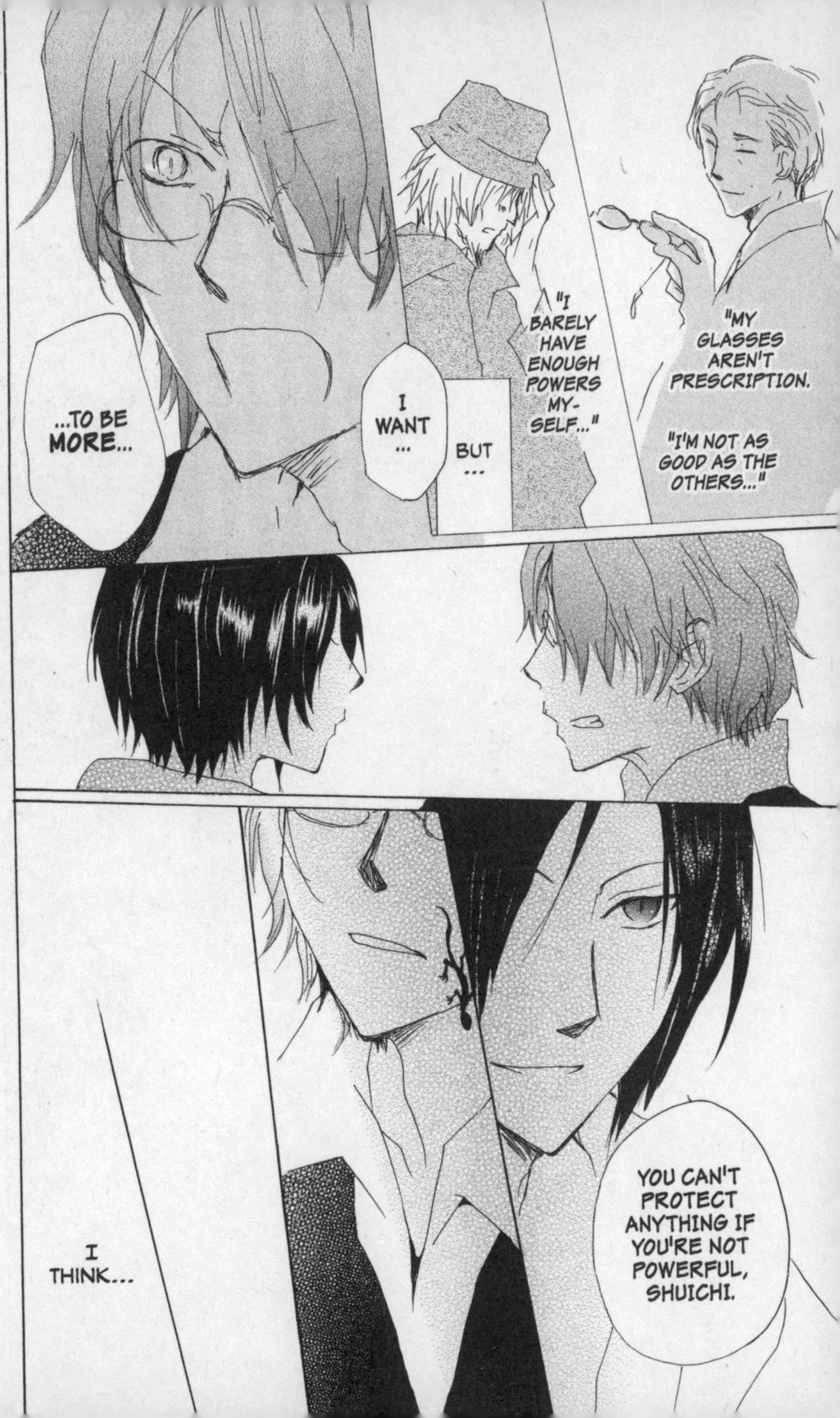
"MY GLASSES AREN'T PRESCRIPTION.
"I'M NOT AS GOOD AS THE OTHERS..."
"I BARELY HAVE ENOUGH POWERS MY-SELF..."
BUT...
I WANT...
...TO BE MORE...
YOU CAN'T PROTECT ANYTHING IF YOU'RE NOT POWERFUL, SHUICHI.
I THINK...

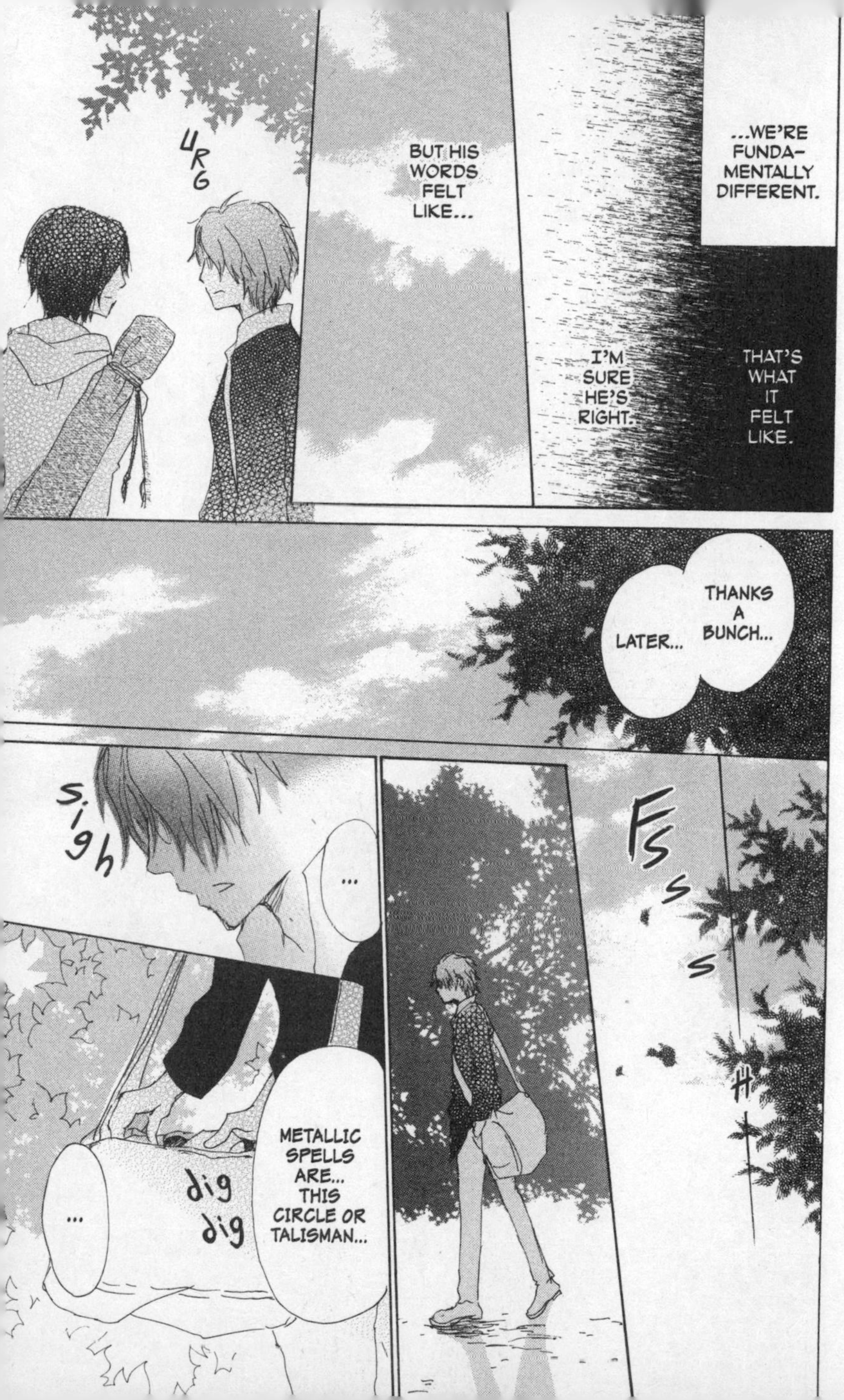
...WE'RE FUNDA-MENTALLY DIFFERENT.
THAT'S WHAT IT FELT LIKE.
I'M SURE HE'S RIGHT.
BUT HIS WORDS FELT LIKE...
URG
THANKS A BUNCH...
LATER...
FSSSH
sigh
...
METALLIC SPELLS ARE... THIS CIRCLE OR TALISMAN...
dig dig
...

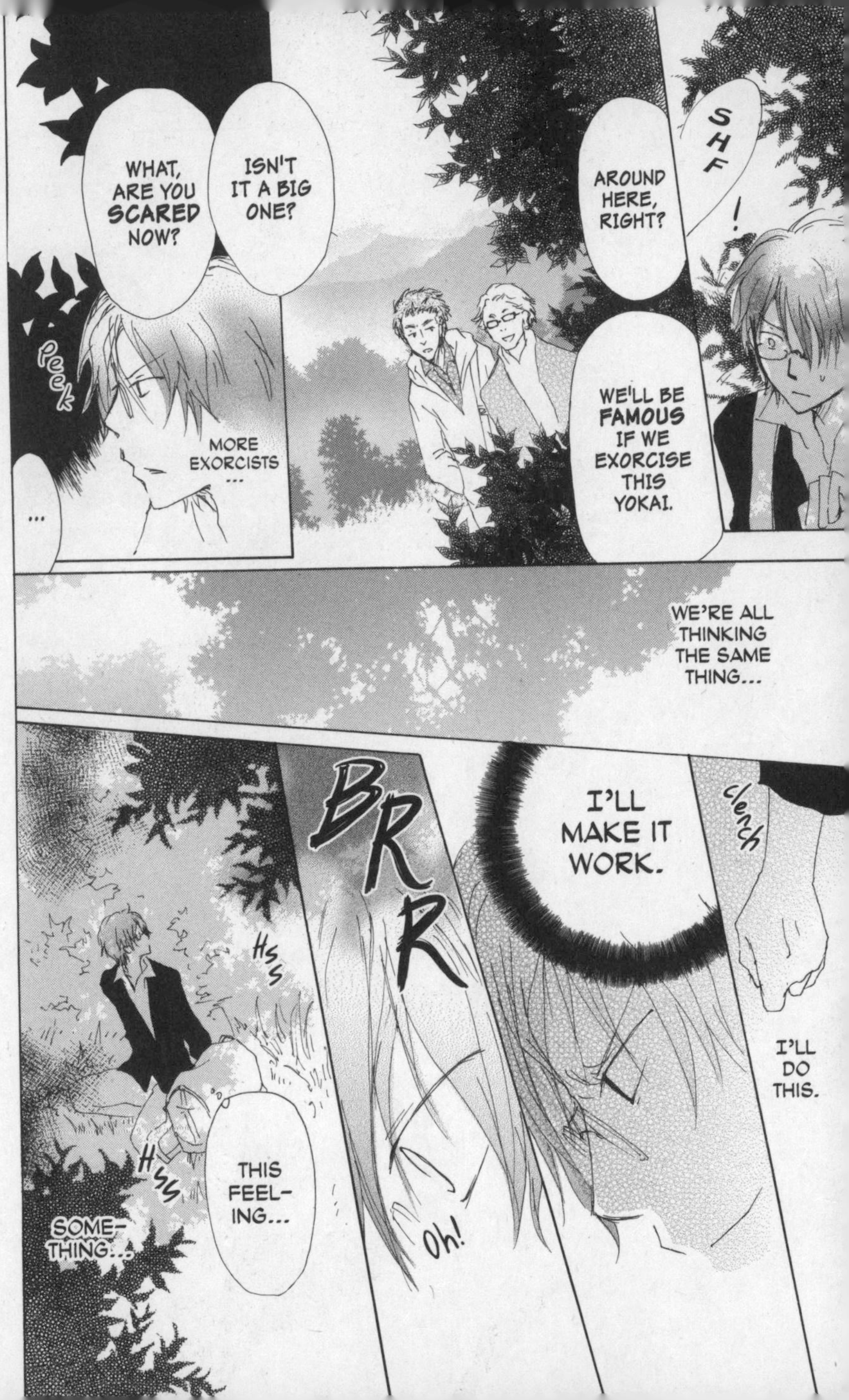
SHF
!
AROUND HERE, RIGHT?
WE'LL BE FAMOUS IF WE EXORCISE THIS YOKAI.
ISN'T IT A BIG ONE?
WHAT, ARE YOU SCARED NOW?
Peek
MORE EXORCISTS ...
...
WE'RE ALL THINKING THE SAME THING...
clench
I'LL DO THIS.
I'LL MAKE IT WORK.
BRR
Oh!
Hss
THIS FEEL-ING...
Hss
SOME-THING...

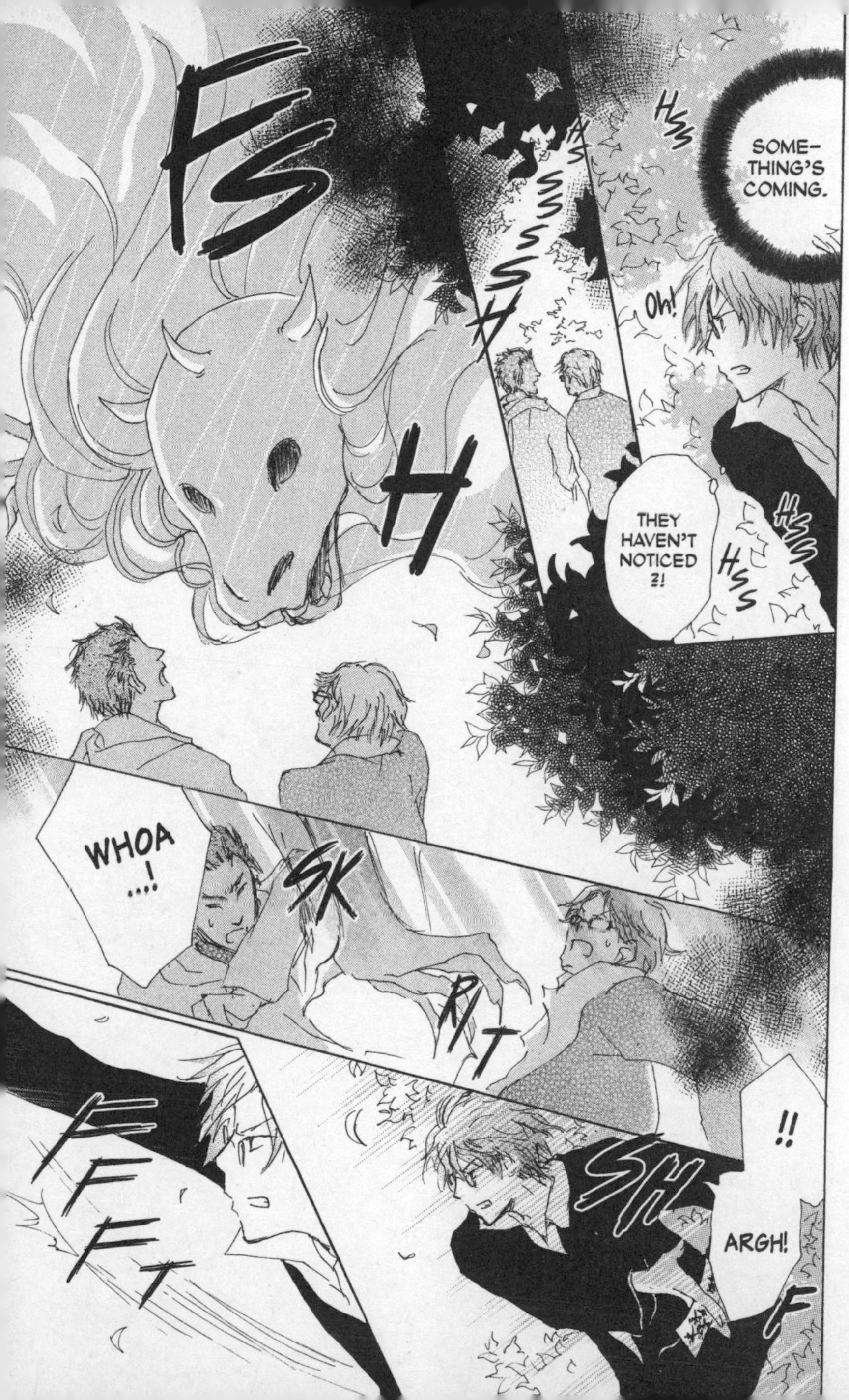
HSS
SOME-THING'S COMING.
Oh!
HSS
HSS
THEY HAVEN'T NOTICED?!
HSSSSSSH
FS
H
WHOA ...!
SK
RIT
!!
SH
ARGH!
F
FFFT

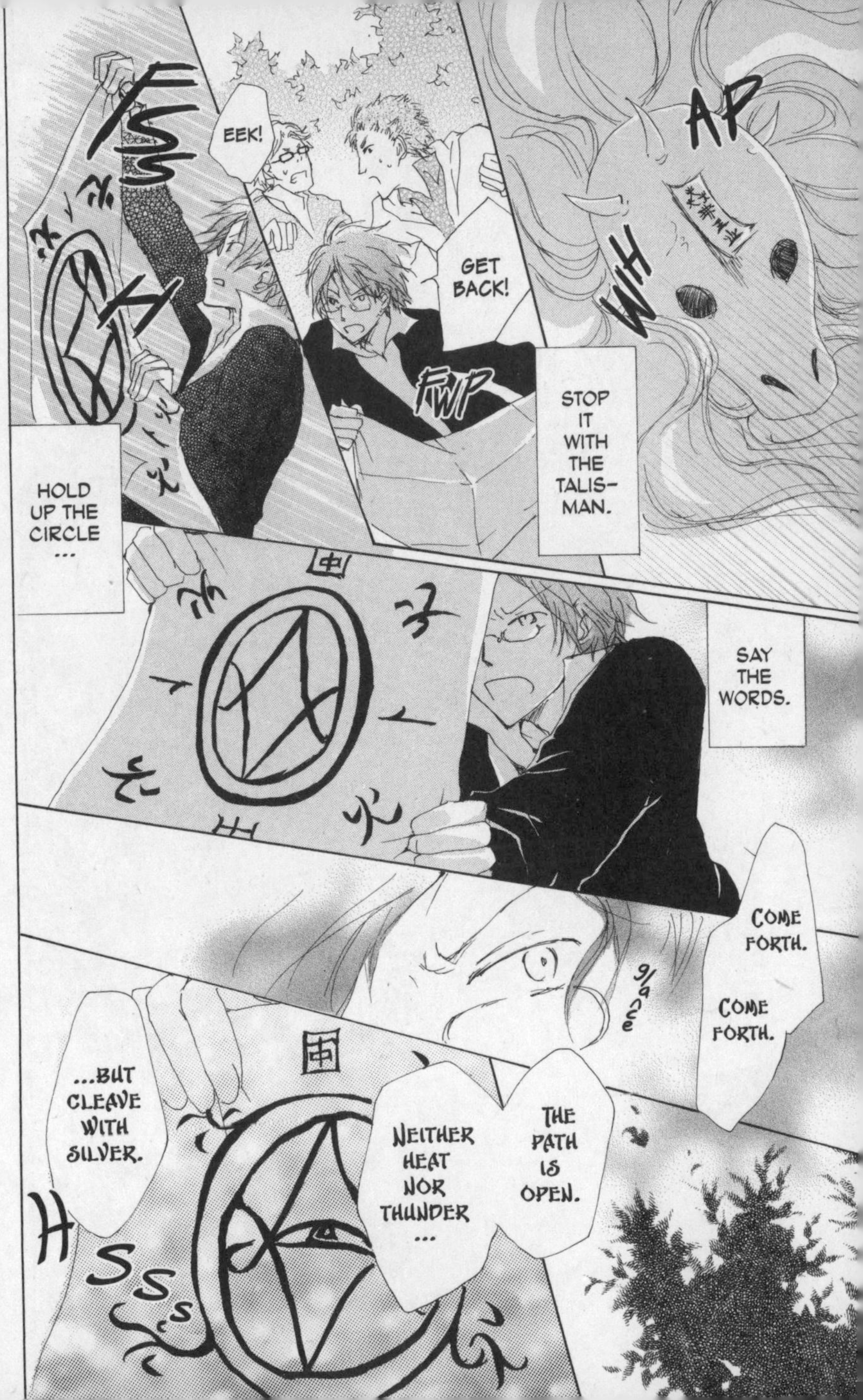
WH
AP
EEK!
GET BACK!
FWP
STOP IT WITH THE TALISMAN.
FSS
H
HOLD UP THE CIRCLE ...
SAY THE WORDS.
COME FORTH.
COME FORTH.
glance
THE PATH IS OPEN.
NEITHER HEAT NOR THUNDER ...
...BUT CLEAVE WITH SILVER.
HSSS

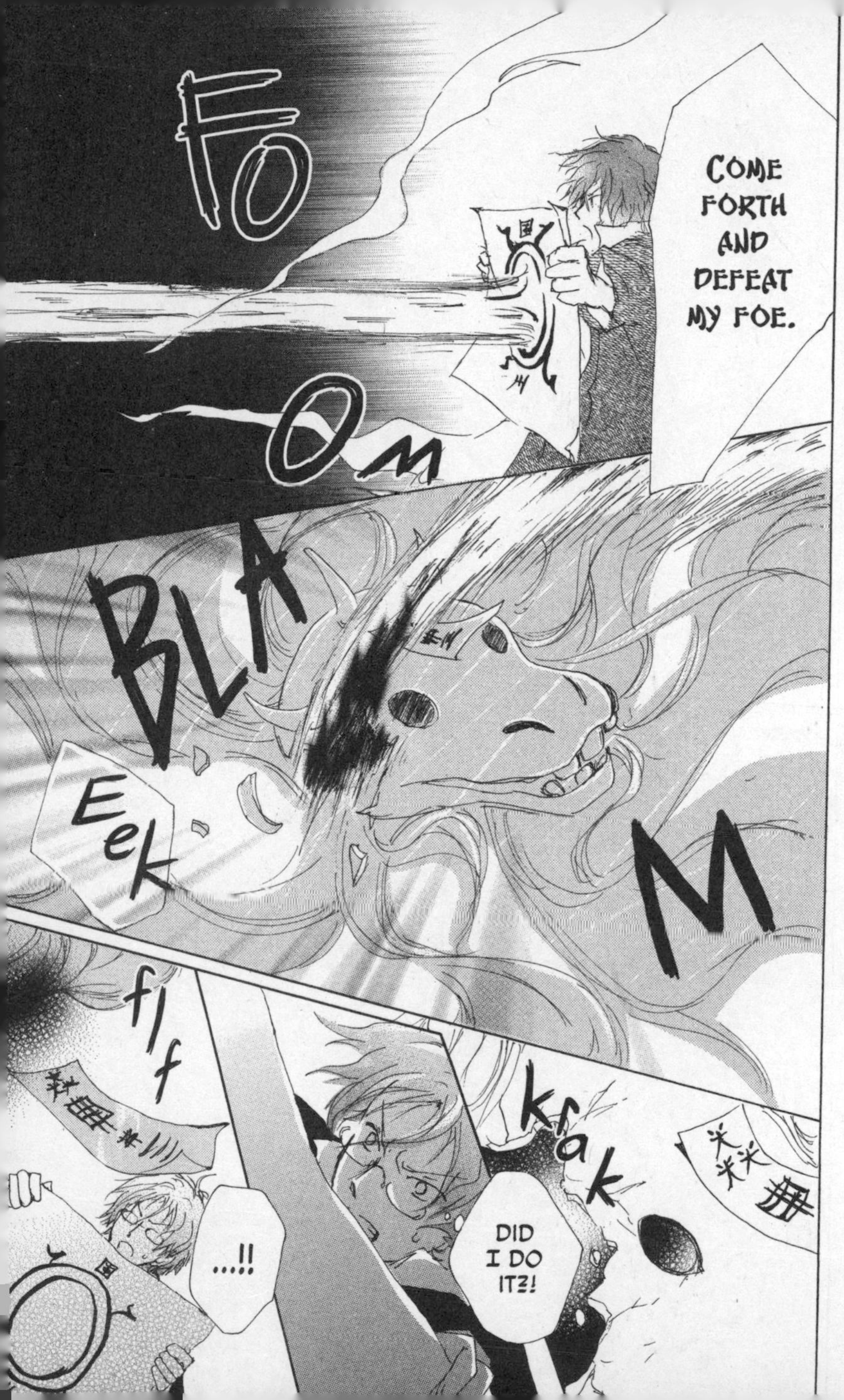
COME FORTH AND DEFEAT MY FOE.
FOOOM
BLAM
Eek
krak
DID I DO IT?!
...!!
flf

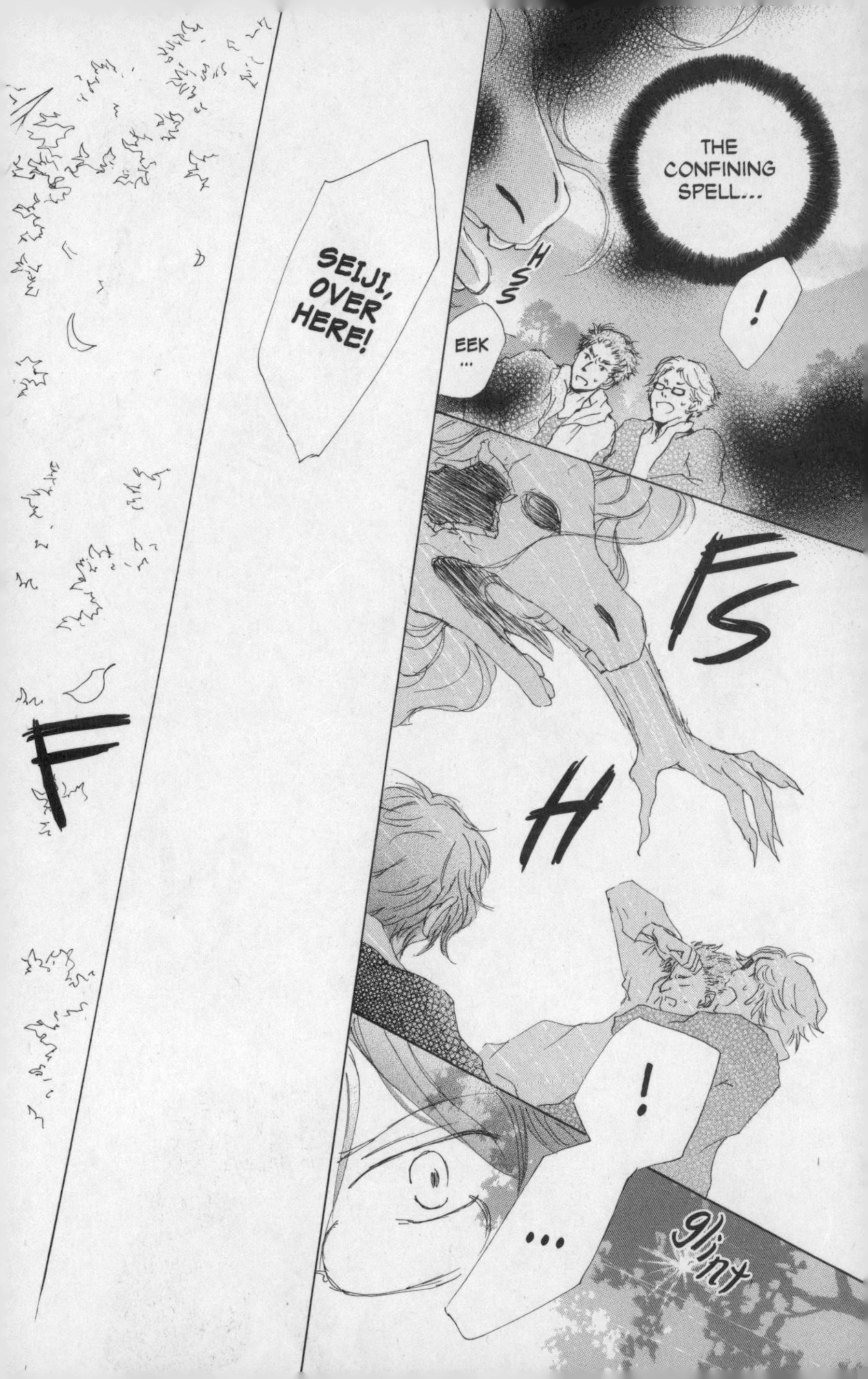
THE CONFINING SPELL...
!
HSS
EEK ...
FS
H
!
...
glint
SEIJI, OVER HERE!
F

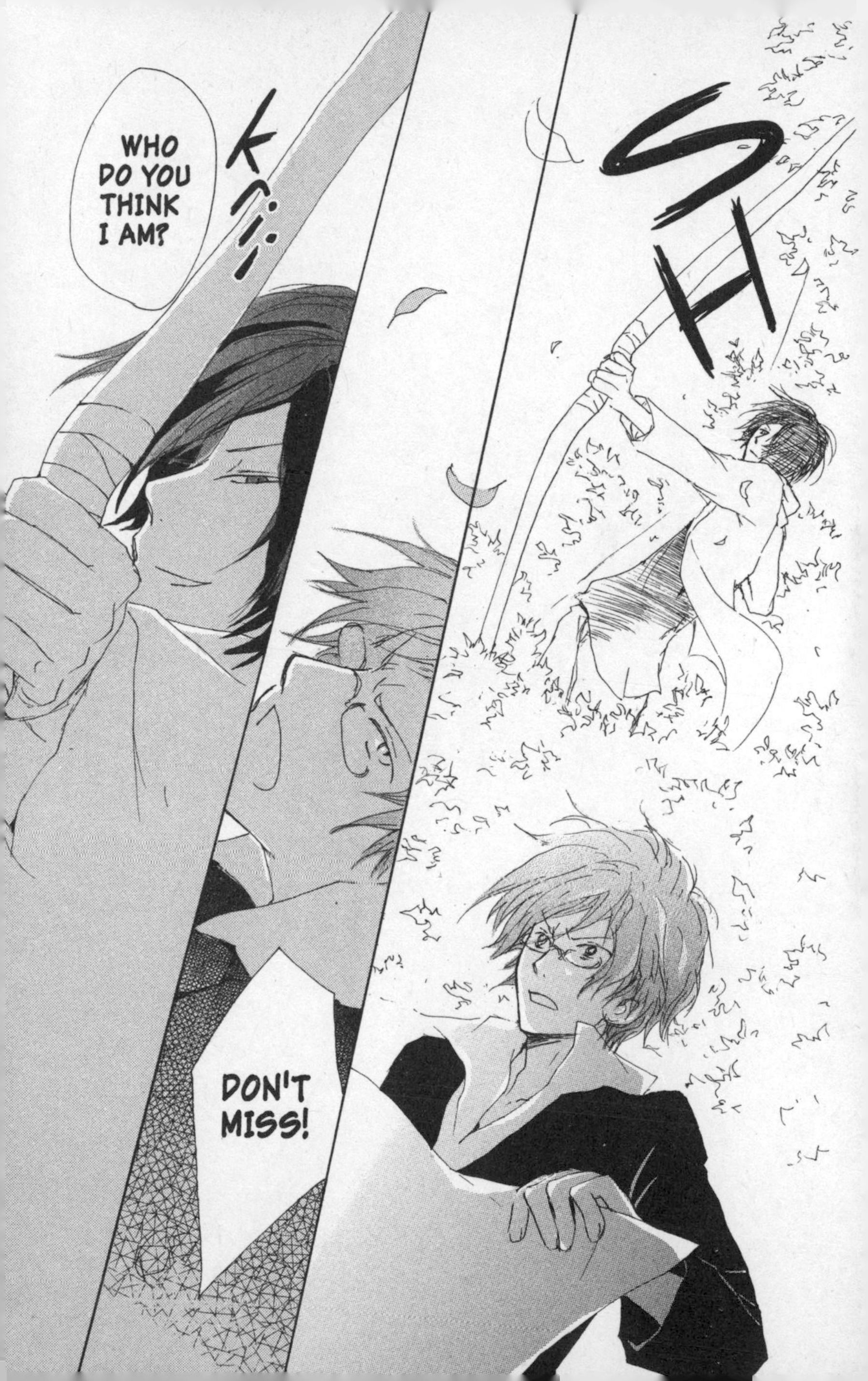

SH
DON'T MISS!
KRII
WHO DO YOU THINK I AM?

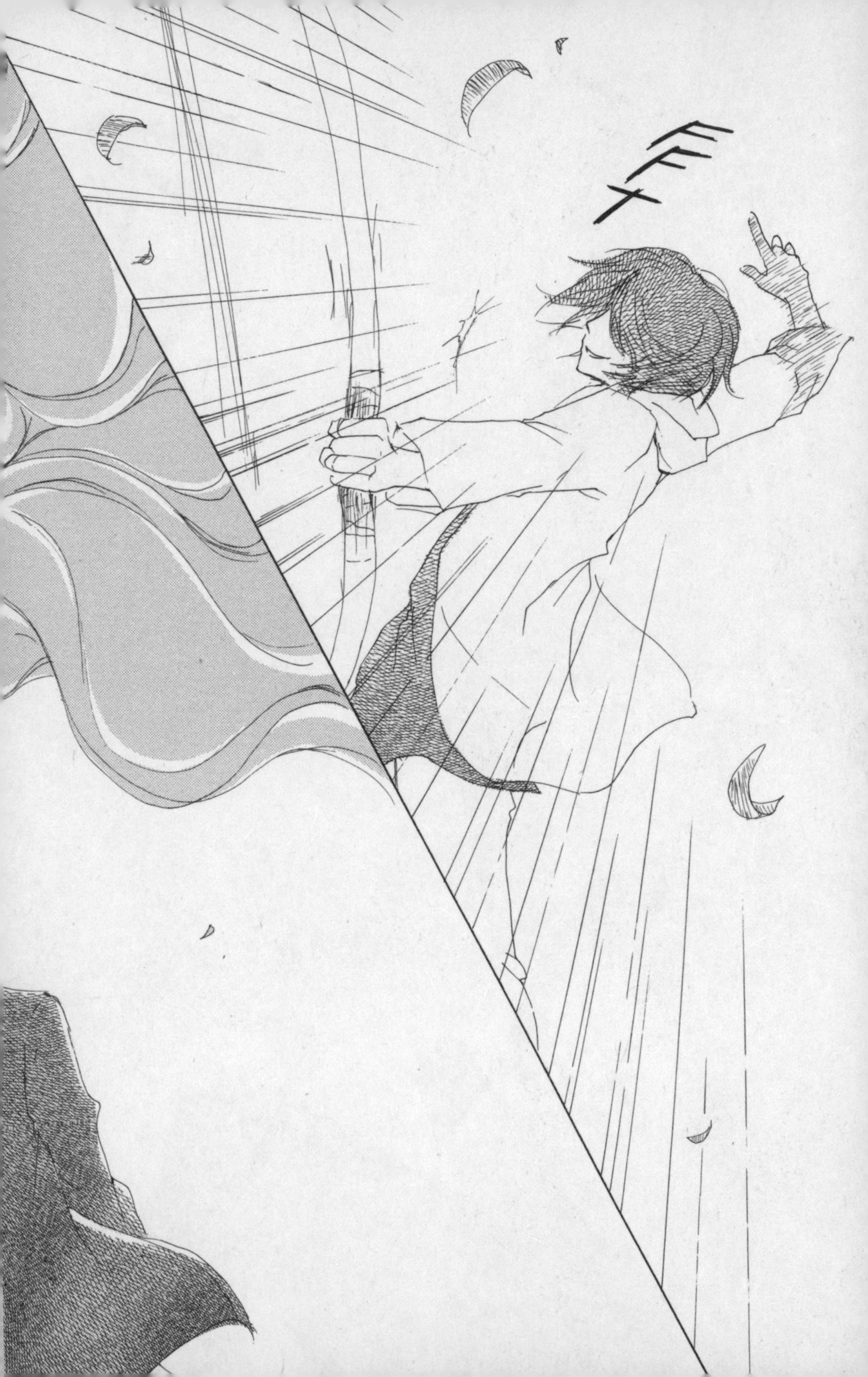

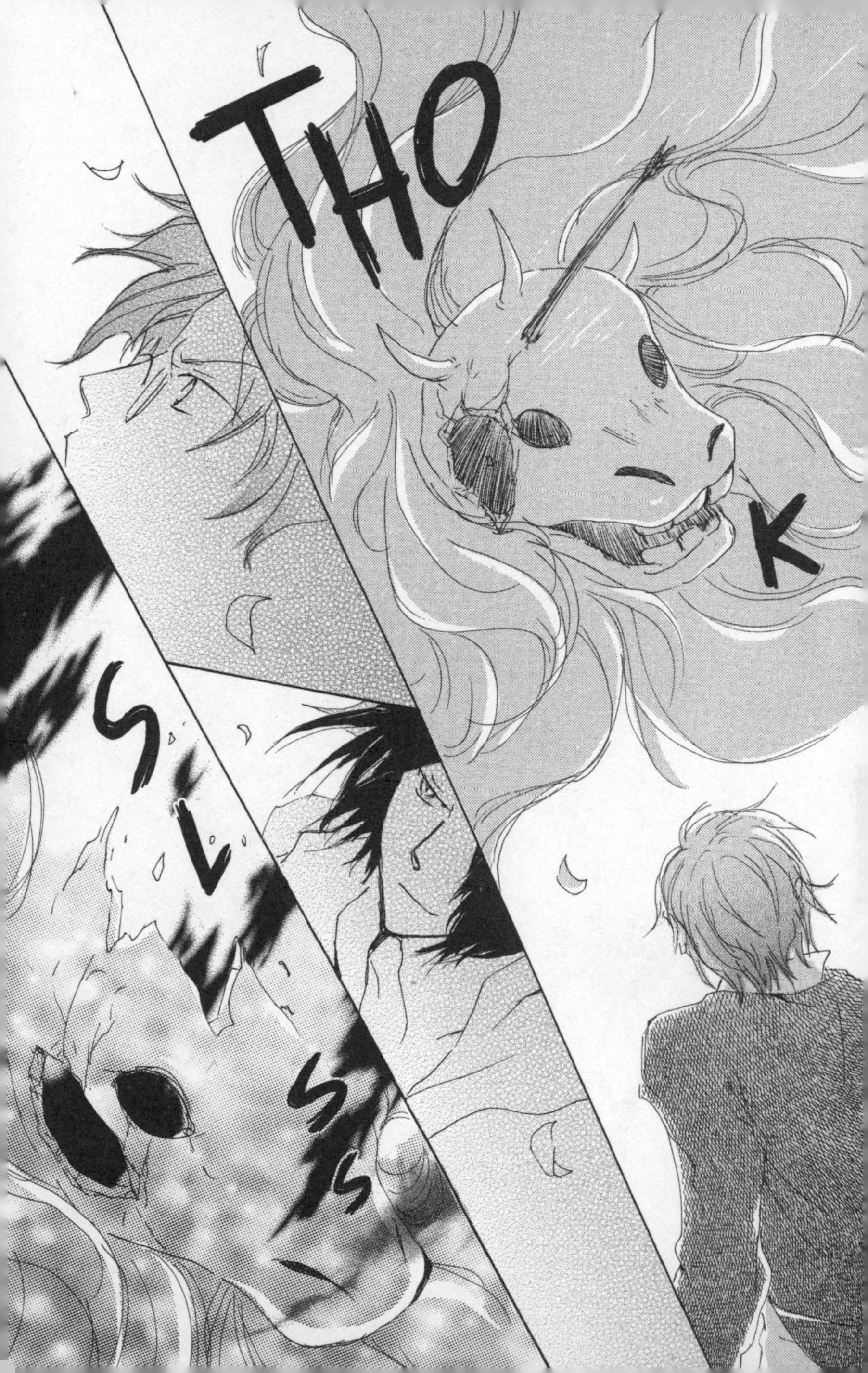
THOK
SLSSS

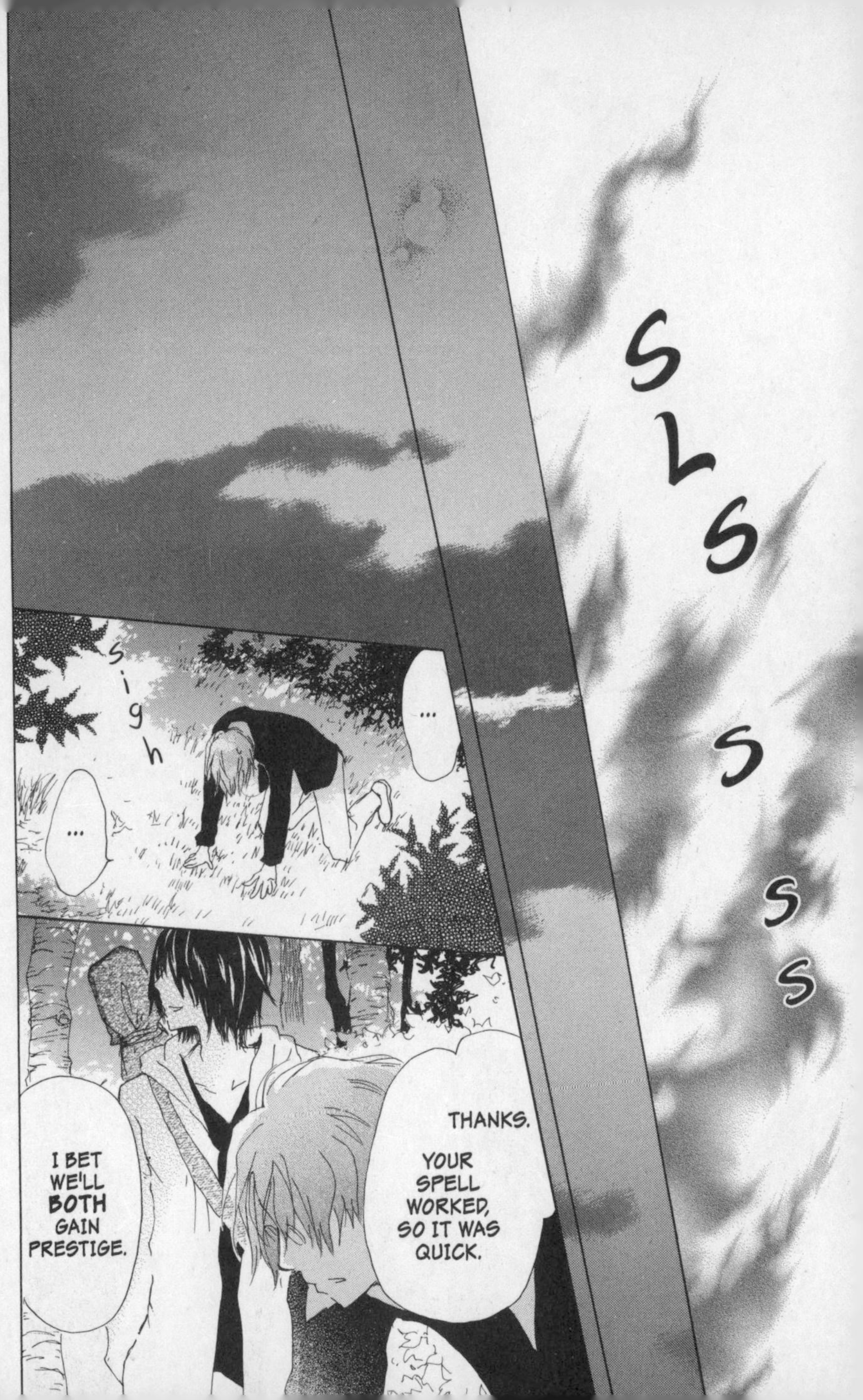
SLSSSS
...
sigh
...
THANKS.
YOUR SPELL WORKED, SO IT WAS QUICK.
I BET WE'LL BOTH GAIN PRESTIGE.

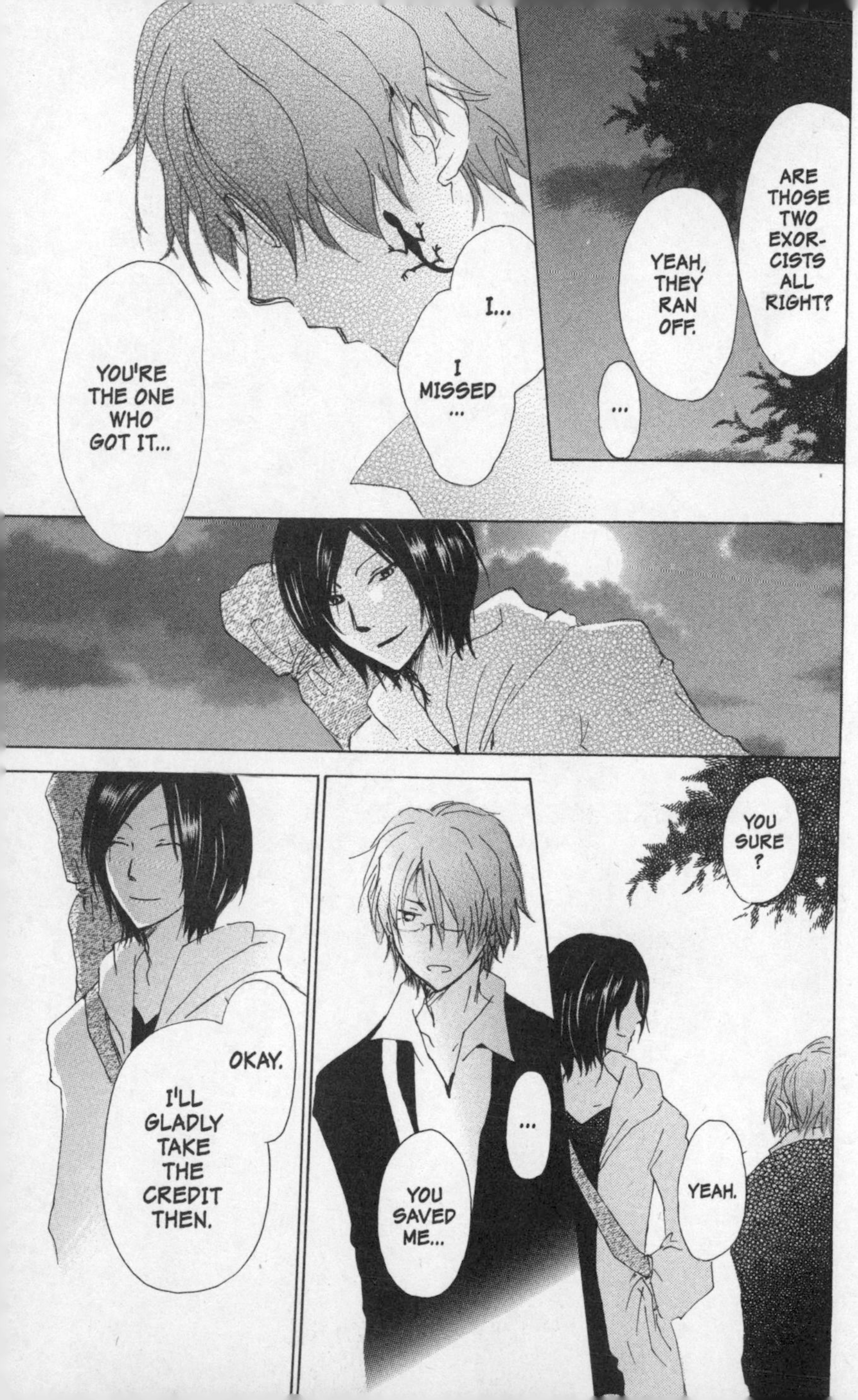
ARE THOSE TWO EXORCISTS ALL RIGHT?
YEAH, THEY RAN OFF.
...
I...
I MISSED ...
YOU'RE THE ONE WHO GOT IT...
YOU SURE?
YEAH.
...
YOU SAVED ME...
OKAY.
I'LL GLADLY TAKE THE CREDIT THEN.

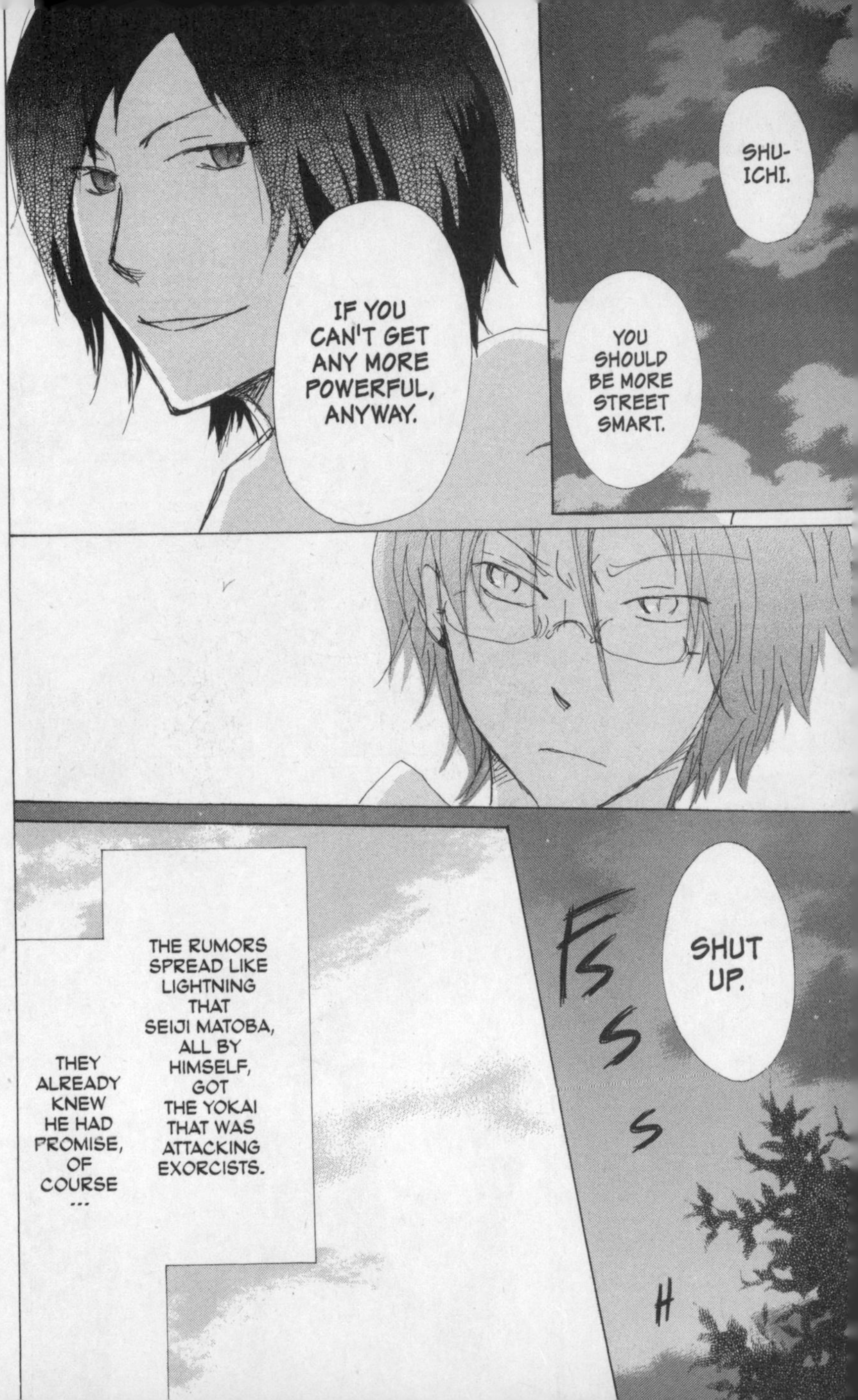
SHU-ICHI.
YOU SHOULD BE MORE STREET SMART.
IF YOU CAN'T GET ANY MORE POWERFUL, ANYWAY.
SHUT UP.
FSSSH
THE RUMORS SPREAD LIKE LIGHTNING THAT SEIJI MATOBA, ALL BY HIMSELF, GOT THE YOKAI THAT WAS ATTACKING EXORCISTS.
THEY ALREADY KNEW HE HAD PROMISE, OF COURSE...

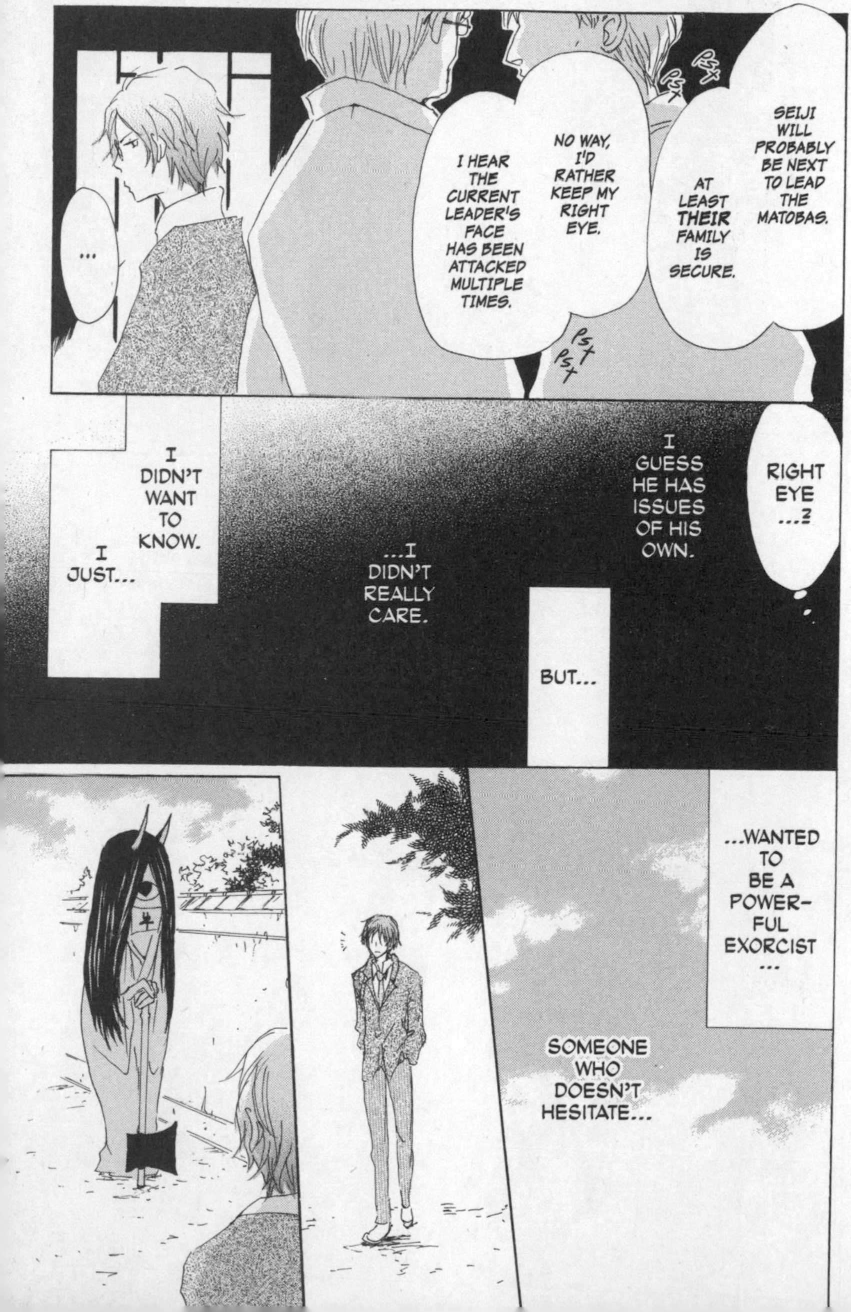
PST PST
SEIJI WILL PROBABLY BE NEXT TO LEAD THE MATOBAS.
AT LEAST THEIR FAMILY IS SECURE.
NO WAY, I'D RATHER KEEP MY RIGHT EYE.
I HEAR THE CURRENT LEADER'S FACE HAS BEEN ATTACKED MULTIPLE TIMES.
PST PST
...
RIGHT EYE...?
I GUESS HE HAS ISSUES OF HIS OWN.
BUT...
...I DIDN'T REALLY CARE.
I DIDN'T WANT TO KNOW.
I JUST...
...WANTED TO BE A POWERFUL EXORCIST...
SOMEONE WHO DOESN'T HESITATE...

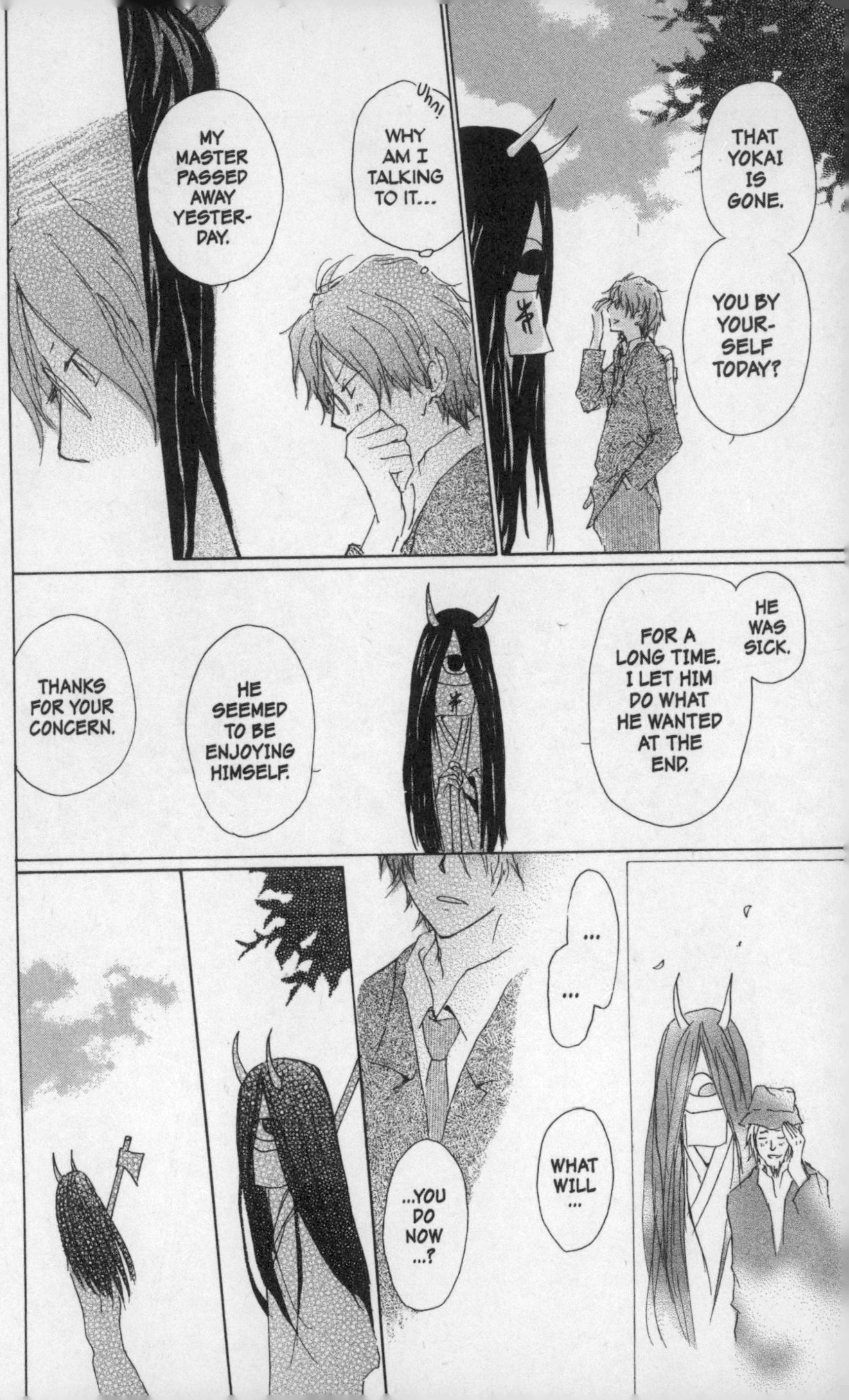
THAT YOKAI IS GONE.
YOU BY YOUR-SELF TODAY?
Uhn!
WHY AM I TALKING TO IT...
MY MASTER PASSED AWAY YESTER-DAY.
HE WAS SICK.
FOR A LONG TIME. I LET HIM DO WHAT HE WANTED AT THE END.
HE SEEMED TO BE ENJOYING HIMSELF.
THANKS FOR YOUR CONCERN.
...
...
WHAT WILL ...
...YOU DO NOW ...?

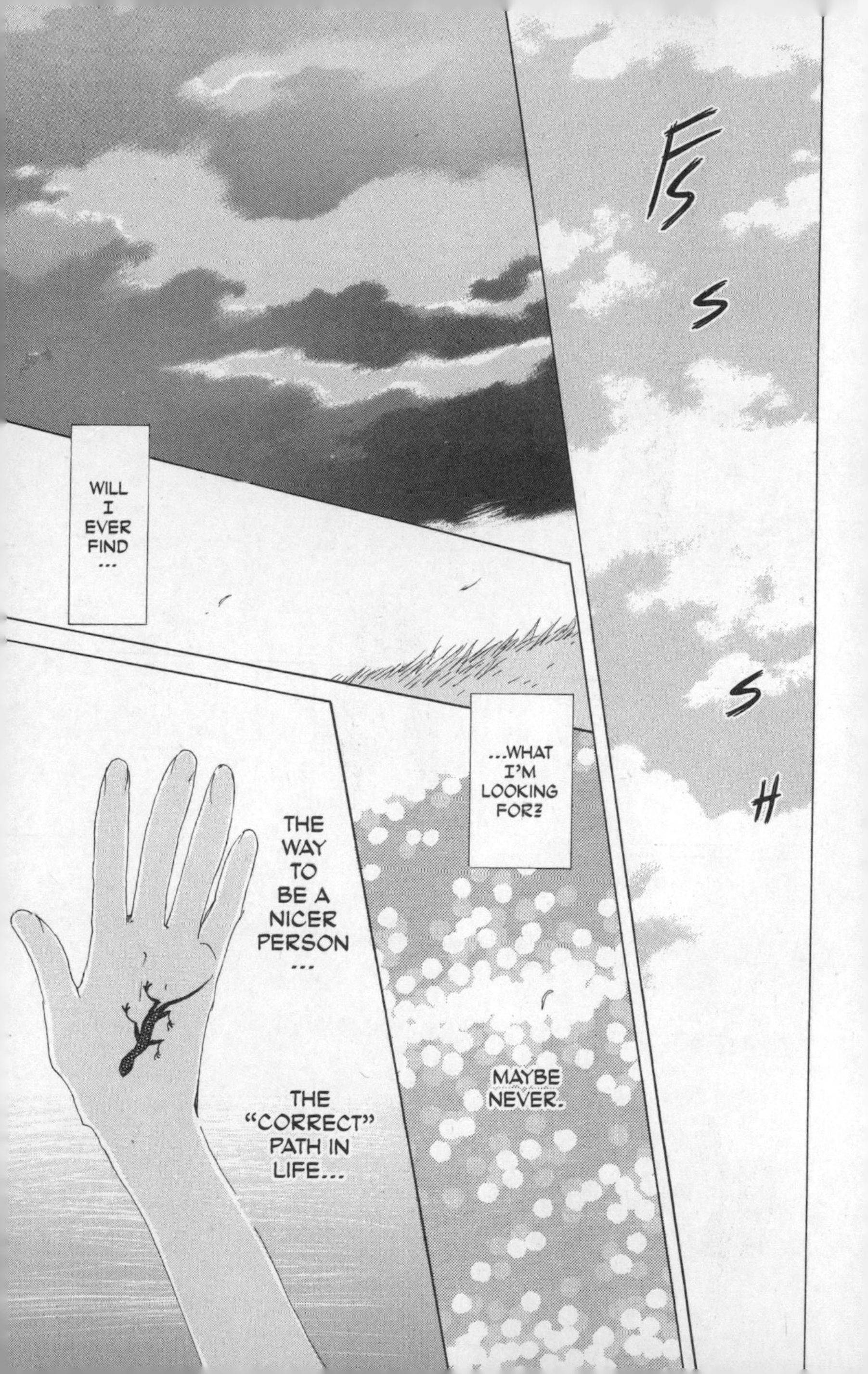
FSSSH
WILL I EVER FIND...
...WHAT I'M LOOKING FOR?
THE WAY TO BE A NICER PERSON...
THE "CORRECT" PATH IN LIFE...
MAYBE NEVER.

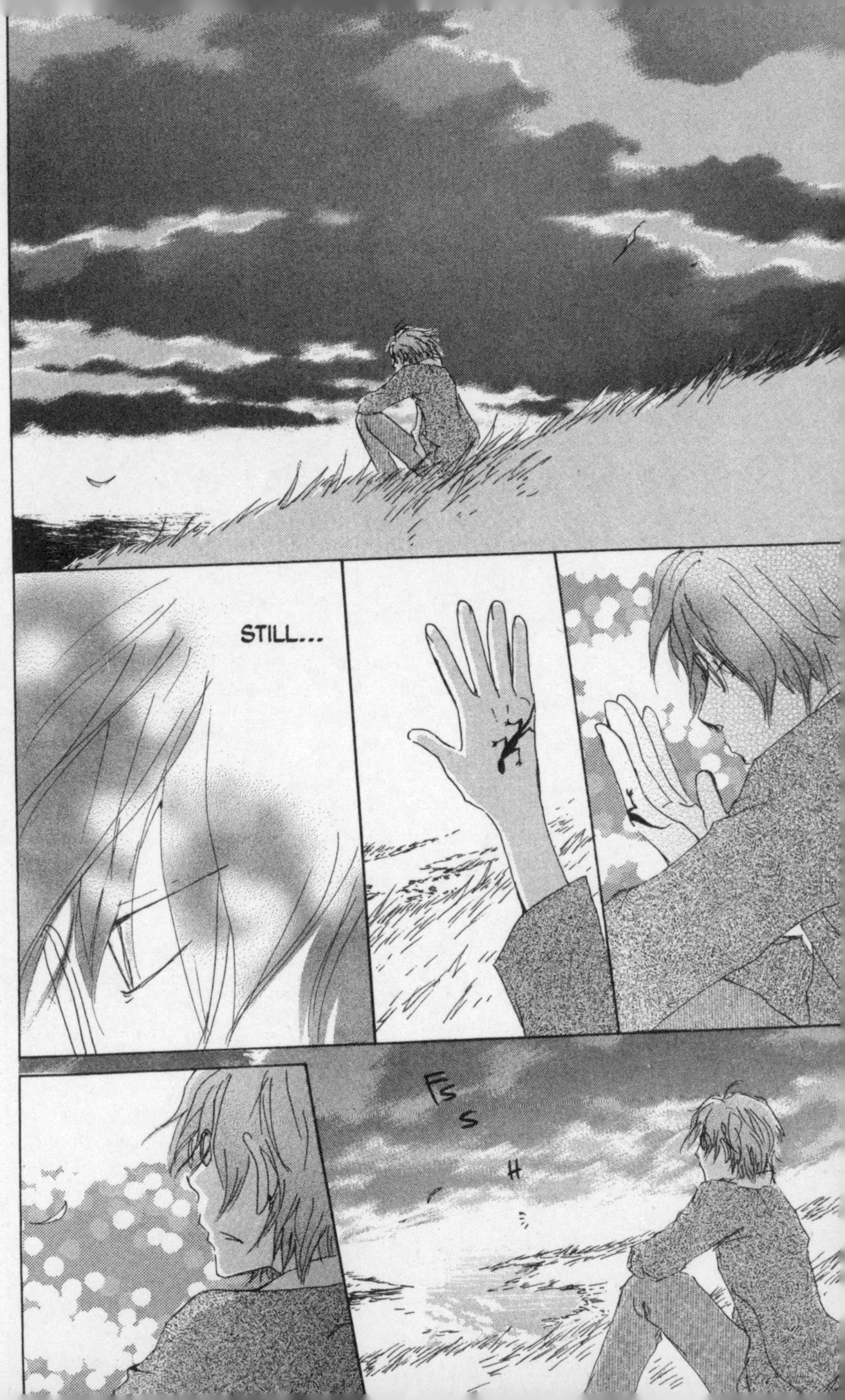
STILL...
FSSH

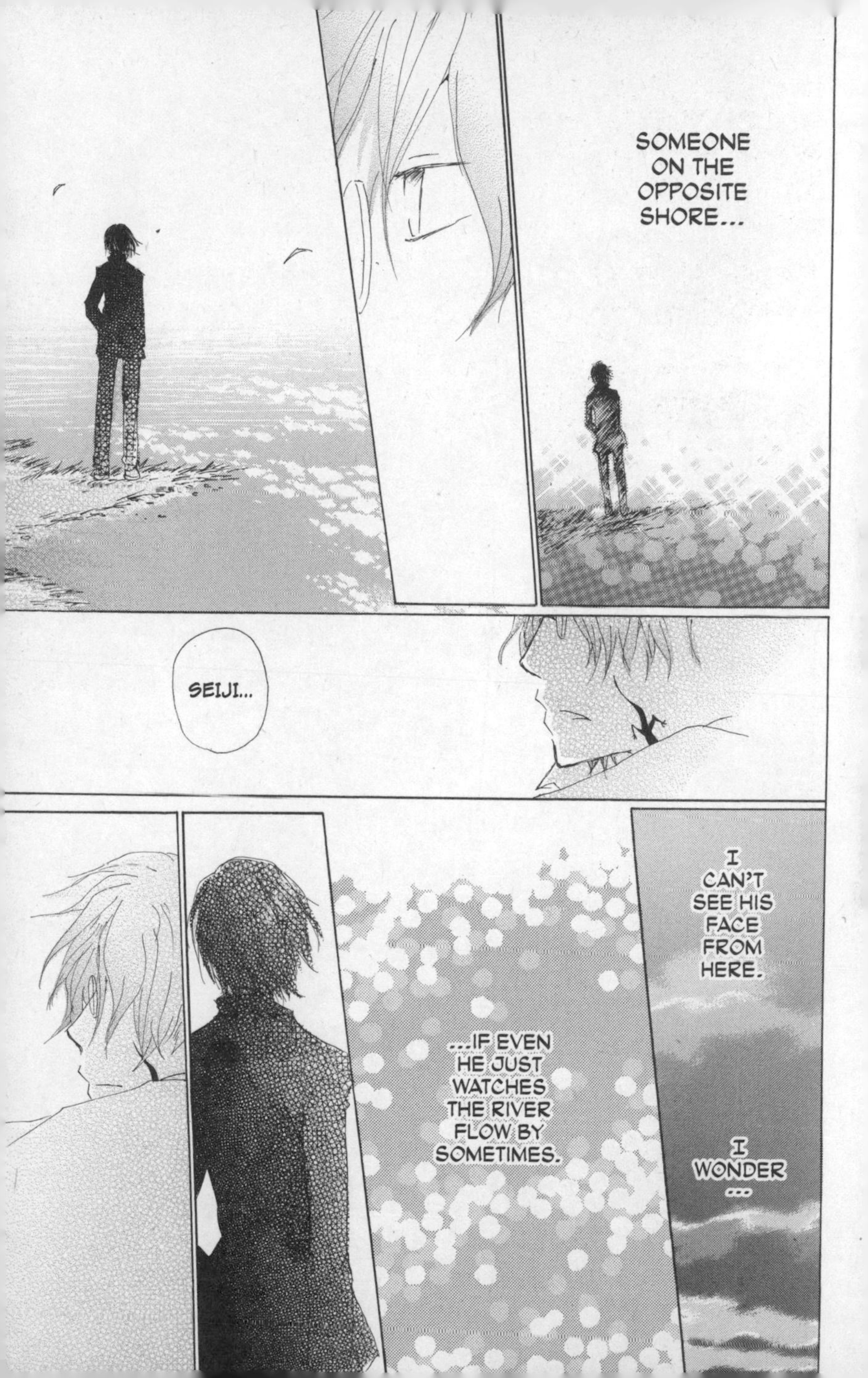
SOMEONE ON THE OPPOSITE SHORE...
SEIJI...
I CAN'T SEE HIS FACE FROM HERE.
I WONDER...
...IF EVEN HE JUST WATCHES THE RIVER FLOW BY SOMETIMES.

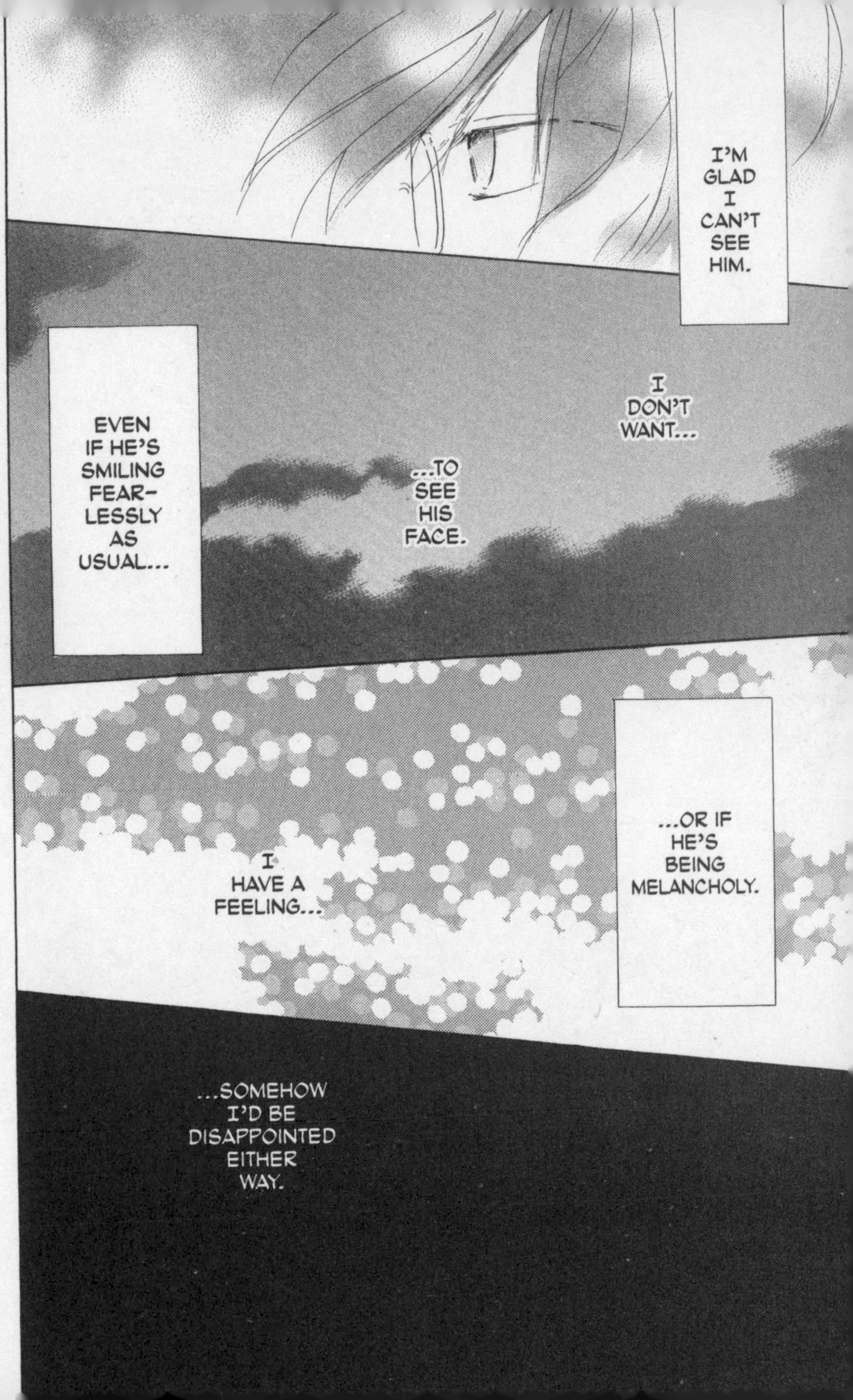
I'M GLAD I CAN'T SEE HIM.
I DON'T WANT...
...TO SEE HIS FACE.
EVEN IF HE'S SMILING FEAR-LESSLY AS USUAL...
...OR IF HE'S BEING MELANCHOLY.
I HAVE A FEELING...
...SOMEHOW I'D BE DISAPPOINTED EITHER WAY.

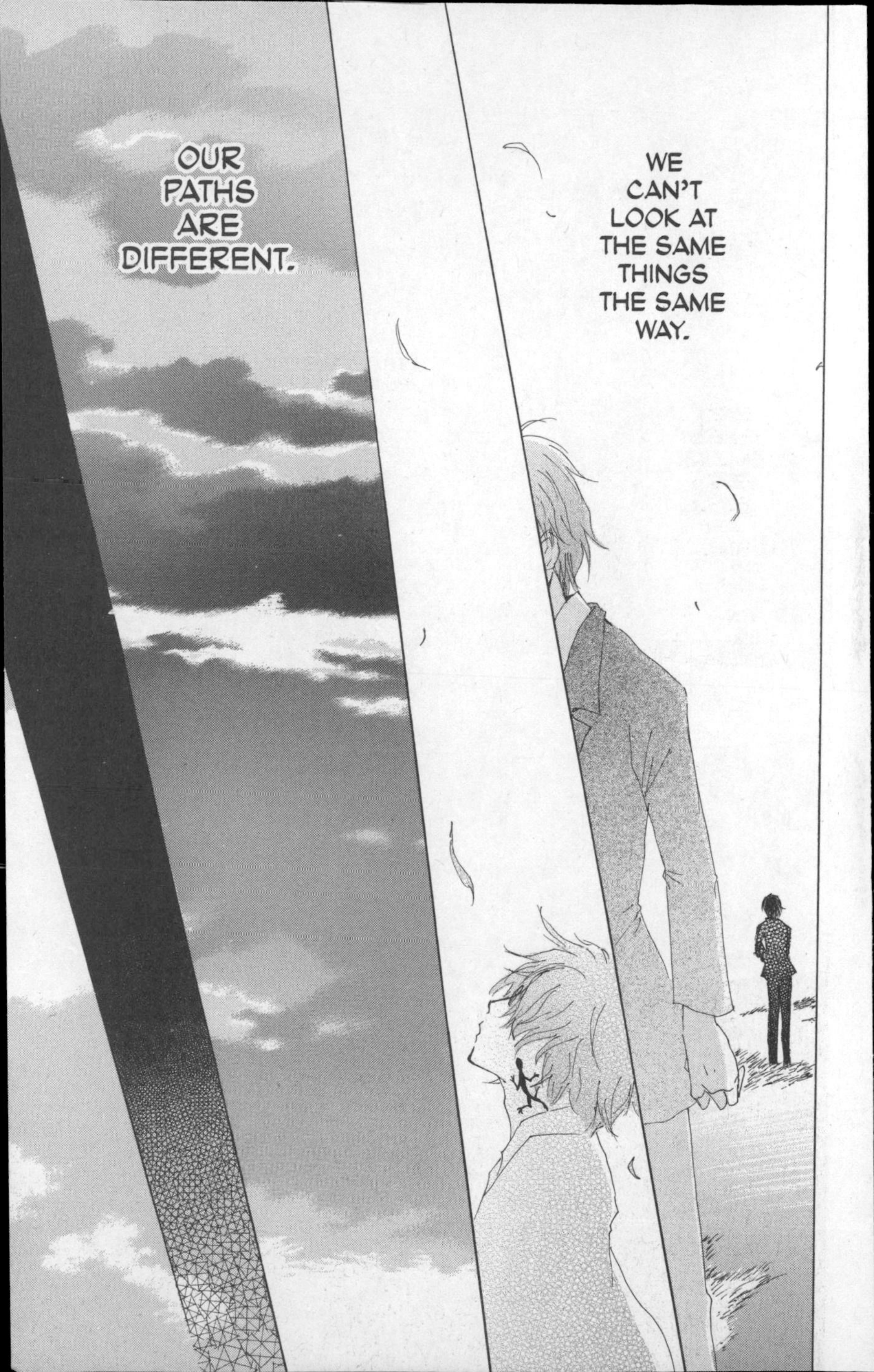
WE CAN'T LOOK AT THE SAME THINGS THE SAME WAY.
OUR PATHS ARE DIFFERENT.

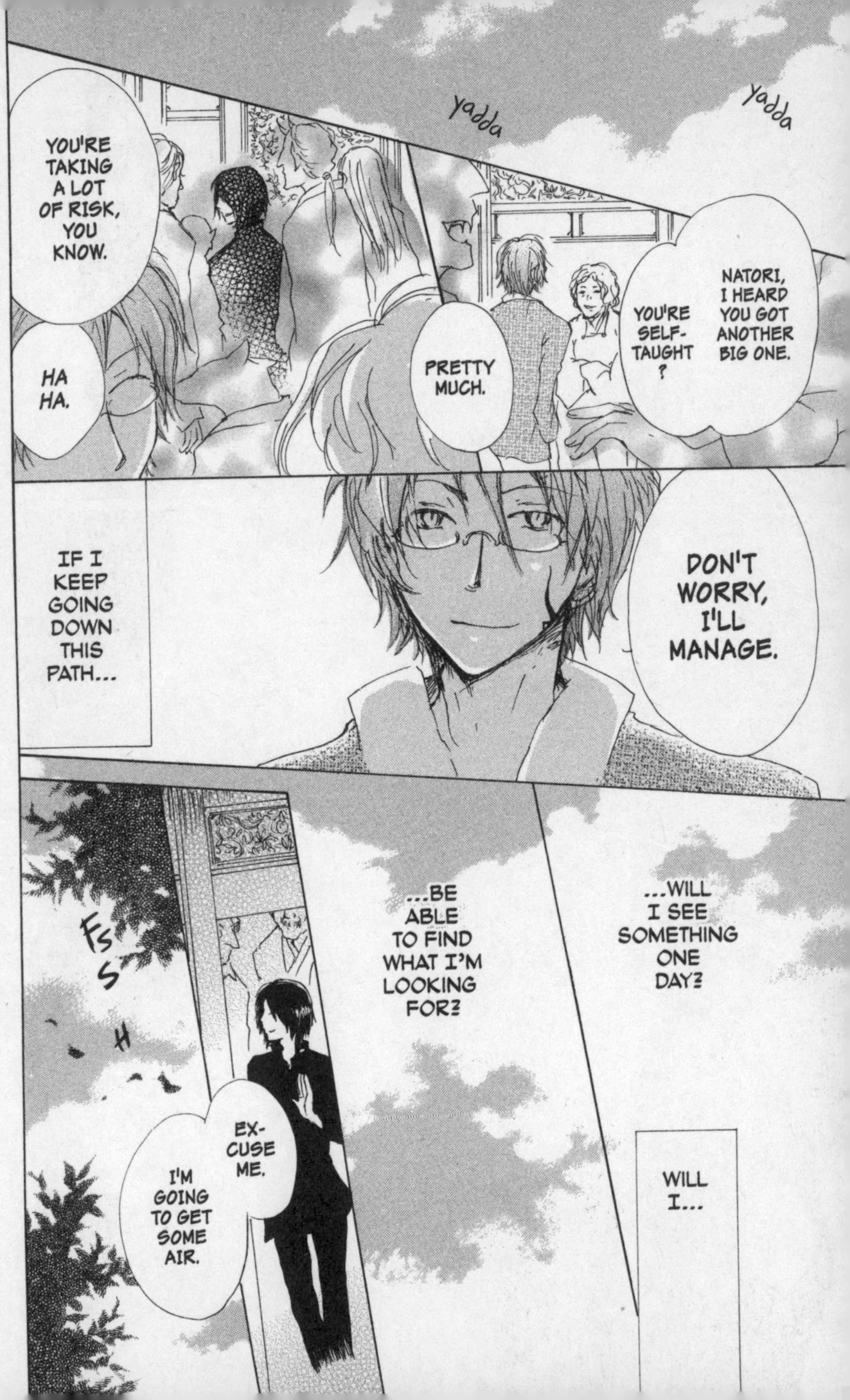
yadda
yadda
NATORI, I HEARD YOU GOT ANOTHER BIG ONE.
YOU'RE SELF-TAUGHT?
PRETTY MUCH.
YOU'RE TAKING A LOT OF RISK, YOU KNOW.
HA HA.
DON'T WORRY, I'LL MANAGE.
IF I KEEP GOING DOWN THIS PATH...
WILL I...
...BE ABLE TO FIND WHAT I'M LOOKING FOR?
...WILL I SEE SOMETHING ONE DAY?
FSSH
EX-CUSE ME.
I'M GOING TO GET SOME AIR.

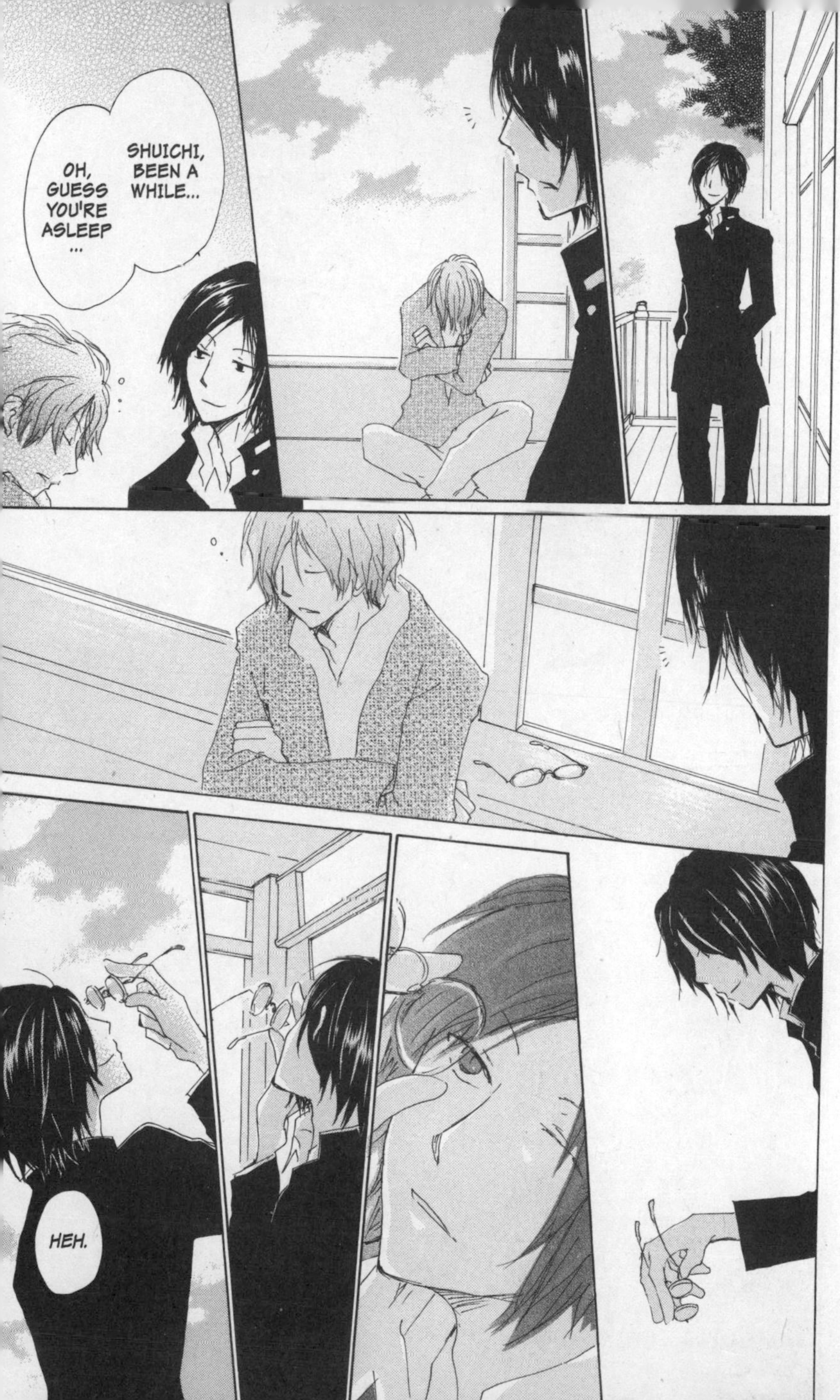
SHUICHI, BEEN A WHILE...
OH, GUESS YOU'RE ASLEEP ...
HEH.

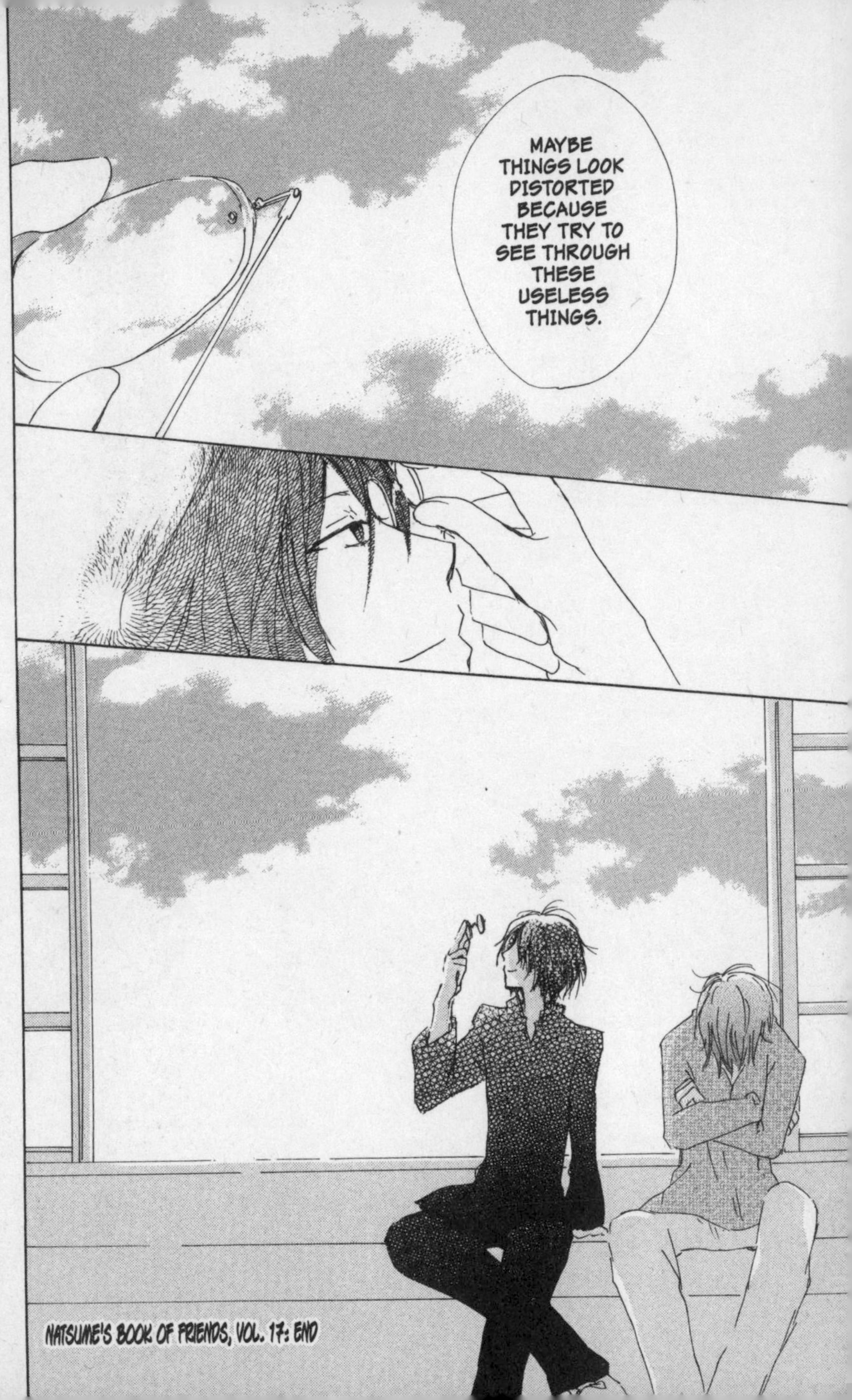
MAYBE THINGS LOOK DISTORTED BECAUSE THEY TRY TO SEE THROUGH THESE USELESS THINGS.
NATSUME'S BOOK OF FRIENDS, VOL. 17: END

AFTER-WORD

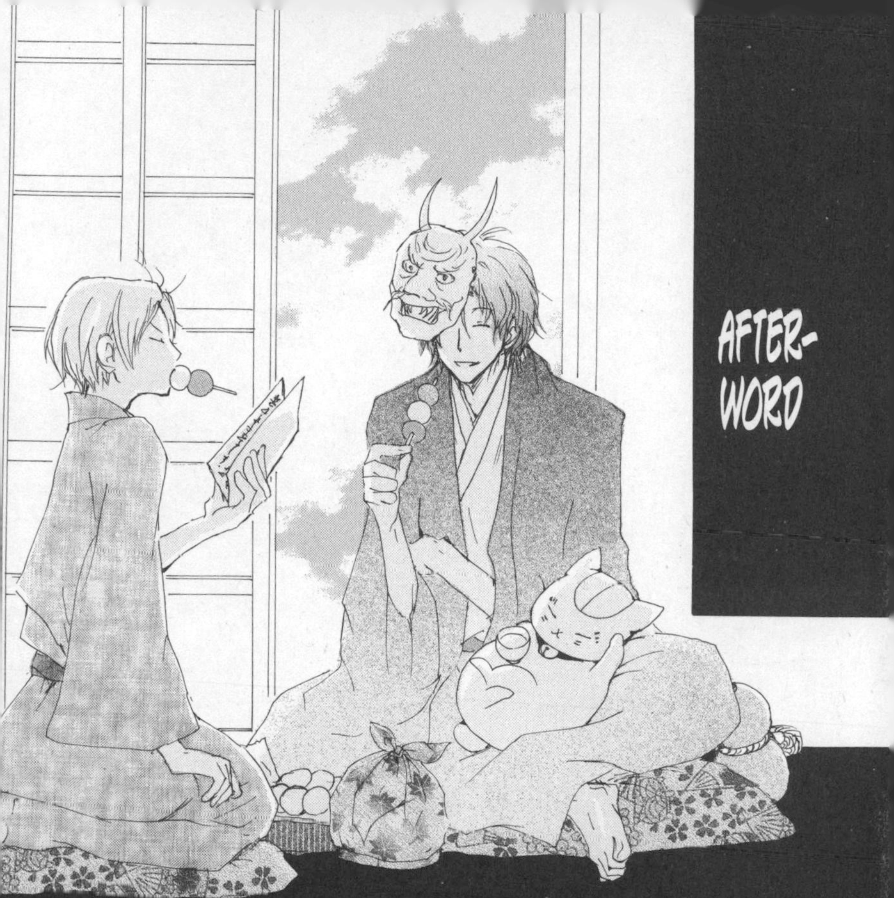

Thank you for reading.

When I'm drawing Natsume slowly learning how to calmly deal with things and how not to take things seriously, I look back upon how he used to be in the beginning and feel a little nostalgic. I'm relieved that the instability is gone, but strangely wistful at the same time.

The capacity of Natsume's heart has changed quite a lot, and I know I have to keep things feeling fresh. I'll work hard to depict the changing circumstances and the resulting emotions.

Please read the rest of this afterword only after reading the entire volume, to avoid spoilers.

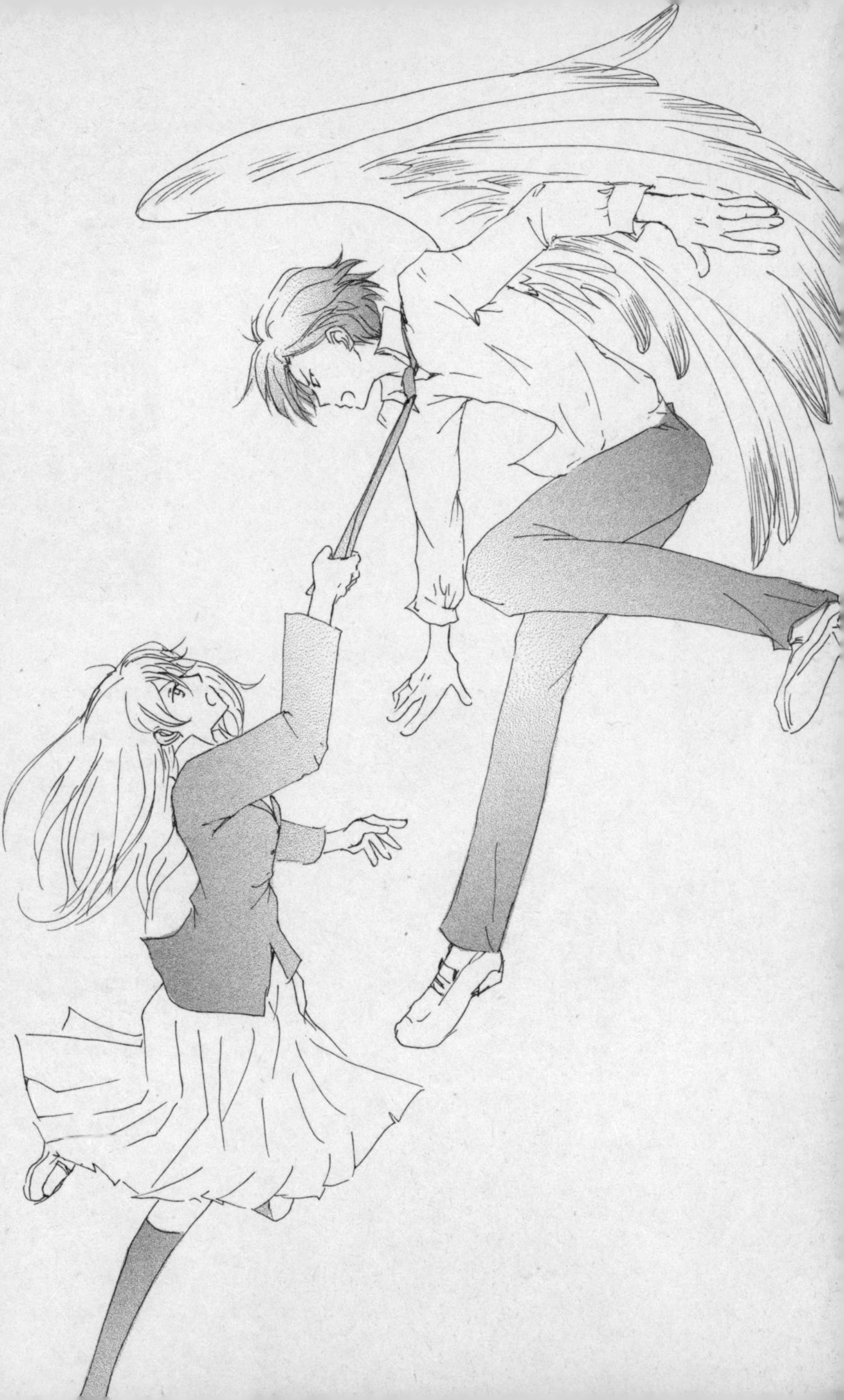

CHAPTERS 68-69 The Coming Days

I thought it was about time to have romance as the driving motive for the story, and decided upon a pair of sickeningly soppy lovebirds, a type I hadn't tackled before. Once I got going though, it was difficult to centralize the romance, and their reunion comes towards the end, so it was too bad I couldn't depict Natsume gagging at how ridiculous they were being. But drawing Aoi and Kaoru was very refreshing. It was a memorable episode that I enjoyed creating.

I figure that the future waiting for them is the one Aoi predicted, so I took great care in writing the story. I also wondered if Natsume having siblings close in age would look like this. It was fun drawing him pressing his luck.

CHAPTER 70 Games Party

I wanted to do a short, 30-page, fun story. It was fun to see Natsume efficiently moving along without Sensei. I wonder if he just matches pace when there's someone he can depend on. I love drawing the fan club, but it's hard to fit them into stories.

SPECIAL EPISODE 15 A World Without Distortion

This was a story I've been longing to work on. I couldn't fit in all the parts I wanted, even though they let me do a two-parter, so I hope to get another opportunity some other time. I'd like to show more of the dilemma and frustration of wanting to do the right thing but having your actions distort your goals.

I've been able to work on
Natsume's Book of Friends for
ten years now. So many people have read
my manga, leading into so many relationships.
The more time passes, the more the memories add up.
Looking back chokes me up, so I'll try to look forward
and put my heart and soul into the work I have
before me. I'll work hard so you'll keep reading.

Thank you so much for your support.

Thanks to:

Tamao Ohki
Chika
Mika
Mr. Fujita
Hinata
My sister
Mr. Sato
Hoen Kikaku, Ltd.
    Thank you.

I'm unable to write replies to all the letters I receive,
but I read every single one. Thank you.

AFTERWORD: END

Natsume's
BOOK of FRIENDS
VOLUME 17 END NOTES

PAGE 17, PANEL 3: *White bean paste*
A sweetened bean paste made from Japanese navy beans. Similar in texture to sweet black or red bean paste.

PAGE 30, PANEL 2: *Bracken mochi*
Warabimochi in Japanese. Similar to rice flour mochi, but made from the starch of the bracken fern and rolled in *kinako* (sweet toasted soy flour used as a coating on traditional sweets).

PAGE 43, PANEL 1: *Cram school*
Supplemental classes after school to help students pass entrance exams. Similar to SAT prep classes.

PAGE 73, PANEL 1: *Ohagi*
A confection of sweet rice coated in a thick layer of red bean paste. Typically made in the autumn.

Yuki Midorikawa is the creator of *Natsume's Book of Friends*, which was nominated for the Manga Taisho (Cartoon Grand Prize). Her other titles published in Japan include *Hotarubi no Mori e* (Into the Forest of Fireflies), *Hiiro no Isu* (The Scarlet Chair) and *Akaku Saku Koe* (The Voice That Blooms Red).

NATSUME'S BOOK OF FRIENDS

Vol. 17

Shojo Beat Edition

STORY AND ART BY *Yuki Midorikawa*

Translation & Adaptation *Lillian Olsen*
Touch-up Art & Lettering *Sabrina Heep*
Design *Fawn Lau*
Editor *Pancha Diaz*

Natsume Yujincho by Yuki Midorikawa
© Yuki Midorikawa 2014
All rights reserved.
First published in Japan in 2014 by HAKUSENSHA, Inc., Tokyo.
English language translation rights arranged with HAKUSENSHA, Inc., Tokyo.

The stories, characters and incidents mentioned in this publication are entirely fictional.

Printed in Canada

Published by VIZ Media, LLC
P.O. Box 77010
San Francisco, CA 94107

10 9 8 7 6 5 4 3 2
First printing, October 2014
Second printing, February 2020

Behind the Scenes!!

STORY AND ART BY BISCO HATORI

From the creator of Ouran High School Host Club

Ranmaru Kurisu comes from a family of hardy, rough-and-tumble fisherfolk and he sticks out at home like a delicate, artistic sore thumb. It's given him a raging inferiority complex and a permanently pessimistic outlook. Now that he's in college, he's hoping to find a sense of belonging. But after a whole life of being left out, does he even know how to fit in?!